SHERLOCK HOLMES
AND
PHILOSOPHY

Popular Culture and Philosophy® Series Editor: George A. Reisch

For full details of all Popular Culture and Philosophy® books, visit www.opencourtbooks.com.

Popular Culture and Philosophy®

SHERLOCK HOLMES AND PHILOSOPHY

The Footprints of a Gigantic Mind

Edited by
JOSEF STEIFF

OPEN COURT
Chicago and La Salle, Illinois

Volume 61 in the series, Popular Culture and Philosophy®,
edited by George A. Reisch

To order books from Open Court, call toll-free 1-800-815-2280, or visit our website at www.opencourtbooks.com.

Open Court Publishing Company is a division of Carus Publishing Company.

Printed and bound in the United States of America.

Library of Congress Cataloging-in-Publication Data

Sherlock Holmes and philosophy: the footprints of a gigantic mind / edited by Josef Steiff.
        p. cm. -- (Popular culture and philosophy ; v. 61)
Includes bibliographical references and index.
ISBN 978-0-8126-9731-5 (trade paper : alk. paper)
1. Doyle, Arthur Conan, Sir, 1859-1930--Characters--Sherlock Holmes.
2. Philosophy in literature. 3. Holmes, Sherlock (Fictitious character) I.
Steiff, Josef. II. Title. III. Series.

PR4624.S46 2011
823'.8--dc23
                                        2011030635

CONTENTS
Things Must Be Done Decently
and In Order

THE TRACING OF FOOTSTEPS   285

A MAN OF HABITS   351

An Extraordinary Genius

for Minutiae

Chapter 1

A Sherlockian Scandal in Philosophy

Kate Rufa

I'm in love with Sherlock Holmes. I'll admit it. He is so tantalizingly (yet utterly, infuriatingly) English. His cool, concise, and unapologetically confident nature enthralls me. Whether he's pacing a crime scene with his trademark magnifying glass or wearing one of his numerous disguises, Holmes is the epitome of confidence and his unruffled and rational persona is absolutely riveting and absorbing.

In my mind the image of Sherlock Holmes will forever remain the talented actor Jeremy Brett who played Holmes in the revolutionary 1980s TV series, *The Adventures of Sherlock Holmes*. And while I feel that other such actors who have taken on the Holmes role have given equally adequate performances—I enjoyed the versions played by Basil Rathbone and Robert Downey Jr.—no one will ever take the place of Jeremy Brett as Sherlock Holmes in my heart.

But while the various movies are fun, I've always held the opinion that the books are far superior and Sir Arthur Conan Doyle's world famous literary character was truly innovative. Holmes's astute logical thinking and objective rationality gives him a distinctive character. He is continuously unimpressed with the crimes and criminals he pursues and his unperturbed countenance makes him an exceptionally entertaining hero.

We're truly astounded by Sherlock Holmes because he is never astounded himself.

Sherlock Holmes is, at his quintessential core, unemotional, objective, and completely rational. He uses logic, science, and strict analytical cognitive processes to solve his mysteries. Whether he's handling the affairs of scandalous royalty as the world's first and only "unofficial consulting detective," chasing a murderer in the dead of night with his trusty hound Toby, or catching a treasure thief in an adrenalin-racing boat chase, one thing remains a constant: his logical and unemotional persona.

Truly, most philosophical doctrine tells us that this state of being—to utilize our reason to overcome our passions—ought to be one of our ultimate goals if we wish to attain non-materialistic happiness. No philosopher embodies this doctrine more than seventeenth-century philosopher Baruch Spinoza. In his most celebrated work, his *Ethics*, Spinoza discusses his view of human passions and explains how the just man can utilize reason to overcome his negative human emotions. Once these emotions have been checked by reason he is able to experience not only freedom but the highest form of human happiness possible.

Sir Arthur Conan Doyle's literary character Sherlock Holmes is the very person whom Spinoza believed that human beings should aim to be. Sherlock Holmes is an unemotional sleuth in search of justice. His cool and precise nature allows him to examine clues without prejudice and place each puzzle piece together until he has a complete picture before him.

The crimes almost appear to the reader (and our beloved Dr. Watson) to be like elaborate illusions. Holmes, like the gifted illusionist, takes random, meaningless bits of information and connects them to show an undeniable chain of events. Once the illusion has been explained the magic disappears and we all believe it to be utterly simple.

No Romantic Illusions

In *The Sign of the Four* Sherlock Holmes criticizes Watson for romanticizing his published stories about his criminal investigations:

> "Detection is, or ought to be, an exact science and should be treated in the same cold and unemotional manner. You have attempted to tinge it with romanticism, which produces much the same effect as if you worked a love-story or an elopement into the fifth proposition of Euclid."

In Holmes's perspective, written works should be purely scientific and informative. Spinoza could not have agreed more. Spinoza himself amusedly called his style of writing in *Ethics* his "cumbersome geometric method." He wrote in a fashion similar to a mathematical treatise, with definitions, proofs, and axioms all lined up in an orderly fashion. Spinoza's *Ethics* is broken down into five parts. Within each part Spinoza states a proposition then proceeds to prove it and occasionally add a scholim, axiom, corollary, or other extremely boring and complex geometric term to his proof. I can see much of a similar style between Holmes's "The Book of Life" (in *A Study in Scarlet*) and Spinoza's *Ethics*.

Similar to their writing styles both Holmes and Spinoza lived their life accordingly. Spinoza advocated a life in which we objectively examine our emotions (or passions) and understand them (what initiated their cause and their effect once in place) and then utilize reason to overcome them through an understanding of the external emotional stimulus. When we use reason to keep our emotions in check we allow ourselves to broaden our minds to the possibility of more advanced forms of knowledge. And with a greater understanding of life, the universe, and ourselves, we experience the highest form of contentment possible.

Sherlock Holmes is the ideal model for Spinoza's concept of the "just man." Holmes must have long ago eliminated the illogical nuisance of uncontrolled passions and chosen to live life through the utilization of reason. Because his mind is not cluttered with irrelevant and, therefore, useless thoughts that might hinder his investigations, Holmes is capable of examining clues and crime scenes with an almost automaton quality.

Indeed, Watson on many occasions in the canons of Conan Doyle's work noted Holmes's perpetual unemotional state of being, and considered him more machine then man. For example, in *The Sign of the Four*, Watson describes Holmes as "an automaton—a calculating machine,' I cried. 'There is something positively inhuman in you at times.'"

And again in "A Scandal in Bohemia," Watson uses the metaphor of a machine to describe Holmes's objective, analytical mind even in reference to Holmes's only potential love interest, Irene Adler:

> It was not that he felt any emotion akin to love for Irene Adler. All emotions, and that one in particular, were abhorrent to his cold, precise but admirably balanced mind. He was, I take it, the most perfect reasoning and observing machine that the world has ever seen, but as a lover he would have placed himself in a false position.

Even when facing the threat of death, Holmes remains his distinguished self. In "The Final Problem" we encounter a somewhat different Holmes than that found in Doyle's previous stories. While confident as ever, we find our calculating consultant detective more cautious and guarded as he faces off against "the most dangerous and capable criminal in Europe:" the maniacal Professor Moriarty. Indeed, while confronting Moriarty's revenge for interfering in his criminal activities, Holmes (in the company of Watson) is eventually forced to leave the country on "holiday."

This dramatic tale begins with Sherlock Holmes's unexpected visit to Dr. Watson's consulting room. Holmes arrives looking thinner and more sickly than usual. One of his hands appears to be injured due to a violent confrontation that occurred that very night on his way to Watson's home. Holmes immediately proceeds to close the windows to the room, securing them with bolts. Watson, aware that something is amiss, concludes that Holmes is frightened by something, though we should know by now that Holmes is never afraid but merely cautious. Holmes begins to relate to Watson his recent actives to bring down the villain Moriarty whom, Holmes believes, is behind all of the major crimes of the last few years.

Moriarty, who is described as being "extremely tall and thin" and almost snakelike in his mannerisms, is described by Holmes as being the "Napoleon of crime." He is Holmes's intellectual equal and his moral polar opposite. After an impressive battle of wits and intellect, Watson is left to conclude, at the end of the story, that during their travels through Switzerland, Holmes and Moriarty fell together while still in battle, plummeting down Reichenbach Falls where they both presumably perished.

Indeed, while a thrilling tale in and of itself, what is most intriguing about this short story, in which we witness what was meant to be the death of one of the greatest detective characters of literary history, is that throughout its entirety, complete with all the death threats and very real possibility of mutually assured destruction, Holmes shows no fear and no regret. His temperament constantly remains calm and cool. If he does express an emotion it is never a negative or pernicious one but one of intrigue or amusement. Indeed, when dueling both physically and mentally against Moriarty's vengeance Holmes was not depressed but energized. He was excited by the challenge of a worthy opponent and the tale played out similarly to a game of chess.

From this we can see that whether engaged against his only potential love interest or battling to his presumed death, Sherlock Holmes maintains a Spinozistic countenance at all times. Spinozistic philosophy maintains that while there is nothing wrong with human emotions as such, they can interfere with higher forms of cognitive processes. When an emotion is provoked by an external cause and is not properly reasoned through it can distract us from understanding the truth about said external cause by adding a personal element to an objective occurrence.

One of the ultimate goals of Spinozistic philosophy is to achieve true happiness, happiness that is found through an intellectual pursuit of the mind instead of any fictional happiness that can temporarily arise from materialistic gains. For Spinoza happiness can be found only through freedom, the freedom that we can experience when we're no longer controlled by our emotions and by our human ignorance. If we allow ourselves to merely react when an external force happens to elicit our uncontrolled emotions, we submit ourselves to forces that are ultimately beyond our control.

Of course we cannot eliminate our emotions. No matter what, they *are* there. Even our renowned Sherlock Holmes cannot eliminate all of his emotions (just primarily the negative or passive ones). What reason does, says Spinoza, is turn our passive human emotions into active emotions by allowing us to understand them as clearly and distinctly as is humanly possible. Once we have a clear and distinct understanding of the emotion, the more control we have over it, and the less passive we are when we encounter it. Because we're no longer passive bystanders to the powerful emotions set into place by external stimuli we experience a kind of freedom, which for Spinoza, is true happiness. Spinozistic philosophy dictates, and Sherlock Holmes demonstrates, the idea that we ought to control our reactions to our emotions instead of allowing them to control us.

The Conatus and Cocaine

One of the more troubling character flaws with Holmes has always been his morphine and cocaine addiction. It doesn't seem to fit with his purely rational persona. As much as it may surprise us, it was Watson in *The Sign of the Four* who reasonably argued to Holmes the illogical choice of utilizing these powerful hallucinogenic drugs:

> "Count the cost! Your brain may, as you say, be roused and excited, but it is a pathological and morbid process which involves increased tissue-change and may at least leave a permanent weakness. You know, too, what a black reaction comes upon you. Surely the game is hardly worth the candle. Why should you, for mere passing pleasure, risk the loss of those great powers with which you have been endowed?"

Sherlock Holmes attempts to justify his substance abuse by claiming the drugs allow his mind to stay in an active state when he has no work or crime to solve. From Conan Doyle's first work about Holmes, *A Study in Scarlet*, we note Holmes's demeanor when he fails to have adequate cognitive stimulation. He not only becomes depressed but utterly torpid:

> Nothing could exceed his energy when the working fit was upon him; but now and again a reaction would seize him, and for days on end he would lie upon the sofa in the sitting room, hardly uttering a word or moving a muscle from morning to night.

Here again we can see Sherlock Holmes as a representation of Spinoza's concept of the just man. He's only happy when engaged in intellectual work and problem solving. Spinoza claims that happiness can only be achieved when we utilize our reason and are in a state of cognitive activity. Intellectual passivity leads to unhappiness. We can note the same feelings in Conan Doyle's Holmes: when Holmes has no work he becomes utterly depressed to the point of lying on the couch for days on end. To alleviate the depression, Holmes abuses powerful hallucinogenic drugs in an attempt to stimulate his mind.

One of the clearest examples of Holmes's drug use and of his excuses for his addiction can be found in *The Sign of the Four*, where Watson, having repeatedly witnessed Holmes's drug use, finally rages at him. Holmes contemplates Watson's argument, but finally states, probably more forcefully and dramatically then really necessary:

> "My mind," he said, "rebels at stagnation. Give me problems, give me work, give me the most abstruse cryptogram, or the most intricate analysis, and I am in my own proper atmosphere. I can dispense then with artificial stimulants. But I abhor the dull routine of existence. I crave mental exaltation."

Holmes will sacrifice his life, not just his physical duration on Earth, but his all-consuming mental facilities to maintain his constant mental activity.

It's here that Holmes appears to separate himself from Spinoza's just man. One of Spinoza's key concepts in the *Ethics* is his notion of 'conatus'. Conatus is the Latin word for striving or endeavor. In the third part of the *Ethics*, "Concerning the Origin and Nature of the Emotions," Spinoza introduces and defines a thing's conatus as its endeavor to persist in its own being. This simply means that everything has an innate sense of wanting to promote its own existence for as long as possible.

Holmes's use of morphine and cocaine, then, suggests that he is acting, consciously or unconsciously, against his conatus in that the use of these drugs will potentially (and drastically) shorten his existence. We can convincingly conclude that he is irrefutably acting against his conatus by purposefully performing actions that instead of promoting longevity perform the opposite.

Why? Why would Sherlock Holmes, the master of logical, analytical thinking, this objective and rational machine that so astounds us, allow himself to make such an obvious miscalculation? Quite simply, Sherlock Holmes is not a machine. He is a human being and, as such, not above human error. He too is prone to inadequate ideas. If he were otherwise the beautiful and talented Irene Adler would not have escaped and several of his clients wouldn't have inconveniently died.

We can attempt to rationalize Holmes's inadequate ideas concerning drugs through our continued examination of Spinozistic philosophy. Spinoza, as a philosopher, believed in a world view in which the only thing that exists is God (otherwise known as Nature or that which is self-caused) and various modes of God (things which are conceived and brought into a transient state of duration through something other than themselves). Human beings are, hence, considered "modes" in Spinozistic philosophy.

God itself is understood as being complete actuality. Which makes sense, in that if God were anything else this would inherently imply that God has the potential to be something God is not, which is absurd if we accept the notion that God is omnipotent. If God or Nature is complete actuality, various human modal units are found somewhere within a scale of potentiality. We as beings have the potential to always be more or less than we currently are.

We can move forward on this imaginary scale closer to actuality if we are active (mentally and physically) and move away from it when we are passive. Moving closer to actuality makes us happy which, in the world of philosophy, ought to be one of our primary goals. We can be cognitively active by utilizing reason to understand and override our emotions and allow for higher forms of knowledge and intellectual fulfillment. The role of reason is to turn passive emotions into active affects. If we were to visualize this scale we would see Watson probably somewhere towards the upper middle of the scale between passivity and actuality and Holmes about as close as a human can get to actuality.

Holmes's drug use is his attempt to stay in an active state (as close to actuality as modally possible) for as long as possible. He ignores his conatus in an attempt to maintain a state of near actuality. Human modal units are not designed to maintain that intense level of activity continuously, since we can only exist within the scale of potentiality. To attempt to exceed this is to endanger shortening the already temporary duration to which we exist.

And so, Holmes's cocaine use is his attempt to maintain a complete form of actuality while still being merely a temporary modal unit. Or, in other words, Sherlock Holmes has a God-complex. Which should not surprise us; he is, after all, a nineteenth-century Englishman.

The Most Impious and the Most Dangerous Man of the Century

Honour is not opposed to reason, but can arise from it
    —Spinoza, EIVP58

Therefore he who is born free and remains free has only adequate ideas and thus has no conception of evil, and consequently no conception of good (for good and evil are correlative).
    —Spinoza, EIVP68

Holmes represents Spinoza's concept of the just man in many ways. The most notable of these is Holmes's unique ability to be unaffected by his negative human passions and maintain an almost constant level of machine-like cognitive performance. Sherlock Holmes is, and always will be a precise, calculating, objective character. Very rarely does anything he sees or observes astound him (and let's face it, he's seen a lot). He simply does not let his emotions get in the way of his intellectual endeavors and lives only to challenge his intellectual prowess.

Furthermore, we as the readers metaphorically gorge ourselves on Holmes's ability to create and maintain this perpetual state of being unimpressed and unperturbed. We love him for literally sticking his nose in the air at a crime as if it is so boring, that its straightforward and uncomplicated structure has some disagreeable smell. So remarkable is it when he finds a case worthy of his abilities, miraculous as it may seem, we the readers, find ourselves excited by the unfolding mystery as if we were Holmes the man, instead of merely his readers. Of course the adventure, and the mystery that lies therein, are all too short-lived. The clues play out in an obvious way that for him is almost always far too predictable. The cycle continues and he falls back into his tall armchair and his experiments.

There's something rather appealing in this almost inhuman attribute to rid ourselves of our emotional burdens and examine life the way Holmes would. When freed (so to speak) from the emotions that can hinder our analytical abilities we encounter a whole new world of possibilities. But can this ability to separate ourselves from being personally involved with things injure our sense of ethical and moral responsibility, not only to each other, but our community, indeed, our humanity?

This was an important question for Spinoza. Dramatically called "the most impious and the most dangerous man of the century" by one disgruntled theologian (as cited by Matthew Stewart in *The Courtier and the Heretic*), Spinoza's almost pantheistic views regarding life, the universe, and well, everything else, defiantly challenged and certainly frightened the ruling classes of the seventeenth-century Netherlands. And with appreciable reason, I might add. Spinoza was two hundred years ahead of his time. This type of forward thinking has the potential to create a hero of Holmes's stature but a villain of Moriarty's capacity as well.

We can see that, similar to Holmes, Moriarty was an objective, abstract thinker. His objectivity, however, led him to a life of depravity and crime. Most interestingly examined in the hit television show *Sherlock*, Moriarty can truly be seen as Holmes's negative image when considered under the title of the world's first and only consulting criminal.

Hence, if we understand Holmes to be as close to as we can humanly get to Spinoza's just man, Moriarty must be considered the negative possibilities that such a life may present. Spinoza, however, was ready for such immoral and unethical interpretations of his work. Found within his arsenal of astute logic and rationality was the ever formidable philosophy of Socrates (dramatic music please, maestro!).

Socrates argued in the *Apology* that when we harm others we inevitably harm ourselves, which we would never knowingly do. Spinoza, in his own way, states the same concept in *Ethics*.

When we follow the dictates of our conatus we are in a sense, being self serving, or more accurately, it allows us to seek our own advantage:

> The more each one strives [utilizes one's conatus], and is able, to seek his own advantage, that is to preserve his being, the more he is endowed with virtue; conversely, insofar as each one neglects his own advantage, that is neglects to preserve his being, he lacks power. (EIVP20)

According to Spinoza, the more we seek our own advantage, the more power we gain. The more power we gain through adequate ideas the more we are endowed with virtue. Thus we choose to participate in actions that positively benefit ourselves and others through the adequate ideas we possess.

To act otherwise (as our evil antagonist Moriarty does) is to act from a basis of ignorance and from inadequate ideas. Because Holmes operates from mostly adequate ideas he is considered virtuous and free. Moriarty, on the other hand, is immoral and entrapped by his passive affects.

The House that Holmes Built

Many of Conan Doyle's stories begin with Dr. Watson praising the wit and brilliance that is Sherlock Holmes's mind and capabilities. Indeed, though often thought narcissistic and conceited by the local authorities whom he assists, Sherlock Holmes deserves every ounce of the self-importance he feels.

And what's more, we love him for it. There's something about the intellectual hero that is simply engaging, especially in today's culture. Our modern day conception of a hero now involves (more often than not) an intellectual crime solver instead of the brash cowboy of recent years. Whether Dr. Gregory House in *House*, Dr. Temperance Brennan in *Bones*, Mr. Spock in *Star Trek*, or Captain Picard in *Star Trek: The Next Generation*, if you prefer, or any number of the characters found on American television shows such as *CSI Miami* or *Criminal Minds*, you'll find that it's the intellect instead of the brawn that saves the day.

And Sherlock Holmes just may have started it all. His cold and impassive nature makes him stand apart from the passionate few whose success rely more on good luck than anything else. I find it fascinating that this creation of nineteenth-century literary genius should follow so closely to the image that a man from the seventeenth century proposed.

I find the correlation found between Spinoza's ethical writing and Sherlock Holmes's sleuthing truly astounding. And it's intriguing to see how these ideas have blossomed into the characters of our modern day protagonists. Whether considered together or separately, Spinoza and Sherlock have seemingly helped pave the metaphoric road for the modern conception of a hero.

Why? Why is this ideal of an intellectual hero so appealing to us? Why is it that we love Holmes's unemotional objectivity or care about Spinoza's ethical implication that such a life presents?

Holmes and Spinoza have already spelled it out for us. Utilize reason and logic when you act and do not let your emotions govern you. Get in control of your own life and your own sense of self. Avoid ignorance, create brilliance. Open yourself up to a whole new world of thinking and understanding and gain the respect (or, quite possibly, the annoyance) of those around you. With study and discipline we can become the House, or the Bones, or even the Sherlock Holmes of any field of study.

Perhaps what's most wonderful about Sherlock Holmes and Spinoza's just man is simply this, that they truly have no superhuman qualities to them, no magic powers beyond our own meager means. What makes them special is what we ourselves have within us. We too can become that which so astounds us.

Chapter 2
Calculating Humanity
Timothy Sexton

The first glimpse of Jeremy Brett's Sherlock Holmes that the viewer gets in every episode of the Granada television series is that of Holmes looking down on Baker Street's activities from his apartment on the second floor.

Brett turns his face slightly toward the camera with a look on his face registering a very definite emotion that is just as definitely impossible for the viewer to identify. Is he amused by what he sees out the window? Is he intrigued? He may even be bored.

It's impossible to read his emotional register as the scene turns into a freeze-frame, but one thing is certain: this Sherlock Holmes—this one—is situated above all other humans and rather than being unconcerned or disinterested about his special status, he is quite satisfied with the nature of the relationship between him and everybody else who exists on a level below. Equality be damned; it's all about the will to power and Holmes has the will lacking in the street urchins, bobbies, and assorted rabble below.

But more on that Sherlock Holmes later. The game is afoot and since I don't want to make it too elementary, you will have to pay close attention to the clues.

Human, Inhuman, or Underhuman?

Man, philosopher Friedrich Nietzsche's titular prophet in *Thus Spake Zarathustra* tells us, is a state of being that must be overcome. Zarathustra's essential contention: comparing modern man to the coming Overman is like comparing a gorilla strutting back and forth in his zoo habitat to Fred Astaire dancing on the ceiling in *Royal Wedding*.

In Arthur Conan Doyle's *The Sign of the Four*, Dr. John Watson turns to his good friend Sherlock Holmes and replies to a statement made by Holmes that he—Holmes—had not even observed that future client Mary Morstan was, and I'm paraphrasing Watson here, one stone cold fox. Watson, accustomed to Holmes's ability to successfully construct an entire biography merely by observing the clothing a person wears, is compelled to cry out: "You really are an automaton—a calculating machine. There is something positively inhuman in you at times."

Sherlock Holmes is inhuman, observes his close companion—who should know—Dr. Watson. Zarathustra does not say that the next evolutionary tiptoe up the ladder to perfection will be inhuman, but rather overhuman.

To Underestimate One's Ability
Is Just as Wrong as Overestimation

"He is a calculating machine, and anything you add to that simply weakens the effect." The words are again being used to describe Sherlock Holmes. In this case, Arthur Conan Doyle is writing entirely in the guise of an author reflecting on his literary creation and he goes on to observe—and he should know—that Sherlock Holmes is just a calculating machine with no room for the addition of common literary characteristics like light or shade or nuance or complexity or, let's finally admit it, a personality. If you go by the description of the author who created him, Sherlock Holmes can only be what your English teachers referred to as a "flat character."

Actors for over a century appeared to pay great respect to Doyle's assessment of the lack of style in Sherlock Holmes. Actors portrayed Sherlock Holmes as an admittedly brilliant seeker of truth and justice with little in the way of style. Whether it was the famous Basil Rathbone or the considerably less famous Alan Wheatley, actors saw in Sherlock a chance to play a character with significant cranial capacity, but not a whole heck of a lot more. Indeed, judging from most performances, apparently you can't be both smart and fascinating. The only time that these Sherlocks even came close to being fascinating was in the scenes where Holmes is telling someone all about themselves based on their gloves or tie.

We shouldn't blame actors for making of Sherlock Holmes something much more inhuman than overhuman. Just as Holmes proudly points out the fact that he is the creator of the job of consulting detective, so was Conan Doyle a co-creator with Edgar Allan Poe of a new literary genre known as the detective story. Today, amid well-rounded characters in the world of crime-solving, from Columbo to Ellery Queen to Monk, it's sometimes difficult to remember that the detective is way too often the least interesting character in a story because he's only there to solve the dang crime. It took a while for writers to learn that crimes could be solved in just as stylish a fashion as they could be committed.

You Don't Think I Put Too Much Color and Life into It?

Watson's exclamation includes a rejoinder that begs further study: "There is something positively inhuman in you at times." What does it really mean to be inhuman? Most dictionaries agree: any material object that is not a human being (like an automaton) or a human being who lacks qualities such as compassion and mercy and also possesses the potential to display cruelty or act in a barbaric fashion.

Remember, this is his good friend Sherlock Holmes that Dr. Watson is talking about. Okay, maybe Doyle's Sherlock and the Sherlock of Rathbone and the rest aren't particularly rounded, but to suggest that their Holmes showed no compassion or mercy? That their Holmes acted barbarically? This description doesn't seem to describe the character as written in the books nor does it seem an apt depiction of Holmes as portrayed on film.

To compare Sherlock Holmes as we know him to the Sherlock Holmes that Dr. Watson describes is like comparing Jerry Lewis's nutty professor to Mr. Spock. A calculating machine could be used to determine the odds that a specific person committed murder by speckled band, but that machine is hardly capable of caring enough to place its own life in jeopardy in pursuit of the proving the hypothesis.

Several generations of actors portraying Sherlock Holmes as a mere calculating machine based on the literary tales of a character described by his own creator as such have conditioned fans to accept without question that Sherlock puts his brilliant mind to work solving crimes because he is interested in Truth, Justice, and the Victorian Way. That Sherlock—that one— often ploddingly goes about collecting clues which he uses as punchcards in his calculating machine of a brain to arrive at the answer to what is, after all, the central component without which no detective story can survive: whodunit? (And howdunit and whydunit in most cases.) While the Sherlock that wormed its way into public consciousness and acceptance was usually quite surprisingly unemotional about everything, including proving himself right, he wasn't exactly what most of us would describe as inhuman.

Maybe if Dr. Watson had been a bit more imaginative, he might have searched the definition of 'inhuman' in his mind before speaking, have found it insanely inappropriate and coined a much more suitable word to describe what he actually meant: underhuman. Then, being as how this was the Victorian Age, he would have necessarily shortened to reflect a more honest appraisal of the gender conventions of the time. "You really are an underman—a calculating machine," Watson might have said.

The Law Is as Dangerous to Us as the Criminals Are

Sherlock Holmes: the Underman. A calculating machine slightly less than human and an automaton who is most certainly a far cry from Nietzsche's promises of those to come who shall be "the meaning of the Earth." The Sherlock Holmes who exists in stories written by his creator and the overwhelming majority of cinematic adaptations is, ultimately, only another member of what Nietzsche termed the herd. He solves crimes in the pursuit of justice fostered by purely traditional notions of good and evil, right and wrong, fact and fiction.

The lack of style in this Holmes is rather astonishing. If you were Sherlock Holmes and you had just solved a crime that the police could not solve, and you had exhibited compassion and mercy by letting someone you know to be a guilty man go free, you, too, might shout out in clear, very human, frustration: "I am not retained by the police to supply their deficiencies! Maybe I am committing a felony, but I may be saving a soul."

Here's the way Arthur Conan Doyle describes the moment that Sherlock Holmes says those very words:

> "After all, Watson," said Holmes, reaching up his hand for his clay pipe, "I am not retained by the police to supply their deficiencies. If Horner were in danger it would be another thing; but this fellow will not appear against him, and the case must collapse. I suppose that I am committing a felony, but it is just possible that I am saving a soul. This fellow will not go wrong again; he is too terribly frightened. Send him to jail now, and you make him a jail-bird for life."

No exclamation points in that paragraph. Perhaps Doyle felt that emotion would weaken the effect of the coldly calculating mind playing over the odds that his decision to break the law would result in an ultimate good that playing by the rules of statutory justice could not match. Sherlock is willing to break a minor law in order to achieve what might be a cosmically greater good: saving a soul.

But where is Sherlock's soul in that scene? In addition to banning light and shade, Arthur Conan Doyle also seems to have banished Holmes's soul. And what's a human without a soul? Inhuman? Unhuman? Underhuman? Certainly not overhuman.

Sherlock Holmes suggests that his action of committing a felony may result in saving a soul, but Jeremy Brett's aristocratic dismissal of the real felon in question makes one wonder if Holmes even believes in such an illogical concept as a soul. Lacking any hint of style, the above scene from "The Adventure of the Blue Carbuncle" is about little more than Sherlock Holmes matter-of-factly admitting that he regularly outsmarts the police.

One's Moral Code Is a Decisive Witness to Who He Is

Now let's examine the exact same scene from "The Blue Carbuncle," but with Sherlock Holmes reinterpreted—Oh, let's go ahead and say it—recreated by Jeremy Brett. The disgusted dismissal of the actual thief of a priceless blue jewel shows Sherlock sitting in profile, left hand held up to his temple. The scene provides us with yet another example of how we know the man is deeply in touch with a certain emotion, but we're not allowed to know exactly what that emotion is. Not yet, anyway.

And then Dr. Watson confesses to being more than a little surprised at the shocking turn of events in which Sherlock Holmes—up to now just an unofficial arm of the prevailing Victorian ideology to punish transgressors of some moral rules codified into statutory law—actually breaks the law by letting a man he knows is guilty of the most famous crime of the moment get away scot-free. Sherlock Holmes does what Nietzsche tells us must be done in order to be an Overman: he has moved beyond good and evil.

The almost violent response about police deficiencies as interpreted by Jeremy Brett includes a raised voice, braying sneer, cocked eyebrow and, finally, a momentary glare at Watson that passes by so quickly it's easy to overlook. Contained within that outburst and especially within that barely perceptible glare resides an acknowledgment that he has moved beyond the concept of good and evil along with recognition that Watson remains a prisoner of the mass culture that accepts a moral code as intrinsically good without questioning where that code came from. There is a word for the kind of Sherlock Holmes that Jeremy Brett reinvented for audiences grown bored with the calculating machines.

Style.

This, more than anything else, has been the addition by Brett to the Sherlock Holmes mythos that Conan Doyle feared so much would weaken the effect of his brilliant calculating automaton. The evolution of Sherlock Holmes in the capable hands of Jeremy Brett bestows upon modern audiences a man who meets, word for word, Friedrich Nietzsche's description of what the Overman—the next step in the evolution of man—must do:

> . . . give style to one's character—that is a grand and rare art. He who surveys all that his nature presents in its strength and in its weakness, then fashions it into an artistic plan, until everything appears as art and reason, and even the weaknesses enchant the eye—he exercises that admirable art.

The art that Nietzsche considers grand and rare is nothing less than the creation of a way to peer into the abyss of a world without meaning, a world without absolute truths, a world in which God has been declared dead . . . and not only still find meaning, but "attain satisfaction with himself." There exists a specific term used to describe the admirable art of fashioning all one surveys into an artistic plan that creates a reason for being rather than acting out against the dread and sublime angst of a world lacking any intrinsic meaning.

Sublimation.

This Fellow Rings True Every Time

With his pronouncement that God was dead, Friedrich Nietzsche unleashed the floodgates of nihilism and existentialism. If a perfect God was a myth created by man then by definition that means that all morality is an invention of imperfect man. Absent the presence of a superior being sitting in judgment of our ability to conform to His morality and the subsequent knowledge that all those moral laws can be traced back to a very fallible culture of men, well, why should it be taken seriously at all?

Nietzsche puts it elegantly: "A morality, a mode of living tried and proved by long experience and testing, at length enters consciousness as a law, as dominating." He goes on to suggest that the origin of any morality is eventually forgotten, but the morality itself becomes holy and unassailable. It dominates the culture; dominates the members of the herd.

The suggestion that the predominant moral codes of the Judeo-Christian society that came to dominate much of the world is actually the work of man eventually, inconsolably, leads to the reality that if there's no such thing as God then that must mean that there's no such thing as absolute morality. Even worse, it means no reward for doing the right thing. Of course, it also means no eternal punishment for doing the wrong thing, but there's a certain inescapable hollow quality to that upside of a life that ends forever at the moment of death on this planet.

Coming face to face with this knowledge initially creates a sense of fear, confusion and nausea, but ultimately the situation calls for some kind of response. If Nietzsche were alive today he would probably refer to those who respond to the nausea and despair by tying their self-esteem to a sports team, and those who define their falsely rebellious non-conformity to the social norm by painting their skin and piercing selected body parts, and those who put their faith in any organized religion, and those who respond to the lack of any absolute morality by declaring that there is no morality at all as "the herd." Sticks and stones may break Holmes's bones, but words will never herd him; at least, not Jeremy Brett's Sherlock.

I Cannot Agree with Those that Rank Modesty among the Virtues

Rather than latching onto naturalized social conventions or escaping into nihilist rejection that any kind of truth exists or escaping into the temporary good feelings supplied by recreational use of narcotics or becoming a literal warrior laying waste to humanity in support of a herd mentality political ideology, Nietzsche suggested there was another way to overcome the sickness experienced when you gain the knowledge that you are alone and the morality you've clung to through even the most boring sermon is nothing but a cultural tool. There exists a better way.

Jeremy Brett's seemingly apathetic and drugged-up Holmes describes it even more stylishly than Nietzsche. "My mind rebels at stagnation. Give me problems, give me work, give me the most abstruse cryptogram, or the most intricate analysis, and I am in my own proper atmosphere. I can dispense then with artificial stimulants. But I abhor the dull routine of existence. I crave mental exultation. That is why I have chosen my own profession, or rather created it, for I am the only one in the world . . . the only unofficial consulting detective . . . . I claim no credit in such cases. The work itself, the pleasure of finding a field for my peculiar powers, is my highest reward." Only it turns out that Holmes hadn't been partaking of his seven-percent solution of cocaine as Dr. Watson feared.

Two significant differences exist between this exchange as it exists in Arthur Conan Doyle's original literary version and how it exists in the television episode starring Brett. The first change is that it is to be found in the Holmes novel *The Sign of the Four* whereas it appears at the beginning of the television episode "A Scandal in Bohemia." Some might argue that's a pretty important difference, but the second stain on literal adherence to Doyle's written word is far more significant. In fact, the second difference is absolutely vital toward understanding how it is specifically Jeremy Brett's interpretation of Sherlock Holmes that brings the character into the domain of the Overman rather than the character himself.

In the book, Sherlock does speak the words while under the influence of cocaine. They are the words of a human machine looking only for the chance to exercise logic. The significance here is that Brett's Sherlock has been giving a performance all along for an audience of one: Dr. Watson. The drug-induced lethargy that stimulates Holmes to pointedly encapsulate Nietzsche's notion of sublimation as the correct response to despair is all part of a very complex game that is, at all times in Brett's refashioning of this calculating machine, very much afoot.

Whereas the Sherlock Holmes of a Nicholas Rowe or a Peter Cushing are avatars of Doyle's inhuman calculating machine who dutifully play out their role as the brilliant detective called in to solve a crime, enact justice and restore proper moral balance to London, Jeremy Brett's Holmes is not in the game to bring justice or even safety to the "great and observant public" who don't "care about the finer shades of analysis and deduction." The manner in which Jeremy Brett delivers this line in its entirety is of deep and profound disgust for those whom he is supposedly trying to protect. No, Brett carries these words with a deeper emotion than disgust for the public: revulsion. You never saw

Basil Rathbone sneer at the very people he had put himself in charge of protecting when the police were not up to the job.

His Work Is Its Own Reward

"That is why I have chosen my own profession, or rather created it, for I am the only one in the world." Even Nietzsche—perhaps the most accessible of all great philosophers in terms of how he uses common language to express profound and often profane ideas—could not have put words into the mouth of Sherlock Holmes that concretizes his concept of using sublimation and the application of style to one's character any better. In Conan Doyle's original literary version of the scene in which this elementally Nietzschean line is delivered, Sherlock, while under the influence of cocaine, leans his elbows on the arms of his chair in a situation that Watson describes as "like one who has a relish for conversation." Under the influence, Sherlock is just being gabby.

The screenwriter of "A Scandal in Bohemia" rewrites the scene so that Sherlock sits almost serenely in the throes of a drug-induced state of relaxation that belies the fact that he's so restless he's bored as a cat. As written, this scene from the TV series is almost as flat as Doyle's original. As played, however, the scene is anything but banal.

The Sherlock Holmes that is recreated in the Granada series is a collective effort between the various screenwriters and directors and actor, but because Brett adds so much to his portrayal that may or may not have been someone else's idea, we must consider Jeremy Brett's performance the key indicator of the realization of the Nietzschean Overman.

Especially at the moment of truth when Jeremy Brett chooses not to draw the veil down over Sherlock's emotions, but to wonderfully—dramatically, perhaps some might even say melodramatically—and subtly give the very first indication in the entire canon of cinematic interpretations of Sherlock Holmes that this alleged calculating machine is far closer to an Overman than an automaton. Nietzsche says that what is needed is "that a human being attain satisfaction with himself." It lies well outside the realm of possibility for Jeremy Brett's Sherlock Holmes to exude satisfaction with himself any more than he does in this scene.

And yet if your knowledge of Sherlock Holmes has come only through the movies featuring Basil Rathbone or the television series featuring Ronald Howard or any of a number of other cinematic representations, you might well find yourself nodding in agreement with Watson. It is almost as if actors are rigidly insistent upon Conan Doyle's contention that Holmes must be played only in the register of logically deductive genius searching for truth, justice, and the Victorian Way. Any portrayal of Holmes that contains the dreaded "light or shade" would appear to be in violation of the central tenet of the character of Sherlock Holmes: he solves crimes to bring bad guys to justice.

But what if that weren't the case? What if Sherlock Holmes solves crimes not because his compassion makes him care about things like justice, truth and morality? What if the drive behind Sherlock's need to solve cases was about "striving for excellence . . . striving to overwhelm one's neighbor, even if only very indirectly or only in one's own feelings?" Can we imagine a portrayal of Sherlock Holmes in which he's not a coldly calculating automaton who solves crimes as a path toward re-establishing the order of justice in polite Victorian society? For this Sherlock the solving of the crime becomes his own private and personal little melodrama and the subject of that melodrama is proving his superority over everyone.

Superiority—with the caveat that this proof of his superiority impacts directly or indirectly on those with whom he comes into contact so that he changes their lives for the better. Jeremy Brett's Sherlock overwhelms all those with whom he comes in contact such as when he despairingly closes his eyes and, using his high-pitched exultation voice, says "Please, tell me the facts," with just the slightest quivering of his voice on the word "me." Is that quiver the suggestion of superiority? I think it is.

Brett also overwhelms in the delightful scene near the end of "The Norwood Builder" when he is using fire to locate the bad guy. He tells the three bobbies, Inspector Lestrade and Dr. Watson to yell fire and when they do so only half-heartedly, Brett immediately and comically says, "Gentlemen, we can do better than that." It's a brilliantly timed moment of comedy, but within the rush to exhort the men to yell louder there is that superiority that is expressed not just in the voice, but in the way Brett nods his head his head and raises his arm. In the hands of a less capable actor, Sherlock would merely be logically encouraging a more robust announcement of fire. The look in Brett's eye when he quietly suggests that the men can do better than that carries with it a much different emotion. It is the look of someone who is tired of asking himself a very contemporary question.

Brett was the very first Sherlock to take the standard scene of Holmes deducing everything about a person when they walk into his room and turn it into a tour de force exhibition of Holmes's absolute and total superiority over those who see, but do not observe. Without Jeremy Brett's invention of a theatrically overwhelming Sherlock Holmes who isn't just a calculating machine, you would not have the twenty-first century Sherlock Holmes of Benedict Cumberbatch or Robert Downey, Jr. (Well, we shouldn't blame Brett entirely for the latter, I suppose; he knew not the extent of his influence.)

The best example of Brett's performance being central to the elevation of Sherlock Holmes from inhuman machine to Nietzschean Overman is most perfectly displayed in a scene from Granada's "The Abbey Grange" that differs considerably from the original as written by Conan Doyle. That version merely describes Holmes asking Lady Brackenstall to tell him the truth. The scene is rewritten to take place outside in the Brett version. With the lightness and dexterity of the dancer he was, Brett positively skips down a row of steps, walks to a spot across from where Lady Brackenstall is sitting, keeping his back to her, digging at the ground with a shoe and dramatically pivoting around on one heel almost military style to finally face the woman. It is theater crafted upon a foundation of pure style.

Chapter 3

Is Holmes Really Just Lucky?

J. Solomon Johnson

"When I hear you give your reasons," I remarked, "the thing always appears to me to be so ridiculously simple that I could easily do it myself, though at each successive instance of your reasoning I am baffled until you explain your process. And yet I believe that my eyes are as good as yours."

—Dr. Watson in "A Scandal in Bohemia"

Sherlock Holmes always knows the answer. This is part of his mystique. However, we readers are often left more closely identifying with Dr. Watson. It seems obvious how and why Holmes reaches his conclusions (once his reasons are spelled out), but until this happens any conclusions that we draw are merely guesses. It's only when Holmes confirms our suspicions that we truly come to *know* the answer.

The more curious (and dare we say Holmesian) reader might then ask what exactly is so special about Holmes? What allows him to arrive at the truth when the rest of us are just guessing? Or, perhaps the even more compelling question: could Holmes himself be merely guessing? While it doesn't seem like Holmes merely "believes" the correct answer, explaining how he knows is tougher than you might think.

The distinction between beliefs and knowledge is central to the difference between Holmes and the layman. Clearly there is a difference between *believing* that someone is guilty and *knowing* that someone is guilty. But what exactly is this difference?

For over two thousand years, there was one dominant theory of knowledge: the "Justified True Belief" (JTB) theory. The JTB theory required three things for knowledge: belief, justification, and truth. Let this be our starting point, our first examination of data that will help us solve this mystery of luck. Let us examine what a belief is. Then why knowing something means it has to be true. And why justification is so important.

It was easier to know it than to explain why I know it.

The real core of any knowledge is belief. Here "belief" just means anything that you think is true. Beliefs range from an inkling that something bad might happen to the virtual certainty that you are reading this book right now. There might be a difference in how *certain* you are in these two sorts of cases, but they are the same sort of thing.

But there's more to belief. In fact, everything you know is also something you believe. The philosopher G.E. Moore showed this through examples like the following: Suppose that Watson notices some bit of evidence and says: "I know your old nemesis Moriarty must be behind this, but I do not believe it!" Assuming this isn't just hyperbole (an expression of utter incredulity) and is said in total sincerity, Watson's statement here is nonsense. Try to think of a time where you knew something, but did not believe it. There are plenty of cases where we do not *want* to believe something, but that is a different matter. Knowing something requires that you believe it. If you're still unconvinced try to think of a case where someone simultaneously knows something but doesn't believe it.

Any truth is better than indefinite doubt.

Now let's examine the second part of the JTB theory: truth. For anyone to really know something, it has to be true. For example, in the story "A Scandal in Bohemia," Holmes explains to Watson that he knows where Irene Adler has hidden a photograph; this fact is central to the case. Later we learn that by the time he relates his tale to Watson, Ms. Adler had already moved the picture. Thus, when Holmes says that he knows where the photo is, he is thinking of the wrong place. Most of us would then say that Holmes didn't really know where it was. We might say that Holmes "thought he knew" or "believed that it was true" but not that he really *knew*. However, had the picture remained where he thought it was, he would have known. This illustrates an important part of the relationship between beliefs and knowledge: a true belief might become knowledge, but an untrue belief never will.

Let us hear the suspicions—I will look after the proofs.

The final facet of the JTB theory is justification. To see why it's important, let's look at examples from the 2010 BBC Production

Sherlock. In the episode titled "The Great Game," Ms. Wenceslas (the curator of the Hickman Gallery) displays a recently discovered (fake) Vermeer painting. Since the gallery is presumably reputable, and the forgery is of the utmost quality, everyone who sees it is justified in believing that it is authentic. However, Holmes discovers reasons to doubt its authenticity. This undermines the justification for his belief that it's real. Thus, even if the Vermeer were genuine, his doubts would mean Holmes no longer *knows* it. If something legitimately weakens your justification, your belief no longer counts as knowledge.

But can justification turn a true belief into knowledge? In some cases, yes! An example is found in that same episode when Alex Woodbridge (the security guard at the gallery) contacts Professor Cairns regarding the Vermeer. Mr. Woodbridge believes that the Van Buren supernova shouldn't appear in the painting (since it was not visible when Vermeer would have painted it). But when he reaches out to Professor Cairns, he needs confirmation of his belief (generally speaking, suspicions and hunches are not well justified). Had Mr. Woodbridge actually reached Professor Cairns, she would have confirmed his suspicion. Confirmation by an expert would provide Alex with stronger justification, and his belief would become knowledge. In short, while hunches and suspicions generally don't give rise to knowledge, with proper confirmation they can become knowledge.

There is nothing more stimulating than a case where everything goes against you.

The JTB model sets up excellent criteria for assessing most cases of knowledge. Even when we feel absolutely certain that we know something, losing any one of those parts (the belief, the truth, or the justification) leaves us without real knowledge. But, strong as it is, the JTB theory isn't perfect. In 1963, a philosopher named Edmund Gettier argued that justified true beliefs don't always count as knowledge. There are in fact cases where you have a justified true belief but you only got there because of sheer luck.

To illustrate the point, Gettier came up with an example much like the following: Suppose that Holmes reveals evidence to Watson that a murder was likely committed by Mr. Jones. Mr. Jones is a former ship hand so Watson rightly forms the belief "the murder was committed by a former ship hand". Unbeknownst to Holmes and Watson, a different former ship hand actually committed the murder. Now, here's the trick: It turns out that

Watson's belief—that the murder was committed by a former ship hand—is justified (Holmes showed good reason to believe it), it is true, and it is believed by Watson. Thus, according to the JTB theory it has all three parts and should count as knowledge. But it doesn't seem as if Dr. Watson *really* knows that a former ship hand committed the murder. It's only a matter of luck that he got it right. After all, Watson came to his conclusion by thinking about the wrong chap, so he might technically be right (the murder *was* committed by a former ship hand) but somehow it's just a lucky guess.

Fortunately for the King and Queen, I was on top of my game.

What exactly is a lucky guess? In epistemology luck tends to be spelled out in terms of the *safety* and *sensitivity* of a belief. If a belief is safe then *in most nearby possible worlds where you form the belief in the same way, it's still true.* A belief is sensitive if *in the nearest possible worlds where it's false, you wouldn't form the belief in the same way.*

But what are "possible worlds?" Think of a possible world as a hypothetical situation, some way you can imagine the world as it might have been. For instance, imagine a world just like ours, but where Holmes was a real man; that's one possible world. Some possible worlds are called "nearby" because they closely resemble our world in important ways (the real-Holmes world you just imagined is reasonably close). Others are considered to be "further away" because they are significantly different to ours (perhaps a world where Earth is populated by robot dinosaurs from Mars). There's a lot more to possible worlds, but this is enough for our purposes.

Let's look again at what safety means now that this "possible worlds" stuff is a little clearer. Essentially, if a belief is safe, then so long as your reasons for the belief don't change, small changes in the world shouldn't make it false. For example, if you flip a coin and see that it came up heads, the belief that it did come up heads is pretty safe. It doesn't matter if you flipped the coin in a kitchen, a den, or on the street. It seems that so long as your reason for the belief (seeing it for yourself) doesn't change, the belief is still probably true.

Additionally, assuming your reasons for forming a safe belief remained constant, falsification would have to involve large-scale changes to the world. Again, by way of example: your belief that

Arthur Conan Doyle wrote the original Sherlock Holmes stories is pretty safe. Why? Because your belief that he wrote them is based on repeated testimony from multiple sources. All of those people would have to be mistaken for your belief to be false. A world where everyone is mistaken about who wrote a famous story seems pretty far away from ours.

In contrast, the philosopher Bertrand Russell gave an example of an *unsafe* belief much like the following: suppose that Watson realizes that his pocket-watch has stopped during the night. So, when he heads out the door, Watson glances at his table clock and sets his watch to match it. However, unbeknownst to him, the table clock also stopped during the night. Luckily for Watson, the clock stopped precisely twelve hours before. Thus, when he glanced at it, it displayed the correct time (because he happened to look at it at precisely the right moment). Assuming that the table-clock is well made and normally accurate, Watson has every reason to believe it is accurate now (he's justified, and does believe it). Further, it did give him the right time (it's true). However, it seems that he might not really *know* what time it is. Since Watson would have formed his belief about the time in the same way even if there were a tiny change that made it false (such as the clock stopping five minutes earlier, or Watson glancing at it five minutes later), this belief is not safe.

Now let's look at sensitivity. If a belief is sensitive, then in the nearest possible worlds you won't form the belief that a fact is true unless it actually is true. For example, your belief that you can read English is probably a sensitive one. If you couldn't read English, you most likely wouldn't believe you could. Sure, we can imagine a world where you were raised speaking Dutch and *thinking* it's English. However, that would require large-scale changes to the world and would be a comparatively distant possible world. All that sensitivity requires is that *in the closest worlds where it's not true, you stop believing it.* In the close worlds you simply can't read English, and everything else is roughly the same. Since in those worlds you wouldn't believe that you could read English, your belief is sensitive.

I have heard your reasons and regard them as unconvincing and inadequate.

So, does Holmes ever get lucky? While Holmes often forms beliefs before the reader or Watson, most of us don't think that Holmes is merely making lucky guesses. Holmes himself denies this possibility in *The Sign of the Four*: "I never guess. It is a shocking habit—destructive to the logical faculty." But why aren't his deductions just guesses? How does he succeed where we do not?

The answer is found in his process of Holmesian deduction. This process is what Holmes is describing when he says: "When you have eliminated the impossible, whatever remains, however improbable, must be the truth." Holmes starts with simple observations and moves to seemingly incredible conclusions. However, our own Holmesian deductions are not *safe*. Even if we rightly deduce "whodunit," we have to acknowledge that things could merely appear that way to us regardless of whether it's true.

How does Holmes avoid unsafe beliefs? He relies on his incredible skill at analyzing evidence, finding the truth, and adopting it as his hypothesis. His skills allow him to seemingly unerringly find the right (the safe) justification for any belief he forms. An example of this is found in the 2009 film *Sherlock Holmes*, starring Robert Downey Jr. Midway through the movie a constable informs Holmes that Lord Blackwood is back from the dead. It turns out the constable's belief that Blackwood is alive is not very safe; It is based upon a combination of his belief that Blackwood was dead, and testimony that Blackwood was seen walking through the graveyard. However, since one of the beliefs justifying his belief that "Blackwood is alive" is false it seems as if there *must* be many nearby worlds where he formed this belief about Blackwood in the same way even though it's not true. Blackwood could really have been dead and the groundskeeper mistaken. Or, he could have never been dead at all, thus the belief that he is "back" is mistaken. Either way the constable's belief that Blackwood lives seems *unsafe*: it's not properly connected to the fact that he is alive.

Holmes, however, realizes that if the groundskeeper really saw Blackwood, then he must have simply faked his own death. Further, he did so convincingly enough to fool Watson (a fact which Holmes plays upon to draw Watson back into the investigation.) From this he deduces that Blackwood must never have been dead in the first place. Thus, Holmes's belief that Blackwood lives, based on the second-hand testimony of the groundskeeper, seems safe. Holmes's superior powers of reasoning allowed him to "rule out the impossible" and thus unerringly determine the real truth by reflection on the facts presented to him. This seems to allow Holmes to zero in on only the relevant facts which can support his beliefs in a "safe" way.

One should always look for a possible alternative, and provide against it.

But that only covers safety. Now let's look at sensitivity. As you may recall, if a belief is sensitive, then you would give it up when the relevant fact turns out to be false. Holmes escapes problems with insensitive beliefs by using his famous powers of observation. The combination of the evidence at hand and the lack of evidence to support alternative theories makes his deductions sensitive.

A very straightforward example of this can be found in the adventure "The Stock-Broker's Clerk." In this story, Holmes notices that Watson's new slippers are fire scorched but retain a paper wafer, near the instep, which is stamped with a maker's mark. Holmes correctly surmises that Watson had a cold and kept his feet near a fire for warmth. The other probable explanation (drying after soaking) would have removed the maker's label, so Holmes rules it out. Any alternate explanation would presumably leave different evidence.

When a belief is sensitive it means that in the nearest possible worlds where the fact is false, you cease to believe it. We can turn this around and instead formulate it as "How many facts about the case could you change before Holmes changed his belief?" Because Holmes would (presumably) notice *any* evidence that undermined his theory, we can assume that if almost anything changed, he would notice. In all the nearest possible worlds where his belief is false (Watson didn't have a cold) we can presume that Holmes would not believe it. He could be deceived, however, doing such a thing would require significant effort (like the earlier example about your ability to read English.) Surely, those possible worlds with huge conspiracies to deceive Holmes are not the *nearest* worlds where he is wrong. Since sensitivity is only concerned with the nearest worlds where the fact is false, huge conspiracies and other large changes to the world don't create problems For Holmes's sensitive beliefs.

Now, there are cases where Holmes *has* been wrong. For example, he didn't realize that Irene Adler knew who he was, a fact which enabled her to elude him. One might wonder if this sort of failure undermines the idea that his methods are reliable. If Holmes's methods are unreliable we might worry that his deductions can't give him the justification he needs for a justified true belief, much less safe or sensitive beliefs! It turns out that, despite his failures, the fact that Holmes himself believes something is sufficient justification for him to form knowledge.

This might sound like Holmes is "cheating" the knowledge system. Surely he can't be justified in believing something just because he believes it, can he? In short, yes he can.

We balance the probabilities and choose the most likely. It is the scientific use of the imagination.

This "cheating" self-justification is far more common than you might think. It's actually very similar to the way knowledge is formed in many scientific and academic fields. Suppose you're an expert in some particular field. If you formulate a theory based on some piece of evidence, you and your colleagues are justified in believing your theory partly because of your expertise. The fact that an expert believes something gives you some justification to believe it, even if that expert is you!

If this were not the case, observations about physics made by any "average Joe" might be as well justified as those of professional physicists. This idea is crazy; when Einstein discovered relativity he was far better justified in believing it than most of us would be if we thought about the same things. When professionals come to conclusions it's different from when the rest of us do. The reason for this difference can be found in the reliability of professional methods. Holmes's self-justification is based on his own history of successfully coming to the right conclusions.

Every time Holmes successfully deduces the answer he is better justified in believing in his own methods. As strange as it might sound, his skills of deduction can be likened to a professional billiards player. Just as we wouldn't say "a professional pool player is 'just lucky,'" so Holmes isn't just lucky when he correctly deduces an answer. The difference between Holmes and us is the difference between a professional and someone with beginner's luck.

When a first-time player successfully makes a difficult shot in billiards, it is rightly considered "beginners luck." However, if that same player were to go on and continue making difficult shots for years, we would say he or she is a naturally talented professional. Similarly, until we build up a long successful history like Holmes's, we're just getting lucky.

Further, as often noted in various stories, Holmes's few failures have caused him to redouble his efforts: he learns from his mistakes. Assuming he properly adjusts his methods to shore up any weak spots and always works to form only safe and sensitive beliefs, he can be justified by his own methods.

Education never ends Watson.
It is a series of lessons with the greatest for the last.

All in all a reasonable case can be made that Holmes doesn't regularly fall prey to problems of luck. However, if we found ourselves in his shoes and deer-hunter cap, we would be lucky (in more ways than one). We've seen that even in very difficult epistemic situations, Holmes somehow manages to keep his head and only form responsible beliefs. Holmes's amazing powers of deduction and keen observational skills allow him to reliably form safe, sensitive beliefs in cases where we cannot. This, combined with the justification granted by his career as a professional consulting detective, ensures that if anyone knows what's really going on in a case, it's Holmes.

Now, it's unclear if Holmesian deduction would ever give anyone in the real world actual knowledge. None of us have access to Holmes's famous powers. Further, even if we assume that we could concoct the sorts of reasonable explanations he comes up with, there's no real way of knowing that there aren't a huge number of plausible alternative theories to explain what we see. For now, the job of consulting detective must be relegated to the realm of fiction. While the character Sherlock Holmes might be able to pull off amazing feats of deduction, it's only because we're willing to accept as fact that there really are no nearby possible worlds that would spoil the safety or sensitivity of his beliefs.

It might be the case that Holmes *does* benefit from occasional lucky strikes (after all, even the best occasionally get lucky). However, when Holmes exercises his due diligence, eliminates all the impossible alternatives, and utilizes his formidable prowess as a detective, he doesn't arrive at the answer merely by chance. It's skill, not an accident of fate. This is why we can rightly say that he's not just the luckiest detective in fiction: he *really* is that good.

Chapter 4

The Adventure of the Candle and the Dumbbell

Fiona Tomkinson

Of course, it was Holmes who, to alleviate an evening's tedium, first introduced the question. It is possible, though not certain, that the whole affair arose out of one of the solutions to a crossword puzzle which could have been either "object" or "things."

At first, Watson expressed bewilderment at the possibility that the terms could be anything other than synonymous. Then he began to think that, though people tend to use the words interchangeably, perhaps a rigorous scientific man such as himself should not. But where does the difference lie? He began to advance tentative theories.

Is a thing natural and an object manufactured? Is *thing* a popular term and *object* a scientific one? Is it a question of value? Is a beryl coronet or a golden pince-nez an object, but a missing three-quarter merely a thing? Yet we always talk of the "object of enquiry", never the "thing of enquiry," even when that object is insignificant!

Then again, we talk of "my things," but never "my objects." Is a thing a possession and an object something still to be purchased? But can the purchase of something really expensive, such as the Mazarin stone, ever reduce it to a mere thing?

His ruminations reminded him of how much he and Holmes had, in the course of their many adventures, lived in a world of things, but still, in the end, he confessed himself defeated in the attempt to come up with a consistent theory concerning them, and he wondered whether it were not all ineffable twaddle. He could not say whether objects and things were the same or whether they deserved such a thing as a theory at all. He could not even say with any certainty, what a thing was.

"Holmes," he asked, "do you think one can assert that a thing is always—well, always the same thing? Was my umbrella, for example, the same thing that I used to shelter from the rain, when you used it as a tool to dredge a moat? And then, can something powdery, such as tobacco ash, of which you have made such an extensive study, really be either a thing or indeed an object? What about that important clue, a footprint, which is really only a hole in something else? Or do you think that perhaps the term 'thing' should be applied to everything material, and we should save the expression 'object' for something mythical, such as, say, the Devil's Foot?"

The Adventures of Things and the Things of Adventure

Holmes, after letting Watson talk, stated his own position decisively. There was a distinction of the most elementary sort. As far as he was concerned, a thing was a thing of no consequence; an object was a thing transformed into a clue.

A thing is usually first transformed into a clue through an insight into its relation with the human body. Just as the footprint implies the foot, and the ash the smoker's hand, so does almost every thing conceal the story of how it was touched or abandoned. When we force it to tell its story, it no longer exists simply in the present. It opens up vast vistas into both the past and the future. It makes us aware of what is absent in even greater measure than that which is present.

His own peculiar genius, he now asserted, was no more and no less than the awareness that every thing was not merely a thing, but a thing which could, in the twinkling of an eye, undergo a metamorphosis into an object. (Here, by way of demonstration, he seized his slipper and placed it on the mantelpiece.)

For the detective of genius, he declaimed, reaching now for his violin, the whole world of thingness forever trembles on the brink of true objectivity! His relation with the thing is such that he understands very well why only a single letter divides the words *think* and *thing*.

Watson, knowing his friend to be badly read in philosophy, is astonished at this kind of idealistic language, and looked around uneasily for signs of the hypodermic needle. Then he asked Holmes if he could perhaps illustrate the matter further using one of the stories from the tin box, or perhaps one of the adventures that he had himself committed to writing?

"Nearly all our adventures could be used as illustrations," said Holmes. "Sometimes our difficulty is to crack a cipher and find meaningful words, sometimes to discover the things certain words refer to, as in 'The Adventure of the Speckled Band,' where, half-convinced that the dying woman's words were a reference to a group of gypsies, we overlooked the possibility that they might refer to a poisonous snake. But more often we begin with the things themselves, do we not? We have the things in our hands, and it is only a question of interpreting them correctly, is that not so?

"However," continued Holmes, "I can think of no event which better illustrates my point than the adventure that you have already brought to mind through your reference to moat-dredging, a certain story of a candle——"

Birlstone Manor Revisited

"A candle?" exclaimed Watson.

"Yes, of a very memorable candle," said Holmes. "I am amazed that you can have forgotten it. But you did not let me finish. I was about to say: a certain story of a candle and of a dumbbell!"

"Are you referring," cried Watson, "to the candle in the study in Birlstone Manor House?"

Holmes nodded, and lit his pipe.

"Sometimes a candle is only a candle," he mused.

"Like a cigar?" asked Watson.

"Precisely," said Holmes. "But sometimes it sheds a great deal more light——"

"Than it emits physically?"

"Indeed, Watson. That is why, if you had grasped the essentials of the matter, you would have avoided the fancifully romantic title, *The Valley of Fear*, and called your report *The Adventure of the Candle and the Dumbbell*. In recording other adventures, you were good enough to make things, or perhaps I should say, objects, the true heroes, though you did not always select the right ones. For example, 'The Adventure of the Blue Carbuncle' might more appropriately have been called 'The Adventure of the Bowler Hat,' and——"

"I seem to recollect that we have had this sort of conversation before. One must make some concessions to popular taste. But to return to the candle . . ."

"You are well acquainted with my methods. You will recollect that upon entering the study where we believed the corpse of Mr. Douglas (as we then thought him to be called) was lying, I noticed, among other things, a candle that had been extinguished before much of it had burned away. This immediately led me to two conclusions: firstly, that the dead man's interview with his assailant had been brief, and secondly, that Mrs. Douglas and her husband's best friend, Cecil Barker, were giving a false account of events when they claimed that they had raised the alarm immediately after discovering the body. For, though it is conceivable that a man who had just discovered his best friend's body would have lit a lamp in order to view the scene better, it is unlikely that he should have thought about saving candle wax."

"And there was also the question of the missing wedding ring," said Watson. "If Barker's account was correct, there was no time for the assailant to remove it after the shooting, and the candle proved that there was no time for it to have been removed before!"

"And the ring was another thing, Watson. A thing which became an object! But to return to the candle. What is behind the use of that candle, indeed of any other candle?"

"The desire for light!"

"Indeed, Watson. But behind that desire for light in the house there is something else. Fear, Watson. Fear of darkness, and of what may lurk therein. Fear of bumping into familiar household objects—which then seem to us no longer objects but things! Yes, and the worse fear of encountering the unfamiliar!"

"It was the fear of fire which made Douglas go the rounds of his property every night. Or so we then believed. It was more likely his fear of his old enemies, the Scowsers!"

"The fear of death is behind both of them, Watson. Perhaps the two were connected in his mind. The mining valley where he first had dealings with the Scowsers was also a place of fire, an infernal landscape, as I believe you describe it."

"Yet he met his fate by water in the end."

"Indeed. In the end, there is escape for no-one."

Holmes sighed deeply, doubtless thinking of the role Moriarty had played in this, and of his own failure to prevent it.

Then he continued, "Yet once we understand the extent to which fear and anxiety underlie ordinary human actions, we can all the better understand how men and women act in exceptional ones. Nowhere is this truer than in our relation to so-called things, Watson. We are motivated by fear, or by care, which is fear under a softer name. And that is how these things become objects! We light candles from the fear of darkness, we extinguish them from fear of fire or fear of poverty. We cast them aside when a greater fear makes it necessary to reach for a weapon!"

"As Douglas did when he reached for the hammer, in order to grapple with his old enemy, Ted Baldwin!"

"The presence of the hammer on the floor testified to that, Watson! As surely as if it had taken an oath in court. That hammer would not have remained in such a position otherwise. A tool or piece of equipment is nearly always removed from the floor by servants, prompted by the fear of losing their livelihood! And such a dismissal could doubtless be traced to their master's primordial fear of tripping over something. But more significant yet was my discovery of the single dumbbell. As I said at the time, no-one uses a single dumbbell, Watson, unless they wish to condemn themselves to curvature of the spine! Such a fear would, in most cases, I believe, outweigh the fear of decrepitude which motivates us to use a dumbbell in the first place. And, as previously stated, in an orderly household, with a fair-sized domestic staff, such items are unlikely to be allowed to wander around, as it were of their own freewill, as they sometimes do in the rooms of a bachelor of irregular habits."

"Indeed, Holmes, had you owned a pair of dumbbells, I should not have been surprised to find one of them in the coal scuttle and the other on the mantelpiece."

"If you had, Watson, there would have been a good reason for it, and behind that reason, would, doubtless, have been the fear of losing my intellectual faculties through simple want of stimulation. But to continue. In seeking to account for the missing dumbbell, again I looked at the problem from the perspective of linking it to the human body and to human fear. That dumbbell had been moved by a human hand. It was not the murder weapon. If it had been used in self-defence, as we later learned the hammer was, then, why should it have been removed when the other weapons were not? Yet fear is the most likely reason for its removal. Fear on the part of the guilty person that their guilt would be revealed and that they would end on the gallows! So, what was the fear? If the dumbbell were not removed for its own sake, it must have been used as the means to remove something else. And the nearness of water strongly suggested——"

"That it was used as a weight to sink that something else!"

"As was proved to be the case, Watson, with the aid of your excellent umbrella, which you imagined I had taken as a weapon. And in a sense that was true! A much more dangerous weapon than if I had banged on the man's head with it! For, mark, Watson, I was not content in having located the mere presence of that dumbbell and that which it had been used to conceal. Having looked into its past, I was also in a position to predict the thing's future. It was no longer a mere thing. It was an object! I knew that just as fear had buried it in the moat, so fear would resurrect it when I circulated the false rumour that the moat was to be drained and searched for evidence. Fear, using the agency of a human hand, Watson."

"And thus were Ted Baldwin's clothes and dagger discovered, and we made the even more important discovery that it was his mutilated body, and not that of Douglas, which was discovered in the study! And that the fair Mrs. Douglas was both a deceitful witness and a faithful wife!"

It was now Watson's turn to sigh a little.

"And with the aid of the pamphlet relating the history of the house in the seventeenth-century, we caused Mr. Douglas, wearing the wedding ring he could not or would not remove, to step forward from the hiding-place, which had once held the fugitive Charles II. See how mere things can be gathered together and woven into a net! It is then as if they have become a single object. Did you know that the Vikings called their Parliament a Thing, and that that meant a Gathering? Etymologies are important, Watson!"

"Would they not have done better to call it an Object, Holmes?"

"We cannot expect such distinctions of abstract thought from them, Watson."

"But Holmes, when we consider the things that we weaved together into our net, we should really have called our adventure the story of the candle, the dumbbell, the hammer, the ring, and the pamphlet!"

"That would not be so pithy," said Holmes.

"I stand by my original title," said Watson. "According to your theory, are not the past and the future both valleys of fear, valleys of the shadow of death? And do not the most innocent of things and the most complex of objects continually lead us into those valleys?"

Holmes said nothing.

Postscript

I am a very old man in this chilly spring of 1926, and perhaps I no longer think as clearly as I once did. Yet, hearing a friend of mine (my closest friend since the sad death of Sherlock Holmes)—a friend who is a great specialist in German philosophy—talk at great length of, and even go so far as to read me some extracts from, a new book which has been published in Germany, by one

Martin Heidegger, it seemed to me that some of his ideas owed more than a little to my old friend Sherlock Holmes, though he uses a much more complicated terminology than Holmes's lucid distinction between the thing and the object!

Here is a philosopher, it seems, if I have understood him aright, who does not want to leave things lying about in the present tense. He wants to open what he calls Being up to the past and the future. What his purpose is in so doing, is far from clear to me. It has nothing to do with bringing the perpetrators of crime to justice. I fear much of what he says may be ineffable twaddle. And I distrust the Germans since the last war. Yet here and there, flashing out like jewels among all that incomprehensible Teutonic verbiage, are Holmes's very ideas, the ideas which motivated his scientific practice and his transcendent success!

This philosopher also understands that we are forever in the grip of care and anxiety, of how the human being, whom he rather fancifully calls Being-here or Dasein, always directs his attention to his coming death, and directs himself towards things as a means of avoiding it for a time! He even talks about directionality as one of the attributes of this Dasein. And if I follow him correctly, he thinks that we understand all this better if we also understand the important distinction between those unused things that we do not even think about using, those things which are merely present-at-hand as he calls them, and things which are ready-to-hand, those things which Holmes would have called objects!

These ready-to-hand things tend to have the character of equipment, equipment which is meant to help us in our daily struggle to stay alive! When they get broken and useless, they become ordinary present-at-hand things again. I would once have thought that this difference was too obvious to concern a great philosopher. But now that Sherlock Holmes is gone from the world, I understand exactly how much his genius depended on this simple ability to see everything in it as ready-to-hand, as something which could really be grasped! It was not just that he saw how others had grasped hold of the world in the past. He grasped it himself. The simplest displaced pebble could become his equipment and his weapon in the struggle against crime and the even greater struggle against our ignorance of the causes of things!

And when this German philosopher actually devotes a paragraph to speaking of equipment as something which either has its place or else is left lying around, I can only think of the significance of that hammer left lying on the floor in the study of Birlstone Manor, and that displaced dumbbell submerged in the moat . . .

If Holmes could have lived to see this, would he have sued this Heidegger for theft of intellectual property? I trust not. He was always willing to let others take the credit for his intellectual labours.

I think, in any case, that we have not heard the last of theories of things. They will probably grow to keep pace with all this newfangled equipment which proliferates in the modern world. And this German professor, who is doubtless a genius in his own way – God grant he be not another Moriarty in the making!—will, I dare say, develop his own ideas more in the future, though I shall not live to read them. Perhaps he will, in the mystical German manner, ponder that connection between the words 'think' and 'thing' which so intrigued Holmes. Perhaps one day he will even find a way of speaking of things which is not relentlessly related to our mortal fears, a way of just letting them be. At any rate, it seems to me that this philosopher is like my old friend in his quest for truth. For me the truth has always resembled the solution to a crossword puzzle. But for Holmes, for all his cold scientific ways, it was something much more concrete, something that had to be violently uncovered and dragged into the light.

—JHW

Chapter 5

Action Man or Dreamy Detective

Sami Paavola and Lauri Järvilehto

> Sherlock Holmes and Dr. Watson were waiting for Miss Violet Hunter to contact them. The young woman had accepted the post of governess at the Rucastle household under the most curious conditions. The master sleuth's intuition told him something was amiss with Miss Hunter's case, but he could not pinpoint what it was.
>
> "Data! data! data!" he cried impatiently. "I can't make bricks without clay."
>
> —"The Adventure of the Copper Beeches"

Sherlock Holmes is renowned for his capacity to single out the essential from a bewildering array of trifles and so crack even the hardest of cases. This capacity has lent the detective an air of the supernatural. Holmes himself, however, would object to such interpretations. For the master detective, his power lies in his methodology.

How does Holmes come up with novel ideas? What's the secret of his masterful problem-solving skills? If he really has invented a method, can it be used for solving problems or making discoveries outside of the field of crime?

Holmes is, he tells us, about to write a textbook on the subject. He often complains that when reporting the cases Watson put too much emphasis on the story instead of instructive and rigorous demonstration. When Watson asks in annoyance why Holmes is not writing on the cases from this angle, Holmes remarks:

> "I will, my dear Watson, I will. At present I am, as you know, fairly busy, but I propose to devote my declining years to the composition of a textbook, which shall focus the whole art of detection into one volume."
> ("The Adventure of the Abbey Grange")

Unfortunately for us, Holmes never had time to write this textbook. And we don't know for sure what he would have written, but we can follow up some clues from his cases.

Asking the Right Question

Sherlock Holmes called his method by many names. It was the "Science of Deduction and Analysis" or simply "Science of Deduction" which demands faculties of observation, and deduction, as well as knowledge on relevant areas of life. It required "curious analytic reasoning from effects to causes". It demanded faculties of deduction and logical synthesis; or analysis.

Jaakko Hintikka, a philosophical Sherlock in his own right, has maintained that Holmes's secret was the skillful use of the old Socratic method: in uniting the art of reasoning with the art of providing proper questions and answers. Other Socratics (like Matti Sintonen) have agreed. Holmes is able to find key issues in problematic situations by framing strategically useful questions. For example, in "Silver Blaze" the key question is the odd behavior, or actually the lack of behavior, of the dog during the robbery of the famous racing horse Silver Blaze:

> "Is there any other point to which you would wish to draw my attention?"
> 'To the curious incident of the dog in the night-time."
> "The dog did nothing in the night-time."
> "That was the curious incident," remarked Sherlock Holmes.

Did the dog bark? No. Why does a watchdog not bark in the middle of the night, if something odd is happening? Because whatever was happening in the night-time, the perpetrator must have been somebody the dog knew well enough not to be disturbed by him.

As with many great discoveries, Holmes's questions seem self-evident after the discovery has been made. But as with many discoveries, coming up with the right questions beforehand is a very tricky task. Good questions are just those questions by which you eventually solve your case. But it takes a Sherlock Holmes, or Holmes's methods, to come up with such questions.

Playing the Guessing Game

Holmes's reasoning does not only rely on knowing the definitional rules of logic. It's about coming up with chains of arguments which support the search for key issues in the case. It's more about having a good strategy for reasoning than about reasoning as such. As Hintikka has emphasized, the master player in games of chess is not the one who knows the basic rules of the game extremely well, but the one who is a master in the strategies and heuristics of the game. The same applies to the art of detection and reasoning.

It's often been claimed that Holmes's method was not, in fact, deduction, but *abduction*. Charles Peirce, the famous American philosopher and logician, maintained that reasoning falls into three categories.

- **Deduction, the pattern of reasoning by clarifying logical necessities.**

- **Induction, reasoning on the basis of what "actually is."**

Induction has attracted philosophers' minds for ages. We use various kinds of inductive reasoning all the time, for instance, when making generalizations. According to Peirce, there is, however, also another form of non-deductive reasoning: abduction.

- **Abduction, the main kind of reasoning we use for coming up with new ideas.**

Abduction is weaker than induction. And it is much more speculative than deduction. Abduction is about crafting hypotheses and fertile possibilities on the basis of clues. Abduction is used when we look for possible explanations for somehow surprising events. Even if abduction is weak as a form of reasoning (it's about *maybe*'s) it's strong and useful where discoveries and novelties are concerned. When we aim at inventing something new we cannot deduce it by necessity or inductively generalize it from existing knowledge. We need ways of inventing and developing new possibilities.

Despite being a fan of Edgar Allan Poe, the grand old man of the detective genre, Peirce himself did not make a strong connection between abduction and detective work. Others, such as Thomas A. Sebeok, Jean Umiker-Sebeok, and Umberto Eco have, however, noticed how Sherlock Holmes's work is often like abductive reasoning. Typically, abduction is about reasoning "backwards" from consequences to causes or explanations. When a murder has happened, various signs are left at the crime scene that tell us something about the crime and the perpetrator. Abduction is coming up with explanations for these signs.

Reasoning backwards is what Sherlock Holmes calls "analytic," as opposed to "synthetic" reasoning. Synthetic reasoning is asking: What happens next? Analytic reasoning is asking: How did this come about?

> "In solving a problem of this sort, the grand thing is to be able to reason backward. . . . In the everyday affairs of life it is more useful to reason forward, and so the other comes to be neglected. There are fifty who can reason synthetically for one who can reason analytically." (*A Study in Scarlet*)

We know the end result. The trick is to use this knowledge for inventing novel hypotheses about how the result came about.

Holmes is always making detailed observations and minute investigations at the crime scene in order to provide materials to start these backward reasonings. Abductive reasoners especially look for strange happenings and little details that don't quite fit, as clues when searching for potential explanations. As Sherlock Holmes says in "The Boscombe Valley Mystery": "You know my method. It is founded upon the observation of trifles."

Details and strange happenings can be used as a starting point for providing logically elegant solutions and chains of reasoning. These details can be so small that at one extreme abductions turn on hints which we're not even aware of. Nonetheless, they can help when guessing and searching candidate solutions.

Abduction is not, however, just wild, intuitive guesswork. While the process of discovery might begin with intuitively forming a hypothesis, such a hypothesis is in the end strengthened in a very Sherlockian manner: by drawing deductive inferences that coincide with the known facts.

Maybes and Must Bes

The beginning phases of Holmes's abductive process involve minute observation, guesswork, and imagination. Holmes can craft several possible scenarios that could be used to crack a given conundrum. He does not, however, commit to any single one before he had enough information to settle on a single hypothesis:

> "I have devised seven separate explanations, each of which would cover the facts as far as we know them. But which of these is correct can only be determined by the fresh information which we shall no doubt find waiting for us." ("The Adventure of the Copper Beeches")

Holmes also holds that imagination has a key role in drawing his impressive inferences:

> "See the value of imagination. . . . It is the one quality which Gregory lacks. We imagined what might have happened, acted upon the supposition, and find ourselves justified." ("Silver Blaze")

While observation, guesswork, and imagination are central to abduction, this peculiar mode of inference involves more than just guessing. Indeed, Sherlock himself objected to plain guesswork in *The Sign of the Four*: "I never guess. It is a shocking habit—destructive to the logical faculty."

Abduction is not pure guesswork but is based on skillful use of clues and constraints. Guesswork and imagination function as the first stage of discovery. The ingenuity of Holmes's method is combining the imaginative capacity with impressive skills in all forms of inference. Holmes firmly objects to speculations on their own. Only once data has been gathered can we draw up a hypothesis: "It is a capital mistake to theorize before you have all the evidence. It biases the judgment" (*A Study in Scarlet*).

Good abductive "guesses" need some material. The inquirer uses clues, previous knowledge, and new observations to trigger and guide guesses. These speculations must then be checked separately. This is not traditional inductive methodology where data is simply compiled together in order to reach more general truths. Rather, data provides triggers for searching explanations and novel perspectives.

While the grounds for abductive reasoning can be based on drawing hypotheses on the basis of clues, the whole process of reasoning also involves deduction and induction. New premises are introduced by anticipating how to draw deductions from them. If the deductions are verified by novel observations, the hypothesis is strengthened, otherwise not. The inquiry process requires three processes of reasoning: abduction, deduction, and induction.

A clear example of the process of Holmes's combining abduction with deduction and induction can be found in the classic encounter of Holmes and Watson near the beginning of *A Study in Scarlet*. When he first meets Watson, Holmes quickly concludes that Watson has been in Afghanistan. Later Sherlock explains this to Watson:

> "The train of reasoning ran, 'Here is a gentleman of a medical type, but with the air of a military man. Clearly an army doctor, then. . . .'"

The start of this train of reasoning is then more like detailed observation.

> "He has just come from the tropics, for his face is dark, and that is not the natural tint of his skin, for his wrists are fair. . . ."

This is an abductive explanation for the darkness of the face, which is clearly not Watson's natural tint (on the basis of a clue concerning his wrists).

> "He has undergone hardship and sickness, as his haggard face says clearly. His left arm has been injured. He holds it in a stiff and unnatural manner. Where in the tropics could an English army doctor have seen much hardship and got his arm wounded? Clearly in Afghanistan."

An abductive explanation for various clues and observations (injured arm, coming from tropics, army doctor) pointed with a key question.

> "The whole train of thought did not occupy a second. I then remarked that you came from Afghanistan, and you were astonished."

And then, if needed, from the hypothesis that Watson is an injured army doctor who has just come from Afghanistan, supported by some additional, commonplace suppositions, all details can be deduced and the whole thing checked inductively.

Three to Get Ready

Besides abduction there is another Peircean idea which illuminates Sherlock Holmes's methods.

Peirce founded his famous theory of signs on an elegantly simple idea of three basic categories: *Firstness, Secondness,* and *Thirdness*. These categories appear in many forms. As metaphysical categories, firstnesses are things in themselves. Good examples are qualities of feeling, possibilities and icons. Secondnesses are two things clashing against each other, such as reactions, actualities and indices. Thirdnesses concern mediation, where some things are brought together with mediating processes which is more complicated than just two things reacting with each other, such as rules, symbols and reasoning.

Even though they are categories, the strength of firstnesses, secondnesses, and thirdnesses comes from combinations and mixtures. For example, abduction is a form of reasoning. Therefore it is about mediation and Thirdness. But its peculiarity comes from using tones, potentialities, iconic resemblances—firstnesses—as a fuel for reasoning: the clues and elements from which the abductive hypotheses are formed.

An important part of Holmes's methods is that he is so good at combining in his work the different Peircean categories: qualities of feeling and imagination, actions and reactions, and different forms of reasoning. It's more typical to be good at one of these areas, or maybe two of them. Holmes is a Peircean savant: an expert in all three categories. Although Holmes doesn't always want to admit it, reasoning includes an element of the dream (especially through abductions) and action (with inductions). Peircean categories work for each other.

Most famously, Sherlock Holmes is uncanny in drawing inference, and he often emphasizes their exact and "scientific" nature. "Detection is, or ought to be, an exact science and should be treated in the same cold and unemotional manner" (*The Sign of the Four*).

Holmes could solve some easier cases just by armchair reasoning. But he's also a man of action. This takes several forms. He is a true forerunner of crime scene investigation with the use of various instruments like a magnifying glass or a tape measure to get the evidence he needs, instead of relying only on what can be seen by the naked eye.

Holmes is keen on making experiments which help him to analyze evidence, like making a test for blood stains, or distinguishing differences in cigar ashes. These kinds of experiments were complemented by his detailed knowledge of crimes and horrors perpetrated down the centuries, which he refers to while searching for apparent novelties. "There is nothing new under the sun. It has all been done before" (*A Study in Scarlet*).

An expert fighter, Sherlock doesn't hesitate to put his fists up and his neck on the line if a case requires it. He's always ready, with Watson, to risk his own life and well-being when grappling with the London underworld. He goes to enormous trouble to find crucial pieces of evidence, sometimes using disguise to elicit information. "'They say that genius is an infinite capacity for taking pains', he remarked with a smile. 'It's a very bad definition, but it does apply to detective work'" (*A Study in Scarlet*).

Finally, in addition to being a man of reason and a man of action, Sherlock is also a man of imagination and day-dreaming. Watson notes in "The Copper Beeches," "As to Holmes, I observed that he sat frequently for half an hour on end, with knitted brows and an abstracted air."

His toolbox did not consist only of his wit, his scientific equipment and his fists, but just as much of his violin and his armchair which he would use to feed his reasoning and to make room for novel insights while pondering the cases. While these elements of his character would sometimes backfire, as was arguably the case with his addiction to intravenous cocaine, the element of reverie was just as central to Sherlock's methodology as was his colder reasoning capacity, or his skills in the field.

Peirce once remarked that there are three classes of human beings related to three categories: those to whom the chief thing is the qualities of feeling and art, secondly the practical men, and thirdly those who emphasize thinking. Sherlock Holmes manages to combine all of these features to serve his methods.

Holmes's methodology covers the entire process of discovery. First, he provides the clay of thought by the way of minute observation and related imagination and reverie. Secondly, his meticulous capacity for chains of reasoning provides the forms into which the clay is molded. And finally, as a man of action, he is also capable of working with the bricks themselves when needed to get constructions ready, or to get more clay for thought. By being a sovereign master of all Peircean categories, the master sleuth is a superb renaissance man. However, this is not because he has somehow magically been endowed with such skill. Quite the opposite, the secret of Sherlock Holmes's detection lies, as he so often emphasizes, in his methods and the practical skills for mastering them.

A Toolbox for Your Holmes

Sherlock Holmes maintains that although his methods seem to be theoretical they are "extremely practical" as well. Here's a short toolkit of Holmes's methods. The list is by no means exhaustive, but gives some advice for those interested in effective methods:

- **Formulate the problem you set out to solve clearly and distinctly.**

- **Observe and make experiments: investigate carefully your area of interest.**

- **Pay attention, especially to surprising details and clues: keep your focus on the concrete but what is easily evanescent.**

- **Keep yourself up to date and focus your work: build an extensive library and index of relevant information.**

- **Theorize, but by taking facts into account: create hypotheses that are viable in terms of the data.**

- **Don't be satisfied with half-baked explanations: do not give up before you have solved the mysteries.**

- **Aim at elegant chains of logical connections: Even the most intricate tangle of things can be sorted out with dedicated inquiry.**

- **Ask specific questions: by formulating questions you can narrow down the applicable data and theories.**

- **Refine the tools and instruments needed in your work: Good work requires good tools, and advanced practice in using these tools.**

- **Test and retest: your favorite ideas can turn out to be wrong or biased.**

- **Surround yourself with people who can help you in various tasks needed in your work: Not even Sherlock Holmes can work alone.**

- **Get involved! Do only those things that really make sense for you and what you love most.**

We can't claim to have unveiled all the secrets of Holmes's methods. Like any art or expertise, learning these methods requires practice and long and patient study. It is not a question of inborn capacities but a result of practice. There will always, no doubt, remain a shroud of mystery around the mastery of the Baker Street detective's methods.

Furthermore, the methods of detection have in some senses changed dramatically during the last hundred or so years. Therefore, modern Holmeses need even more elaborate methodologies, techniques, and collaboration for problem solving than was the case in Holmes's day. Nonetheless, making observations, asking questions, using all forms of reasoning, and combining aspects of imagination, action, and intelligence, will no doubt remain some of the most useful tools for people involved in any line of detection.

By applying these very same methods, we can also learn more about the mystery—and the mastery—of Sherlockian methods themselves.

A
DOG REFLECTS
THE
FAMILY LIFE

Chapter 6
From the Mean Streets to Baker Street
Francine J. Sanders

It's hard to recall the first detective who stole my heart. I'm sure he was wrapped in a trench coat, blowing smoke in someone's face, but there have been so many through the years. As a young girl, I crushed on Charlie Chan and an assortment of detective heroes on Saturday morning television, curled up on my parents' basement couch, alone, just me and my screen sleuths.

My serious relationships began with exposure to hard-boiled PI's—the stuff of Raymond Chandler and Dashiell Hammett. These guys—and they almost always were guys—were the heroes of film noir, the film tradition rooted in post-World War II disillusionment, inspired by the grit and grime of hard-boiled pulp fiction. Even before I knew I wanted to be a detective, I was turned on by the world in these films. And especially by the detectives who inhabited it. They spit out cool dialogue, knew strange, interesting people in every pocket of the city, and always attracted the most alluring and resourceful women. It didn't hurt that they also brought down one or two bad guys.

And they did it on their own. They were lone wolfs, private dicks, ex-cops who had been cast out from their former departments. It made perfect sense that I would be a sucker for them. Even at a young age, I saw myself as a loner and aspiring rebel.

Sherlock Holmes, the most famous sleuth of them all, was noticeably absent in my little black book of detectives. In movies, I always associated Holmes with Basil Rathbone. When I caught his detective on the screen, I routinely turned the channel for more colorful personas, or waited for the next Saturday morning's detective to make his appearance.

The Evidence

Recently, while channel surfing on early morning cable, I stumbled upon *Sherlock Holmes and the Secret Weapon* (1943), one of fourteen films in a series of Sherlock Holmes mysteries released between 1939 and 1946. These were the films that likely introduced me to Conan Doyle's world and his Baker Street detective. But this time, I didn't find myself switching channels. To my surprise and pleasure, I liked what I saw. Although Holmes hadn't changed through all these years, I had.

I know works of art don't change through time, but certain ones seem to transform themselves in response to the spectator's own transformation. So it wasn't surprising that this recent viewing of *The Secret Weapon* jumpstarted my reevaluation of Holmes and Rathbone, and my relationship to them.

Similar to the setting all those years ago, I watched the Holmes film on an early Saturday morning. But much had changed. I was no longer in my parents' basement, curled up on their couch in my PJ's. My parents—and their home—are long gone. I don't think I even own a pair of pajamas. My life is no longer a mysterious journey waiting to unfold—it's a journey that is already more than half over. And, in the years since my first exposure to Holmes and my early fixation on detectives, I had fulfilled my fantasy—I worked as an investigator with the Chicago Police Department's Office of Professional Standards, a civilian investigative unit that handled misconduct charges against police officers. The work was a long way from Scotland Yard, but it was close enough. Holmes and I now had something in common: We were both investigators.

Now I could appreciate Holmes, especially Rathbone's portrayal. It was as if I was meeting him for the first time. Despite his faraway world drenched in London fog and his Baker Street address, Holmes didn't feel like a distant, remote figure. He was no longer the brittle, mechanical sleuth-robot that I recalled from my youth. He was now the witty master of disguise, fully loaded with a dry sense of humor and razor-sharp mind. He was modern. He was cool. He was even a bit sexy in a tweedy kind of way.

Tea For Two versus Table For One

While Holmes on screen offered some new satisfactions all these years later, I still wondered how he stacked up to my noir heroes.

In an early scene in *The Woman in Green* (1945), the action slows down while Holmes prepares a cup of tea for himself and Watson. After he pours Watson's tea, he drops a splash of milk into the cup. He doesn't ask—he just pours.

This familiarity—this intimacy—was one of the most striking discoveries and satisfactions during my investigation of the early Holmes films. There's something touching here, as if Holmes and Watson are an old married couple, aware of the subtlest details of each other's lives, an awareness cultivated by a long life of togetherness. Holmes clearly has been paying attention to clues and details beyond the scope of an official investigation.

Unlike Holmes, the hard-boiled detectives are defined by their loner status. It's not that there aren't people in their world: cops from their police days before they were kicked out of the department; good-looking secretaries who know the right kind of booze to keep stocked in their desk drawer; and an assortment of marginalized oddballs that they can call on day or night. But when push comes to shove, these detectives are alone—and they know it. They don't have sidekicks or partners. If they do—like Sam Spade in *The Maltese Falcon*—the partner usually gets knocked off a few minutes into the story.

Even Holmes's flat reminds us of this key difference between the Baker Street detective and his American cousins. Holmes's flat is stuffed with evidence of a full life—souvenirs and mementoes reflecting a history crowded with relationships and a world beyond Baker Street. This is in stark contrast to the typically sterile apartment of the noir detective. In many of the hard-boiled stories, we don't even visit the hero's home. When we do, it provides insight only through the absence of clues. And the hard-boiled hero's office offers little more. Its location in the shabbiest part of town and the drab, beat-up space are constant reminders of the hero's place in the world. This man travels light—whether it's because he's on the run or because he knows there's nowhere to go. But Holmes has roots and seems comfortable and comforted by his surroundings. He's a classic hero who is both respected and respectable, unlike the noir anti-hero, who is usually looked down upon and alienated.

Same Tools, Different Problems

As an investigator, I, too, worked in a drab, beige office devoid of color and hope. My mean streets were the streets of Chicago. For more than eight years, I looked for witnesses, victims, alleged

victims, and clues on a wide range of police brutality cases—
everything from people complaining that a cop handcuffed them
too tightly to allegations of severe beating—even shooting—by
a cop.

It didn't take long to learn that I was nobody's friend and
everybody's enemy. It took only a little longer to learn that
everybody told lies and that nothing was what it seemed. This
cold reality was one of the greatest challenges of the job; it was
also one of the draws that kept me there.

The theme of deception is prominent in both detective
worlds, although it is often played out in different ways. In
rediscovering the old Holmes-Rathbone movies, it was no
surprise to see Holmes's adversaries adopt an assortment of
disguises and personas. What caught my attention was Holmes's
own mastery in the art of deception. Unlike the noir hero who is
often the victim of deception, Holmes employs deception as an
investigative tool.

In *The Secret Weapon*, Holmes is introduced in disguise, one
of several that he adopts throughout the film. We meet him in
a Swiss chalet, where his elderly, white-haired, German book
peddler has a rendezvous with a couple of shady characters.
Holmes as book peddler amusingly pokes fun at "this Detective
Sherlock Holmes." This witty introduction establishes Holmes
as chameleon, a versatile performer who is able to transform
himself into myriad personas in the service of his investigation.

But Holmes's skill as masquerader offers more than witty
play. Later in the film, Holmes disguises himself as a roughneck
sailor, a physical and emotional antithesis to his pipe-smoking,
well-bred detective. I was surprised—and delighted—to see
Rathbone's cerebral, logical Holmes give way to this rough-
and-tumble character. Not only does he do some serious tough-
talking, he also gets flat out physical. Sure, he's no Mitchum or
Bogart, but the brawn seems real enough, a part of Holmes and
not just an external trapping.

In *The Spider Woman* (1944), Holmes again reveals his skill
in the art of masquerade. After Holmes fakes his own death,
we discover him in disguise as an elderly, bushy-browed postal
worker. He arrives with a delivery to the Baker Street flat just as
a grief-stricken Watson and Mrs. Hudson are sorting through
Holmes's possessions. During his exchange with Watson, he
spews out, in a heavy Cockney accent, one verbal assault against
Holmes after another. Mrs. Hudson catches on, but Watson,
always the loyal partner, is ready to fight for Holmes's honor.
Of course, the audience is onto the deception and Holmes's fun.

The real pleasure in scenes like this is being part of the game: waiting and watching as Holmes plays with his colleague who's always a couple of steps behind. Here, the game of deception reminds us, once again, of that essential element in the Holmes stories—Holmes and Watson's relationship.

In one of *The Secret Weapon*'s most memorable instances, Holmes also poses as Herr Hoffner, one of four scientists who have been given secret information that will aid the allies. Holmes stages his own abduction in order to gain entry to Moriarty's lair—he will do whatever it takes to solve the crime and stop the evil. He is obsessed.

The 3:00 A.M. Moment

I understand obsession. Maybe that's what drew me to investigative work. I'm sure it's one of the reasons I had to get out. During my years on the job, I saw a lot of decent investigators. But the best ones, whether they were civilian investigators like me or sworn police detectives, were the ones who couldn't let go. The ones who woke up in a sweat at 3:00 A.M. choked by the question they should have asked.

Holmes is obsessed, but it's a different obsession than the kind associated with my hard-boiled dicks. These guys also want answers. But their obsession is to make double-crossers pay for their duplicity, especially the femme fatales who betrayed them. Holmes's obsession is all about the work—he needs to solve the puzzle.

The investigator in me was newly inspired as I watched Holmes bear down on each of his cases. He sizes up Sir George's daughter when she pulls up to the flat in *Woman in Green*. She must have something in her purse, he tells Watson, because "it was picked for size not style." And she must have left home in a hurry, because she's not wearing gloves. In *The Spider Woman*, Holmes calls out Watson for reading a newspaper while they're on holiday. The tip-off: Watson's hat is on backwards, cluing Holmes that he must have a newspaper stuffed inside. But Holmes's power of observation is not limited to extracting clues. "Nobody ever looks twice at a postman," he tells Watson, after revealing his postal worker get-up. He is also a keen observer of human nature.

In his book *Adventure, Mystery, and Romance*, John G. Cawelti points out that both the hard-boiled formula and classical detective story have similar patterns of action: They both move from the introduction of the detective and the presentation of the crime, through the investigation, to a solution and apprehension of the criminal. But there are differences in the way this pattern gets worked out. One significant difference is "the subordination of the drama of solution to the detective's quest for the discovery and accomplishment of justice."

My attraction to the hard-boiled detective probably comes from my identification with this hero's need for justice. I have always related to the noir hero's interior struggle and quest for justice, rather than with the machinery of the crime. However, in re-watching the early Holmes films, I discovered an immense satisfaction in watching Holmes move through each case, one detail and observation at a time. His brand of obsession was an inspiration to the investigator in me. It reminded me of my own obsession and pleasure in the art of deductive reasoning and close observation. For me, there have been few highs as satisfying as those delicious investigative moments—asking the case-breaking question, exacting the truth from someone's body language, or piecing together the mystery of what really happened at the scene of an incident.

Great Villains Make Great Heroes

In a way, it's similar to the satisfaction of doing battle with a worthy adversary. As I've often told my writing and storytelling students, your protagonist is only as good as your villain.

The hard-boiled side of me has always enjoyed seeing my heroes rise up against an assortment of villains. But the greatest conflict for the hard-boiled hero has always been himself. The noir detective—at least the ones that have most intrigued me— is caught in a trap, partly the result of a corrupt world and often a corrupt woman, but largely the result of his own flawed machinery. In the world of Holmes, it's the weight of an evil opponent that sets everything in motion.

In many stories, especially classical detective stories, the antagonist is in some ways a reflection of the hero. Alex Epstein writes in *Crafty Screenwriting*: "They can be two sides of the same coin. Batman and Joker are both angry, violent men who dress strangely and pursue their own ends outside of the law. Batman just happens to be fighting for good and the Joker for evil."

In studying Holmes and his most famous adversary, Professor Moriarty, we can't help wonder if detective and criminal are more alike than different.

One of the highlights in *The Secret Weapon* is a wonderful scene between Holmes and Moriarty in Moriarty's seaside lair. The two foes, sitting across from each other in comfy-looking armchairs, chat casually about the challenge of finding a suitable approach to offing each other. Holmes, who's been captured by Moriarty (or more accurately has allowed himself to be caught), lets his adversary know that any pedestrian method would be offensive. He suggests rigging up a device that would extract his opponent's blood—drop by evil drop. Moriarty one-ups him by choosing this approach to destroy Holmes.

Of course, Holmes ends up getting away and traps Moriarty by tampering with his escape route, a secret elevator. During their final exchange, Moriarty falls down the empty shaft to his death. As Holmes looks down into the dark abyss, I can't help thinking that he probably feels not only a sense of relief, but also a sense of loss. Like all great heroes, he must know that his power and strength are defined by the prowess of his enemies.

There's something similar at play in *The Woman in Green*, the story of Holmes's attempt to stop a series of grisly "finger" murders. Holmes quickly adds up the facts and realizes that his greatest adversary, Moriarty, is behind the scheme. When Watson reminds Holmes that Moriarty swung from the gallows and accuses him of having "Moriarty on the brain," Holmes says he doesn't believe Moriarty's dead. He knows his enemy, just as he knows himself.

One of my most memorable adversaries was an officer who had been the "accused" on more than one of my cases. I recall our first meeting when he came in for his Q and A. I had a fair number of investigations under my belt at the time and felt pretty confident. However, even before the officer started answering my questions, I realized I was playing a very different game. The way he spoke, his flinty black eyes staring back at me, even the way he repositioned his chair, told me that I was up against something more dangerous and formidable than in the past.

Months later, I learned that the same officer would once again be sitting across from me, responding to my questions on a new investigation. I still remember the moment when I saw his name in my case file. I wasn't upset that I had to face off with him again. I looked forward to it! I knew that his responses, his silences, his deceptions would all ultimately elevate my performance. I felt like a boxer or tennis pro or any other athlete who knows that her best game is the one played with the most skillful opponent. Just like later in *The Woman in Green*, when Holmes learns of Moriarty's resurrection from certain death and that his suspicions were right, we see his frustration, but we also detect a sense of excitement: The game is still on.

Femme Fatales and Remarkable Women

For the noir hero, no adversary presents a greater challenge than the femme fatale, one of the staples of the genre. Without her and the sexual hold she has on the hero, the detective might not be forced to make a moral choice. And it's justice and the moral world—rather than the law of Holmes's world—that defines noir.

While I had expected women and temptations in the world of Conan Doyle's Holmes, I was surprised to discover Holmes, especially in the early Rathbone films, as a sexual creature. (In *The Woman in Green*, he notes the "lustrous eyes" of Moriarty's accomplice.) Even more exciting was to see him face off with a strong female adversary—Adrea Spedding, Gale Sondergaard's villain in *The Spider Woman*. Like Moriarty, she offers an opponent worthy of Holmes's hero.

Early on, Holmes determines that his newest adversary must be a woman, noting that there's something "subtle and cruel" about the crimes, murders caused by deadly spiders released into the victims' rooms through air vents. He even calls her a "femme fatale." As usual, Holmes's reasoning proves right. Spedding, the mastermind behind the plot, proves a worthy adversary. She and Holmes spend most of the film in a tense—and flirtatious—cat-and-mouse, both putting on and taking off personas—and each aware that the other is doing so.

The movie ends in the perfect setting for a story built on duplicity and the grotesque: carnival fairgrounds. Spedding attempts to use Holmes as a human target in the shooting gallery, but her plan fails. As she's led away by Lestrade, she smiles. If she's going down, at least it's at the hands of Holmes. And for Holmes, the feelings seem to be mutual. "Remarkable woman," he says, and gives her props for picking the most logical spot to commit his murder.

What's absent from Holmes's interactions with Spedding, though, and in other encounters in these early films, is the sexual tension and frustration that oozes from encounters between the deadly woman and the hard-boiled hero. Still, there's just enough hint of a sexual dimension to Holmes's character: Under the right circumstances, who knows what might happen?

A Man and His City

While the Holmes stories do take us on occasion to carnival grounds and country inns, and the noir detective does break free of the urban setting once or twice, it's the city that defines the detective genre. Cawelti writes:

> The importance of the city as a milieu for the detective story has been apparent from the very beginning . . . We can hardly imagine Doyle's Sherlock Holmes far from his famous lodgings at 221B Baker Street in late-Victorian London, surrounded by hansoms, fogs, the Baker Street Irregulars, and the varied and ever enchanting mysteries of a great urban area.

The modern city as a place of fascination and mystery is evident in the early Holmes films, as much as it is in the hard-boiled films. But in the hard-boiled films, the city is darker, scarier. The menace seems larger than any one source of evil. In the films I revisited—all set in modern England—the evil is out there, but we sense that it can be rooted out—as long as Sherlock Holmes is on the case.

In the final scene of *The Woman in Green*, after Holmes has foiled Moriarty's sinister plot, he looks out at the city, Watson at his side:

WATSON: What are you thinking of?
HOLMES: I'm thinking of all the women who can come and go in safety on the streets of London tonight. The stars keep watch in the heavens, and in our own little way, we too, old friend, are privileged to watch over our city.

This scene, like others throughout the Holmes films, provides a portrait of a city in which hope and order are possibilities. This rarely exists in the world of the doomed noir hero. Each set of films, Holmes-Rathbone and film noir, reinforces hope (or its absence) in its own language, an unexpected discovery as I revisited the Holmes I had once turned away.

I've always been attracted to the language of noir. In the best of these stories, the heroes speak a language that is part toughness and part poetry. Holmes addressing a woman as "My dear lady" doesn't have the impact of a Chandler character saying "Listen, sister." Where else but in noir can you find brutality wrapped up in beautiful words like Sam Spade's closing lines in *The Maltese Falcon* or Joe Morse's voice-over narration as he descends the steps at the end of *Force of Evil?*

But there is another passage ("This blessed plot, this England . . .") delivered by Holmes at the end of *The Secret Weapon*. Sure, Holmes and the noir hero are both detectives, but they draw on two different literary traditions, one that offers a world where heroes can change their fate; the other where they are doomed by it.

Final Recommendations

In his iconic essay about the detective hero, "The Simple Art of Murder," Raymond Chandler writes:

> Down these mean streets a man must go who is not himself mean, who is neither tarnished nor afraid. The detective in this kind of story must be such a man. He is the hero, he is everything. He must be a complete man and a common man and yet an unusual man. He must be, to use a rather weathered phrase, a man of honor . . .

In the end, there are more similarities than differences between Sherlock Holmes and his American counterpart. Like Holmes, many of my noir favorites are men of honor. They, too, have lines they won't cross. And just as the hard-boiled detective has a soft center, Holmes's detective can pull out the tough guy when he needs to. Both men need answers, and they will persist until they get them. They are detectives.

I will always be true to my hard-boiled heroes. Maybe it's a question of loyalty, one of the central themes of film noir. I can't turn my back on these guys. But I now see that maybe there's room in my heart for another type of detective: a detective who's capable of leading with instinct and brawn, but instead chooses reason and logic. Maybe I've discovered that there's something nice about a world with partners and friends and people who have your back. Maybe I like the idea of a detective who is not alone. And a world filled with hope.

Still, I don't think I'll be trading in my trench coat for tweed any time soon. But who knows? The investigation is far from over.

Chapter 7

The Mystery of the Horrible Hound
Rafe McGregor

May 1902 *Publisher's Weekly* printed two statements about Conan Doyle's *The Hound of the Baskervilles*: that it was the finest detective story ever written, and that no one would be reading it in 2002.

A hundred and nine years later, it seems as if the anonymous advertiser couldn't have been more wrong about the novel's endurance. A brief look at Amazon's online database shows forty-five editions published in English in 2010 alone, and a "hound of the baskervilles" search on Google produces a little over a million results. I think *Publisher's Weekly* was wrong on both counts: not only has *The Hound* endured for longer than a hundred years, but it wasn't the finest detective story of its time.

No, I'm not suggesting that *The Sign of the Four* (1890) was superior, or that Wilkie Collins's *The Moonstone* (1868) deserves pride of place. *The Hound* isn't the finest detective story ever written simply because it isn't a detective story at all.

Deconstructing Doyle's Dog

How can I convince you that *The Hound* isn't a mystery? By drawing your attention to the following passage from a paragraph at the climax of the narrative (Chapter 14):

> Never have I seen a man run as Holmes ran that night. I am reckoned fleet of foot, but he outpaced me as much as I outpaced the little professional. In front of us as we flew up the track we heard scream after scream from Sir Henry and the deep roar of the hound. I was in time to see the beast spring upon its victim, hurl him to the ground and worry at his throat.

The problem for *The Hound* as a detective story is that this is the second curious incident of the dog in the night-time on Dartmoor. Like the first, in "Silver Blaze," this dog does nothing. It is a very poor murder weapon, as the lines that follow the quotation reveal. Holmes discovers that the beast is corporeal, a bloodhound-mastiff crossbreed whose natural savagery has been exacerbated by starvation. Yet Watson writes, "We saw that there was no sign of a wound." Perhaps Holmes destroyed the dog before it could bite Sir Henry? This explanation would require a creative interpretation of the text, and would in any event be insufficient because the hound never bites anyone.

Does it matter? I'll answer this question by borrowing from the work of Jacques Derrida, the controversial philosopher famous for commentating on—and perpetuating—the postmodern condition.

The what? The radical changes that occurred all over the world in the second half of the twentieth century, changes driven by the mass media, multiculturalism, the digital revolution, globalisation, and an increasing belief that everything from personal identity to truth was relative rather than absolute. Language was regarded as particularly suspect, because the words it employed didn't refer to reality, but to human conceptions of reality, conceptions which were often misinformed. Derrida believed language was inherently unstable, and he exposed the extent of this instability with his introduction of deconstruction in *Of Grammatology* in 1967.

Deconstruction involves the identification of a pair of opposing concepts in a piece of writing. For example, we might examine an encyclopaedia entry on liberal democracy and recognise that the term contains a necessary tension between the freedom of the individual and a requirement for social justice. Usually, where there is a set of oppositions in a work, one will be given priority. In this case the author might define liberal democracy as a political system that maximizes individual freedom. A deconstructive reading involves a re-conceptualisation of the distinction with the aim of showing how the language of the text undermines the selected priority. Just like what is at play in *The Hound of the Baskervilles*.

The novella is presented as a mystery that borrows elements from the horror genre. There is a relationship between mystery and horror in the work, the distinction mystery-horror, where mystery seems dominant. Derrida's idea in deconstruction was that the text would contain a specific point beyond which its inherent logic could not progress, and he called this the aporia.

So the aporia in *The Hound* would be the passage which exposes how the narrative undermines the apparent dominance of mystery in mystery-horror.

So far, so good. Derrida also believed that every piece of writing contained a re-mark, which was an indication of the genre of the work by the author, a feature of the law of genre, whereby every piece of writing belonged to a particular category. We should find at least one part of *The Hound* which explicitly announces that it is a detective story. But Derrida didn't achieve his reputation for complexity by accident: his distinctive idea was that the re-mark was paradoxical because it was itself outside the genre that it marked. The re-mark was thus both a part of and apart from the writing. Now *The Hound* is a particularly good candidate for a deconstructive reading because the aporia and the re-mark interlock in the single passage above.

The dog is a very poor murder weapon, one that is only able to kill victims with weak constitutions (Sir Charles) or bad balance (Selden). In the first murder, the savage, starved hound doesn't even take a nibble of its quarry. Holmes explains to Watson: "Of course we know that a hound does not bite a dead body and that Sir Charles was dead before ever the brute overtook him." Could Doyle—highly intelligent, widely-travelled, and a qualified doctor—really have believed that dogs only ate live prey? Had he never seen a tame, replete dog gnawing the last scrap of flesh from a raw bone? The novella's logic fails at the aporia of the dog that doesn't bite as a murder weapon.

Holmes's especial energy in saving Sir Henry is due to his sense of responsibility for the events described. He has arranged for the aristocrat to walk across the moor at night in order to present Stapleton with an opportunity to use the hound. The ruse is risky, as Holmes is aware that the beast has been trained to target Sir Henry specifically, and that the death of Selden was caused by the fact that he was wearing Sir Henry's clothes. Given this harsh lesson in failure, one would expect the master sleuth to have prepared for every possible contingency.

Yet, when the fog on the moor begins to obscure Holmes's view of Merripit House, he says to Watson: "Very serious indeed—the one thing upon earth which could have disarranged my plans." Doyle is asking us to believe that a brilliant detective has constructed a plan that fails to account for the possibility of fog—on Dartmoor, at night—despite having recently spent several nights upon the moor himself. Anyone who has ever visited any of England's moors will understand how ludicrous the idea is, and Dartmoor is renowned for being one of the most inhospitable in the country. This impossible oversight by Holmes is the re-mark that announces the genre of *The Hound*. The fact that the oversight is made by an ineffective detective—that mainstay of the mystery genre—meets Derrida's criterion that the passage which announces the genre of the work as horror is itself apart from that genre.

The Philosophy of Horror

Why horror? Even if I have convinced you that *The Hound* is a seriously flawed mystery, why should it be a horror story when there are plenty of other genres from which to choose? I think the context in which the work was created provides several clues. The genesis of the novel is the subject of heated debate, but it seems as if the idea was suggested to Doyle by his friend Bertram Fletcher Robinson while they were golfing in Norfolk in April 1901. Doyle had laid Sherlock Holmes to rest in 1893 in order to concentrate on his literary historical romances, and the new project was envisaged as a collaboration. There appear to have been three main sources of inspiration: the legends of black dogs and Wisht hounds widespread in the British Isles; "Followed" (1900), a short story by Dr. Robert Eustace and Mrs. L.T. Meade; and "The Brazilian Cat" (1898), one of Doyle's own horror titles.

Doyle was already an accomplished author of tales of supernatural horror, and amongst his numerous and varied contributions to the genre was "Lot No. 249" (1892), which is the first appearance of a reanimated Egyptian mummy as a monstrous antagonist in literature. He twice used the phrase "a real creeper" to describe his work in progress, but made two important decisions at some time prior to August 1901. First, to introduce Holmes into the story; and second, to write the novel on his own (with an acknowledgement to Fletcher Robinson). The choices may well have been related, and the selection of Holmes as the protagonist—likely motivated by financial considerations—would effectively disguise the tale as a mystery.

Amongst his many other achievements, Noël Carroll is the leading philosopher of film, and one of the foremost writers on genre. He claims that although different genres are identified in different ways, mystery, suspense, horror, and melodrama are designed to elicit specific emotions. In *The Philosophy of Horror, or, Paradoxes of the Heart*, Carroll identifies horror as part of a wider family of stories about monsters, and monsters as "beings that do not exist according to the lights of contemporary science." Horror is distinguished by involving monsters that disturb the natural order, and the essence of horror is that it produces a compound reaction of fear and disgust.

For something to disgust rather than scare us, it must be impure or grotesque, and this can occur in three ways.

● First, we have an aversion to incompleteness. The long list of fictional villains who either have parts missing (like Captain Ahab in *Moby-Dick*) or parts that don't work (like Mr. Potter in *It's a Wonderful Life*) reflects the real-life discrimination with which physically disabled people have to contend.

● Second, we're uncomfortable with contradiction. The reanimated mummy in "Lot No. 249" is not just frightening because of the physical threat it poses, it is revolting because it is un-dead, dead and alive.

● Third, and related, is that we not only react to contradiction, but to creatures that cross accepted cultural categories. The mummy is a cross-contamination between "live things" and "dead things" in the same way that a crab is a cross-contamination between "things that live in the sea" (which usually swim) and "things that walk" (which usually live on land).

The hound straddles the distinction life-death in the same way as Doyle's mummy. Throughout the novel the monster is identified both as a fearsome physical antagonist and as a frightening otherworldly creature. The following descriptions come immediately before and after the slaying of the hound respectively:

> an enormous coal-black hound, but not such a hound as mortal eyes have ever seen. . . . Never in the delirious dream of a disordered brain could anything more savage, more appalling, more hellish, be conceived than that dark form and savage face . . .
>
> In mere size and strength it was a terrible creature which was lying stretched before us.

The hound produces fear by being physically strong and revulsion by being a crossbreed dog-ghost. In addition to this compound reaction that defines horror, Carroll notes four factors that provide supplementary support for his theory: the prevalence of monsters with insufficient strength to instil fear in protagonists, a geography that locates monsters in marginal or unknown places, a predominant concern with knowledge, and the link with mass aesthetic satisfaction. All of these are relevant to *The Hound of the Baskervilles*.

There is a sense in which the hound should not inspire fear. Either Holmes, Watson, and Lestrade are facing a real dog that they are well-equipped to kill, or a ghost dog that cannot wound them. We have already seen that the hound, whatever it is, doesn't bite. Nonetheless, Watson—frequently noted for his bravery—feels fear, an emotion which is, I imagine, shared by many readers. With regard to the geography of horror, the hound is a denizen of Dartmoor, a grim, lonely, and forbidding landscape. The moor is very much one of the "marginal, hidden, or abandoned sites" that Carroll mentions as figurative spatializations of the unknown lurking beyond cultural categorisation. The effect is increased by the hound's kennelling in Grimpen Mire (grim-pen). The habitat is not only the most secluded place on the moor, but deadly to living creatures because of the bog holes.

So,

1. The combination of remarkable success and flawed mystery should make us think twice about what kind of story *The Hound of the Baskervilles*. really is.

2. A horror story is a plausible alternative: there's a monster in the story, and the characteristics of this monster match those that Carroll identifies as definitive of horror.

3. There is further evidence for *The Hound* as horror in the irrational quality of the horror induced and the geography of horror.

Convinced? Not yet? Then let's look at the rest of the evidence.

Re-Solving *The Hound*

The third supplement to Carroll's definition is his description of horror-story plots as repetitive and having a link with knowledge, and he categorizes the two main structures as the discovery and overreacher plot clusters. The latter is the well-known "mad scientist" story, made famous by Mary Shelley's *Frankenstein, or, The Modern Prometheus*. A case could be made for *The Hound of the Baskervilles* as a version of the former, where the protagonists discover that a monster is responsible for unexplained deaths. If we consider the novel in terms of the typical sequence Carroll identifies (onset, discovery, confirmation, and confrontation) the idea is very tempting. But the discovery plot structure overlaps with many mysteries, so this seems more like an instance of Derrida's law of genre—where hybrid genres are the rule, not the exception—rather than proof that *The Hound of the Baskervilles* is a horror story.

There are a surprising number of mystery elements absent from the novel, however, the most important of which are: the detective is a bodyguard rather than an investigator; there is a complete lack of crime scene work; there is a general lack of detection and deduction; and there is a cast of only three serious suspects (Mortimer, Barrymore, and Stapleton). In the original manuscript, Doyle also erased procedural detail in Chapter 11, when Watson reflects on his interview with Laura Lyons. So it seems there's good reason to think that *The Hound* isn't a pure mystery, but do I really need to insist it's a horror story when I could call it a crossbreed, a mongrel mystery-horror?

Close attention to the plot exposes the combination of Gothicism and Romanticism characteristic of classic Victorian horror fiction like *Frankenstein*, *The Strange Case of Dr Jekyll and Mr Hyde*, and *Dracula*. In *Nightmare: The Birth of Horror*, Christopher Frayling cites *The Hound of the Baskervilles* as completing the quintessential gothic horror quartet, and I think he is right. *The Hound* as horror also explains the host of attempts to account for the numerous differences between the most famous Holmes story and the many others in which he appeared, including early suggestions that Fletcher Robinson had written large parts of the novel, and recent claims that Holmes failed to catch the real villain.

The engine that drives the plot of *The Hound of the Baskervilles* is the conflict between protagonist and antagonist, a conflict that underlies much—if not all—mystery and horror fiction. The protagonist is obvious: Holmes, ably assisted by Watson. The antagonist appears to be Stapleton, but is really the hound, a monster whose existence is only explained in the final chapter. Where Stapleton has a relatively minor role, the presence of the hound is felt throughout the work: from the title to its first mention in the second chapter to Holmes's elucidation in the closing paragraphs. Contrast the following two references to the antagonist:

> I told you in London, Watson, and I tell you now again, that we have never had a foeman more worthy of our steel.

> Always there was the feeling of an unseen force, a fine net drawn round us with infinite skill and delicacy, holding us so lightly that it was only at some supreme moment that one realised that one was indeed entangled in its meshes.

Despite what Holmes says, Stapleton is an incompetent antagonist. He chooses an appalling murder weapon; he conducts his personal relationships without discipline (he has a dangerous affair with Mrs. Lyons and his uxorial jealousy almost ruins his plan); and he lacks a definite means of securing the Baskerville fortune in the unlikely event of success (even Holmes admits that Stapleton could not have claimed his inheritance without suspicion). Stapleton is a worthy foe, but only to a master detective who fails to predict fog on Dartmoor.

The clash of the incompetent criminal and ineffective detective is of only secondary interest, however, because the real conflict is between man and monster. The ultimate triumph isn't the capture of the culprit, but the slaying of the beast. While Holmes and his allies battle the hound at the climax of the story, Stapleton's death is an anticlimax, occurring off-stage in Grimpen Mire.

The Postmodern Condition

In "Watson's Weird Tales: Horror in the Sherlockian Canon," Philip Shreffler writes: "It is the book's supernaturalism that has brought generations of readers to *The Hound*." Holmes's status as an international cultural icon is also responsible, but he appeared in three other novels, none of which have proved as successful.

Shreffler's commentary reiterates the final factor in Carroll's philosophy of horror, the mass appeal of the genre. Carroll believes that the popularity of horror fiction and film is a symptom of the late-twentieth-century concern with meaning, value, and relativity captured in the term "postmodernism". The idea that values are relative rather than absolute, and that concepts are created by human beings rather than reflections of things-in-the-world mirrors the horror story's focus on monsters that defy cultural categories, and our fear and revulsion of the unknown. The prevalence of horror is the popular expression of the postmodern condition:

> Contemporary horror fiction, then, articulates the anxieties attending the transition from the American Century to the "we know not what" for mass audiences, in a manner analogous to the way postmodernism articulates intimations of instability for intellectuals.

The link with postmodernism is astute, and it explains the dominant position of horror fiction in mass culture through its production in motion pictures. In this respect, the early and repeated appearance of *The Hound of the Baskervilles* in the mass media of radio, film, and television is a self-fulfilling sign of the fascination the story holds for mass audiences. The Internet Movie Database (IMDb) cites twenty-two film and TV productions from 1915 to 2002, and the list is by no means exhaustive.

With such evidence at hand, I'll make a further observation in support of Carroll: all four of the Victorian classics exerted a similarly strong attraction at the end of the nineteenth century.

The period that preceded postmodernism—modernism—was itself characterized by the collapse of certainty. Beginning with *The Birth of Tragedy* in 1872, Friedrich Nietzsche wrote a series of prophecies about the end of the dominance of Christian values, values which had been exported to the world through the empires of Western Europe and the United States. As civilization slid towards the mass destruction of its first global conflict, no accepted truth about human existence escaped scrutiny. Everything everyone had ever believed was doubted, and intellectuals held nothing sacred: capitalism (Marx), society (Durkheim), religion (Frazer), science (Einstein), language (Saussure), the mind (Freud), and even humanity itself (Darwin). No country prospered from The War to End All Wars, and the resulting disenchantment is revealed in works like T.S. Eliot's "The Waste Land."

For the first time in history, there was constant change, and people didn't know how to deal with it. We still don't, though I hope we have learned something from two hot world wars and one cold.

The Hound of the Baskervilles was written and published at a time of uncertainty. If the narrative reflected that uncertainty, there is no surprise that it is even more popular in an age of heightened uncertainty. Which brings us back to Derrida, who is often considered the arch-postmodernist because his overall philosophical project was to show that truth was something with which human beings could never be acquainted. He used elusive tools like the aporia and the re-mark, and abstruse methods like deconstruction, to illustrate that meaning is not self-sufficient, and that truth itself is flexible. What do we have left without the possibility of truth?

Anxiety.

And that anxiety is the essential clue in the solution of the real mystery of *The Hound*, the secret of its remarkable success. If we follow the novel's own logic to its conclusion, and identify the dramatic finale in the fog of Dartmoor as an announcement of a genre to which Holmes and Watson do not really belong, we can see how neatly the narrative fits into the category of horror.

Doyle, it seems, had it right from the very beginning: the real appeal of *The Hound of the Baskervilles*—now more than ever—is because it's a real creeper.

Chapter 8

The Case of the Dangerous Detective
Ronald S. Green and D.E. Wittkower

During an idle hour, we took up the question of why it is that the detective, as a literary figure, is viewed as 'dangerous'.

"It is not so strange," I said, "for the detective is always uncovering facts that guilty persons have very good reasons not to want known."

"Yes," said Wittkower, "but if that were the end of it, there would be little difference between a detective story and a thriller. The hero of a thriller wishes to set things right and escape with her life—but the detective wants knowledge which is itself dangerous, not knowledge which is simply dangerous because it's somebody's dirty secret."

"I'm not sure I follow. What do you mean, exactly?"

"Well, take for example the first detective in Western literature: Oedipus. In Sophocles's *Oedipus Rex*—or perhaps we could call it 'A Scandal in Thebes'—Oedipus must solve a murder. He is warned away from finding the truth by Tiresias, a prophet of Apollo, a god of light and truth. Despite having been told by the god's representative that he should not seek the truth, he cannot resist his thirst for knowledge, and it is this which brings his downfall.

"There's a similar social history throughout antiquity. Those who claim to know a hidden truth about the world are treated as dangerous and are made to pay for their forbidden knowledge, and even seeking such knowledge is viewed as immoral—from the Athenians' prosecution of philosophers like Anaxagoras, Socrates, and Aristotle; to the Roman persecution of early Christians; and to Roman Christian persecution of Gnostics and Pagans. Society, it seems, has long had the habit of putting to death those who ask too many questions."

This seemed to me too quick. "But," I said, "in the cases of the Greek philosophers, early Christians, and Gnostics, each of these groups were undermining political authority by adopting doctrines which went against the religious doctrines of the state. For example, when Anaxagoras claimed that the sun was a giant burning rock, he wasn't just making a claim about astronomy or physics, as we would interpret this today. Rather, since the Athenian state based its legal tradition on the stories of the gods and heroes, when Anaxagoras said that the sun was an object, not Apollo, he implied that we could get rid of all the stories of the state and replace them with more scientific knowledge. So, he was put to death not because he claimed that the sun was a burning rock, but because he undermined the state by encouraging Athenians to reject traditional knowledge, belief, and authority. In this case, as well as the others you mention— Isn't this a simple matter of a political crackdown on dissidents?"

"Surely this is a significant motive," he said, leaning forward. With a curious, playful look in his eyes, he went on. "But there's something much more distinctive and unusual in these cases. You said Anaxagoras was 'encouraging Athenians to reject tradition'—I suppose that's true, encouraging by example if nothing else, but he wasn't exactly leading riots in the streets!"

"No, that's true."

"And the early Christians and the Gnostics as well; they weren't trying to convert the majority or overthrow the state. Mostly, they were just trying to keep to themselves and maintain their small and unpopular communities of belief."

"Yes," I had to admit, "that is so."

"Tell me, doesn't it seem strange that Western society, which values understanding and knowledge so highly, views some knowledge claims as undermining society itself?"

"Yes, now that you mention it, this does strike me as a bit odd."

"Now, if these 'dangerous' claims are false, why didn't these political authorities simply *disprove* them?"

"Why, these claims about fundamental reality and religion aren't the sorts of things that can be disproved!" I paused for a moment. By prompting me to this response, Wittkower had given me the next step I needed to see what he was getting at. "So, you think these claims are dangerous because they undermine the *ideology* of society—the basic beliefs about humanity and the world which justify the society's laws and ways of life, but which can't be justified, since they can't be proven or disproven. And this fits with the other evidence we have: the great scandals of knowledge in the history of the West, ranging from persecution of Jews and atheists, to the individualism of democracy and Protestantism, to the 'scandal' of Darwin. *Some* of these forms of 'dangerous' knowledge were direct threats to established power, but *all* of them were threats to foundational ideas about what it is to be human. But how does this explain anything about 'the detective' as a character type?"

"Green, tell me: isn't there a 'dangerous' school of thought that you've left out? One that was prominent in the late nineteenth and early twentieth centuries, when detective stories really came into their own as a genre?"

"Yes, hundreds I'm sure. But perhaps you are thinking of Marxism?"

"Precisely. In the Golden Age of detective stories, most famously including the stories of Sherlock Holmes, the basic premise is that there are dark, violent secrets under the genteel veneer of upper-class English society. Holmes does not simply find a truth that some guilty party tries to hide—by finding an ugly truth in high society, he reveals the far more dangerous truth that the ruling class is not fundamentally better than or different from the lower classes. He is *in danger* because he goes up against criminals, but he is *dangerous* because he goes up against the idea that those who are privileged in society are better than those who are downtrodden."

"Ah, but surely there are plenty of detective stories where the guilty persons are career criminals, or other 'outsiders' . . ."

"Yes—like the more distinctly American genre of hard-boiled detectives and film noir. If the idea that our society is a just society were being supported, it is true that the criminal would be from a 'seedy' element in society, as he often is in these stories. But tell me, is the detective part of established authority?"

"No, I suppose not. Usually, the detective is a PI—and if not, then he is a police officer who rebels against authority; a 'cop who plays by his own rules'."

"And so here, the claim is that the established power in society—in this case, the police force—is not able to fix society, and only a detective who acts as an outsider can get to the truth. So the hardboiled detective is *in danger* because he goes against society's undesirables, but he is *dangerous* because he shows us that authority cannot deliver on its promise. Stories about by-the-book police work or FBI investigations are thrillers, not detective stories—only the detective, as an outsider, can represent how *ideologically* dangerous seeking knowledge is."

"So, even though these genres are quite different in their mood and their subject matter, in either case the detective is a dangerous figure because he shows that society is unjust, or unjustified."

"Yes, Green, you've quite got it. And, in that way, 'A Scandal in Thebes' never was a detective story, but more simply a tragedy. Oedipus's story tells this ugly historical truth, but the story is itself part of this social control." Wittkower paused for a moment, pressing his fingertips together, an abstracted look on his face. "The Oedipus myth speaks the truth when it depicts the foundation of society as a crime. How could the founding of a society, in which some rule and others are ruled, be fair or honorable, when there would not have been any rules or justice agreed to by all before that society existed? And then the myth that the poor and disadvantaged are lazy, or undeserving, or genetically inferior; all this is the alibi and the cover-up."

Wittkower sat up, elbows perched against his knees. "Oedipus is a tragic figure because he knows the truth, that society is based on crime, and he suffers from and regrets this forbidden knowledge. In the story this is also expressed in the sexual crime of incest, to represent how forbidden this knowledge is, and how shameful it is to desire this knowledge. And this is what makes Oedipus's story a tragedy: the audience is meant to identify with him, and to suffer with him, and through that, to be prevented from rebelling against society's injustices themselves. Aristotle called this 'catharsis'; I prefer to call it 'oppression' and 'ideological enforcement'. Oedipus questions society's foundations, and discovers a truth he cannot bear—and so we are told never to question society's foundations, so we do not discover the truth which society cannot bear."

I sat back and considered this novel perspective on a play I have long known. Wittkower, though, had not quite finished his account. "The detective story though, my dear Doctor Green, is no tragedy. The detective suffers in a way from his knowledge. He becomes an outsider, but often he is as much an outsider from his unusual abilities to see the truth as he is from his possession of such dangerous knowledge. He is, on the whole though, an appealing and romantic character rather than a warning and cautionary figure, and the rise of the detective story may be a sign that a culture is becoming increasingly open to criticism from within."

"The detective story is on the whole dangerous and liberal, while the thriller is typically conservative or reactionary."

"Perhaps, Green, perhaps. Now, Doctor, you spent time in Afghanistan. What is the view of the detective in Asian traditions of inquiry?"

"An apt reference for the flow of ancient ideas, perhaps from Mesopotamia to all directions, into Europe and India through

Afghanistan. Somewhere along the way speakers of Proto-Indo-European languages must have bade farewell in groups as classical Greek and Latin bear marked resemblances to Sanskrit. They carried, I venture, the seeds of European and Asian inquiry. In the case of India, we might call Vyasa the primal detective as he appears in the earliest of Indian literature, tentatively dated to around 1700 B.C.E., and a man of danger as well."

"I've never heard of this sleuth Vyasa. Pray continue. What was his most renowned case?"

"Let us say it was 'A Case of Identity'. Hereby he established the grounds for three millennia of dangerous detective work that followed. Aiming high, Vyasa set about to hear the cosmic sound a thousand years before Pythagoras."

"Good heavens!"

"Quite. Examining the extent of knowledge itself, which is called 'Veda' in Sanskrit. He splits knowledge into four categories which became the four written *Vedas*, perhaps the oldest writings in any Indo-European language."

"What was his mode of examination?"

"Vyasa turned his search within, like an ancient Descartes but with a rather different conclusion. The 'I' of the "I think" was, for Vyasa, not the true self. As the story goes, he risked it all and lost it all, transcending his own beliefs about who he was and who we are by moving to a depth of his heart which lay outside of word-thoughts. For lack of a better descriptor, he thereby heard the cosmic sound, the vibrations that are the essence of matter. By transcribing this into a language we might understand, the *Vedas* were penned."

"This talk of exalted visions and, I imagine, sparse monk-like lifestyle does remind me of Holmes, and not a little of you I confess."

"I thought you were the Holmes character here. But never mind that for now. Have a pinch. You're on to something vastly more interesting." I noticed the "*oṃ*" symbol on the wooden snuffbox Green proffered, as both stood in contrast to his homely and simple lifestyle. Something in this question of identity also rang true, for I had become the narrator.

Green continued, "In Chapter 2 of the *Bhagavad Gita*, Krishna speaks of two distinct paths for conducting investigation, each with its own assumptions and motivation but ultimately leading to the same outcome. The simpler of these involves deductive reasoning. A consequence of this path in various cultures has been versions of Cartesian dualism, such as found in the ancient Samkhya school of Hindu philosophy. An adherent to this is very formulaic in approach, strictly following set steps of inquiry."

"Somewhat like Holmes, I'd say. Appropriate for dealing with large crimes and academic undertakings."

"Somewhat. But while the larger crimes may be simple to solve using such methodology, Holmes regarded the finer ones as more interesting. Krishna says Samkhya's proclivity for formulae springs from the desire to secure better positions in this world and in future lives if such should come about."

"Why, that's little else but enlightened self-interest, then!"

"Precisely. However, Krishna considers the desire for material gains to be contrary to the better path. The better path is to do good things because those things are good."

"On what basis are we to judge which things are good and which lesser?"

"Krishna says both the realization that this is the better path and the understanding of what is good are achieved through meditation. Meditators proceed from the vantage point of self-knowledge and may disregard rules that appear in doctrinal writings, quite a dangerous task considering the institutions that penned and protected the sanctity of those doctrines. Such a person alone, he says, deserved to be called a yogi."

"I must object that this sounds most anti-intellectual and not at all like Holmes, although he did at times disregard social standards in pursuit of truth."

"It is only anti-intellectual in the terms historically imposed on this mystery that is consciousness. Although we would be remiss to impose the term yogi on Holmes, let us also admit that Watson awarded him the grade of zero in philosophy, called him eccentric in chemistry, unsystematic in anatomy . . ."

"Yes, and as I recall a self-poisoner by cocaine and tobacco," said Green, grinning at these entries to the list. "Here we come to another Indian version of the prototype for dangerous detectives," he said. "While Vyasa deals with matters outside of ordinary social acknowledgments, his discrimination makes the extraordinary accessible to the ordinary. This means the "cosmic sound" he heard was not really heard. It was the experience of absolute unbroken monism without the differences that make our reality comprehensible, differences such as you-me, day-night, past-present, material-non-material and so forth. He makes this indescribable experience intelligible through ordinary language that uses such categories. However, in the same *Vedas*, a different type of dangerous detective appears. These long-haired ones are given to ecstatic flight in the opposite direction. Away from the mundane, their detective work is by way of enduring fire, gazing full on heaven while drinking poison from a cup."

"This does sound remotely like Holmes. But is this not simply dangerous to one's well being and ultimately to mental health?"

"We find something of a counterpart in Euro-American literature detective stories, in the psychic detective or psychic who assists the detective. The "existential detectives" in the film *I ♥ Huckabees* also operate outside methods ordinarily considered logical. The detective in the film *Zen Noir* proceeds in accord with the *modus operandi* of the genre before abandoning the noir method upon realizing its shortcomings in terms of examining his life."

"This intuitive or non-discursive detective indeed differs from the tragic hero, the film noir PI, and from Holmes," I said. "It reminds me a bit of Monk, from the television series by that name. I'm not sure his is always the logical method. But these people are harmless and nigh-invariably turn out to be frauds, at least in Euro-American writing."

"Danger sometimes seems to be in the eye of the beholder. In the late 1990s the Chinese government arrested and tortured members of the group Falun Gong on charges of sedition for practicing a mystical form of Tai Chi in the parks of Beijing. It is in a similar vein that the long-hairs of the *Vedas* appear to threaten the orthodoxy by challenging not only the need for sacrifice which is at the core of Brahmanical social structure, but also the underlying dualistic worldview that most of us share, the view that there is a gap between self and other which Derrida says we can never bridge. Care for that pinch now?"

"The rantings of a few demagogues hardly seem so consequential," I objected, waving off his snuff box. "Such is not so dangerous to a sound of mind, I should say. Although history might not bear me out, as I think of it."

"There's more than that at issue. Consider a counterexample in the most famous of Indian epics, that exemplary case of *The Ramayana*."

"Ah yes. Let us call it 'A Scandal in Lanka'."

"Let us. You will recall in the story, Rama is set to become king of Ayodhya in northeast India. Before this happens however, his wife Sita is kidnapped by a mysterious man disguised as an ascetic."

"As with the Bohemian gentleman, Holmes might have deduced this masked man was the king of Lanka in the south of India."

"For the bulk of the story, Rama forges his way southward through the forests of the subcontinent. On the way he forms alliances with forest dwellers to battle an array of demons and evil doers, all the while gathering clues as to the whereabouts of his beloved Sita. Throughout the story, Rama is portrayed as the representation of order in the world. Indeed he is the very incarnation of order, the manifestation of the supreme god Vishnu, although he forgets this for most of the epic. After a year of subduing the non-Vaishnavites of south India, spreading wide what is represented as righteous social stratification in gender and caste . . ."

"This is generally termed imperialism."

". . . he discovers where Sita is being held. In the climactic battle, Rama kills Ravana and regains Sita. The story ends not there however. After their return to the north and subsequent coronation, the people of Ayodhya begin to wonder if Sita was not raped or, what is apparently worse, if she had willingly succumbed to Ravana's charms. After all, she was with him for over a year."

"I suppose succumbing to his charms means she became attracted to chaos or at least came to reject certain aspects deemed essential to civilization."

"You have hit directly upon the matter. The danger faced by Rama, Sita and all of us according to the *Ramayana* and the *Bhagavad Gita*, is *adharma*, the violation of dharma or righteous duty. The motivating factor in the story is the maintenance of cosmic order. It is for this the sacrificer keeps his fire ablaze, the warrior battles even faced with defeat, the householder reproduces society, all for fear of chaos courted by the renunciate, Ravana and the long-haired ones."

"I now believe your snuff box to be of Lankan design. A reward advance for the present cultural dissemination I surmise. And what of Sita?"

"When Rama asks her of her trials she denies being touched. But the people are not convinced. Rama asks Agni, fire, to test her. Sita is insulted but walks through fire thereby receiving Agni's testimony on her behalf. Yet Rama and his subjects persist in conventional, civilized cruelty and Rama finally casts out his queen. This tragic event is considered the utmost sacrifice for the sake of social order."

"It is also punishing the victim, is it not? Which is truly more dangerous, ruling with truth or by upholding a lie to placate subjects? It is a strange application of deontology indeed, this strict adherence to rules at the expense of breaking a few."

"An alternate outcome to the story appears in the recent Hindi film adaptation called *Raavan*. The film features two glamorous stars, Aishwarya Rai as a Sita character named Ragini and her real-life husband Abhishek Bachchan as the Ravana persona named Beera, meaning Brave. In the film, Dev, a modern police detective whose name means god, reminding us of Rama, investigates his wife's kidnapping. This leads him to south India and the criminal Beera he has indicted before. Beera has kidnapped Dev's wife to show the injustices of the detective past and present, charging that Dev only persecutes south Indians because they are poor and uneducated. As time goes on, Ragini comes to realize the truth in this and sees that her husband's obsession with Beera is stronger than his desire for her release. As in the *Ramayana*, once his wife is returned, the detective questions her fidelity and rejects her. But here Ragini returns to Beera. Dev then kills Beera even as Ravana is killed. Again, conventional social order triumphs. But in this case the outsider dies with a smile, the ideological winner for having gained both the love of Ragini and the audience."

"What of Holmes, then? Does he plummet at Reichenbach Falls with a smile on his face? And, if he does, is it because he has enforced order in society, or because Moriarty's defeat is also a defeat of the ideology that those who are 'respectable' are in fact deserving of respect?"

"Ah, but my dear Doctor Wittkower, you have all the evidence you need to form the proper conclusion, and if I spell everything out for you, we both shall find it so painfully dull!"

Chapter 9

I Suppose I Shall Have to Compound a Felony as Usual

Mihaela Frunză and Anatolia Bessemer

> **HOLMES:** You don't mind breaking the law?
> **WATSON:** Not in the least.
> **HOLMES:** Nor running a chance of arrest?
> **WATSON:** Not in a good cause.
> **HOLMES:** Oh, the cause is excellent!
> —"A Scandal in Bohemia"

Sherlock Holmes is a much better detective than the best of Scotland Yard. So it's no surprise that Holmes has scant respect for their investigative abilities. As he caustically remarks in *The Sign of the Four*, "When Gregson, or Lestrade, or Athelney Jones are out of their depth—which, by the way, is their normal state . . ."

But not only does Holmes deride the official law enforcers' analytic skills, he also feels free to over-ride the typical policeman's sense of justice, and even to go against the law itself. Holmes often commits crimes and gets away with it. He freely engages in fraudulent deception, breaking and entering, or suppression of evidence, whenever he believes that "the cause is excellent."

When he pretends to be an innocent clergyman in order to trace the disputed memento of a royal personage ("A Scandal in Bohemia") he clearly misleads his victims in order to induce them to show what they are trying to hide. (In this case it is Holmes's client who has done wrong, not the woman, Irene Adler.) Occasionally, he commits trespass on property ("The Greek Interpreter") in order to accomplish his detective work. Sometimes he fools the authorities in order to protect a lady against a ruined reputation ("The Adventure of the Second Stain"). He has even been known to let persons guilty of a serious crime get off scott-free (most notably in "The Adventure of the Abbey Grange" but also in "The Adventure of the Blue Carbuncle" and "The Adventure of the Devil's Foot").

By contrast with Holmes, the police seem to always want to stick to the letter of the law. "Now, gentlemen," says Lestrade, "the forms of the law must be complied with . . ." (*A Study in Scarlet*). The police in the Holmes canon are dull-witted but honest; we never see them planting evidence or deliberately twisting an investigation to arrive at a particular outcome.

Occasionally the police will indulge Holmes and Watson by permitting something strictly irregular (though not seriously unlawful), as when Athelney Jones in *The Sign of the Four*, permits Watson, at Holmes's suggestion, to bring the supposed Agra treasure to Miss Mary Morstan. But much of what Holmes decides to do is never brought to the attention of the police, because he is so much better at concealing crime than they are at finding it.

Whose Justice?

When someone decides to put their own sense of justice above the law, how can we adjudicate? If we may sometimes flout the law, what court of appeal can decide when this is right and when it's wrong?

The philosopher Alasdair MacIntyre has proposed in his book *Whose Justice? Which Rationality?* that modern man has lost any common sense of justice. There is no longer a universal tradition which everyone respects, so appeals to justice tend to become mere camouflage for pursuit of self-interest or group-interest. Conflicts between different conceptions of justice seem to be beyond the reach of any judicial verdict.

> There is no standing ground, no place for enquiry, no way to engage in the practices of advancing, evaluating, accepting, and rejecting reasoned argument apart from that which is provided by some particular tradition or other. (*Whose Justice? Which Rationality?*, p. 350)

MacIntyre's solution to the problem is, not to recapture an all-embracing theory of justice, but to understand each separate tradition of justice. MacIntyre tells us that a diversity of perspectives on justice is not necessarily a bad thing. It is rather the normal way of being. It is not only natural and normal to have many views on justice, those views may be incompatible because they are justified by a certain way of reasoning. And this very habit of reasoning is different from one category of persons to another, and even from person to person.

The Holmes Tradition

But to which tradition does Sherlock Holmes belong? We could link him with the tradition of late-nineteen-century England. But we could also place him in the tradition of fictional private detectives, who have always worked around the law when it suited their own sense of morality.

Holmes has predecessors (Poe's Auguste Dupin) and famous successors (Agatha Christie's Hercule Poirot). These characters and many others belong to the same tradition because they all contribute to a peculiar, independent way of accomplishing justice: not by relying on the tools of external law and its police officers, but by relying on their own logical and physical powers.

Holmes claims that "from a drop of water, a logician could infer the possibility of an Atlantic or Niagara without having seen or heard of them" (*A Study in Scarlet*). The image of the exceptional, almost magical detective has become an icon of the mystery story.

What these fictional characters also share is their passionate commitment to their work. Although both Holmes and Poirot end up by supporting themselves financially from their hobby (Dupin was an aristocrat), they would do this job even in the absence of a material reward, for the sheer pleasure of doing it. This places them in opposition to the police detectives, who are only doing their job, and are not always motivated by an inner impetus. In exchange for a salary, they agree to follow the rules. Hence, different social and economic situations generate divergent traditions.

Holmes's Law

While prepared to disobey the law, Holmes also often thinks of himself as an instrument of the law, and always as an instrument of justice.

In "The Adventure of Shoscombe Old Place," Holmes coldly informs the baronet Sir Robert Norberton that "my business is that of every other good citizen—to uphold the law." And after he has heard the baronet's explanation and is somewhat more sympathetic, he still insists that "the matter must, of course, be referred to the police," even though Norberton did not kill his aged sister, but merely concealed her death for a few weeks.

The story which gives us the most detailed insight into Holmes's sense of justice is "The Adventure of the Abbey

Grange." Here we have Holmes's clear statement that he regrets having brought some criminals to justice, that it is his conscience which induces him to flout the law, and that this conscience is basically utilitarian:

> "No, I couldn't do it, Watson," said he, as we re-entered our room. "Once that warrant was made out, nothing on earth would save him. Once or twice in my career I feel that I have done more real harm by my discovery of the criminal than ever he had done by his crime. I have learned caution now, and I had rather play tricks with the law of England than with my own conscience."

Holmes gives the official detective Hopkins a vital piece of evidence, but holds back from helping him any further, to put the police on the track of the resourceful killer. Holmes explains to Watson:

> "You must look at it this way: what I know is unofficial, what he [Hopkins] knows is official. I have the right to private judgment, but he has none. He must disclose all, or he is a traitor to his service. In a doubtful case I would not put him in so painful a position, and so I reserve my information until my own mind is clear upon the matter."

And having finally confronted the guilty man, Captain Croker, Holmes gives him a trick question, which the forthright Captain answers with a splendid display of chivalrous honor. Holmes decides to let him off because he's a decent fellow at heart:

> "I was only testing you, and you ring true every time. Well, it is a great responsibility that I take upon myself, but I have given Hopkins an excellent hint and if he can't avail himself of it I can do no more. See here, Captain Croker, we'll do this in due form of law. You are the prisoner. Watson, you are a British jury, and I never met a man who was more eminently fitted to represent one. I am the judge. Now, gentleman of the jury, you have heard the evidence. Do you find the prisoner guilty or not guilty?"
>
> "Not guilty, my lord," said I.
>
> "Vox populi, vox dei. You are acquitted, Captain Croker. So long as the law does not find some other victim you are safe from me. Come back to this lady in a year, and may her future and yours justify us in the judgement which we have pronounced this night!"

This exchange brings out very clearly an invariable feature of Holmes's transgressions of the law: when Holmes breaks the law, Watson always agrees with him, Conan Doyle always agrees with him, the reader always agrees with him, and no doubt Lestrade, Gregson, Athelney Jones, Hopkins, and the rest would always agree with him, if only they were not bound by their professional code.

Probably Holmes's most dubious occasion for letting the criminal go free is in "The Adventure of the Three Gables." Holmes tells the *femme fatale* Isadora Klein "I am not the law, but I represent justice so far as my feeble powers go." Her own story shows that she was desperate, but still reveals her as ruthless and inclined to employ brutal methods.

"Well, well," says Holmes, after hearing her side of it. "I suppose I shall have to compound a felony as usual." He lets Klein off, only demanding a check for five thousand pounds, which he will pass on to Mrs. Maberley, the mother of Klein's latest victim, so that Mrs. Maberley can take the round the world trip she has always yearned for. Here we see Mr. Justice Holmes holding his own court, evidently one guided more by principles of restitution than retribution—or more likely, by the Victorian gentleman's acute sense of gallantry when confronted by a pretty ankle.

An Eye for an Eye

Very often the criminals have their own sense of justice, which, like Holmes's, may contradict the law of the land. In *A Study in Scarlet*, *The Sign of the Four*, and several of the short stories, the criminals defend their actions by reference to a code of justice which is at variance with the law.

At their most sympathetic, the criminal's motivation is revenge, or personal retribution for past wrongs. John Sholto, the murder victim in *The Sign of the Four*, had once committed a horribly treacherous act that partly motivates Jonathan Small's later revenge.

The most dramatic case of justified revenge is the motivation of Jefferson Hope in *A Study in Scarlet*. Hope remarks to Holmes and Lestrade: "You may consider me to be a murderer, but I hold that I am just as much an officer of justice as you are."

In deference to his own sense of retributive justice, Jefferson Hope doesn't simply kill Drebber and Stangerson, but makes them choose one of two pills, one poisoned, the other harmless. And so God, not Hope, decides who dies. "Let the high God judge between us. Choose and eat."

Enoch Drebber and Joseph Stangerson, the two victims, were actually the perpetrators of murder and oppression in Jefferson Hope's Mormon past. As Hope states: "I knew of their guilt, . . . and I determined that I should be judge, jury and executioner all rolled into one."

Holmes must understand this, because he too is often judge, jury, and executioner.

Chapter 10

The Game Has Virtually Stumbled
Tom Dowd

I can't be Sherlock Holmes. And I'm somewhat annoyed by that.

Well, obviously I can never really be any fictional character in the truest sense, short of a full schizophrenic break (*They Might Be Giants*, anyone?). The best I can hope for is to settle into a comfortable chair with a good book or television show—or do similarly in a darkened movie theater—and in a figurative or literal sense watch the experiences of a fictional character and be engaged.

But I'm not that character. I'm an observer, not a participant The story, the plot, and the actions of the people on the screen or on the page are all predetermined. Yes, in some circumstances, I can pause, rewind or fast-forward, but that actually changes nothing. The only control I really have is to watch or not to watch, which only affects me, not the narrative I was experiencing before I disgustedly stabbed that red button on my remote. I detach, but somewhere else the story goes on.

But can't I be the master of disguise, too? Well, no. I can choose my favorite incarnation of Sherlock Holmes and garb myself up in his likeness—classical Paget, cinematic Rathbone, televised Brett, contemporary Cumberbatch, or a multitude of other manifestations—but that's the best I can do. The costume remains a costume, and the self that I am doesn't change because of it. In a sympathetic company or environment others may play along, but in the end I am I and not he.

In my imagination, of course, I can be whoever I want.

Interpreting the Facts

When we act as the passive observer of a narrative while reading or viewing we're (hopefully) carried along. We may attempt to interact sometimes by inappropriately shouting commands ("No, you idiot! Don't open the door!"), but for the most part we're strapped into the roller-coaster and along for the ride. Mihály Csíkszentmihályi's idea of flow—single-minded immersion that brings about a loss of self-consciousness and a distorted sense of time—is in full control.

When we're the observer, we identify with the characters in the narrative before us, perhaps even sympathize or go so far as to empathize, but we do not project ourselves onto them right then and there. That comes later, in our after-the-fact minds, when we place ourselves into the role of the character, seeing what they've seen, saying what they've said, doing what they do, with our own spin. We reproduce our interpretation of the story or events in our imagination and adjust things to our liking.

And when I'm out and about with friends, I can act the part and quote and misquote with dramatic abandon. With a wry smile I can scan once-over my good friend—or if I'm feeling daring—the pretty young thing at the bar—and spin them some yarn about what I can deduce from looking at them . . . more than enough to hang myself with, unless I am very, very good or somehow already in the know (which works best, trust me).

Alternatively, leaning back, I can imagine myself as Sherlock Holmes. The textures and sounds (and heaven help me, the smells . . .) of Victoria's London roll out before me in my mind. I can place myself there, in Holmes's shoes, and be the Great Detective as I wish him to be. All of the pieces are mine to control—the plot, the characters, the setting, all respond to my machinations. I notice the pale scuff mark, deduce adultery with the handsome cab driver, and of course I'm right. Of course.

We're back to immersion again, yes? It is a sensation we're all familiar with from a good book, or movie, or game. We speak about becoming lost in a good book, and everyone relates. We become lost because the world conjured up on the page or by the image on the screen envelopes us and we settle into it willingly. It surrounds us, and because we believe enough in that world we can imagine peaking around the corner and being satisfied with what we find there.

Lost in Reality

Marie-Laure Ryan looks into the question of narrative and immersion in her book *Narrative as Virtual Reality*, but flips the usual direction of the analytical lens and looks at prior narrative art (among other things) in the context of virtual reality, primarily in the contexts of immersion and interactivity. This expression of "virtual reality" occurs entirely within the mind and it is the place that a good successful narrative takes us. It's that place we become lost within. Ryan argues that this has always been the case and that any type of art has the ability to transport us to a "virtual reality" that is defined by what we can see in the art and what we can imagine as lurking around the corner.

One of the clear successes of the Conan Doyle stories is the ability to conjure up that reality. It's a simplified evocation of the actual time and place of Victorian London, certainly, but in many ways it lives and breathes. That is what we draw from when we imagine ourselves as Holmes . . . but it's difficult to sustain (again, short of that full schizophrenic break). We can generate moments of satisfaction as both mental author and character, but it is only fleetingly satisfactory and difficult to maintain for a prolonged time.

A curious part of the problem is that there is no challenge. The pale scuff mark leads to adultery every time because I choose that it does, and therefore I'm right, every time. The game is not afoot; it is in fact quite rigged. For some that may be enough, but . . .

Where can I be Sherlock Holmes with the requisite challenges to overcome?

In a video game, or interactive narrative, of course.

But there's a catch . . .

Realization Hits

In interactive narrative (which video games are a kind of) the concept of agency refers to, using Janet Murray's explanation from *Hamlet on the Holodeck*:

> The more realized the immersive environment, the more active we want to be within it. When the things we do bring tangible results, we experience the second characteristic delight of electronic environments—the sense of agency. Agency is the satisfying power to take meaningful action and see the results of our decisions and choices.

Agency has become a powerful term in discussion of virtual reality and interactive narrative. Regardless of the term employed, this sense of being able to take a meaningful action and observe the result of that action is critical to interactivity. That, coupled with Donald Norman's concept of "perceived affordance," or those possible actions the user perceives as achievable within his or her current environment, are the foundations for the interactive part of interactive narrative.

Affordance, however, is perceptual—it is not just all possible uses or actions, but those deemed most likely within the user's personal context. (There's that self again.)

Agency and affordance are both tools and goals of the author of a piece of interactive narrative. A significant point of interactive narrative is the sense of participation, that interaction allows the user to create a new narrative by changing the sequence of events (plot) or the emotional, contextual underpinnings (story).

Traditional narrative devices, such as books, film, or television, are examples of linear narrative, where the order of events in the plot or story play out in chronological order, some use of flashbacks notwithstanding. Works of nonlinear narrative, such as the movies *Memento* or *Pulp Fiction*, or the TV series *Lost*, use non-chronological storytelling as their primary structure. Very often, games are referred to as having a nonlinear narrative and although a few may have, most have a story expressed in as linear a manner as any movie or television show. Games, especially story-driven games, often have nonlinear gameplay, which means that the player can travel through the world using any route he chooses and undertake various subplots in nearly any order, though the main story remains nearly linear.

So what does this have to do with Sherlock Holmes and my not being able to be him?

Run, Jump, Shoot, Screw . . . but Don't Think

Interactive narratives, and especially video games, do a great job at providing agency and affordance for certain acts. I can shoot a gun like a Black Ops sniper, skip across the rooftops of Venice as a highly-trained assassin, take a tight corner at Le Mans as a pro racer, or even hop, skip and bounce my way across the world grabbing gold rings as a blue-haired hedgehog. Games provide mechanisms that allow a new set of affordances and a different sense of agency from that which I have in real life. I am not expected to be able to ride a horse like an Old West outlaw seeking vengeance in real life in order to be just that in *Red Dawn Redemption*. Nor am I expected to have the smooth moves required to get me some sweet inter-species lovin', like in *Mass Effect*.

Video games, however, fall back to the abilities of the player when it comes to reasoning. Many games, especially role-playing games, give characters sets of knowledge skills that come into use during the game, but these are most often simple indicators that determine if the character can or cannot perform a physical, intellectual, or knowledge task. For example, in *Fallout 3* the Science skill is used to determine if the player can or cannot fix a broken robot. I don't need to know how to fix the robot; the game mechanic handles it for me.

Abstract reasoning—deduction—is entirely up to me. And I am, therefore, screwed.

The Art of Deduction

I can't ever satisfactorily play Sherlock Holmes because my brain doesn't work like his does, and video games provide no mechanisms to assist me. To date, there have been dozens of various forms of computer game adaptations of Sherlock Holmes, the oldest in 1984. Many of them have been casual hidden object or simple puzzle-solving games, but a number have been story-driven adventure game attempts to portray Sherlock Holmes with a truly interactive structure. While all of these have had nonlinear gameplay, at least to some limited extent, none have had a truly interactive story where the outcome varies based on the player's actions.

That said, they have all attempted to create the Sherlock Holmes experience with varying degrees of success. They've all, however, avoided requiring real deductive reasoning to resolve the story. The puzzle or problem solving in games like *Sherlock: The Riddle of the Crown Jewels*, *The Lost Files of Sherlock Holmes: The Case of the Rose Tattoo*, or the more recent *Sherlock Holmes: Nemesis* is primarily there as an obstruction to physical progress (solve the puzzle to open the secret passage) or plot progression (solve the puzzle to trigger the story-advancing movie segment).

The most recent release, *Sherlock Holmes vs. Jack the Ripper* (2009), introduces the concept of a "Deduction Board" where the player can organize clues (objects and observations obtained at a crime scene), literally form links between them and then draw conclusions based on those links. The system does help the player out by allowing him to connect strings of clues, but ultimately he can reach the conclusions by simply finding everything and arranging and rearranging until successful. It's a step in a better direction, but ultimately there's no true deductive reasoning in that it helps the player follow the clue trail a little easier, but it does not allow the intuitive leaps that Holmes is best

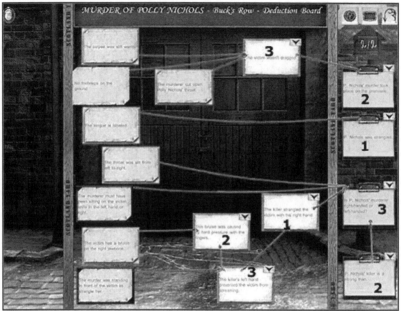

Screenshot from Sherlock Holmes vs. Jack the Ripper (C) 2009 Frogwares

known for. It's not truly abstract and deductive reasoning, but maybe, though, that's for the best.

In many Sherlock Holmes video games while Holmes is the primary character, when it comes time to figure out the clues the burden shifts to Watson—standing in for the player—and Holmes confirms or refutes the conclusions, which he has already reached. Some of the games shift control between the two depending on where matters are in the investigation.

If Not Holmes, then Watson?

Aha! I'm Doctor John Watson.

Well, no, I'm not him either, but in the Conan Doyle stories I am somewhat.

Conan Doyle uses Watson as the source of the first-person narrative perspective in the Holmes tales. We see through Watson's eyes as he recounts Holmes's adventures. In addition to the choice being a dramatic literary one, it's a practical one as well: By putting us in Watson's head as the narrator Conan Doyle doesn't have to put us in Holmes's.

For Conan Doyle as a writer, it must have been hard enough to work up the chain of clues that leads Holmes to his brilliant conclusions, but to put the reader in Holmes's head while it runs through all of the possible permutations of what lies before him would have been painful for both reader and author alike. Fortunately, he chose Watson and spared us all, and himself, that madness.

The presence of a Watson-like figure is standard in any fiction where another character is smarter or has more knowledge or expertise than the other characters. Often this is the protagonist (as in the Holmes's stories) but not always. The smarter character has to have some reason to verbalize his conclusions or intentions, and the presence of the not-quite-as-smart characters provides exactly that. Sometimes the verbalization involves the process prior to reaching a conclusion, or the reverse order where the conclusion is expressed and then by way of explanation the process that achieved it. (Gil Grissom from the CBS Television's *CSI: Crime Scene Investigation* often has to explain himself in this manner, as does Gregory House in the thinly disguised translation of Holmes to the world of diagnostic medicine in the Fox television series *House*.)

Occasionally, efforts have been made to put us in the head of the genius; the most recent relevant example comes from the 2010 contemporary update of Sherlock Holmes, the BBC *Sherlock* TV series. In that series, predominantly in the first episode "A Study in Pink," floating text is used to show what

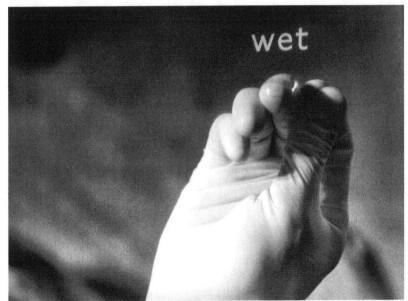

Frame from *Sherlock* "A Study in Pink" © 2010 2 entertain Video Limited

Holmes notices. The audience sees the clues, but then has to wait for Holmes to pronounce the startling conclusion. It's an interesting technique that is used to a lesser degree in later episodes in part, I suspect, because it just duplicates information that Holmes himself relates when he explains his conclusions to those around him.

Sticky Paint

When we look at Sherlock Holmes we often talk about his deductive reasoning skill, which involves using a rule and its precondition to reach a conclusion. For example, "When a wall has been very recently painted, the paint remains sticky for some time. The paint is currently sticky; therefore the wall was recently painted." As Didierjean and Gobet point out, Holmes also uses abductive reasoning, which involves starting from observed data and then deriving the most likely explanation or hypothesis. Holmes himself explains this methodology to Watson in *A Study in Scarlet*:

> "In solving a problem of this sort, the grand thing is to be able to reason backward. That is a very useful accomplishment, and a very easy one, but people do not practise it much. In the everyday affairs of life it is more useful to reason forward, and so the other comes to be neglected. There are fifty who can reason synthetically for one who can reason analytically." "I confess," said I, "that I do not quite follow you."
>
> "I hardly expected that you would. Let me see if I can make it clearer. Most people, if you describe a train of events to them, will tell you what the result would be. They can put those events together in their minds, and argue from them that something will come to pass. There are few people, however, who, if you told them a result, would be able to evolve from their own inner consciousness what the steps were which led up to that result. This power is what I mean when I talk of reasoning backward, or analytically."

Some may think of this more as "guessing," but what it really digs into is the idea of expertise and domain knowledge, which is valid knowledge in a specific area. Holmes can be the master detective because he is able to use both deductive and abductive reasoning in combination with expert knowledge in a wide variety of domains (fields). Holmes, however, is not an expert in everything. Again in *A Study in Scarlet*, Watson himself created a list of Holmes's domain knowledge:

Sherlock Holmes–his limits

1. Knowledge of Literature. —Nil.
2. Knowledge of Philosophy. —Nil.
3. Knowledge of Astronomy. —Nil.
4. Knowledge of Politics. —Feeble.
5. Knowledge of Botany. —Variable. Well up in belladonna, opium, and poisons generally. Knows nothing of practical gardening.
6. Knowledge of Geology. —Practical, but limited. Tells at a glance different soils from each other. After walks has shown me splashes upon his trousers, and told me by their colour and consistence in what part of London he had received them.
7. Knowledge of Chemistry. —Profound.
8. Knowledge of Anatomy. —Accurate, but unsystematic.
9. Knowledge of Sensational Literature. —Immense. He appears to know every detail of every horror perpetrated in the century.
10. Plays the violin well.
11. Is an expert singlestick player, boxer, and swordsman.
12. Has a good practical knowledge of British law.

Often, Holmes speaks directly to or infers that he simply sees thing differently than everyone else. Didierjean and Gobet quote a variety of sources in saying "Experts literally 'see' situations taken from their domain of expertise differently from novices" and connect back to A.D. de Groot's 1946 work *Thinking in Chess* which, while talking about chess expertise, pointed out that "this perceptual advantage is one of the keys to experts' superior performance."

The Game Is (and Isn't) Afoot

Without Holmes's deep domain knowledge (in key areas) or his capacity for deductive and abductive reasoning, I cannot solve crimes as he does. I just simply can't.

Video games currently provide the mechanism for simulating a variety of physical and social actions that I cannot perform, but they haven't yet figured out how to model the vast breadth and depth of knowledge and the intuitive cross-linking necessary for Holmesian crime solving.

Conan Doyle himself in the original works didn't believe it was necessary for his readers to match wits with Holmes. The Sherlock Holmes stories are not whodunits—we can't figure it out because we do not have Holmes's domain knowledge and expertise or his intellect. The stories are about the characters and the chase. We see through Watson's eyes in part because if we could see through Holmes's eyes, the matter at hand would be somewhat less dramatic. Holmes himself is often thrilled primarily by his ability to problem solve, and the fact that the problem gets solved is a serendipitous result.

We still want to be Sherlock Holmes, however, and the continuing popularity of video games shows that clearly. As I write this, Frogwares is planning to release *The New Adventures of Sherlock Holmes: The Testament of Sherlock Holmes*. The game promises a new deduction system and improved questioning and interrogation systems, but will it bring us closer to truly being Sherlock Holmes, or will his superior intellect and cunning forever counter our desire to be the Great Detective, even if only virtually?

Chapter 11

The Curious Case of the Controversial Canon

Ivan Wolfe

Sir Arthur Conan Doyle wrote fifty-six short stories and four novels about Sherlock Holmes.

There—that's all I need to write, clearly. Those texts are the official "canon" and any other texts are apocryphal at best and spurious at worst. It may be fun for other authors to create short stories, novels, comic books, movies, and TV shows about Holmes's adventures, but they can never be considered official. Only the true tales, written by Doyle himself, can be considered our source for determining the truth about the one true and original Sherlock Holmes.

My edition of *The Complete Works* contains four novels and fifty-six short stories. I have other books by other authors—a personal favorite is the H.P. Lovecraft/Sherlock Holmes crossover collection *Shadows Over Baker Street* with Neil Gaiman's brilliant "A Study in Emerald," and I also rather enjoy the collection *Holmes for the Holidays* despite the groan worthy title—but I recognize they aren't the real Holmes.

But I belabor the point. There can be no doubts about the nature of the canon.

And then I pick up a copy of a French edition of Sherlock Holmes—okay, I haven't actually picked up a copy; I can read and write Laotian in addition to my native English, and I minored in Classical Greek, but I cannot read French, so in this case, I'm relying on the word of others and hopefully, this won't get me into too much trouble—and it seems that this French edition contains fifty-eight short stories. And the two additional tales are also written by Doyle.

Wait—what's going on here? Have I and other English speakers been cheated? What does this say about the supposedly fixed nature of the canon? Why do the French get more Holmes then we do? Is there some secret conspiracy to hide two missing

103

tales from the English-speaking world? Or are the French just easily fooled?

Later, I find there are several other short stories about Holmes written by Doyle and published during his lifetime, and yet they aren't considered canon. It's a similar feeling to the one a Protestant sometimes gets when leafing through a Catholic (or Orthodox) Bible and realizing it has a several additional books in the Old Testament—though I guess it depends on which Orthodox Church as well; growing up in Alaska, I became more familiar with the Russian Orthodox; most people, in my experience, are only aware of the Greek Orthodox church due to the movie *My Big Fat Greek Wedding*. But that's another topic for another time. Now where was I?

For Those Who Came in Late

I'm tossing around terms like "canon" and "apocrypha" the way Holmes tosses around seemingly insignificant observations that solve cases. Some of my readers are likely already familiar with these terms. Often, I find the people who are most familiar with them are either religious (or at least study religion) or are hardcore *Star Trek* or *Star Wars* fans. In a very simplified form, for those unaware of these debates, in *Star Trek*, anything other than the movies and TV shows—novels, comics, games, and so forth—are apocrypha. In *Star Wars*, it's more complicated, but Lucasfilm has people whose job it is to determine which novels, comics, games, or other creations are canon and which aren't.

For those of you not too familiar with these terms, a brief examination of their definitions will help move the discussion along, and help us decide whether the English or French editions of Sherlock Holmes are the more correct canon (or if both are incomplete).

We shall start, as one always should, with the *Oxford English Dictionary* (OED). It defines "canon" as "a piece of ordnance; a gun or firearm of a size which requires it to be mounted for firing." Actually, that is a "cannon"—and "canon" is an archaic spelling for that weapon of war. That is NOT what we are talking about here. So—one "n" for important texts, and two for a weapon of destruction. To help remember the difference, think of having two as overkill, or twice as much power, or something (whatever works for you). Back in the days when spelling was not standardized, this wasn't a problem—but now, it can cause problems online. Imagine discussing where a particular story fits into the overall chronology of a series—you start arguing about "using the cannon to show them all," and then the FBI shows up at your doorstep.

The kind of "canon" that we are discussing is

> The collection or list of books of the Bible accepted by the Christian Church as genuine and inspired. Also . . . a body of works, etc., considered to be established as the most important or significant in a particular field.

The OED, being as comprehensive as it is, has several other related definitions, but this is the one (actually, a combination of two) most suited to our purpose here.

The OED defines the related term "apocrypha" this way: "Of unknown authorship; not authentic, spurious; uncanonical . . . A writing or statement of doubtful authorship or authenticity." The term comes from a Greek word meaning "hidden." For example, "The Apocrypha" (capitalized, thus used as a solid Proper Noun) refers to several books in the Old Testament that were rejected by Protestants, but are still in use (to various extents) by Catholic and Orthodox churches.

By analogy, then, any work called "apocryphal" usually has some claim on being official, but it is only accepted by certain adherents (or, if not accepted by any adherents, a decent percentage of informed adherents have to agree there is "something" to the texts, even if it is not enough to raise the texts to official or binding status). If it has no real claim or no one accepts its authenticity, then it's merely non-canonical.

Some apocryphal works are rejected by pretty much everyone today but historically have been accepted by various groups. A canonical work is accepted as official and authoritative. There may be disputes about how to interpret the text, but not about whether the text is official or not. Many religions have a "closed canon" meaning that no new authoritative texts are allowed. Some, such as the Latter Day Saints (or Mormon) church have an "open canon" meaning they can accept new texts into their canon (though they don't accept every possible new text, and getting a new text accepted can be difficult).

Why It Matters

If you belong to a religion and are seeking salvation, then what serves as canon likely matters quite a bit. When we're discussing Sherlock Holmes, though, it may not seem as important.

However, if you are a devotee or a scholar or even a rabid fan, knowing what is and isn't canon allows for fruitful discussion with other fans, scholars, or devotees. You have to have a common ground of some sort, or else discussion cannot happen. Also, among aficionados of Holmes, there's a considerable body of literature that discusses how Holmes could have fit into "real" history and even treats his adventures, for the sake of study, as part of history. Many Sherlockian scholars try to fill in the blanks or read between the lines in the stories to determine more about the background of Holmes and Watson. Some even write whole books dedicated to creating elaborate backstories and end of life explorations for Holmes, Watson, Lestrade, Moriarty, and others. However, to be taken seriously by others with similar interests, these texts have to be grounded in something everyone who talks about Holmes considers authoritative. If there is no "shared language" based in commonly accepted texts, the Holmesian conversation would descend into gibberish.

Having a commonly accepted set of texts allows for the community of Holmes buffs to fruitfully communicate with each other, the way a set of scriptures or laws allows a religious or secular community to determine what is acceptable or how to proceed with life. We all have "canons" of some sort, even if we don't realize it. There are books we consider authoritative and base our lives around, whether they are scripture, self-help, diet, or academic; we also have friends whose advice we trust and consider more important than advice from other people.

An example of how this can play out in a less abstract realm deals with the Guy Ritchie/Robert Downey, Jr. Sherlock Holmes films. In those, Holmes does not wear a deerstalker cap and seems to be something of an action man—even engaging in some bare-knuckle boxing. In the popular imagination, it seems, Holmes is something of an atrophied recluse—a genius, but one who rarely gets his hands dirty. Now, no one would consider the film "canon," but many defenders of the film pointed to areas in the canon that supported the movie's interpretation of the world's greatest sleuth. In particular, many pointed to a passage from *The Sign of the Four*:

> "Oh, yes you do, McMurdo," cried Sherlock Holmes, genially. "I don't think you can have forgotten me. Don't you remember the amateur who fought three rounds with you at Alison's rooms on the night of your benefit four years back?"
>
> "Not Mr. Sherlock Holmes!" roared the prize-fighter. "God's truth! how could I have mistook you? If instead o' standin' there so quiet you

had just stepped up and given me that cross-hit of yours under the jaw, I'd ha' known you without a question. Ah, you're one that has wasted your gifts, you have! You might have aimed high, if you had joined the fancy."

Many also pointed to Holmes's claim in "The Adventure of the Empty House" that "I have some knowledge, however, of baritsu, or the Japanese system of wrestling." Of course, this is likely a misspelling of "bartitsu" an actual system of martial arts developed in England by Edward William Barton-Wright, who had lived and studied in Japan for several years. But the point has been made. And there are other references to Holmes's fighting abilities in many of the stories. In these cases, being armed with canon can help win debates and settle issues about how well a particular version of Holmes fits with the original. (Okay, okay, I'm stealing this phrase "armed with canon"—but not its meaning—from the TV Tropes wiki. But, to paraphrase T.S. Eliot: good writers steal, bad writers borrow.)

Back to Baker Street

So, how does this affect the Holmesian canon, and why do the French get two more short stories in their canon? Well, for that, we need to consider the tales that, for the time being, are not considered canonical, but have at least some claim on the status. For the most part, there are pretty clear rules about the canon, but enough fuzziness on the edges to make things difficult when it comes to certain texts.

There are several collections of apocryphal material, and they do not all agree on what is or should be considered canonical or apocryphal. The four I am aware of (all worth getting for any Holmes reader, regardless of your stance on canonicity) are *Sherlock Holmes: The Published Apocrypha*, edited by Jack Tracy; *The Uncollected Sherlock Holmes*, edited by Richard Lancelyn Green; *The Final Adventures of Sherlock Holmes*, edited by Peter Haining; and *The Apocrypha of Sherlock Holmes*, edited by Leslie S. Klinger.

A few clear criteria for canonicity (with some attendant problem areas) have emerged, though:

- **It must be written by Arthur Conan Doyle.** This may seem obvious, but Doyle's son co-wrote a collection called *The Exploits of Sherlock Holmes* that was intended to be "official" and J.M. Barrie wrote several pastiches for his friend

Doyle (which have sometimes been mistakenly identified as written by Doyle). In one instance, Doyle even paid another writer for a story, in case he ever wanted to use the idea. He never did, but the story was mistakenly published as having been written by Doyle. Also, Doyle collaborated with the actor William Gillette on *Sherlock Holmes: A Drama in Four Acts*, which went through several revisions, making it difficult to tell how much is Doyle and how much belongs to Gillette.

• **It should have been published during Doyle's lifetime.** While there have been some posthumous publications of unpublished plays, story outlines, and the like, the general consensus seems to be that if Doyle didn't publish it, he didn't like the tale, couldn't make it work, or lost interest.

• **It must be about Sherlock Holmes (or possibly Watson).** The dispute over some apocryphal tales is whether or not they actually are about Holmes. The two found in French editions of the complete works actually never mention Holmes by name—though some have speculated they refer to Watson (or even Mycroft) rather than Holmes. Other scholars and writers have argued for mystery tales written by Doyle that predate Holmes but were clearly proto-Holmes or Holmesian in spirit. There is even a case of a play (*The Angels of Darkness*) written by Doyle that adapts the American parts of *A Study in Scarlet* and features Watson (in America!), but not Holmes. This play also falls under #2 above, as Doyle never published this play, likely realizing it did not fit well with the direction his Holmes stories were taking (Watson is wildly out of character, though it was written before Doyle had firmly established Watson's character).

• **It cannot radically contradict the rest of the canon.** While the accepted canon is not free from contradiction, anything that is wildly out of line is clearly not a candidate. The play *The Angels of Darkness*, mentioned above, does this in many ways, most notably with its treatment of Watson.

• **It should be prose fiction.** Several collections also include essays by Doyle about Holmes, but as these are treated as interesting insights from the creator, and not as canonical tales (since, most obviously, they aren't tales).

With these basic ground rules in effect, we can discuss several apocryphal texts and hopefully come to a conclusion about whether they deserve a place in the canon. As stated above, not every collection agrees on what the apocryphal texts are, but even in those collections, the editors admit several of the texts would not pass muster. Instead, the editors include them in the collection as historical curiosities or for entertainment value. *The Angels of Darkness*, for example, would never seriously be considered for canonicity. Likewise, the story "The Case of the Man Who Was Wanted" was written by Arthur Whitaker, who sent a copy to Doyle suggesting the two collaborate on a tale. Instead, Doyle paid Whitaker ten pounds for the rights to the story idea, but then never did anything with it. The short comic play "The Painful Predicament of Sherlock Holmes" is almost certainly written by the actor William Gillette, and therefore also fails in consideration. Several other collected apocryphal texts fail similar tests.

That said, a few texts do exist that seem, at the very least, borderline canon. Let us consider them one at a time, and the go where the evidence leads us.

Canon Fodder

There are the two tales that appear in French editions and are often considered the two apocryphal stories with the best case for being canon (several critics have jokingly called them "canon-fodder"): "The Man with the Watches" and "The Lost Special." They each deal with a seemingly impossible event (a man with thirteen watches in his pockets is found dead in a railway carriage he couldn't have possibly entered; in the second tale, a specially commissioned train vanishes with no indication of how it vanished or where it has gone). Sherlock Holmes is not consulted during these tales, and in both cases a confession well after the fact reveals how the events actually happened. However, in both tales an unidentified letter writer offers potential solutions.

In the first tale, he is identified as "a well known criminal investigator" and in the second as "an amateur reasoner of some celebrity." These identifications have caused many scholars to argue these are clearly meant to be Holmes. The letters use similar language and reasoning as Holmes, including the phrase "when the impossible has been eliminated the residuum, however improbable, must contain the truth."

In both cases, however, there are problems with this identification. One is that the tales take place during the time Holmes was in hiding, after faking his death at the hands of Moriarty. It seems unlikely Holmes would reveal his survival to the world at large through highly speculative letters to the press, especially on cases where he was unable to see the evidence firsthand (such a tactic seems more akin to Poe's Dupin, someone Holmes did not admire). Additionally, the "well known reasoner" is spectacularly wrong in both cases. These details have led some to argue that perhaps the reference is to Watson or maybe Mycroft. It would seem unlikely that it was Mycroft, as he is just as unlikely to get it wrong as Sherlock, but there is, perhaps, a case for Watson, who is known for attempting to reason like Holmes and failing at it. However, calling Watson "a well known criminal investigator" seems somewhat unusual.

These tales were written during the time Doyle had "killed off" Holmes, and so he may have been working out some issues. Perhaps they were a sort of "Take That!" or an affectionate bit of gentle jabbing at the detective. In any case, Holmes was still "dead" at that point, making it even more unlikely the detective was meant to be Holmes, rather than a tribute or passing reference.

Bizarre Lack of Adventure

Edinburgh University asked Doyle (and several other prominent authors) to write a short tale for a newsletter that would be sold to raise funds for expanding athletic facilities. While not a mystery, "The Field Bazaar" does read like the beginning of many of the canonical short stories, with Watson and Holmes at breakfast, Holmes making brilliant deductions that baffle Watson, and then Holmes explaining how he made those deductions to an impressed Watson.

Though nearly every editor refers to this as a "parody," there appears to be very little parody about it. It is humorous, but very little distinguishes it from the opening of many other Holmes tales. Its most unique features are its brevity and that it does not immediately lead into an adventure of some sort.

Tricky Man

Perhaps the most unusual of all the tales, "How Watson Learned the Trick" was a very brief story written for a miniature book to be placed in the library of Queen Mary's Dolls' House. It was also published in a collection (*The Book of the Queen's Dolls' House Library*) along with several other books from that library, as many authors of the day contributed very short stories for the project.

This short tale deals with Watson attempting to show Holmes that he has mastered deduction and failing miserably. Also referred to by many as a "parody," I see little reason to label it as such. While short, it would fit right in place at the beginning of any tale. Not only that, as many others have noted, the tale provides a clue as to Sherlock Holmes's birthplace (or at least his hometown).

At Play

Sherlock Holmes: A Drama in Four Acts contains many items of interest to Holmes fans, including the first recorded use of "Elementary, my dear Watson." Though it contains several new scenes and borrows heavily from the short stories, it is clear that actor William Gillette made many revisions and changes. However, the play ran for over thirty years, so it was a clear success.

The Stonor Case is a theatrical version of "The Speckled Band," but differs in many key areas. *The Crown Diamond* is similar to "The Adventure of the Mazarin Stone," but as with *The Stonor Case*, it differs in many key areas. It seems that the general consensus is that *The Crown Diamond* came first, and this helps explains why this tale has a third-person narration. However, the short story is solidly canonical, whereas the play is not. And while some of the short stories and novels accepted into the canon have some disagreements and discontinuities, the plays, if accepted, would create too many problems because they radically contradict the tales they are based on.

Interlude

If it were up to me (and, of course, it isn't), I would reject most of the above tales, even the ones found in French editions of the complete works. It seems quite clear that "The Man with the Watches" and "The Lost Special" do not concern Holmes. The various plays contradict too many other well-established canonical tales, and are best looked at as adaptations or alternate universes.

The two that I feel most likely belong in the canon are "How Watson Learned the Trick" and "The Field Bazaar." They fulfill nearly all the criteria—they are fiction, they were written by Doyle, they were published for public consumption during his lifetime (even if in a very limited way in both cases), they concern Holmes, nothing in them contradicts other strictly canonical tales, and they even provide informative background information on Holmes and Watson. The largest complaints against them are that they are "parodies" or that they are not strictly mysteries. While they're humorous, there is no clear evidence Doyle meant them to be parodies; instead they read more like anecdotes or snapshots from the life of Holmes and Watson – pleasant interludes in between cases that shed light on their relationship and histories. And while they are slight and short, each one does involve some deduction.

But the Contradictions! What about the Contradictions?

Many different versions of Holmes exist, and in some sense, they all have their own canons. The Basil Rathbone films (and radio series) can be said to be their own canon, though one clearly built on "The Canon." The various cartoons, movies, TV shows, comics, and whatnot can all be said to be separate canons, though clearly subservient to the original canon created by Doyle. None could even be considered as important as the original, but often they can flavor how we interpret the original tales (witness the debates over the recent movies, as discussed above). When they contradict the original canon, there's no need to worry.

But—how to deal with contradictions in the official canon? The canon of Sherlock Holmes, with or without the additions I have argued for, is not entirely self-consistent either. Many, many trees have died in attempts by Sherlockian scholars to explain away or harmonize these problems. Perhaps the most common one is the list of things in *A Study in Scarlet* that Watson claims Holmes does not know, including politics, literature, and philosophy. However, later tales show Holmes very knowledgeable about these fields.

As for how to deal with them, I generally leave that to those more knowledgeable on the issues. However, I do have a few, final suggestions. As far as religious canons go, many believers either find ways to harmonize the contradictions, deny there are any, or admit they are still working on it.

A similar approach applies to Sherlock Holmes. The most common approach is to harmonize the contradictions, usually by coming up with fancy and convoluted explanations. Another common tactic is to argue that there are no contradictions at all, but that perhaps Watson (or Doyle) changed a name or date to protect the innocent or made a mistake when transcribing the details of the case. The third approach is to admit the contradictions are there, but to act as though further research will reveal the truth.

So, to use the example above, perhaps Holmes was playing some game with Watson upon their initial acquaintance, Watson was jumping to conclusions based on incomplete knowledge about someone he just met, or that some other reason exists for the apparent contradiction.

If you want to join in on the study of Sherlock Holmes (or even just argue on Internet chat boards), feel free to add your own contributions on how to deal with any potential problems. But in order to do that, of course, we need a canon to argue over in the first place.

I Think
You Might Want

a Little
Unofficial
Help

Chapter 12

How Marriage Changed Sherlock Holmes

Amy Kind

"But love is an emotional thing, and whatever is emotional is opposed to that true cold reason which I place above all things. I should never marry myself, lest I bias my judgment."

> —Sherlock Holmes on the occasion of Watson's engagement in
> *The Sign of the Four*

"You do realize how potentially disastrous this whole thing is?" he said. "I am old and set in my ways. I will give you little affection and a great deal of irritation, though heaven knows you're aware of how difficult I can be."

> —Sherlock Holmes proposing to Mary Russell in *A Monstrous Regiment of Women*

As a young man, Sherlock Holmes was a confirmed bachelor. But most readers of Conan Doyle probably don't realize that later in Holmes's life, after he had retired to his Sussex cottage, he met and married a precocious young woman named Mary Russell. Or at least this is how Sherlock Holmes's later years have recently been imagined (Conan Doyle aficionados might here insist: *re-imagined*) in a series of books by the author Laurie R. King.[1]

Though she's young and untutored in the art of detection when she first meets Holmes, Russell's intellect is a match for his own. We might naturally think of her as a female version of Holmes—or, perhaps, as a female version of Holmes who is not

---

[1] The series now consists of eleven Mary Russell novels—King has long insisted that her works are Mary Russell stories, not Sherlock Holmes stories. Russell was introduced in *The Beekeeper's Apprentice* (1994); she and Holmes get engaged in *A Monstrous Regiment of Women* (1995). Other books from the series discussed in this chapter include *A Letter of Mary* (1997) and *The Moor* (1998).

117

only of the twentieth century but also a serious scholar of theology. Both Russell and Holmes realize that they are kindred spirits from almost the moment they meet. As Russell herself describes it, Holmes "towered over me in experience, but never did his abilities of observation and analysis awe me as they did Watson. My own eyes and mind functioned in precisely the same way. It was familiar territory" (*The Beekeeper's Apprentice*, p. xxi).

Laurie King herself offers similar reflections in her essay "Mary Russell's World." Thinking of the mind like an engine, free of gender and nurture considerations, King suggests that Russell and Holmes are "two people whose basic mental mechanism is identical. What they do with it, however, is where the interest lies."

The partnership between Holmes and Russell—first a purely professional pairing, and then a domestic one as well—changes them both in many ways. Holmes, a man who's fiercely independent and used to being completely unencumbered, must approach his work differently once Russell comes into his life. And in many ways, both the love between them and their marriage change not only the way that Holmes looks at his work but also the way that he looks at himself.

And, of course, the way that we look at him as well. Sherlock Holmes, a married man? The man who, according to Watson at least, would be as disturbed to find himself having a strong emotion as he would be to find dirt in one of his sensitive measuring instruments? One would be forgiven, at this point, for wondering whether a married Holmes would still be Holmes at all.

The Woman (or The Girl?)

It's not at all surprising that a man of Holmes's temperament—a man who so craves mental stimulation that he turns to cocaine and morphine during the lull between cases to escape the dull routine of day-to-day existence—would be unsatisfied with the slow pace of life in retirement.

When Watson confronts the great detective about his drug use, Holmes explains that his mind "rebels at stagnation. Give me problems, give me work, give me the most abstruse cryptogram, or the most intricate analysis, and I am in my own proper atmosphere. I can dispense then with artificial stimulants. But I abhor the dull routine of existence. I crave for mental exaltation" (*The Sign of the Four*, p. 92).

What's perhaps more surprising is that he would also mind the solitude. We see glimmers of his loneliness as early as 1907: "My house is lonely. I, my old housekeeper, and my bees have the estate all to ourselves" ("The Adventure of the Lion's Mane"). These sentiments had presumably only deepened by the spring of 1915 when he first bumps into the fifteen-year old Russell while he's out observing bees on the Sussex Downs. Actually, their initial meeting is more accurately described as Russell bumping into Holmes. Walking along with her nose in a book, she nearly steps right on him.

Even for those untrained in the science of deduction, the mention of Russell's age might naturally give rise to immediate concern. Wasn't Sherlock Holmes already practically middle-aged when he took up residence with Watson in Baker Street in the early 1880s? That's certainly how the *Strand* illustrations portray him. So isn't he well into his seventies by the time he meets Russell? When he and Russell marry in 1921—after she reaches the age of majority—isn't he easily old enough to be her grandfather?

Upon meeting Russell, Holmes is able to deduce all manner of things about the teenage girl before him: that she was raised in southwestern London though her father hails from Northern California; that her parents were killed in an accident sometime the previous fall, an accident that has left her scarred both mentally and physically; that she now lives with a tight-fisted and unsympathetic relative; and that she reads and writes Hebrew. Displaying a sharpness of mind that instantly endears her to the great detective, Russell is able to match him at his own game of observation and deduction. Though many facts about Holmes had previously been disclosed in Watson's published case files, she's able to tell that he no longer smokes cigarettes though he still frequently uses a pipe, that he's kept up with the violin, that he's unconcerned about bee stings, and that he hasn't entirely given up his former life. When she then guesses him to be in his early fifties, he tells her that he's fifty-four (and, unsurprisingly, admonishes her for guessing).

Leslie S. Klinger, who has published numerous scholarly articles and books on Sherlockiana, has compiled a comprehensive chronology ("Major Events") of key occurrences in Holmes's life that puts his birth in 1854. This would make him sixty-one at the time he meets Russell. Laurie King discusses her own scientific deduction of Holmes's age in "A Holmes Chronology."

Holmes also provides Russell with an easy explanation for the discrepancy between his actual age and the earlier *Strand* illustrations, an inconsistency Russell herself comments upon. Since a youthful detective would not have inspired confidence in readers, Conan Doyle and the editorial staff at the *Strand* sought to make him appear more dignified by exaggerating his age. So we should not be concerned that Holmes was already a doddering old man when beginning his association with Russell, though the thirty-nine-year age difference between the two might still give us considerable pause. It gives Holmes himself pause. After Russell finishes her incisive characterization of him, he cryptically murmurs: "Twenty years ago . . . Even ten. But here? Now?" (*The Beekeeper's Apprentice*, p. 26).

Indeed, not only does love often find us when we least expect it, but it also finds the people of whom we'd least expect it—even someone who has long seemed incapable of love. In Watson's assessment, emotion and passion were distractions incompatible with the cold precision of Holmes's mind, and thus "as a lover, he would have placed himself in a false position" ("A Scandal in Bohemia"). Of course, Watson makes this claim long before Russell comes into Holmes's life. The doctor might have been right that there is but one woman for Holmes, but he was surely wrong about who *the* woman really is.

Two into One

One of the earliest sources for philosophical reflection on love is Plato's *Symposium*, a dialogue that depicts a Greek drinking party in which the participants take turns singing the praises of the god of love. Although Socrates is usually the hero of Plato's work, here the Greek playwright Aristophanes has the scene-stealing speech. According to his tale, we humans were once quite different from what we are now; as originally created, we were spherical beings with four arms, four legs, and a single head. But when our human ancestors offended the gods—and don't humans always end up offending the Greek gods in some way or other?—Zeus decided to teach us a lesson by splitting each of us in two.

Humanity might have been better off had we just been punished with the usual thunderbolts. Having been bisected into the two-legged creatures we are today, we are left feeling desperately incomplete and always yearning for our missing half. As Aristophanes concludes his paean to Love: "The happiness of the whole human race . . . is to be found in the consummation of our love, and in the healing of our dissevered nature by finding each his proper mate." In love, we attempt to restore ourselves to our former natures, "to make two into one, and to bridge the gulf between one human being and another" (*Symposium*, p. 544).

As much as we might want to reintegrate ourselves, however, doing so is not always easy. Even after two years of marriage, Holmes and Russell are each still adjusting to their partnership—a partnership that far transcends the marriage bed into every area of their lives together. As he tells her, in terms strikingly reminiscent of Aristophanes' tale, "I still find it difficult to accustom myself to being half a creature with two brains and four eyes. A superior creature to a single detective, no doubt, but it takes some getting used to" (*A Letter of Mary*, p. 85).

Holmes's quiet declaration startles Russell. Having known him for over a third of her life, she has long recognized how much she has been shaped by him. But what she is now only coming to realize is that she, too, has been shaping him.

Crazy Love

Philosophers interested in theories of personal identity—the question of what makes an individual the same person over time—are known for inventing unusual and often outlandish cases in an attempt to test our intuitions. Would you still be the same person if your body were completely disassembled and the molecules beamed across space, later to be reassembled in their original configuration on Mars? What if we took a detailed imprint of your complete molecular configuration, destroyed your physical matter here on earth, and then imposed that molecular configuration on completely new physical matter on Mars? Would the Mars human be you? Or what if we imposed the molecular pattern on the completely new physical matter on Mars without destroying your body here on Earth? Would the being newly created on Mars be you? But then who's on Earth? Are you somehow in both places? Holmes might never have needed cocaine to keep himself stimulated in the downtime between cases had he only turned his mind to reflection of these sorts of cases!

A different outlandish case, and one more relevant to our purposes here, is raised by philosopher Derek Parfit in his influential discussion of personal identity. Imagine a world in which fusion was a natural process: "Two people come together. While they are unconscious, their two bodies grow together into one. One person then wakes up" (*Reasons and Persons*, p. 298). Different people value autonomy differently, and some people accord a greater sense of importance to their sense of individuality than others do, but it's hard to believe that any of us would fail to be anything but completely horrified by a world in which this kind of fusion was commonplace. Parfitian fusion looks remarkably like death.

But this presents us with something of a puzzle, because romantic love itself is often understood as a kind of fusion. Granted, lovers—even in the very act of love—do not literally become a single physical entity. We do not literally achieve the kind of reintegration that Aristophanes claims we're searching for. But the merger that occurs between lovers, both physically and psychologically, is not just metaphorical. When we fall in love, we are no longer fully separate and independent beings.

In love, as the song lyric says, two hearts do beat as one. Our desires, values, and interests change in accordance with those of our lovers. We no longer make decisions individually. We make joint plans and coordinate our activities. We find ourselves thinking differently about things. We are as highly sensitized to the moods of each other as we are to our own moods, if not even more so. As Russell herself finds, "Marriage attunes a person to nuances in behaviour, the small vital signs that signal a person's well-being" (*A Letter of Mary*, p. 27). Simply by noticing that Holmes has not read the newspaper for three days, for example, Russell can tell that something is troubling her husband.

Many philosophers have taken the fusion of identities to be central to the very notion of romantic love. For example, on Robert Nozick's view, love involves wanting to become a *we* rather than merely an *I*, and this involves the creation of a new, joint identity. Neil Delaney argues that lovers want to merge with one another in profound psychological and physical ways. One identifies with a lover; one takes the needs and interests of one's lover to be one's own. Roger Scruton too talks of the union of interests achieved by lovers; when we are in love, the distinction between *my* interests and *your* interests is wholly eroded. And Robert Solomon argues that in romantic love the self expands to include another. As he puts it, "shared identity is the intention of love."[2]

---

[2] See Robert Nozick, "Love's Bond"; Neil Delaney, "Love and Loving Commitment"; Robert Solomon, "The Virtue of (Erotic) Love"; and Roger Scruton, *Sexual Desire*.

The psychiatrist Willard Gaylin is perhaps even more explicit than these philosophers about love being a kind of fusion. On his view, all love involves the blurring of boundaries between individuals, the merging of the self with another individual to create "a fused identity." Moreover, the notion of fusion here sounds eerily like Parfitian fusion:

> The concept of fusion as I will use it literally means the loss of one's identity in that of another; a confusion of ego boundaries; the sense of unsureness as to where I end and you, the person I love, begin; the identification of your pain with my pain and your success with my success; the inconceivability of a self that does not include you . . . (*Rediscovering Love*, p. 103)

But here something seems to have gone awry. Although there's something deeply plausible about the understanding of love as a kind of fusion, once the account gets spelled out in detail, it starts to seem more puzzling. How can a loss of identity be a good thing? As even Gaylin himself notes, an uncertainty about the boundaries of one's identity is a feature of psychosis. Watson may have been right that Holmes once viewed emotions such as love as incompatible with the achievement of a properly balanced mind, but surely even Holmes wouldn't want to suggest that falling in love means literally going insane.

From I to We

Just a couple of weeks after turning twenty-one, while involved in a difficult investigation, Russell is kidnapped by a band of criminals, held captive for ten days, and repeatedly injected with opium against her will. In a noble effort to keep her mind clear, she forces herself to engage in a variety of forms of "mental gymnastics." She conjugates verb forms in the many languages she knows, works on difficult mathematical problems, and tries to solve logic puzzles. Eventually, however, her mind turns to a more personal puzzle: Her relationship with Holmes.

She has been working by his side for six years, first as his apprentice and then as his equal. Trapped in her basement prison, she finally comes to acknowledge the depth of her affection for him: "I loved him, I had loved him since I met him, and I doubted not that I should love him with my dying breath." What shape, exactly, does that love take? It's not a love of frenzied infatuation. But that's not to say that it's not impassioned. Rather, as Russell comes to realize, "For me, for always, the paramount organ of passion was the mind.

Unnatural, unbalanced, perhaps, but it was true: Without intellect, there could be no love" (*Monstrous*, p. 266).

Theirs may be a passion born of the intellect, but that's not to say it was a purely intellectual passion. Once married, they do engage in the activities rendered legal by their marital status (*Moor*, p. 7). But what's critically important about their relationship for Russell is that she not "lose herself" in love—thereby hitting upon precisely what seems problematic about the fusion view of love. If, in becoming a *we*, I have to give up my very autonomy as an individual—if, in becoming a *we* I can no longer be an *I*—then falling in love would be a loss of self. So if, like Russell and Holmes, we value our individuality, our autonomy, our very *identity*, then love would be simply unthinkable.

But perhaps there's a way of understanding the fusion involved in love that allows us to avoid these unpalatable consequences. Nozick tries to ward them off when he suggests that being part of a *we* "involves having a new identity, an additional one. This does *not* mean that you no longer have any individual identity or that your sole identity is part of the *we*. However, the individual identity you did have will become altered." But Nozick doesn't do much to help us understand what this means. To spell it out in more detail, we might look to an intriguing suggestion by Delaney that the merger involved in love be understood as akin to what happens when a group of sovereign states opt to come together into a republican nation.

In a discussion of the potential threat to autonomy posed by romantic love, Marilyn Friedman develops this suggestion of Delaney's. When states come together in a federation, they combine without ceding all of their previous powers. The states themselves continue to exist as states, even as a new joint entity—their federation—comes into being. On Friedman's view, we should say something similar about romantic joinings. In the merger that is love, there is indeed the *emergence* of a new entity, a new *we*, but our own identities are not themselves wholly *submerged* by it. The merger is thus both partial and flexible:

> Each lover remains, in some sense and for some purposes, a separate self with her own capacities for the exercise of agency. On this view, a romantic merger does not obliterate the separate existence of two lovers. Instead it produces a new entity out of them, but only to some extent, only at some times, and only for some purposes—while leaving them as two separate selves. Each lover remains, like each state in a federation, a separate self with capacities to make choices and to act on her own.
> (*Autonomy, Gender, Politics*, p. 119)

For Friedman, then, love is best understood as involving a sort of threesome—though not of the kinky variety. In becoming *we*, neither you nor I cease to exist. The two individual lovers continue to exist along with "the flexible romantic 'federation,' or merger, that they become," and these three entities co-exist in "a dynamic, shifting interplay of subjectivity, agency, and objectivity."

Our identities are shaped and shifted by all sorts of activities in which we engage, love among them. And there's nothing wrong with that. In living our lives, we're constantly engaged in the shaping and reshaping of our own identities, whether through education, exercise, or analysis. The psychotherapy that Russell undergoes after the car accident that kills her parents, and the hypnosis employed by her psychoanalyst over the course of the therapy, enables her to get past her own guilt at having caused the accident. Clearly her identity was shaped both by the accident and by the resulting therapy. But although she became in some sense a new person as a result of those experiences, we don't see them as a threat to her very selfhood. As long as what's involved in a romantic fusion is the shaping of an identity, rather than its obliteration, we have nothing to fear from love.

Granted, as Friedman notes, this can't be the end of the story. Not all mergers of identities are *mutual* mergers, and thus not all of them are *fair*. An unfair merger robs us of our autonomy and drains us of our individuality. In contrast, a fair merger is both nurturing and affirming, and it promotes our autonomy and individuality rather than denigrating it. To love well, then, we have to make sure to hold on to ourselves.

Perhaps this is why Russell doggedly persists in her pursuit of theology. It does occasionally cross her mind to wonder whether she'd chosen a course of study that Holmes regarded as an "irrational pseudodiscipline" in part to maintain her identity "against the tide of Holmes's forceful personality" (*A Letter of Mary*, p. 29). Perhaps it's also why she prefers to be addressed as "Miss Russell" rather than as "Mrs. Holmes," and why she finds it so irritating when the Dartmoor locals, who affectionately refer to Holmes as "Snoop Zherlock" give her the nickname "Zherlock Mary"—a nickname that doesn't reflect her identity in her own right, but rather fuses her with her husband (*The Moor*, p. 132). And perhaps, in a way, it also explains why Holmes gives the advice he does to one of those same locals who has just been abandoned by his fiancé: "You look around for a woman with brains and spirit. You'll never be bored" (p. 70). Upon hearing this advice, Russell isn't sure who was the more nonplussed: the young lad or herself.

Surviving Fusion

Even if Watson had been a woman, Holmes could never have loved him the way that he loves Mary Russell. As Watson himself admits, he was hardly a partner to Holmes in any real sense of the word. He may have in some sense served as a "whetstone" for Holmes's mind, but that's more a matter of his mere presence than any positive contribution that he made. In fact, conversations between Holmes and Watson are really best described as instances of Holmes's thinking aloud:

> His remarks could hardly be said to be made to me—many of them would have been as appropriately addressed to his bedstead—but none the less, having formed the habit, it had become in some way helpful that I should register and interject. If I irritated him by a certain methodical slowness in my mentality, that irritation served only to make his own flame-like intuitions and impressions flash up the more vividly and swiftly. Such was my humble role in our alliance. ("The Adventure of the Creeping Man")

No, for Holmes to fall in love, he needed to find someone who could be a true partner to him—someone who could fuse with his strong personality, and still remain herself. Her ability to do so is important not only for her own sake, but for Holmes's sake as well. Marriage to Mary Russell does indeed change Sherlock Holmes, but just as he does not sacrifice his identity to their pairing, neither does she sacrifice hers. And it's for precisely this reason that their partnership, however surprising and unconventional it may be, is a successful one. It's even—dare I say?—elementary.

This chapter is dedicated to the Holmes to my Russell, Frank Menetrez.

Chapter 13

A Study in Friendship
Ruth Tallman

From their first meeting in *A Study in Scarlet*, in which they each run through their laundry list of flaws to determine if they'll make compatible roommates, Sherlock Holmes and John Watson are a match made in . . . well, they're a match, anyway. Watson grumbles about Holmes's slovenly habits, and Holmes usually maintains his "too cool for emotions" veneer, but anyone who has followed the pair through adventure after adventure intuitively recognizes friendship in both men's actions.

Despite the fact that Holmes and Watson obviously seem to be friends, the long-standing gold standard for a philosophical account of friendship comes from Aristotle, and on his account, it turns out that Holmes and Watson are not friends at all. This leaves us with two mysteries: first, what clues can we deduce from Aristotle's account of friendship that will help us learn why he thinks Holmes and Watson cannot be friends? Second, who is the better friend, Holmes or Watson?

Good Friends?

Aristotle was the first philosopher to offer a systematic account of friendship, and he deserves credit for getting a whole lot right. He recognized that we often use the word 'friend' loosely, and that many people that we casually call friends are at best fair-weather friends. These are people that spend time together because it suits their self-interest, but they part ways when one or both of them cease to benefit from the relationship.

True friends, Aristotle explains, bear some resemblance to this other, lesser type of friend, but true friendship is markedly different. True friends can be distinguished from the other types of friendships, according to Aristotle, because true friends want what is good for their friend, even when that good comes at the expense of their own good (*Rhetoric*, lines 1380b35–1381a).

So far, Aristotle's description of true friendship seems perfectly in accord with the relationship between Watson and Holmes. Both men have risked their own lives for the other, the pre-eminent example of putting another's good before your own. What's more, they clearly have genuine affection for each other. While Watson wears his heart on his sleeve—and chronicles his affection for the detective faithfully in his writings—Holmes also demonstrates his love of Watson, generally in more subtle ways, such as the care he takes to explain the steps in his reasoning process that allow him to solve mysteries.

The usually impatient Holmes is always willing to take the time to help his friend understand what is intuitively obvious to himself. Probably the clearest instance of the demonstrated recognized reciprocity of the friendship is shown in "The Adventure of the Three Garridebs," when Watson suffers a gunshot wound, and Holmes fears he has been killed. In his moment of panic, Holmes's normal reserve is dropped, revealing deep raw emotion for his friend. That unguarded revelation was, to Watson, "worth many wounds . . . to know the depth and loyalty of love" his friend feels for him.

So, Watson and Holmes have deep affection for each other, and their love is such that they each want the best for the other, even at their own expense. Yet, Aristotle's account would have us conclude that the two cannot be true friends. How is this possible?

The problem, according to Aristotle's account, is that he holds that true friends must be "equal in goodness." He says, "Perfect friendship is the friendship of men who are good, and alike in excellence; for these wish well alike to each other qua good, and they are good in themselves" (*Nichomachean Ethics*, Book VIII). Here is where we run into a problem for Watson and Holmes. Aristotle's moral philosophy holds that "the Good" is a single, unified object, something that individuals can be more or less alike with regard to.

Aristotle thinks that true friends must be equally good, for if one friend is morally better than the other, the superior friend's goodness will be diminished by spending time with the worse friend. This makes a lot of sense if you buy into Aristotle's understanding of the way humans develop morally. Remember when your parents didn't want you to hang out with the "wrong crowd"? That's because Aristotle's view, that we model our behavior on those around us, has been highly influential in Western thought and culture. If you have a "bad friend," chances are, that friend is going to pull you down, and a friend who would corrupt you is no true friend at all.

Good for Me, Good for You

But wait a minute, you might be saying. Aren't Holmes and Watson both good? Maybe, but they are certainly not both good in the same way. Aristotle's account of morality holds that good people must conform to a particular model of virtue, and for him, the good of a friend is that the friend helps you to perfect yourself in a virtuous way. He explains that friends should serve as mirrors, allowing each other to see their moral flaws in a more objective way, so that they can work to correct them, constantly seeking to better themselves morally. But who's the mirror to whom in the Holmes and Watson friendship? Should Watson try to be more like Holmes, or should Holmes strive to model himself on Watson? You might think that there's no right answer—that neither should have the goal of becoming more like the other. The problem with trying to understand the way the relationship of Holmes and Watson fits into this account stems largely from the fact that the two men hold entirely different moral codes.

Aristotle was a *moral naturalist*. Moral naturalism holds that there are objectively right and wrong ways for human beings to behave, and that the standards of human behavior can be known through a scientific study of the kind of biological beings we are. Sometimes an individual might not realize what's best for himself, but what is best for him is an objective fact, whether he knows it or not.

A moral naturalist would say that Watson is right to continually condemn Holmes's cocaine habit, even though cocaine was not seen as a particularly objectionable substance at the time. Regardless of what individuals or society think, there are objective standards of behavior to which we ought to conform, and we behave immorally when we choose to behave differently. Good actions are those that promote human flourishing, and bad actions are those that thwart it. Cocaine use is wrong, on a naturalistic account, because it inhibits the body's ability to flourish.

Some examples, like that of cocaine, make Aristotle's account seem correct, but is there really always one clear answer regarding what is good for a human? We all need food, shelter, rest, and so forth, but what about all those values we disagree about? Is a life of physical exertion more valuable than a life of intellectual study? Does telling the truth always lead to human flourishing, or do we sometimes flourish better through the use of a selective white lie? Should humans try to promote their own goodness, or should we strive to maximize the social good? Many people, called *moral pluralists*, think there is no single right answer to questions regarding what is best for a human being.

If you hold that there are objective truths about morality, and that these truths are the same for everyone, regardless of their personal values and beliefs, Aristotle's rule about friends needing to be equal with regard to goodness makes some sense. However, moral pluralists do not think that there's one objective standard of the Good that is the same for everyone, and so it's not necessary or even desirable to choose only friends who "match" you morally. Moral pluralists believe that there can be more than one moral code that a human could follow and live a good life, and just because I choose to follow one path, this does not mean that you must follow the same path.

What's more, there are many possible "good lives," and they are not the sorts of things that can be measured against each other, as there is not just one Good that applies to everyone, but rather there is "good for me" and "good for you." "Good for Holmes" might include the ingestion of a hearty amount of lung blackening and mind-altering substances, while "good for Watson" would include fastidious dedication to the purity of his internal organs. A good human life involves attention to the many factors that feed into the overall best life for each of us. The pleasure Holmes derives from tobacco and cocaine is considerable, but Watson derives no such pleasure from these things. Watson experiences a good from his devotion to clean living that Holmes would experience merely as unpleasant deprivation. According to moral pluralism, there is no "good for humans," but rather "good for this human" and "good for that human."

Moral pluralists are likely to find Aristotle's claim that friends must be equally good a little puzzling. After all, how can a plurality of goods be measured? Who's better, the heart-on-shirtsleeves physician sidekick, or the tough-as-nails loner detective? Are you a better person if you work within the law, allowing many guilty people to go free, or outside of it, using methods that allow you to bring more criminals to justice? Is it better to adhere to an unbreakable code of conduct, or to hold that good ends justify questionable means?

Because moral pluralists say there is no single answer to these questions, and that most of the answers will depend on the particular values and preferences of the individual moral agents involved in the business of living their lives, we often can't tell whether those who live according to differing moral codes are "better" or "worse"—in fact, there might not even be an answer. Holmes might sleep very well at night knowing he spent his day deceiving and manipulating innocent people, because at the end of it all a criminal is behind bars, and those he harmed are at peace. Watson's more reverent attitude toward the law means some of the methods acceptable to Holmes are unacceptable to Watson.

Sometimes, differences in moral codes determine whether two individuals will become or be interested in or able to maintain a friendship. For example, James Moriarty's values are so much at odds with Holmes's that it seems unlikely that the two could ever be friends. Mutual affection cannot shine through a complete revulsion for the other person's life goals and projects. Even so, it is not typically the case that friends' moral codes exactly line up. Many of us probably count among our friends someone whom we think goes wrong on at least one moral point. Given this, we are left with an interesting question. How ought we to respond when our friends profess and enact values that are different from our own?

An Act of Persuasian

One option is to be a proselytizing friend—to try to persuade your friend to adopt your own values. This approach is tempting, as most people who have given careful thought to their moral code think is the best path to follow, otherwise, they wouldn't accept it themselves. Thus, having come to this wisdom, a person might feel the need to share it with those he cares about.

This is the approach that Watson accepts. Not only does he reject the ingestion of cocaine into his own body, he does his best to talk Holmes out of using it as well. Watson complains when he thinks Holmes is behaving inappropriately, judging him with the familiar refrain, "Surely you have gone too far!" The proselytizing friend sees himself as looking out for the best interests of his friend. He's interested in helping him develop and act in accordance with what he sees as the "right" moral code. Although he recognizes differences between his friend's values and his own, the proselytizing friend deems his own values to be superior to his friend's, at least with regard to some matters (the ones he proselytizes about). This model of friendship seems to be about helping those you care about to make moral progress, but this progress must be on the proselytizer's own terms.

Recognizing the Difference

In contrast to proselytizing friends, some friends recognize differences between their own values and the values of their friends, but do not seek to modify the friend's values to match their own. While the proselytizing friend sees himself as helping his friend recognize the error of his current way of thinking, this type of friend, which I will call "integrity-promoting," is interested in helping his friend live up to his *own* moral code. This sort of friend demonstrates a great deal of humility, as he does not assume that he has all of morality figured out. This friend, though living according to an alternative moral code, does not suppose that his code is necessarily superior to that of his friends.

What's important to the integrity-promoting friend is that he and his friend are *internally consistent* and that they live lives of *integrity*. Internal consistency means not endorsing contradictory moral beliefs (beliefs that cannot possibly both be true), such as believing that homosexual behavior is an abomination because it says so in Leviticus and every word of the Bible is God's law to be followed explicitly, but also believing there is nothing wrong with eating a bacon cheeseburger (which double-violates the dietary laws laid out in Leviticus). Those striving to be internally consistent, while they might not think there is one right answer to how one ought to live, think they should modify their belief set when it turns out to be self-contradictory, as contradictory beliefs means at least one of them is necessarily wrong. Internal consistency, then, is to be valued because it helps us eliminate false beliefs and get closer to truth.

Integrity means living in accordance with your own belief system. People who lack integrity are those who act against their moral code—they believe one thing but do another. It seems that this is just what the proselytizing friend is asking us to do, and this is just what the integrity-promoting friend encourages us not to do. Now, the proselytizing friend will probably protest that he doesn't want you to act against your own belief system, but rather that he wants you to modify your belief system so that it's more like his. Maybe so, but it is likely that he would take as a second choice that you merely modify your actions, if you can't manage to modify your beliefs. Let's think about Watson again for a minute—surely his first choice would be for Holmes to adopt his belief that he ought not ingest cocaine. However, since it seems Holmes simply will not be brought around to this belief (given Watson has been hounding him for years), certainly Watson prefers that Holmes merely act against his own belief system and in accordance with Watson's, and lay off the drug. This lends further support to the thesis that Watson is a proselytizing friend.

Holmes, on the other hand, is concerned to help Watson stick to his own moral code, even when his beliefs don't match Holmes's. In "The Adventure of Charles Augustus Milverton," Holmes strives to convince Watson to stay home while Holmes breaks into Milverton's house to steal the letters he is using to blackmail a woman. Holmes almost certainly wants Watson to accompany him and provide back up on this dangerous excursion—this would be in Holmes's own best interest. Yet, he urges Watson not to accompany him, because Watson has already voiced his belief that the act of breaking and entering is wrong and ought not be done. Rather than pressure Watson to conform to Holmes's moral code, Holmes actually pressures Watson to *stick to his own code*! This is what an integrity-promoting friend does.

Despite Holmes's urging, however, Watson repeatedly violates his own moral code in the name of friendship. He thinks breaking into the house is wrong, but scampers along after Holmes anyway. He thinks Holmes's cocaine habit is wrong, but enables him by providing care when the drug gets the better of him. These actions suggest that Watson, despite his friend's efforts, lacks integrity. He puts friendship ahead of morality, and asks Holmes to do the same. This is characteristic of a proselytizing friend, and antithetical to the integrity-promoting friend, who feels that, rather than friendship getting in the way of one's efforts to behave morally, part of the responsibility of friendship is to help each other maximize their own conception of moral goodness. While Watson clearly thinks these two values come into conflict, and require a choice, Holmes doesn't see it this way. In respecting Watson's opposing moral code, Holmes recognizes that this means he and Watson will not always engage in the same behaviors, and he feels that part of being a good friend involves not asking your friend to act against his own conscious.

The Best Kind of Friend

Although Watson is a loyal and loving friend, Holmes provides us with a better model of friendship. He demonstrates a respect for Watson that Watson doesn't return. A person who helps his friend become the kind of person he wants to be is better than one who tries to make his friend over into the kind of person *he* thinks he should be. The proselytizing friend assumes an attitude of moral superiority that is actually quite demeaning, even though it is done with a spirit of goodwill. The Watson model of friendship assumes a friend who follows an alternative moral code cannot possibly know what is best for himself, and thus seeks, out of love, to "fix" his behavior. Holmesian friendship respects the friend's ability to choose the best life for himself, and works to help him stay on that path when challenges come his way. Holmes's interactions with Watson throughout Doyle's stories provides us with a powerful model of respectful and integrity-promoting friendship.

Chapter 14

Out of House and Holmes

Julia Round

When Lord Robert Baden-Powell launched the British Boy Scout movement with his book *Scouting for Boys* (1908), he advised scoutmasters to demonstrate "Sherlock-Holmesism" and to use examples from Conan Doyle's stories as puzzles for their boys to solve.

Holmes's rationality, logic and comradeship with Dr. Watson are masculine traits that helped set the pattern for masculinity at the start of the twentieth century. But how would Holmes fare in today's society?

The American television series *House* pays homage to Holmes in various ways, not least through its antisocial, drug-taking lead character—but has also made significant changes. What does this tell us about the changes that have taken place over the past century?

Model of Perfection

Victorian masculinity was strongly associated with rationality, logical thought, and a lack of emotion. Although Holmes is not a scientist, he's introduced to the reader in a scientific laboratory and chapters called "The Science of Deduction" appear in both *A Study in Scarlet* and *The Sign of the Four*. Holmes also uses the logic and language of medicine—for example when finding a key clue he says: "It confirms my diagnosis" (*The Sign of the Four*). He claims that his theories "are really extremely practical—so practical that I depend on them for my bread and cheese" (*A Study in Scarlet*). Defining his intellectual activity as everyday work also emphasises his masculinity.

Logic and rationality form the basis of Sherlock's thought processes, and are emphasised throughout the stories. In *The Sign of the Four,* Holmes claims he values "true, cold reason . . . above all things." Watson describes his friend's mind in "A Scandal in Bohemia" as "cold, precise but admirably balanced" and Holmes as "The most perfect reasoning and observing machine that the world has ever seen"—in fact their mutual friend Stamford says he is even "a little too scientific for my tastes—it approaches cold-bloodedness" (*A Study in Scarlet*).

Sherlock Holmes is a man of science and reason; the perfect model of Victorian masculinity. Or is he? Did such a model ever really exist?

The Essential Man

The nineteenth century was marked by a "crisis of masculinity" in society. The industrial revolution had affected men's lives more than any other change in history by moving work outside the home. This reduced contact between boys and men, challenging patriarchy, which should have provided more diverse options for male behavior. But in fact this meant that men of all classes stubbornly clung to basic notions of what a "real man" should be, with what Peter Stearns (in *Be a Man!*) describes as a "self-conscious assertiveness." So Baden-Powell could endorse the Holmes tales because they confirm qualities associated with the masculine: "observation, rationalism, factuality, logic, comradeship, daring and pluck."

Asserting set male characteristics in this way is a clear example of essentialist masculinity. Essentialism is the idea that everything can be precisely defined and described, and that each thing has a set of characteristics or properties that all things of that kind must possess. So, there are set characteristics of being "male" that all men will possess, regardless of their particular situation or personality type; equally there is an inherent "Englishness" that can be defined.

But this idea is difficult to reconcile with Victorian masculinity, which (despite the simplistic definition offered above) was a troubled concept, for instance regarding class, sexuality, and nationality. The accepted general view is of the bloodless and repressed Victorian man, cultured and upper-class; and the working-class proletariat, illiterate and often dishonest, who lived in abject poverty. But both types are only a half-story. The upper classes were not all repressed sophisticates; the lower classes were not all thieves and drunks.

Victorian men's lives were constructed in dual roles that relied upon processes of exclusion and antithesis in order to balance social and moral respectability against class and gender expectations. The upper-class Victorian man was expected to be refined, cultured, and above his baser urges—and yet also to complement Victorian femininity by being worldly-wise and sexually experienced; and possess manly skills such as boxing, fencing, and so forth. It therefore seems doubtful that essentialist definitions of class or gender can be valid, although at this time these were accepted and asserted.

Sherlock Holmes is an image of the self united in exactly this type of division, and *The Sign of the Four* provides numerous examples of this dual nature. He is first and foremost a man of thought, and sometimes mocked for this; for example referred to as "Mr Theorist" by disgruntled detectives. Conan Doyle presents Holmes as a refined man, whose "long, white hand" is able to play the violin with "remarkable skill," and who also enjoys listening to music while deep in thought. On the surface, he is a cultured and intellectual gentleman.

But (like a good Victorian hostess), he can also sustain varied dinner conversation with "gaiety"—"on miracle plays, on medieval pottery, on Stradivarius violins, on the Buddhism of Ceylon, and on the warships of the future." He has sophisticated culinary knowledge; as he quips "I insist on you dining with us . . . I have oysters and a brace of grouse, with something a little choice in white wines. Watson, you have never yet recognised my merits as a housekeeper."

Holmes is also what one might call the feminised half within his and Watson's friendship—for example in his emotional moods and changeability. These qualities and the use of the domestic sphere (their rooms at Baker Street) for his professional activities begin to suggest a critique of essential "maleness."

A Man's Man

However Conan Doyle also makes sure he defines Holmes as a man's man, tempering his intellect and enthusiasm for music and art with experience of fencing, boxing and martial arts. He "is an expert singlestick player, boxer, and swordsman" (*A Study in Scarlet*), and many writers have pointed out that our hero's name is a combination of sportsmen Mordecai Sherwin and Frank Shacklock. Both of these were famous Victorian cricketers.

Shacklock and his fellow fast-bowler William Mycroft made a sensational impression at Lord's cricket ground in 1885, two years before the cricket devotee Arthur Conan Doyle wrote his first Holmes story.

Holmes shows great daring and bravery: climbing at night time atop a "breakneck" roof with little fear, "like an enormous glow-worm crawling very slowly along the ridge," and attempting the dangerous descent with a simple "Here goes, anyhow." He carries a revolver and is at ease with the necessity of using it: "if the other turns nasty I shall shoot him dead" (*The Sign of the Four*). It seems key to Holmes's character that he walks the line between the cerebral and the physical, and this allows Conan Doyle to subtly challenge the Victorian ideal of essential masculinity.

Holmes is also stoic in the face of danger—for instance later in *The Sign of the Four* when a poison dart narrowly misses Watson and himself: "Holmes smiled at it and shrugged his shoulders in his easy fashion, but I confess that it turned me sick to think of the horrible death which had passed so close to us that night." British qualities of stoicism and "stiff upper lip" are apparent here, but the early Holmes stories also interrogate these sorts of national stereotypes. For example, Jefferson Hope (the killer in *A Study in Scarlet*) is an American whose name and characteristics are emblematic of the frontier stereotype: courage, dauntlessness and daring. But despite being a murderer, his crime seems validated by Conan Doyle as he ultimately dies of an aneurism, rather than by hanging.

There is a subtle critique of ethical essentialism here that is replicated at other points in the tale, where Holmes also challenges ethics; by being willing to do anything necessary to solve a case. He frequently behaves outside Victorian notions of appropriateness. In "A Scandal in Bohemia" he asks Watson:

"You don't mind breaking the law?"
"Not in the least."
"Nor running a chance of arrest?"
"Not in a good cause."

Irene Adler's ultimate outwitting of Holmes in this tale therefore serves a dual purpose: it gives all characters a "deserved" outcome (she is not deprived of her photograph, while Holmes's client, the King, is appeased) and also undercuts innate masculine superiority. Conan Doyle would continue to query the British Empire along similar lines in the rest of the series: Watson's wounding at the battle of Maiwand (a notorious defeat) is just one example.

So it seems that although Conan Doyle created a masculine figure so successful that it was used as a template for a subsequent generation of boy scouts, Sherlock Holmes also challenges the idea of gendered essentialism. The character subtly contradicts fixed notions of masculinity, and the stories also test the limits of ethical essentialism and nationalism.

By contrast, masculinity today is a changing concept with shifting definitions. The emergence of the "new man" in the 1980s (caring, well-groomed, able to do household chores, pro-feminist) gave way to the "new lad" in the 1990s (knowingly abrasive, adolescent, beer-drinking, pre-feminist). Since the millennium, newer models such as the "metrosexual" (straight, young, affluent, enjoys personal grooming and shopping) have blurred the gender lines still further.

Current cultural theorists such as Judith Butler put forward the idea that gendered behavior is no longer linked to biological sex: our gender is simply an (unconscious) performance we put on according to social norms and the situation we find ourselves in. Women in high-powered jobs may adopt a masculine performance (British Prime Minister Margaret Thatcher famously took elocution lessons to lower the pitch of her voice); men relating to or negotiating with partners may adopt a feminized one. Although we have recognised that gender today is not an essentialist concept, masculinity still seems in crisis. So, might a modern Holmes reflect these traits rather than the Victorian model of near-perfection?

Who Says a House Is Not a Holmes?

David Shore's American medical television series, *House*, offers some interesting answers to this question. Rather than a standard medical drama, the show was intended to be more like a police procedural, but quickly became more character-driven. Lead character Dr. Gregory House is an antihero who diagnoses patients by uncovering their secrets and lies. House is obviously based on Sherlock Holmes; as Shore confirms in a videotaped interview: "Anytime one says 'puzzle' and 'brilliant deduction' in the same sentence, one can't help but think of the great fictional detective Sherlock Holmes and his trusty sidekick, Dr. Watson. And indeed, Holmes—and the real-life physician who inspired him, Dr. Joseph Bell—were very much inspirations for House."

The *House* series contains some obvious references and name checks, and there are also multiple professional and personal links between the characters. "House" was chosen as a synonym for "home" (based on the British pronunciation of "Holmes"); both live at 221B Baker Street (Season 7, Episode 13). House is shot by a man named Moriarty (Season 2, Episode 24); his first patient is named Adler (Season 1, Episode 1); Dr. Wilson later tells a story about House's unhappy love affair with a nurse named Irene Adler (Season 5, Episode 11), called "the woman" by him (referring to "A Scandal in Bohemia"). At other points, House is given copies of Conan Doyle's books (Season 4, Episode 10; Season 7, Episode 5) and also Joseph Bell's *Manual of the Operations of Surgery* (Season 5, Episode 11).

Both characters are eccentric and arrogant personalities; both are drug addicts (Holmes to cocaine, House to Vicodin, and both to morphine); and both have a supportive best friend (Dr. Watson–Dr. Wilson) who is something of a womanizer (Watson marries twice during the Holmes series; Wilson has three ex-wives).

Both solve their cases through inductive reasoning and logical thought—dismissing all the incorrect solutions until only the correct one remains: "Eliminate all other factors and the one which remains must be the truth." House's cases, like Holmes's mysteries, are often couched in factual and masculine terms: for example the mathematical. In Season 2, Episode 24, House claims "numbers don't lie" (speaking metaphorically about physical attractiveness) and Dr. Chase uses a similar metaphor to describe their diagnostic process in the same episode, saying: "the equation has changed." Just like Conan Doyle, mathematical and rational symbols are used to emphasize the masculine process of deduction.

However, despite this use of metaphor, House is certainly not an essentialist model of traditional masculinity; but rather can be read as embodying and critiquing traits of the new man and new lad (themselves critiques of previous concepts of masculinity). Whereas manliness had previously been characterized by aggression, competition, emotional coldness, and an emphasis on penetrative sex, a counter-argument emerged which focused on the fears and anxieties that men felt about these established scripts of masculinity.

Boys to Men

The new man emerged in the 1980s as a response to the "new woman"—coinciding with changes in the market such as a growth in menswear, men's grooming products, and men's magazines. As an advertising product, he is voyeuristically and passively constructed through a series of visual codes. He is not afraid to show his feelings, or to occupy roles traditionally filled by woman (for example in the home, the kitchen, or the nursery).

In some respects House fills this role, by displaying behavior and skills that might traditionally be considered feminine: he is an excellent cook (although this is attributed to his masculine knowledge of chemistry—Season 6, Episode 2), watches soap operas (Season 1, Episode 20) and, like Holmes, is very musical (House plays the piano, guitar, and harmonica, and listens to opera in the toilet at work for the sake of the acoustics—Season 2, Episode 2). Despite his curmudgeonly exterior, he even exhibits caring and romantic behavior on occasion: for example buying Dr. Cameron a corsage for their date together (Season 1, Episode 20), organizing a mariachi band as a surprise for Dr. Cuddy at a hospital event (Season 7, Episode 14), or collecting Thirteen on her release from prison with a fresh martini complete with olive (Season 7, Episode 18).

However, House also critiques the new man's emotional and caring outlook by being cynical and mistrustful; and often repeats the maxim "everybody lies." Much like Holmes, he sees through the emotional responses of those around him. In *The Sign of the Four*, Holmes says "love is an emotional thing, and whatever is emotional is opposed to that true, cold reason which I place above all things." House comments similarly: "the thing about emotional reactions is they're definitionally irrational or . . . 'stupid'" (Season 5, Episode 8). In this regard he goes further than Holmes by openly mocking emotion and empathy, traits that his best friend Wilson possesses in abundance: for example when knocking on his office door: "I know you're in there! I can hear you caring!" (Season 2, Episode 11) and forcing Cameron through the emotional process of taking an HIV test.

But although he critiques the new man's nurturing traits, he undeniably embodies many (perhaps more negative) feminine and emotional characteristics. For example, House often relies on manipulation (frequently emotional) to solve his cases and keep his team working for him; such as encouraging student

Martha Masters to lie and manipulate patients in order to get an internship with him (Season 7, Episode 19). As he comments: "The only value" of people's trust "is that you can manipulate them" (Season 3, Episode 21). He is also bitchy ("I thought I'd get your theories, mock them, then embrace my own. The usual"—Season 3, Episode 10) and sarcastic ("Oh thank you, Rationalization Man, you've saved the village!"—Season 5, Episode 14).

However, this manipulative behavior means he depends on others for much of his strength—as well as a team of doctors working under him, he has his best friend Wilson and friend/lover Lisa Cuddy. Relying on such a support network or "family" might also be seen as domestic (and therefore feminized) behavior. In these ways he often seems more "spinster" than "bachelor" and his relationship with Cuddy in Season 7 sees the confirmed misanthrope becoming a family man for a short time—a role he plays surprisingly well, helping her daughter get into the pre-school of her choice (Season 7, Episode 10) and even attempting to support Cuddy against her mother—although this ultimately ends with him drugging the mother; behavior undeniably more suited to the immaturity of the new lad (Season 7, Episode 9).

Men to Boys

The 1990s saw the emergence of the new lad: an attempt to recover conventional forms of masculinity in response to the new man. The new lad, according to Tim Edwards, is "Selfish, loutish and inconsiderate to a point of infantile smelliness. He likes drinking, football and fucking, and in that order of preference . . . defensively working class which also means defensively masculine." Although it's difficult to view House as working class (despite his upbringing as an army brat), he certainly fits the criteria of selfish and infantile. His behavior is designed to put himself first; he is, as Cuddy puts it, "an egomaniacal narcissistic pain in the ass" (Season 2, Episode 11). He is (in general) sexually misogynistic, preferring to use prostitutes than date (Season 2, Episode 12), and although not a "lager lout", he frequently overindulges in recreational drugs and alcohol.

But infantile behavior is the strongest evidence of his new lad status. For the first six seasons, his ongoing flirtation with Cuddy is based around playground-type behavior, as he consistently insults the size of her ass (Season 5, Episode 10) or her clothes

("Love that outfit. Says, 'I'm professional, but I'm still a woman.' Actually, it sorta yells the second part"—Season 1, Episode 6). Cameron describes his behavior towards her similarly: "like an eighth-grade boy punching a girl" (Season 1, Episode 20).

Romantic relationships aside, House is a big kid: he often plays with a tennis ball or yoyo (Season 1, Episode 20) in his office (fans can even buy these oversized monogrammed balls online) and watches monster trucks at his desk (Season 2, Episode 11). He plays mean practical jokes (such as the hand in warm water) on his friends and colleagues (Season 2, Episode 16) and makes ridiculous bets with Wilson (such as who can keep a chicken in the hospital for longest without getting caught—Season 7, Episode 1). In later seasons his behavior becomes more extreme: he spends days devising a complicated and dangerous practical joke (where he pretends to shoot a prostitute with a crossbow) and parties in a hotel swimming pool with college students (Season 7, Episode 16). In Season 7, Episode 17 he hires a monster truck; plays ping pong with a female companion during a differential diagnosis; installs a flat-screen TV on the wall of his office; and travels everywhere on a Segway. Gadgetry, game-playing and immaturity are all hallmarks of his character. Even "infantile smelliness" is conveyed through his typical outfit of wrinkled t-shirts and sneakers.

Rubik's Complex

In *The Sign of the Four* Holmes complains, "I cannot live without brainwork." House claims "Knowing is always better than not knowing" (Season 2, Episode 11). Like Holmes, his triumph comes only when he has "solved my case" (Season 7, Episode 14)—the fate of the patient is irrelevant. As Cameron accuses him, "All that matters is your stupid puzzle!" (Season 2, Episode 1) and Wilson agrees: "You know how some doctors have the Messiah complex—they need to save the world? You've got the Rubik's complex; you need to solve the puzzle" (Season 1, Episode 9). Using a toy metaphor to describe House's case again calls attention to his juvenility.

When Holmes famously tells Watson "The game is afoot" (first used in "The Adventure of the Abbey Grange"), the primary meaning of "game" refers to the "quarry" of their hunt ("the criminal is on the move")—"amusement" is a secondary meaning in its Victorian context. House's "Rubik's complex" has no such dual meaning, referring only to entertainment: his "puzzle" is even dissociated from the fate of the patient to emphasise this. As House says: "The sign on the door says I'm a diagnostician. Full diagnosis means I'm finished." Even if the patient dies, "I'm fine with that. I wanted a diagnosis, I got it" (Season 7, Episode 19).

House can therefore be seen as a "new lad" who dissociates maturity from masculinity. While maturity was strongly associated with Victorian essential masculinity, today it seems typically rejected. Gary Cross suggests that definitions of masculinity have changed so that now maturity is no longer a requirement (although he notes that "maturity" is also a constructed term with a changing definition). Today it is okay for men in their twenties (and beyond) to indulge in the latest technological gadgets; to play computer games; to live with their parents beyond their teens; to wear a baseball cap and jeans; to prefer sports or online gaming to dating; or even to date a string of women rather than be married to one.

Implicit in this immaturity is the idea that men are no longer perfect or idealized, and fallibility is a significant addition to the Holmes-House character, who describes himself as "damaged" (Season 1, Episode 20)—not just physically, but mentally (in Season 3, Episode 12 he claims his father abused him). Imperfection and failure are a regular part of the process in *House*.

Although Holmes talks a lot about the science of deduction, both "detectives" ultimately rely on inductive reasoning: where particular events are used to make generalizations. Holmes uses deduction (reaching a specific conclusion based on generalizations) but his judgements are based on principles which are the result of inductive study (such as his monograph on cigar ash or his study of the different types of mud found in London). In such a process, it's entirely possible that, even if all the premises relied upon are correct, the conclusion can still be false.

But whereas Sherlock Holmes's conclusions are seldom wrong (a notable exception would be "The Adventure of the Yellow Face"), House is often mistaken and in each episode his patient often gets worse, not better. However each new symptom or clue then allows him to adjust his diagnosis. Fallibility is emphasized in the series, and (aside from House's "eureka" moments) the audience work through the differential diagnosis alongside House and his team—rather than being spellbound as Holmes offers what seems an impossibly accurate conclusion from very little evidence.

Defiant Male Behavior

Like Holmes, House defies ethics and rules nearly constantly; again undercutting the idea of essentialism, as each episode emphasises that context is all that matters when defining appropriate behavior (his successful manipulation of Masters in Season 7, Episode 19 also testifies to this). He invades patients' privacy on a regular basis (breaking and entering their homes to search for "clues") and is unconcerned with the social norms or who he might offend. In Season 2, Episode 16, he "kidnaps" a teenaged patient in an elevator to look for a tick that he is sure must be there and is causing her illness—her outraged father sees House apparently sexually assaulting his daughter, before House reveals he has found the creature he is looking for.

It may even be possible that, as well as ethical essentialism, a critique of cultural essentialism (or stereotyping) is apparent here. House (played by English actor Hugh Laurie) is sarcastic and superior, often delivering deadpan witticisms—traits arguably more suited to a British stereotype than an American one. His lines frequently play off his own bad behavior, such as replying to Cuddy's question "Don't you think this is a little manipulative?" "No, I think it's hugely manipulative" (Season 2, Episode 14), or offering a cynical commentary on events: "The kid is having nightmares. Only happen at night. It's right there in the name" (Season 3, Episode 2).

House's behavior contains the sort of ironic self-awareness often found in contemporary masculinity, which acknowledges its stereotypes and shortcomings while nonetheless following them (for example in men's magazines which perpetuate sexist images and articles while commenting critically on these—the magazine *Loaded*'s slogan "For men who should know better" illustrates this).

Both Holmes and House attack essentialist ideas of culture, gender, and ethics. Holmes subtly challenges conventional essentialist Victorian masculinity through his combination of the physical, intellectual and emotional. House, a product of today's society which offers multiple options for male behavior, embodies and critiques the constructed categories of the new man and the new lad. His type of contemporary masculinity is characterized by immaturity and fallibility.

The goal-oriented and rationally deconstructed mysteries that make up the plots of both the Sherlock Homes and the Gregory House stories are complemented and challenged by lead characters whose contradictions undermine these themes.

In this way, both Homes and House challenge social convention and gender stereotypes, offering multi-faceted alternatives.

Chapter 15

A Feminist Scandal
in Holmes's Generalizations

Mona Rocha and James Rocha

If the eighteenth-century Scottish philosopher, David Hume, met up with the nineteenth century fictional British detective, Sherlock Holmes, David would surely tell Sherlock that it isn't simple deduction, but induction.

And, really, induction is not all that elementary—in fact, it can be quite dangerous. Imagine a husband drawing a conclusion about his wife based on a clear pattern that he regularly witnessed among all of his ex-girlfriends: "But Sweetie, all my girlfriends liked it when I did that to them, so it is simple deduction that you should like it as well!" David Hume argued that we should never assume the future will be like the past. Hume did not care how many similar instances you had in the past. None of those instances can tell you what would happen next because they are all stuck in the past. This poor husband has no idea how his wife is about to react to him drawing conclusions about her based on his previous girlfriends. His induction from past girlfriends to his present wife is quite a dangerous move!

In the twenty-first century, we know the dangers of generalizing about gender. Not all men are alike, and neither are all women. Men can be feminine; women can be masculine. There are no real differences between the genders in intelligence, personality types, or even physical abilities. Top female weight lifters can lift more than almost any men. And, you certainly should never assume your significant other is exactly like your exes. We overcome sexism (as well as racism and other forms of bigotry) in large part by refusing to put individuals in boxes based on their gender, race, religion, or sexuality.

But a large part of what Sherlock Holmes does is induction (not deduction), which relies on treating like people as alike. Deduction occurs when you move from a set of premises to a conclusion that is certain to be true based on those premises. All women are human. Irene Adler is a woman (let's ignore that she is a fictional character). Therefore, Irene Adler is human.

Induction occurs when you move from a set of premises to a conclusion that is probably true based on those premises. Most women have two legs. Irene Adler is a woman. Therefore, Irene Adler has two legs. That's probably true. Of course, Moriarty could have intervened and done something horrible to maim Adler! Contrary to what Hume thinks, induction often works out fine. This example seems to be a good case: the conclusion might be false—but it is probably true that Adler has two legs.

At the same time, induction can be quite dangerous when it comes to gender. Let's try another argument. Most women are not as intelligent as a great British detective. Irene Adler is a woman. Sherlock Holmes is a great British detective. Therefore, Irene Adler is not as intelligent as Sherlock Holmes. There is much that is wrong with this argument (the logic appears to be fine, but it is not a cogent argument that should convince us that the conclusion is probably true). We can tell because the conclusion is not probably true: Adler outwits Holmes in "A Scandal in Bohemia." We should not assume that women are not as smart as British detectives – even great ones. We should not even assume that women cannot be British detectives, which might be implied by the first premise.

It is the kind of premise, which is found in many inductive arguments, that asserts "Most women are this way . . ." that troubles us. It's this kind of premise that often falls prey to the fallacy of hasty generalization. That fallacy occurs when a generalization is made on flimsy evidence. How can we know what most women are like? When we say most women have two legs, we're walking on pretty safe ground. But how about when we refer to the intelligence of most women or what most women desire? We can't really know those sorts of things, and that is why we have to be careful about making hasty generalizations.

It Is a Capital Mistake to Theorize before You Have All the Evidence

Sir Arthur Conan Doyle's female characters are often irrational and gullible, hysterical and vengeful, and always thinking with the stereotypically one-track mind of a woman who does everything for her family or man. They are also often too frail under the monumental stress of the situations they find themselves in and need a man, such as Sherlock Holmes, to save them. In reality, gender patterns (most women are a certain way) are likely to yield some dangerous inductive conclusions (therefore, this woman must be that way). But, in Doyle's universe, most women really do fit into well-established patterns.

Holmes often assumes it will be easier to trick a woman than to ask an honest question. This kind of assumption fits into the idea that women are likely to be gullible and dishonest. For example, in *The Sign of the Four*, Holmes needs to find a boat that contains his primary suspect. Mrs. Smith, the wife of a simple boatman, has the information Holmes requires. Rather than just coming out and requesting the information, Holmes assumes that Mrs. Smith won't relay it honestly. He uses a ruse against her that plays on her motherly instincts: he compliments her son and gives him money to curry her favor. Holmes then pretends to be confused about what the boat looks like. Mrs. Smith feels she's correcting his mistaken information when, in reality, she is giving him the description he is after. But there is no need for this deceitful move. Holmes seems to have generalized from his views about women to the conclusion that this woman is unlikely to be honest and helpful, but will be easy to trick.

Holmes often generalizes about females, and although these generalizations should be dangerous, they often work out fine for him. Consider Mary Sutherland, who comes to see Holmes in "A Case of Identity." Holmes, observing her behavior under his window, works his infamous inductive skills. He analyzes her back and forth movements on the pavement, and quickly decides that her jerky movements and fidgeting behavior indicate that she is of two minds about seeking help. Further, he infers that her distraught behavior is due to a love affair.

We can see the generalizations stirring in Holmes's mind in this case. How did he figure out it is a love affair? Well, it would have to be something that was not too serious since the woman is not certain she wants to hire the detective. But surely there are dozens of random problems that could fit into that category. So, why love affair? Because that's what most women trouble themselves about! We have stepped right into a hasty generalization!

Fortunately, Mary Sutherland's love affair problem is not too serious, since "when a woman has been seriously wronged by a man, she no longer oscillates, and the usual symptom is a broken bell wire" ("A Case of Identity"). If a woman is unsure of whether to hire a detective, then she has a mild love problem. If a woman is sure of her need for a detective, then she has a severe love problem and is likely to break down the detective's door—

that's why detectives need extra security, not to protect them from super-villains like Professor Moriarty, but from scorned women! By this reasoning, Holmes would have assumed a love problem the moment any female showed up at his door. It's just a matter of measuring how bad the problem is by checking how little control she has over her emotions.

In spite of these rather poor characterizations of women, Doyle does not write even his minor female characters as stupid. Mary Sutherland manages her yearly income adequately, and is rather adept at understanding the stock market. Holmes recognizes this insight, and is approving of it. Having generalized her as overly emotional, he comes to see that she has a rational side as well.

Still, Holmes does over-complicate matters in the end by not fully accepting that this smart woman could handle the truth. Holmes figures out that Mary was actually engaged to her stepfather in disguise. Instead of telling her that she had been duped, he merely scares away the stepfather. But since Holmes will go on to other cases, and neither Mary nor her mother know that her stepfather is carrying on this ruse, this solution will probably only lead to new problems after the events of the story. Because he assumed that this woman would not be able to understand the solution to her problem, Holmes left Mary Sutherland unable to protect herself in the future if her stepfather returns.

Finally, let's look at Lady Frances Carfax, who appears in "The Disappearance of Lady Frances Carfax." We learn right at the outset of this story that Lady Frances, who is single, is also "the drifting and friendless woman . . . the inevitable inciter of crimes in others. . . . She is a stray chicken in a world of foxes. When she is gobbled up she is hardly missed." All in all, we can sum up by saying she is a, "rather pathetic figure."

But what provides the basis for these conclusions? It's unclear that there is any basis, other than that she is an older, single woman. By the events of the story, Watson learns that she's "not more than forty. She was still handsome and bore every sign of having in her youth been a very lovely woman." We must imagine that what makes her such a pathetic figure is her inability to find a man, in spite of having been very lovely in her youth.

It is this kind of quick thinking that throws Holmes off in the case at hand. Lady Frances disappeared because a couple is attempting to bury her alive in the coffin of a woman who died of natural causes. Holmes almost misses this clever ruse, which forces him to admit that he is indeed mortal. Though he also thinks of himself as the best kind of mortal since he is the kind that can always "recognize and repair" his mistakes in time. In fact, he does arrive in time to save Lady Frances, but not in time to catch the couple who tried to bury her. We must be on the lookout for whether he eventually "recognizes and repairs" his tendency to form hasty generalizations about women. But, we shouldn't just isolate Holmes's hasty generalizations without noticing that Dr. Watson is even guiltier when it comes to generalizing unfairly about women.

Watson, the Fair Sex Is Your Department

Where Sherlock Holmes often risks drawing hasty generalizations about gender, Dr. John H. Watson is even worse as he consistently objectifies women in his generalizations about them. Feminist philosophers worry a great deal about sexual objectifications where a person treats someone like they are an object, such as when we concentrate on a human's shell—her body—and miss what's inside—the person. Hasty generalizations are a big part of this problem. If you meet some people who can be judged quite accurately based on what's on the outside, it's natural to think that you don't need to keep looking for people's insides. But we can already see how dangerous that is: some of the most interesting people in life are the ones who cannot be judged by how they look. Dr. Watson's generalizations often involve forming opinions on women based only on their looks.

We see this from the first moment he meets his eventual wife in *The Sign of the Four*:

> Her face had neither regularity of feature nor beauty of complexion, but her expression was sweet and amiable, and her large blue eyes were singularly spiritual and sympathetic. In an experience of women which extends over many nations and three separate continents, I have never looked upon a face which gave clearer promise of a refined and sensitive nature.

We see the basis for Watson's generalizations: he tells us all about his wealth of experience with women from all over the world. More importantly, we see how Watson has completely figured out Miss Mary Morstan, his future wife, merely by looking at her. She is not beautiful in terms of having a symmetrical face or an attractive complexion, but he can tell that she is sweet, amiable, spiritual, sympathetic, refined, and sensitive just from looking at her facial expression.

Dr. Watson is quick to judge other women based on their appearances. As another telling example, we can look at a situation where Holmes gives Watson the chance to try out induction for himself. Watson's immediately concentrates on the woman's outward display:

> Well, she had a slate-coloured, broad-brimmed straw hat. . . . Her jacket was black. . . . Her dress was brown. . . . Her gloves were grayish. . . . Her boots I didn't observe. She had small round, hanging gold earrings, and a general air of being fairly well-to-do in a vulgar, comfortable, easy-going way. ("A Case of Identity")

What's really interesting about this passage is not just the fact that Watson zooms in on colors (Sherlock responds, "It is true that you have missed everything of importance, but . . . you have a quick eye for colour"), but that he has deemed that there is something vulgar about the fact that the woman has a comfortable, easy-going way about her. Watson is drawing an opinion about the woman's character just from the air about her.

Not only does Watson make quick judgments about women's appearances, but beautiful women get special treatment from Watson, and from Holmes. When a "beautiful intruder," in "The Adventure of the Solitary Cyclist," interrupts Holmes's and Watson's evening, the doctor states that, "it was impossible to refuse to listen to the story of the young and beautiful woman, tall, graceful and queenly." Yet, an "elderly, motherly woman of the buxom landlady type" coming in the afternoon gets no special treatment in "The Adventure of the Veiled Lodger." In fact, Holmes explains to Watson that he should not hold himself back in front of such a woman, and that he should feel free to smoke in her presence. It's as if there is some sort of correlation between attractiveness and respect or courtesy.

Holmes and Watson are enthralled with the beautiful intruder and her story, and Watson is inclined to view her as having great "clearness and composure." But all Watson says about the old lady is that "she waddled out of the room." In both cases, the women's mysteries are solved: but there's a clear indication of differential treatment. With the young, beautiful intruder, the two inquire after her marital status; with the elderly woman, they simply get down to business and dismiss her promptly so that they could have lunch.

Doyle's Proto-Feminist: Irene Adler

Both Watson and Holmes engage in occasional generalizations about women. That raises the question of whether Doyle thought that it was safe to paint women in such universal strokes. We can tell that he did not by looking at the one case where Holmes was outwitted. As if the dangers of all of these generalizations were adding up to the one big mistake, it turns out that he was outwitted by "the woman." As Watson explains:

> To Sherlock Holmes she is always *the woman*. I have seldom heard him mention her under any other name. In his eyes she eclipses and predominates the whole of her sex. . . . there was but one woman to him, and that woman was the late Irene Adler, of dubious and questionable memory. ("A Scandal in Bohemia")

We've already seen that Holmes is likely to think that women will be too emotional for their own good, and that this makes them easy to trick. For this reason, Holmes did not think he would have any trouble when he set out to trick Irene Adler into giving up her most prized possession (a picture that could cause a scandal for the King of Bohemia). Irene Adler is the exception that turns Holmes's sexist generalizations upside down, and one of the few individuals, of either gender, to beat him at his own game. Irene Adler, a woman—or "the woman," as Holmes thinks of her— outwits, outmaneuvers, and out-sleuths the usually incomparable Sherlock Holmes, teaching him the dangers of hasty gendered generalizations.

Holmes's entire plan is based on gendered generalizations. Holmes task is to get the picture away from Adler. To do so, he needs to know where she keeps it. He feels it is safe to assume that it will be in her home because, "Women are naturally secretive, and they like to do their own secreting." Having assumed she is like all other women, Holmes thinks he can trick her into letting him into her house and into showing him where she keeps the picture.

Of course, Watson—judging character from outside appearances as always—feels guilty about tricking her since she's a pretty woman: "I never felt more ashamed of myself in my life when I saw the beautiful creature against whom I was conspiring."

The trick appears to work as Holmes does get into Adler's home. Once in her home, Holmes's ruse takes form. Holmes continues to think he can draw conclusions about any woman from past experiences of other women: "When a woman thinks that her house is on fire, her instinct is at once to rush to the thing which she values most."

When Holmes returns to her home the next day, he's shocked to find that Adler not only knows who he is, but also has left a note for him. Though Holmes uses his disguise to trick Adler, he does not realize that she has been using a disguise of her own to trick Holmes. She actually wished him "Goodnight" while dressed as a man. Adler out-prepared Holmes, and when he came to trick her, she was ready for him, and he is unable to get the photograph for the King of Bohemia.

The Honorable, *the* Woman

This moment—where Adler outwits the greatest detective in literary history—is incredibly important as a response to the dangerous gendered generalizations we have been discussing. If Holmes and Watson always got away with their gendered generalizations, that would be a problem. If the female characters always confirmed their negative stereotypes of women, we would have to think that Doyle himself created a sexist fictional universe. But the exception not only proves the danger of hasty generalizations, but it also indicates that Doyle was aware of this danger.

In Irene Adler, Doyle created a proto-feminist: a strong female character who was just as smart as the smartest man—a female character that stood for everything any woman is capable of. For this reason, it makes sense to refer to her as "the woman." She is not only the woman who beat Holmes, but she is also the woman who shows why it is always wrong to treat women as a group instead of treating them as particular individuals. Each woman, of course, deserves to be referred to in singular terms to capture her unique personal traits that set her apart as a real individual who cannot be judged simply by her sex or outer appearances.

Notice how important this point is, historically speaking. "A Scandal in Bohemia" is published in 1891, and yet it presents a female antagonist just as intelligent as Sherlock Holmes. It is incredibly difficult to find a female antagonist going head-to-head against a great male hero, and coming out on top. Over thirty years after Holmes's defeat, Agatha Christie's Hercule Poirot goes up against Countess Vera Rossakoff, but he easily sees through her framing of another man and collects the jewels she stole. Forty years after Doyle's "Scandal," Dashiell Hammett's

Sam Spade goes up against Brigid O'Shaughnessy, but she ends up falling in love with Spade who turns her over to the cops. Fifty years after Irene Adler's tale of success, Raymond Chandler's Philip Marlowe goes up against Helen Grayle, who manages to escape Marlowe's clutches, but ends up killing herself.

Clearly, Doyle was ahead of his time in appreciation for the ability of a woman to equalize his great detective in an intellectual dispute. His characters may have lagged behind him with all of their inductive arguments that moved from previous experiences with women to a conclusion that the next woman would be the same. But, surely, they learned their lesson when they were bested by the woman. As Watson says:

> the best plans of Mr. Sherlock Holmes were beaten by a woman's wit. He used to make merry over the cleverness of women, but I have not heard him do it of late. And when he speaks of Irene Adler, or when he refers to her photograph, it is always under the honorable title of *the woman*.

THERE ARE

UNEXPLORED
POSSIBILITIES

IN YOU

Chapter 16

The Many Faces of Deception
Don Fallis

> If, like truth, the lie had but one face, we would be on better terms. For we would accept as certain the opposite of what the liar would say. But the reverse of the truth has a hundred thousand faces and an infinite field.
> —Montaigne

> Why are they lying, and what is the truth which they are trying so hard to conceal? Let us try, Watson, you and I, if we can get behind the lie and reconstruct the truth.
> —Sherlock Holmes, Esq.

Sherlock Holmes is renowned for observing several minute details and then being able to draw amazingly accurate inferences about what has happened. At their first meeting in *A Study in Scarlet*, Holmes quickly notices that Watson has a military bearing, that his face is darker than the skin on his wrists, and that he holds his left arm in "a stiff and unnatural manner." From these clues (together with his knowledge of the recent Anglo-Afghan War), Holmes famously concludes, "You have been in Afghanistan, I perceive." But obviously Holmes didn't mention all the clues he had employed, because based on that evidence alone, Watson could also have been in South Africa, where the British had been fighting the Zulus at about the same time.

However, the sorts of "deductions" that Holmes regularly makes in order to solve crimes are even more impressive. In these cases, Holmes manages to uncover something that (unlike Watson's military service) someone else is actively trying to keep hidden. In other words, he's dealing with liars and deceivers who attempt to make the world appear to be one way when the reality is actually quite different. And in order to see through their ruses to the truth, Holmes has to understand the various ways in which people try to deceive other people.

Philosophers from Plato and Saint Augustine to Immanuel Kant and Friedrich Nietzsche have been primarily interested in *moral* questions about lying and deception, such as whether it's always wrong to lie and whether lying is worse than other forms of deception. But philosophers are also concerned with the purely *epistemological* questions of how people can be deceived and how deception can be detected. In other words, how can we acquire knowledge in a world of liars and deceivers?

All types of deception involve manipulating people's beliefs by altering the way the world appears to be. However, as we see from reading the "Reminiscences of John H. Watson, M.D.," deceit comes in a wealth of different varieties. Thus, philosophers, such as Augustine, Roderick Chisholm and Thomas Feehan, J. Bowyer Bell and Barton Whaley, Jonathan Adler (no relation to Irene), and, most recently, Thomas Carson, have attempted to classify the different possible types of deception.

As well as writing a technical monograph enumerating the various types of tobacco ash (*The Sign of the Four*), Holmes was also interested in categorizing the various types of crime and deceit. As he points out, "There is a strong family resemblance about misdeeds, and if you have all the details of a thousand at your finger ends, it is odd if you can't unravel the thousand and first" (*A Study in Scarlet*).

Why They Might Deceive Us

Saint Augustine (*De Mendacio*, pp. 86–88) was the first philosopher to explicitly classify different types of deception. In particular, he categorized various kinds of lying based on the *purpose* for which it is done. For instance, there are lies that harm someone and help no one, lies that harm someone and help someone else, lies that harm no one and help someone, and lies told "solely for the pleasure of lying." However, this taxonomy is not very helpful when it comes to classifying deception in the Sherlock Holmes stories (a.k.a. the "Canon").

There may be a few lies in the Canon that harm no one and help someone. In "The Adventure of the Second Stain," Holmes is asked by the Secretary for European Affairs to retrieve a sensitive document that has been stolen from his "despatch-box." Holmes discovers that the document has been removed by the Secretary's own wife. But instead of exposing her, he secretly replaces the document in the despatch-box and tells the

Secretary, "the more I think of the matter the more convinced I am that the letter has never left this house."

Since the document is safe, the lie arguably does no harm and it saves the wife from potentially losing her husband. But almost all of the examples of deception that Watson records fall into the category of helping the deceiver and harming someone else. In fact, even the lie in "The Adventure of the Second Stain" ends up making the Right Honourable Trelawney Hope look a bit foolish for having thought that the document was stolen in the first place.

But fortunately, there is a more useful way to classify the deceptions in the Canon according to their purpose. Most notably, criminals use deception *to conceal who committed the crime*. For instance, Colonel Valentine Walter and Hugo Oberstein steal the "Bruce-Partington Plans." But they kill the junior clerk at Woolwich Arsenal and plant several of the documents on his body to make it look as if he was the thief.

Criminals sometimes attempt to hide the fact that a crime has been committed at all. In "The Adventure of the Speckled Band," Dr. Grimesby Roylott of Stoke Moran kills his step-daughter so that she cannot get married, and he does so in a way that conceals the fact that she was murdered. (As we'll see below, there's a veritable epidemic of parents in Victorian England who are willing to take extreme measures to keep their daughters from getting married.) He sends a venomous snake down a bell-rope into her locked bedroom to bite her, which leaves no visible evidence of foul play.

But in addition to covering up the crime, criminals also use deception *to commit the crime* in the first place. Most notably, Vincent Spaulding (a.k.a. John Clay) deceives Jabez Wilson about there being a "vacancy on the League of the Red-headed Men." The ruse keeps Wilson out of his pawnshop for several hours a day so that Clay and his accomplice can dig a tunnel into the vault of the neighboring City and Suburban Bank.

In "The Adventure of the Norwood Builder," Jonas Oldacre plants false evidence to suggest that he has been murdered by the unhappy John Hector McFarlane. He uses a little of his own blood, and McFarlane's thumbprint from a wax seal on an envelope, to place a bloody thumbprint on the wall.

Some of Holmes's own clients try to deceive him simply *to avoid embarrassment*. In "The Problem of Thor Bridge," Mr. Neil Gibson tries to deceive Holmes about the nature of his relationship with the governess of his children (at least until Holmes accuses him of lying). Dr. Gregory House, a fictional *medical* detective who is loosely based on Sherlock Holmes (see Jerold Abrams, "The Logic of Guesswork in Sherlock Holmes and *House*"), has the same sort of problem. ("I don't ask why patients lie, I just assume they all do.") In fact, Holmes explicitly draws the analogy between a client lying to him and a patient lying to a doctor. ("And it is only a patient who has an object in deceiving his surgeon who would conceal the facts of his case.")

Holmes himself regularly uses deceit in order *to solve the crime*. In "A Scandal in Bohemia," Watson throws a "plumber's smoke-rocket" through a window so that Irene Adler will think that there is a fire and will reveal the location of the indiscreet photograph that Holmes has been engaged to retrieve. In "The Adventure of the Empty House," Holmes puts a wax bust of himself in the window of 221B Baker Street to convince Colonel Sebastian Moran "that I was there when I was really elsewhere." In "The Adventure of the Mazarin Stone," Holmes does the exact opposite. He pretends to be a wax replica of himself so that Count Negretto Sylvius will think that he is elsewhere when he is really there.

Holmes even goes so far as to fake his own death at the Reichenbach Falls to protect himself from the Moriarty gang ("The Adventure of the Empty House"). The "tragedy" at the falls occurred before the "Norwood Builder" faked his own death. But Holmes might have gotten the idea from John Douglas in *The Valley of Fear*. In addition to faking his own death, Douglas (while working as a Pinkerton in America) was a counterfeit counterfeiter ("I never minted a dollar in my life. Those I gave you were as good as any others").

Holmes often deceives Watson as well as the criminals he's chasing. Just like the rest of the world, Watson is completely convinced that Holmes died with Moriarty at that "fearful place." And, as if Watson had not already suffered enough grief, Holmes later persuades him that he (Holmes) is dying of a rare tropical disease ("The Adventure of the Dying Detective"). But Holmes usually only deceives Watson as a means of deceiving the criminals that he's chasing. For instance, Watson had to believe that Holmes was dead because "it is quite certain that you would not have written so convincing an account of my unhappy end had you not yourself thought that it was true."

It's not completely clear why Holmes needs to maintain this fiction for three years. After all, a "confederate" of Moriarty was a "witness of his friend's death and of my escape." Holmes has a much better excuse for deceiving Watson in "The Adventure of the Dying Detective." He wants Watson to fetch Mr. Culverton Smith ("the man upon earth who is best versed in this disease") and, as he later explains to Watson, "if you had shared my secret you would never have been able to impress Smith with the urgent necessity of his presence, which was the vital point of the whole scheme."

As the great German philosopher Friedrich Nietzsche pointed out just a few years before Holmes supposedly fell into that awful abyss, "men believe in the truth of that which is plainly strongly believed."

And finally, Sir Arthur Conan Doyle himself engages in deception. He's always trying *to deceive his readers* about what's really going on, until Holmes reveals the solution to the mystery. As Doyle explains in his autobiography, "having got that key idea, one's next task is to conceal it and lay emphasis upon everything which can make for a different explanation." In *The Hound of the Baskervilles*, Doyle provides us with several possible suspects. In addition to being the butler (always a suspicious character in murder mysteries), Mr. Barrymore has "a full, black beard" just like the man that followed Sir Henry Baskerville in London and he could have the motive of keeping Baskerville Hall for himself. The escaped convict Selden, the Notting Hill murderer, is loose on the moor and is "a man that would stick at nothing." There is also the suspicious, unidentified "man on the tor" that Watson sees silhouetted against the moon (who turns out to be Holmes himself). Or the curse of the Baskervilles could actually be true and there is a "hound of hell" roaming the moor.

How They Might Deceive Us

It's useful to know about the different reasons *why* people deceive. This can make us more aware that a person might have a motivation to deceive us. But it's even more important to understand *how* people deceive. According to J. Bowyer Bell and Barton Whaley and to Paul Ekman, there are two main ways to deceive. You can "hide the truth" or you can "show the false." For instance, Dr. Roylott just hides the truth that he murdered his step-daughter. By contrast, Colonel Walter and Oberstein show the false that Cadogan West stole the plans for the submarine (as well as hiding the truth that they did it).

Either way, the ultimate goal is the same. As several philosophers have pointed out, in order for something to count as deception, the goal must be to foster in someone a *false belief*, or at least to lower that person's confidence in a true belief. For instance, Dr. Roylott wants people to believe that his stepdaughter was not murdered and Colonel Walter and Oberstein want people to believe that West stole the plans.

Admittedly, it's possible to hide the truth from someone just in order to "keep him in the dark." I might steal the latest copy of *Variety* from your mailbox so that you will not learn that the new *Sherlock Holmes* film is going to be written by the guy that accused George Costanza of double dipping. However, with only a few exceptions, philosophers don't count this as deception. Similarly, Holmes is not deceiving anyone when he keeps his chain of reasoning secret. As he explains to Watson in *A Study in Scarlet*, "I'm not going to tell you much more of the case, Doctor. You know a conjuror gets no credit when once he has explained his trick, and if I show you too much of my method of working, you will come to the conclusion that I am a very ordinary individual after all." When the same issue comes up in "The Red-Headed League," Holmes quotes the Roman historian Tacitus, "Omne ignotum pro magnifico" (Everything unknown appears magnificent). Likewise, the "cipher messages" used in "The Adventure of the Dancing Men" and in *The Valley of Fear* are not intended to deceive. They are simply designed to keep everyone but the intended recipient *ignorant* of the contents of the message.

A Master of Disguise

As Bell and Whaley have pointed out, there are several different techniques for hiding the truth and showing the false. These techniques can be illustrated by looking at the various ways that *disguises* function in the Canon.

Several of the villains that Holmes chases down disguise *themselves*. Most notably, Mr. Neville St. Clair becomes "The Man with the Twisted Lip" because he could make more money as a professional beggar than as a journalist. In "A Case of Identity," James Windibank "disguised himself, covered those keen eyes with tinted glasses, masked the face with a moustache and a pair of bushy whiskers, sunk that clear voice into an insinuating whisper, and doubly secure on account of the girl's short sight, he appears as Mr. Hosmer Angel, and keeps off other lovers by making love himself."

Sometimes criminals even disguise *other people*. Mr. and Mrs. Rucastle of the "Copper Beeches" make their governess (without her knowledge) appear to be their daughter. The goal is to convince the daughter's fiancé that she's no longer interested in him. In fact, criminals sometimes disguise *animals*. Silas Brown dyed the distinctive white forehead of "Silver Blaze" so that he would blend in with the other horses at Mapleton.

And as we all know, Holmes himself is a master of disguise. He often pretends to be a member of the working class so that he can conduct his investigations with greater anonymity. He appears as a "rakish young workman" ("The Adventure of Charles Augustus Milverton"), a "mariner who had fallen into years and poverty" (*The Sign of the Four*), a "drunken-looking groom" ("A Scandal in Bohemia"), an "ill-dressed vagabond" ("The Adventure of the Beryl Coronet"), and a "doddering, loose-lipped" opium fiend ("The Man with the Twisted Lip"). And he has set up various locations around London where he can change into these disguises ("The Adventure of Black Peter"). Unlike Clark Kent, Holmes cannot just hop into the nearest phone booth to change his identity.

According to Sherlock Holmes in "The Great Game" (from the first season of *Sherlock* with Benedict Cumberbatch), "the art of disguise is knowing how to hide in plain sight." But hiding the truth is not the only possible goal of putting on a disguise. Disguises can also be used to show the false in several different ways. In addition, there are actually several different ways to hide the truth with a disguise.

Hiding in Plain Sight

One way that disguises can hide the truth is called *masking* (or *camouflage*). This is when the person or the thing disguised is not intended to be seen at all. A prime example is a chameleon changing its color to blend in with the surrounding environment. Similarly, a criminal might use the thick London fog to hide himself. As Holmes explains to Watson, "See how the figures loom up, are dimly seen, and then blend once more into the cloudbank. The thief or the murderer could roam London on such a day as the tiger does the jungle, unseen until he pounces, and then evident only to his victim" ("The Adventure of the Bruce-Partington Plans").

Holmes himself is really good at this technique. In "The Adventure of the Devil's Foot," when Holmes tells Dr. Leon

Sterndale that he was followed, Sterndale says, "I saw no one," to which Holmes replies, "That is what you may expect to see when I follow you." As Holmes explains in the Jeremy Brett adaptation of "The Man with the Twisted Lip," the goal is to "merge with the surroundings." The murderer in *A Study in Scarlet* is quite good at it too. When he's finally caught, he says to Holmes (in the Benedict Cumberbatch adaptation), "See, no one ever thinks about the cabbie. It's like you're invisible. Just the back of a head. Proper advantage for a serial killer."

Another way that disguises can hide the truth is called *repackaging*. This is when the person or the thing disguised is made to look like something else. For instance, several species of insects have evolved to look like sticks or leaves. In a similar vein, "Silver Blaze" is made to look like just any other horse. Unlike with masking, this is not an attempt to keep people from seeing the disguised item, but just to keep them from recognizing it for what it is.

The most famous example of this technique from detective fiction is *The Purloined Letter*. The stolen letter was made to look like a different letter and then hidden by the thief in plain sight. While the ruse fools the Parisian police, the letter is discovered by Edgar Allan Poe's C. Auguste Dupin. I'm somewhat hesitant to bring up this example as Holmes thought that "Dupin was a very inferior fellow" (*A Study in Scarlet*). Dupin had a confederate create a commotion to distract the villain, so that he could recover the purloined letter. Despite Holmes's disdain for his French counterpart, this event may have inspired Holmes's attempt to trick Irene Adler.

Disguises are often a combination of these two techniques. Frequently, something (or someone) is disguised with the hope that no one will even notice it (masking). However, the disguise is such that, if someone does notice it, she will not recognize it for what it really is (repackaging). This is probably what the murderous cabbie really had in mind. Similarly, in "The Final Problem" and "The Adventure of the Empty House," Holmes disguises himself as an Italian priest and as an "elderly deformed" book collector so that the Moriarty gang will not notice him at all. But if they do notice him, as they probably do when Watson bumps into him and upsets his books, they are unlikely to recognize him as the famous consulting detective.

Finally, *dazzling* is yet another way to hide the truth. When pursuers know that a particular person or thing is in a particular location, masking and repackaging are not going to be effective techniques. However, it's still possible to confound the pursuers.

An octopus might shoot out ink to confuse a predator and escape. Similarly, law firms sometimes provide boxes and boxes of documents so that the opposition will not be able to find the one incriminating document in the "haystack."

Since we don't know "the whole story concerning the politician, the lighthouse, and the trained cormorant" ("The Adventure of the Veiled Lodger") or the "story for which the world is not yet prepared" about "the giant rat of Sumatra" ("The Adventure of the Sussex Vampire"), I cannot say for sure whether or not Holmes ever faced dazzling. But the readers of the Holmes stories certainly have. Doyle himself was engaged in dazzling when he pointed to multiple false explanations of the crime as he did in *The Hound of the Baskervilles*. With several possible suspects in each of her mysteries, Agatha Christie is the queen of this technique.

Creating a False Impression

In addition to hiding the true, disguises can also be used to show the false. One way that disguises can do this is called *mimicking*. This is when the person or the thing disguised is made to look like something else, not just to remain hidden, but to gain some other advantage. For instance, several species of cuckoo lay their eggs in the nests of other birds so that these other birds will raise them (believing them to be their own offspring). Similarly, when Mr. Windibank pretends to be his stepdaughter's young suitor, he certainly wants to hide his true identity, but it is equally important that he display his false identity to her.

It's possible to mimic a *type* of person, as when Neville St. Clair disguises himself as a beggar. And it is also possible to mimic a *particular* person as when the Rucastles' governess is made to appear to be their daughter. In addition, mimicry does not always involve a disguise *per se*. For instance, the bloody thumbprint that Oldacre created "mimicked" an actual bloody thumbprint left by McFarlane.

Another way that disguises can show the false is called *inventing*. This is just like mimicking except that something (or someone) is disguised as something else that never existed before. In other words, a new reality is created. A good example of this is *The Hound of the Baskervilles* itself. As Watson describes it,

> A hound it was, an enormous coal-black hound, but not such a hound as mortal eyes have ever seen. Fire burst from its open mouth, its eyes glowed with a smouldering glare, its muzzle and hackles and dewlap were

outlined in flickering flame. Never in the delirious dream of a disordered brain could anything more savage, more appalling, more hellish be conceived than that dark form and savage face which broke upon us out of the wall of fog.

However, Jack Stapleton had simply painted a large hound with phosphorus to make it appear to be a "hound of hell."

Finally, *decoying* is yet another way to show the false. A bird will sometimes lure predators away from its nest by pretending that it has a broken wing. In *A Study in Scarlet*, when the murderer (who was an American and not a German) wrote the German word for revenge in blood on the wall, "it was simply a ruse to divert inquiry into a wrong channel." And in "The Adventure of the Missing Three-Quarter," Dr. Leslie Armstrong literally leaves a false trail for Holmes. He leaves home in his brougham in the opposite direction from his true destination and then he doubles back. In other words, he "disguises" his destination.

Decoying can certainly involve showing the false. Pretending to have a broken wing is actually a type of mimicking. Also, decoying can be carried out by inventing. But despite the fact that Bell and Whaley classify decoying as a type of showing the false, the ultimate goal is to hide the truth. Moreover, it can be carried out without showing the false at all. For example, if the bird actually does have a broken wing, it can still lure predators away from its nest.

By the way, according to Holmes, Stapleton used his wife, who was pretending to be his sister, as a "decoy" in *The Hound of the Baskervilles*. But this was not decoying in the sense that Bell and Whaley have in mind. Stapleton "hoped that his wife might lure Sir Charles to his ruin" rather than away from anything. In other words, he was using her in the way that a hunter uses a decoy duck. So, this is just another case of mimicking.

Deceived by Words

The principal distinction drawn by philosophers is between lying and other forms of deception. For instance, in *The Valley of Fear*, Cecil Barker told "a great, big, thumping, obtrusive, uncompromising lie" about the shooting at Birlstone. By contrast, Jonas Oldacre merely planted false evidence to frame John Hector McFarlane. He did not actually say anything false. Of course, prevaricators typically engage in both verbal and nonverbal deception. For instance, Barker also planted a "smudge of blood like the mark of a boot-sole upon the wooden sill." And when he is finally caught, Oldacre does lie about his motivations. He claims that "it was only my practical joke."

This distinction is important, as several philosophers have argued, because all other things being equal, lying is worse than other forms of deception. Most notably, the great German philosopher Immanuel Kant argued that, while it is *always* wrong to lie, it is sometimes okay to deceive in other ways.[1] But this distinction is also important for the epistemological questions of how people are deceived and how deception can be detected.

If it becomes known that a piece of evidence has been placed somewhere intentionally, it is immediately suspect. Since it was not there the first time that he searched Oldacre's house, Holmes knew that the bloody thumbprint must have been put there on purpose by someone other than John Hector McFarlane. In other cases, he is able to rule out the possibility that a clue has been left intentionally. For instance, in "The Problem of Thor Bridge," the note from the governess is clutched so tightly in Mrs. Gibson's hand that "it excludes the idea that anyone could have placed the note there after death in order to furnish a false clue."

As Harvard philosopher Richard (a.k.a. "The Colonel") Moran points out, "ordinarily, if I confront something as evidence (the telltale footprint, the cigarette butt left in the ashtray) and then learn that it was left there deliberately, even with the intention of bringing me to a particular belief, this will only discredit it as evidence in my eyes. It won't seem *better* evidence, or even just as good, but instead like something fraudulent, or tainted evidence."

However, things work differently when someone deceives us by *telling us* something false. When someone tells us something, it's always clear that she's doing so on purpose. In fact, we believe what someone tells us precisely because she explicitly offers her assurance that what she says is true. So, some indication other than the intentionality of the act is needed to cast doubt on the veracity of testimony.

Infernal Lies

What exactly is a lie? According to most philosophers, a *lie* is a false statement that is intended to deceive someone. But a false

---

[1] Kant is probably more famous for this view than for being my dissertation advisor's advisor's advisor's advisor's advisor's advisor's advisor's advisor's advisor's advisor's advisor.

statement is still a lie even if it does not *succeed* in deceiving that someone. In particular, Holmes is rarely taken in by the lies that he's told. For instance, he can tell immediately that what Barker says to the police "is a clumsy fabrication which simply could not be true." In "The Final Problem," Holmes saw that "the letter from Meiringen was a hoax." And in "The Adventure of the Three Garridebs," after a visit from the conman John Garrideb (a.k.a. James Winter), Holmes asks, "I was wondering, Watson, what on earth could be the object of this man in telling us such a rigmarole of lies."

But it must be conceded that even Holmes is occasionally fooled by deceivers. For instance, in "The Adventure of Wisteria Lodge," Inspector Baynes arrests Mr. Aloysius Garcia's cook for his murder. Although the inspector's real suspect is Mr. Henderson of High Gable (a.k.a. Don Murillo, the Tiger of San Pedro), he "arrested the wrong man to make him believe that our eyes were off him." And his ruse fools Holmes as well as his suspect.

In addition to showing that Holmes is fallible, this case illustrates an interesting fact about lying. In most cases, a liar intends to deceive his audience about what he is saying. For instance, Barker intends the police to believe that the shooting at Birlstone occurred just as he describes it. But as James Mahon points out in the *Stanford Encyclopedia of Philosophy*, a liar may intend to deceive about *his believing* what he is saying rather than about what he is saying. Baynes does not expect or intend Holmes or Don Murillo to believe that the cook is the murderer. After all, both Holmes and Don Murillo know full well that the cook is innocent. But Baynes does convince them that *he thinks* that the cook is the murderer. In fact, Holmes used this sort of technique himself. For instance, he is tempted to confront John Garrideb about his lies because "there are times when a brutal frontal attack is the best policy—but I judged it better to let him think he had fooled us."

But a few philosophers, such as Thomas Carson and Roy Sorensen, claim that some lies are not intended to deceive at all. In fact, *bald-faced lies* are told with complete seriousness even though everyone knows that the speaker is insincere. When Dr. Armstrong catches Holmes following him on a bicycle, he walks back and says that "he hoped his carriage did not impede the passage of my bicycle" on the narrow road. Both of them know quite well that Holmes was not trying to pass the carriage and that Armstrong would not have cared if he were in the way. Although Holmes is not at all misled, the comment serves its purpose. Since he is not willing to admit that he was following Armstrong, Holmes has to continue along past the carriage and he loses Armstrong that day. As Indiana University philosopher Marcia Baron points out, lies can manipulate even when they do not deceive.

But in order to lie, one does have to *intentionally* say something false. In his search for the "Bruce-Partington Plans," Holmes interviews the clerk at Woolwich Station. And in the Jeremy Brett adaptation, the clerk says, "I was saying to the wife only on Sunday night. No, I'm a liar. It was Saturday. I said, there is no safer railway than the London Metropolitan." However, the clerk was not lying, strictly speaking. He was only misspeaking because he did not intend to say something false.

I Didn't Say So, Mr. Holmes

Lying is not the only form of verbal deception that is intended to deceive. Philosophers agree that, in order to lie, you have to say something false (or at least something that you believe to be false). But as Adler points out in "Lying, Deceiving, or Falsely Implicating," you can also deceive by saying something true. Strictly speaking, Inspector Baynes's deception was a *false implicature* rather than a lie. When Holmes asks him if he thinks that he has evidence that the cook is guilty, Baynes replies, "I didn't say so, Mr. Holmes; I didn't say so."

In "The Adventure of the Missing Three-Quarter," Holmes tells Lord Mount-James that "it is entirely possible that a gang of thieves have secured your nephew in order to gain from him some information as to your house, your habits, and your treasure." Now, it was certainly *possible* that the nephew was kidnapped. However, as Holmes admits to Watson, that theory "does not appeal to me as a very probable explanation. It struck me, however, as being the one which was most likely to interest that exceedingly unpleasant old person."

Of course, there are also many occasions on which Holmes tells outright lies. In addition to lying to Secretary Hope, he lies to a telegraph clerk about having sent a telegram so that he can get a look at the telegram that the "Missing Three-Quarter," Godfrey Staunton, sent before he disappeared. In fact, in *The Hound of the Baskervilles*, he even lies to Watson about having to stay in London to work on a case of blackmailing. Thus, even if Kant is right that simply deceiving is not as bad as actually lying, it does not get Holmes off the hook.

You can also deceive simply by failing to say something. After solving "A Case of Identity," Holmes does not tell his client Miss Mary Sutherland that her missing suitor was really her stepfather in disguise. His silence helps to ensure that she continues to believe falsely that he has not solved the mystery. It is what the great epistemologist Roderick Chisholm and his student Thomas Feehan call "deception by omission." As Tom Carson explains, "withholding information can constitute deception if there is a clear expectation, promise, and/or professional obligation that such information will be provided." But since he does not actually say something that he believes to be false, such a "lie of omission" is not a lie, strictly speaking.

It's a Conspiracy

As well as illustrating *how* we might be deceived, Holmes's cases can teach us something about *who* might deceive us. Sometimes criminals work alone. For instance, Dr. Roylott kills his stepdaughter, and attempts to kill his other stepdaughter, all by himself. (That is, unless you count his swamp adder as a co-conspirator.) But more often than not, a small group of people carries out a crime, and then works to keep its nefarious activities secret. For instance, as Holmes notes, "Mrs. Douglas and Barker are both in a conspiracy to conceal something." Also, Mr. Windibank tries to keep hold of his stepdaughter's money "with the connivance and assistance of his wife."

Moreover, it's quite reasonable to believe that these conspiracies are responsible for bringing about the events that have been attributed to them. But many philosophers argue that it's irrational to believe in most conspiracy theories. For instance, it's clearly crazy to think that the Freemasons were behind the assassination of JFK or that water fluoridation is part of an Illuminati plot to take over the world. It would be almost miraculous that such undetected criminal conspiracies exist, yet no concrete evidence of their secret activities has come to light. Explaining away this lack of evidence requires extreme skepticism about many of our main sources of information about the world. The police and journalists would have to be incredibly incompetent, or they themselves would have to be involved in the conspiracy.

However, in at least one notable instance, this is precisely the sort of thing that Holmes, who "was pre-eminent in intelligence" ("The Adventure of the Greek Interpreter"), believes in. He thinks that Professor Moriarty "is the organizer of half that is evil and of nearly all that is undetected in this great city. . . . He sits motionless, like a spider in the centre of its web, but that web has a thousand radiations, and he knows well every quiver of each of them. He does little himself. He only plans. But his agents are numerous and splendidly organized" ("The Final Problem"). Among other crimes, Moriarty is responsible for the death of John Douglas in *The Valley of Fear*. Also, in the television adaptation with Jeremy Brett, he is really the mastermind behind *The Red-Headed League*.

Such conspiracies theories certainly have their attractions. They imply that things do not just happen at random, that human beings are able to control the course of events. Also, from what Watson tells us, Moriarty actually *is* "some deep organizing power which forever stands in the way of the law, and throws its shield over the wrong-doer." But is it *reasonable* for Holmes to believe that this is true?

According to Watson, "it will be within the memory of the public how completely the evidence which Holmes had accumulated exposed their organization" ("The Final Problem"). However, it is interesting that we only ever hear about two meager pieces of circumstantial evidence against Moriarty. First, he owns a painting by Jean Baptiste Greuze that he could not possibly afford on his "professor's salary." Second, he writes checks on at least six different banks, which suggests to Holmes "that he wanted no gossip about his wealth. No single man should know what he had" (*The Valley of Fear*).

In fact, like most conspiracy theorists, Holmes even takes a lack of evidence to be evidence of the very existence of the conspiracy. He says to Watson, "Ay, there's the genius and the wonder of the thing! . . . The man pervades London, and no one has heard of him" ("The Final Problem"). Moreover, Holmes has trouble convincing intelligent people about the threat of Moriarty. Inspector Alec MacDonald of Scotland Yard tells him, "I won't conceal from you, Mr. Holmes, that we think in the C.I.D. that you have a wee bit of a bee in your bonnet over this professor. I made some inquiries myself about the matter. He seems to be a very respectable, learned, and talented sort of man" (*The Valley of Fear*). And even Watson wonders whether Holmes might sometimes suffer

from some huge self-deception? Was it not possible that his nimble and speculative mind had built up this wild theory upon faulty premises? I had never known him to be wrong, and yet the keenest reasoner may occasionally be deceived. He was likely, I thought, to fall into error through the over-refinement of his logic—his preference for a subtle and bizarre explanation when a plainer and more commonplace one lay ready to his hand. (*The Sign of the Four*)

This sort of deception is not the same as the *interpersonal* deception we've been discussing so far. Self-deception is usually not intentional. In fact, some philosophers argue that it is not even possible to intentionally deceive yourself.

In Holmes's defense, he does have independent reasons to think that the police and journalists are incompetent. With regard to the police, Holmes notes that Gregson and Lestrade "are the pick of a bad lot" and that being "out of their depths . . . is their normal state" (*A Study in Scarlet*). And with regard to journalists, Holmes finds it easy to mislead them whenever he needs some false information to appear in the papers as he does in "The Adventure of the Six Napoleons" and in "The Adventure of the Illustrious Client."

The press never seems to give Holmes sufficient credit for his successes. He remarks that "out of my last fifty-three cases my name has only appeared in four, and the police have had all the credit in forty-nine" ("The Adventure of the Naval Treaty"). This also may have to do with Holmes misleading them, as "nothing amused him more at the end of a successful case than to hand over the actual exposure to some orthodox official, and to listen with a mocking smile to the general chorus of misplaced congratulation" ("The Adventure of the Devil's Foot").

Detecting Deception

Holmes claims that "What one man can invent another can discover" ("The Adventure of the Dancing Men"). But exactly how do we go about detecting deception? These days, the most common technique is to use a polygraph, which monitors physiological indicators of stress, such as perspiration and increased blood pressure, that are associated with lying. The polygraph was developed after Holmes retired to the south of England to keep bees. However, the technique that Holmes actually uses turns out to be even more effective than the polygraph.

Paul Ekman is a psychologist at the University of California, San Francisco and is perhaps the greatest living expert on lying. He is also the inspiration for another fictional detective,

Cal Lightman, from the television series *Lie to Me*. Ekman has trained himself and others to observe extremely short-lived facial expressions that reveal people's emotions. And when these "microexpressions" do not fit with what a person is saying, it can be a very good indication of deceit.

In a similar vein, Holmes "claimed by a momentary expression, a twitch of a muscle or a glance of an eye, to fathom a man's inmost thoughts. Deceit, according to him, was an impossibility in the case of one trained to observation and analysis" (*A Study in Scarlet*). In "The Adventure of the Norwood Builder," Holmes observes that Oldacre's housekeeper, Mrs. Lexington, has "a sort of sulky defiance in her eyes, which only goes with guilty knowledge."

Also, in "The Resident Patient," he uses this technique to read Watson's thoughts and then gives the following explanation: "The features are given to man as the means by which he shall express his emotions, and yours are faithful servants." "Do you mean to say you read my train of thoughts from my features?" "Your features and especially your eyes." This technique is so important that Holmes and Watson had exactly the same conversation twice. However, in "The Adventure of the Cardboard Box," the conversation takes place in August 1888 rather than October 1881. But any lie detection technique can be beaten. For instance, Professor Moriarty's "soft, precise fashion of speech leaves a conviction of sincerity" ("The Final Problem").

But despite the power of this technique, Holmes does not usually discover that someone is lying to him because of what he observes in their features. Just like the rest of us, when he catches someone lying, it's typically because what she says doesn't fit with what he already knows or with what he later finds out. As Holmes puts it, "we must look for consistency. Where there is a want of it we must suspect deception" ("The Problem of Thor Bridge").

In "The Problem of Thor Bridge," Holmes figures out that someone is trying to deceive because it just does not make sense "that after carrying out so crafty a crime you would now ruin your reputation as a criminal by forgetting to fling your weapon into those adjacent reed-beds which would forever cover it, but you must needs carry it carefully home and put it in your own wardrobe, the very first place that would be searched." In a similar vein, regarding Cecil Barker's story,

> "Consider! According to the story given to us, the assassin had less than a minute after the murder had been committed to take that ring, which

was under another ring, from the dead man's finger, to replace the other ring—a thing which he would surely never have done—and to put that singular card beside his victim. I say that this was obviously impossible."

Finally, regarding John Garrideb's story, "Here is a man with an English coat frayed at the elbow and trousers bagged at the knee with a year's wear, and yet by this document and by his own account he is a provincial American lately landed in London."

Useless Facts

If we want to be able to detect deception, it's important not to clutter our minds with a lot of other unimportant stuff. As Holmes tells Watson, "there comes a time when for every addition to knowledge you forget something that you knew before. It is of the highest importance, therefore, not to have useless facts elbowing out the useful ones" (*A Study in Scarlet*).

About a hundred years later, the Princeton philosopher Gilbert Harman rediscovered this important fact about our *cognitive economy*. He said,

> there is a practical reason to avoid too much clutter in one's beliefs. There is a limit to what one can remember, a limit to the number of things one can put into long-term storage, and a limit to what one can retrieve. It is important to save room for important things and not clutter one's mind with a lot of unimportant matters.

At least in Billy Wilder's *The Private Life of Sherlock Holmes*, it seems that Holmes has trouble following his own advice. He laments that "some of us are cursed with memories like flypaper, and stuck there is a staggering amount of miscellaneous data, mostly useless."

Yet it's hard to say ahead of time which facts will turn out to be useful. In *A Study in Scarlet*, Holmes is not concerned that he does not know that "the earth travelled round the sun." However, such astronomical ignorance gets him into trouble in "The Great Game." It almost takes Holmes too long to recognize that a Vermeer is a fake because it depicts in the sky a supernova that did not appear until almost two hundred years after the painter's death. As Holmes ironically admits in *The Valley of Fear*, "All knowledge comes useful to the detective," even a "trivial fact."

Wrapping Up the Case

As we learn from Holmes, in order to avoid being deceived, we have to ask *why* someone might want to deceive us, *how* she might go about doing so, *who* she might be, and *how* we might detect the deception. Philosophers can help us to answer these questions by enumerating what the different possible answers are. And, as we have seen, the illustrious career of the world's first private "consulting detective" provides concrete examples of all these different types of deceit. In addition, studying these examples through the "powerful magnifying lens" of philosophy illuminates why Holmes was such a successful detective.

Although Watson claims in *A Study in Scarlet* that Holmes knew "next to nothing" about philosophy, he was certainly well-versed in the *epistemology of deception*. And once Holmes had retired to the south coast of England, Watson records in the preface to *His Last Bow* that "his time is divided between philosophy and agriculture."

Before most philosophers who have written about deception were even born, Holmes was well aware of the various different methods of deceiving people. Not only did he foil numerous criminals who tried to use these methods to "get away with murder," but he employed many of these methods himself. He was also ahead of his time in developing techniques for detecting deception (as with the use of "microexpressions"). And he probably would have beaten these philosophers into print on the varieties of deception if his planned "textbook, which shall focus the whole art of detection into one volume" had been published. But it must also be granted that his penchant for conspiracy theories may sometimes have led Holmes to see deception even when it was not really there.

I would like to thank Tony Doyle, Daniel Griffin, Sydney Johnson, Peter Lewis, Kay Mathiesen, and an audience at the School of Information Resources at the University of Arizona for many helpful suggestions on this chapter.

Chapter 17

Watson's a Liar!

Rory E. Kraft, Jr.

While this may be an odd place to start, I want to emphasize from the beginning that I am not one of those freaks who wanders around in a deerstalker hat, muttering things like "Elementary my dear Watson." Those poor people seem not to be able to separate fact from fiction. We find no mention of either the ridiculous hat or that silly line in the recognized John Watson memoirs (to which I add the two accounts penned by Holmes himself and the two stories we don't know who wrote.)

But like many, I dismiss the possibility that the Holmes stories were written by Sir Arthur Conan Doyle. Doyle was a failed physician and sometime spiritualist who also published works related to Atlantis and living dinosaurs in South America. It would be quite unreasonable to assume that he was able to "invent" the quite rational Holmes. Clearly Watson, in order to greater protect his own and Holmes's identities, used pseudonyms and utilized Doyle as a literary agent. It is worth noting in passing that the famous address 221B Baker Street did not exist at the times of Holmes's adventures, Baker Street then numbering only up to 100. This bit of misdirection is sufficient enough to show that just as their flat was obscured, so were Holmes and Watson's real names.

To be clear however, just because Holmes did something is not a reason to follow along. I am unlikely to take up cocaine anytime soon, even if Sherlock believed the seven percent solution was "so transcendently stimulating and clarifying to the mind" (*The Sign of the Four*).

In any event, I seem to have wandered away from my proper beginning point. Those of us who study Holmes do so for a simple reason: we seek truth. In these adventures we see not only good reasoning going on, but puzzles about the nature of reasoning, and puzzles about the nature of truth itself.

Do Not Trust Watson. Ever

A central problem in reading the Holmes stories is that we're generally being led by what literary types refer to as an untrustworthy narrator. Watson throughout the stories tells us that he has changed information in order to protect confidences. (For example, consider that we never learn in which college the "Adventure of the Three Students" occurs, because revealing this would be "injudicious and offensive.") Further, as some of the stories are recounted years after they occurred, based upon notes, and given Holmes's desire not to have more accounts published, we find that many of them can be considered "carefully guarded" and "somewhat vague in certain details" ("Adventure of the Second Stain").

No doubt some of these omissions and changes were at Holmes's request, as he believed that "Some facts should be suppressed, or, at least, a just sense of proportion should be observed in treating them" (*The Sign of the Four*).

Watson, however, assures us (in a comment to Holmes) that he "could not tamper with the truth" by leaving out the romantic elements of *A Study in Scarlet*. But it is just those romantic elements that cause us problems. Who exactly is the author of the Utah-section of the memoirs, and how did Watson come to integrate it into his work? Even if we grant that perhaps Watson shifted to a third-person narrator for these aspects he was not directly witnessing, we still have the problem of determining how he came to know these events, as Jefferson Hope died shortly after being arrested.

But even when it comes to aspects that need not be obscured, we find that Watson is less than reputable. Perhaps the most famous example of this is Watson's wandering wound. We discover in the second paragraph of *A Study in Scarlet* that Watson was wounded while fighting in Afghanistan. He "was struck on the shoulder by a Jezail bullet, which shattered the bone and grazed the subclavian artery." But later in *The Sign of the Four* we find Watson nursing his wounded leg, which "had a Jezail bullet through it some time before" and "ached wearily at every change of the weather." While it is always possible that Watson was hit through the leg, with the bullet then hitting the shoulder causing the other damage, I have yet to determine how anyone can contort himself such that a single bullet would travel in such a manner. Watson would have had to be folded in upon himself.

Nor is it likely that he would omit mentioning a larger (multi-shot) wound initially. Watson after all tells Holmes of his own pet dog, which never appears again in the stories. If something as minor as a quickly forgotten pet is mentioned at the outset, I assume that something as major as a double wound would have been acknowledged.

Even the casual reader of Holmes is likely to have heard of the struggles that some go through to properly date the various adventures. But few realize that given Watson's fast and loose way with facts, even some of the most obvious clues are suspect. For example, we have ample evidence in *A Study in Scarlet* that Holmes and Watson met in 1881. Given that the conversation between Watson and Holmes on the nature of 'deduction' (as explained in "The Book of Life") is closely followed by the appearance of Gregson's note, most assume that the Drebber-Stangerson murders occurred in March of 1882. However, the notice in the *Standard* that Watson reprints in Chapter 6 of *A Study in Scarlet* clearly puts the murder as occurring on Tuesday, March 4th. The closest Tuesday, March 4th to the 1881 meeting is 1879, prior to their meeting. The next is in 1884. But we know that the "Adventure of the Speckled Band" occurs in April of 1883.

Our choice then seems to be between Watson copying the newspaper clipping incorrectly (I assume here that the newspaper would not make such a large mistake as to misstate the day of the week of a recent crime) which allows the *A Study in Scarlet* narrative to remain as written, or to imagine that given Watson's "pledge to secrecy" in the Band case, he made it seem as if the events of *A Study in Scarlet* occurred prior to the events of "Speckled Band." The second seems plausible given that in *The Sign of the Four* Holmes does not point out the factual error of the day of the week, instead objecting to the "romantic" element as unnecessary.

If Only We Could Ask the Book. Or Holmes

Perhaps it's because it's impossible to "separate the sensational from the criminal" ("Adventure of the Cardboard Box") that Holmes's attempts to be his own chronicler come across just as adventurous as when Watson writing. After all, the stories must be written such that they "may interest the reader" ("Adventure of the Blanched Soldier"). Complain as he might, Holmes refrained from simply advancing from the data to the conclusion, preferring instead to mimic Watson's method of keeping the reasoning process hidden until the case has been solved.

"Blanched Soldier" even includes the classic Holmes trick of telling another about his background in an astounding case of observation. If Holmes truly wrote this tale, it no doubt would be far more straightforward. We do see something more like a Holmesian reticence in "Adventure of the Lion's Mane," the 'other' Holmes narrated tale. Therein Holmes admits to his own slowness in determining the cause of death, and refuses to accept the thanks of those involved. So what are we to make of "Blanched Soldier" and the third-person narrated "Mazarin Stone," "Last Bow," and the Utah chapters of *A Study in Scarlet*? None of these seem to match the methods and style of Watson and it seems unlikely that Holmes would have written them in the manner given. Perhaps they are, like Pseudo-Platonic writings, early attempts to write in the literary style of another. Early pastiche pieces, so to speak.

All of this confusion points back to a shortcoming of texts that no doubt you have already experienced in reading this volume. In many ways written texts are inferior to a person recounting an event or telling a story. Indeed, Socrates in the *Phaedrus* explains that a problem with writing is that it stands in "solemn silence" when questioned (line 275d). Thus it can be difficult to find truth through writing because the writings are not able to defend themselves against attacks, always in need of a "father's support" but remaining alone (line 275e). Similarly when we try to unravel some of these problems in the Holmes's stories, we have no proper audience to ask. The texts themselves cannot respond to our queries, and careful examination leads to more confusion. Given that our narrator is obscuring facts and shifting both times and locations, we are faced with an even more insurmountable task than Socrates had envisioned. Further, as Watson and Holmes are clearly pseudonyms, we lack even the ability to know for certain who it is that we wish to question. (If only we knew Watson's real name we might be able to track down his original notes and thus solve some of the problems.)

No Holmes-related puzzle is perhaps more needing of an honest interlocutor than the question of Watson's wives. While he clearly had at least two, some Holmes scholars have placed the number as high as six! How marvelous it would be to simply ask the texts a question and get an answer, but alas it is not to be. The best we can hope for is to attempt to use our reasoning process to discern the answer to this and other puzzles. I will therefore leave the puzzle of enumerating Watson's wives to the reader, though I will helpfully point out that Watson wife is visiting her mother in "Five Orange Pips," that Mary Morstan's mother is dead in *The Sign of the Four*, in "Blanched Soldier" Watson is with his wife, and that Holmes knew of Watson's "sad bereavement" in "Empty House." That should be enough of a start to work out the puzzle for yourself. Or at least to become puzzled.

But It Is Not Deduction!

But it is just at the process of reasoning that we begin to have problems. Throughout the corpus of Holmes adventures we are continually informed that he is doing deduction. Indeed, in the "Science of Deduction" chapter of *A Study in Scarlet*, we read a reprint of Holmes's "Book of Life" wherein he refers to "The Science of Deduction and Analysis." But of course, as demonstrated elsewhere in this tome you are now reading, Holmes is (generally) not utilizing deduction itself in his reasoning. With few exceptions, Holmes is utilizing inductive reasoning, or more precisely in most instances abductive reasoning. Induction is probabilistic reasoning wherein more information can change the strength of the conclusion. Deductive reasoning involves an argumentative structure such that in valid deductions the conclusion follows with certainty from the premises. No additional information can change the valid deduction to an invalid deduction, whereas more information can either strengthen or weaken the conclusion of an inductive argument.

This distinction is one which philosophers are more apt to make than non-philosophers, and we might be inclined to forgive Watson's use of the wrong term as his usage does conform with how physicians and scientists tend to use the term. For non-philosophers, we utilize deduction if we move toward a particular conclusion from a larger set of possibilities. Yet, Holmes's use of the term is puzzling. Certainly we read early on that Holmes had no knowledge of philosophy (*A Study in Scarlet*), or more precisely "Nil." But this flies in the face of Holmes's later spending his retirement years studying agriculture and philosophy (Preface, *His Last Bow*). Of course it's always possible that someone as interested in precision would late in life come to find solace in the theoretical purity of philosophy, so this might well be a dead end. (Or indeed, it could be the case that Watson's early list of Holmes's shortcomings was based upon Holmes's own playing a prank on his new friend and flat mate.)

Even if we grant Holmes's general ignorance of things philosophical, it would seem odd indeed for Holmes not to know the works on logic done by John Stuart Mill and C.S. Peirce. Mill's *System of Logic* was published in London in 1843—nearly forty years before Watson and Holmes meet. In Mill's amazing advancement of inductive logic he explains various approaches that have come to be known as Mill's Methods. Consider for a moment this description of the Method of Residues: "Subducting from any given phenomenon all the portions which, by virtue of preceding inductions, can be assigned to known causes, the remainder will be the effect of the antecedents which had been overlooked, or of which the effect was as yet an unknown quantity" (p. 464). Now consider this from *The Sign of the Four*: "Eliminate all other factors, and the one which remains must be the truth." Or this, "when you have eliminated the impossible, whatever remains, however improbable, must be the truth"—this appears first in The Sign of the Four, then throughout the corpus.

Surely Holmes owes a debt to Mill. Mill's writings on inductive reasoning predate Holmes's work, feature systematic analysis on reasoning and determining causes for events, and are in the same vein as Holmes's work in "Book of Life." That Holmes repeatedly uses 'deduction' for 'induction' seems to indicate either that Holmes did not have a grounding in the theory of reasoning—which seems unlikely as he publishes a monograph on the subject—or that someone (Watson? Doyle?) edited Holmes's own work to ensure that a non-philosophically astute readership would not be confused by a technical difference in terminology between philosophers and the rest of the world.

We could perhaps go so far as to wonder if the American philosopher C.S. Peirce's development of the terminology of 'abduction' to refer to those instances wherein we move from facts to theory was an attempt to smooth over this gap. Peirce's work was being published around the same time as Watson's accounts of Holmes's exploits, so Peirce might have seen his neologism as a way to address this difficulty. Peirce's abduction is one where we "start from the facts, without, at the outset having any particular theory in view, though it is motivated by the feeling that a theory is needed to explain the surprising facts" (p. 137). Slightly later, Peirce notes that "Abduction seeks a theory." It is the job of induction to test that theory. But it remains the case that we can only get certainty from a deduction. Surely with Holmes as interested in reasoning as he was, he would have been keeping current with discussions on the nature of the scientific method and logical reasoning—precisely the topics Peirce is writing on during the time period of Holmes's adventures.

All We Want Is the Truth

Holmes's own passion for discovering the truth took many forms, from the laboratory, to the streets, to reading and writing treatises in the sitting room at 221B Baker Street. This voracious search is in keeping with Plato's remark that "we all ought to be contentiously eager to know what's true and what's false about the things we are talking about" (*Gorgias*, line 505e). In light of this, we should consider again Watson's list of Holmes's knowledge gaps. Perhaps it's because he has found no need to discuss literature or astronomy that he had not sought out the truth of these subjects. But surely there would be some aspects of these disciplines which could lead a consulting detective to solve a case more quickly. Of course Watson's inclusion of not only literature but also sensational literature complicates matters. Indeed, it seems more and more likely that Watson's early accounting of Holmes's knowledge base is off. So much so that William Baring-Gould quotes Edgar Smith's statement that this list should be "headed by the specification: 1. Knowledge of Sherlock Holmes. —Nil" (Volume 1, p. 156n).

Holmes's own use of abduction reasoning largely operates through the elimination of false possibilities. This is in many respects in agreement with Aristotle's belief that "everything that is true must in every respect agree with itself" (*Prior Analytics*, line47a8). By understanding that no individual truth can be self-contradictory, we can come to understand that an understanding of the larger Truth would involve a larger investigation. This investigation is one in which, for Aristotle, "no one is able to attain the truth adequately, while on the other hand, no one fails entirely, but every one says something true about the nature of things, and while individually they contribute little or nothing to the truth, by the union of all a considerable amount is amassed" (*Metaphysics*, lines 993a30–993b4).

Here, perhaps, we can see the genius of Sherlock and Mycroft Holmes displayed. Each can determine with high probability the cause of a given aspect of the world—from the source of the soil on ones cuffs to the birthplace of a visitor—but also can bring together a vast amount of information such as to draw upon the wisdom of the masses in forming a particular conclusion. The Holmes brothers' analytic ability comes from their knack of being able to "amass" a considerable contribution to our understanding of the truth of the world.

Failing the Truth. Or the Truth in Failing

Certainly throughout the canonical stories we see many attempts by Holmes to display for Watson what it means to find the truth of a situation. Strangely for a successful physician/scientist, Watson seems to never be able to quite get the hang of the situation. I say strangely because surely Watson's diagnostic ability depends at least in part on the observation of particulars of a patient and placing them together in a meaningful fashion. Indeed, Holmes is greatly worried about Watson's ability to diagnose him at a glance in "The Dying Detective." So we should take seriously that Watson's faults in the stories are not actual faults, but instead faults included in order to throw the serious reader off of the hunt for the truth of the situation. But in all of his carefulness, Watson may have gone a bit too far. Consider the problem of dating the "Disappearance of the Lady Francis Carfax." Unlike the problems raised above in regards to dating the Drebber-Stangerson murders in *A Study in Scarlet*, here we see issues arising not out of our own assumption of facts, but from conflicting possibilities.

Consider that the story was first published in 1911, perhaps making it one of the later adventures. Indeed, Watson complains of feeling "rheumatic and old" that seems to point to it being so. But beyond this tidbit, which may be a false signal on Watson's part, we know that Holy Peters's ear was bitten off in a saloon fight in 1889. Further, we know that Watson is not currently married—he was sitting with a woman in a hansom cab, which limits the possibilities somewhat. This case is not one of those provided in "The Golden Pince-Nez" as having occurred in 1894. In 1896 and 1902 we know Watson was not living at Baker Street ("Veiled Lodger," "Blanched Soldier"). So how are we to date this story?

Baring-Gould dates it to July 1902, which we know cannot be correct as Watson was away with a wife at that time. (Though to his credit, Baring-Gould does state that this dating is rather arbitrary.) Jay Christ places the story in 1903, based upon the discovery of a case of a missing "Miss Sophie *Francis* Hickman, a lady M.D." (emphasis added). This Lady Francis disappeared in August of 1903, and Christ thus believes that he has found both the actual identity of Lady Francis Carfax and the date of the adventure. Ernest Zeisler is far more reticent, placing it as occurring in either 1895 or 1897–1901.

But again, how are we to date this story? It seems as if we both have too little information and too much. Too little in that barring Christ's discovery of a likely case we have nothing external to utilize. And unless we go the way of Baring-Gould and guess, we are apparently left with Zeisler's rather unsatisfactory multiple possibilities. We also have too much in that we have again encounterered the problems of Watson's wives and a singular reference to a date (1889) that may or may not be accurate. Watson has foiled us again.

But in our failure to see how to go forward here, we can see something very telling about the nature of truth. As long as we rely upon external data and coherence with other known facts, we will be hampered by the uncertainty of various aspects surrounding us. To use a far more contemporary example, if we struggled to date a mentioning of the "eight planets of the solar system," we could be dealing with a pre-1930 or a post-2006 statement.

The seventy-odd year reign of Pluto as a planet is something which provides us with information, but only in a circuitous fashion. And indeed, given that many reject Pluto's downgrading we might be tempted to place it in the earlier time frame. There is always the possibility that the speaker misspoke. Or that the statement was edited following the later categorical shifts. Pluto, like Holmes, can vex us in determining the truth of the situation. Surely there is a truth as to how many planets the solar system has. Yet testing a statement against that truth can quite escape us. As we find in "The Red Circle," we are in a situation wherein there is "a ragbag of singular happenings! But surely the most valuable hunting ground that ever was given to a student of the unusual."

Is It All Meaningless?

Returning again to the question of Holmes's supposed ignorance of things philosophical, it may well be that given the amount of controversy on matters metaphysical, Holmes had taken an early move toward what Rudolf Carnap would later declare, that the statements of metaphysics were "meaningless," in that metaphysical claims are not statements as they cannot be empirically observable. As seen above, much of the analysis of Holmes that we can do continues to stumble across moments where we cannot go forward. From Watson's deceptions to Doyle's amendments, to lack of information necessary in order to properly place the cases, we may be forced to find that in Holmes we can find little that is certain, observable, or meaningful. Consider also Ludwig Wittgenstein who famously quipped at the close of the *Tractatus Logio-Philosophicus* that "Whereof one cannot speak, thereof one must be silent." Holmes, perchance, was a logical empiricist before they had even come into being. But alas, we cannot be certain of that so we ought not speak.

As for the larger question of the truth of Watson's accounts, it seems prudent that we rely upon the advice of Jacques Derrida. In his consideration of truth, Derrida states that "Truth is always that which can be repeated" (p. 246). We can certainly repeat the process of Holmes's induction, and get—with a great amount of probability—the same answers. Further, our continual rereading of the Holmes canon causes us to rethink and reconsider puzzles. Thus, we cannot say that any given number of Watson's wives is true, nor any complete chronology, or even partial dating. But we can say with certainty that Holmes did not wear that fool hat. That is true. We can repeat it. Those who do so should stop falsely imitating the master detective and reasoner par excellence.

Chapter 18

Dark Rumors and Hereditary Tendencies
Sawyer J. Lahr

What Holmes does is poetic. His work as a consulting detective is an art like poetry or sculpture. He can't be confined to the category of forensic detective as we know it from television series today, *CSI* or *Law and Order*. The title never existed in the late 1800s yet our unofficial poet detective certainly pioneered the occupation in fiction.

In two recent BBC adaptations of the Holmes stories, actors Rupert Everett and Benedict Cumberbatch portray the detective as a cryptic poet trapped in the body of a consulting detective. Holmes can see the reflection of criminal artists in the evidence left by their dirty work. It takes a dark imagination to retrace a murder plot. He puts himself in the perpetrators' shoes and asks himself what he would do if he were the criminal. He goes as far as breaking and entering homes, endangering others, and donning disguises to identify with the offender in order to meet him face-to-face, but Holmes's ultimate goal is not always to put someone behind bars. His reckless nature sometimes leads to a criminal's death rather than his arrest, escape, or release.

Like his gay contemporary Oscar Wilde, Holmes lives an artist's life in the realm of ideas. His methods are better thought of as the work of a true artist and aesthete, and Plato might say that Holmes sees only the perfect forms on which all reality is based. That's why Holmes's perceptions are rarely inaccurate whereas his sidekick Dr. John Watson is a philistine who fails to the see the ingenious master plans behind the crimes he helps Holmes investigate. Sherlock Holmes is an aesthetic philosopher and scientist of beauty who can appreciate the poetic nature of things, however perfect or perverse. With his super powers of aesthetic sight, he sees the bigger picture in all the details.

Aestheticism is the science and philosophy of beauty, poetry, and fine arts. The word aesthetics comes from the Greek word *aísthēsis*, meaning perception. A true aesthete as Doyle's contemporary Walter Hamilton defines it in *The Aesthetic Movement in England* is one who can recognize true beauty and agrees upon standards that govern the perception of what is beautiful.

What makes Holmes, like Wilde, so revered is his ability to see beyond the surface and find connections, meanings, and stories told by clues and circumstances. Both Holmes and Wilde understand that things are much more than what they seem. Holmes recognizes the most beautifully crafted criminal master plans. He points out flaws and imperfections in the best crimes and never stops searching for the criminal who is a better aesthete than he. It's not surprising that Holmes never marries because he is rarely equaled. In "The Final Problem," Holmes meets his match, Professor James Moriarty, "the Napoleon of crime" who had to resign from a small university in provincial England because of "dark rumors" and "hereditary tendencies of the most diabolical kind."

And it is these hereditary tendencies that empowers these queer beings of detective fiction with such extraordinary senses for sniffing out criminals or committing their own crimes.

Holmes admits that his brother Mycroft Holmes, "one of the queerest men," has greater powers than his own. Unlike Sherlock, Mycroft lives out all of his days working and lodging in the same few blocks radius and spending leisure time in the unsociable Diogenes club where many London men "some from shyness, some from misanthropy, have no wish for the company of their fellows." Holmes calls it the "queerest club in London," and Graham Robb writes in *Strangers: Homosexual Love in the Nineteenth Century* that the word "queer" had taken on its modern sense by 1894.

The Holmes brothers' grandmother was supposedly the sister of the French painter, Horace Vernet (1789–1863)—as Holmes says to Watson, "Art in the blood is liable to take the strongest forms."

The work of every artist, including gay artists, relies on superficial details and appearances to convey the deeper messages of their work or, in Holmes's case, to solve a mystery. Holmes detects great criminal minds whose strange motives and queer natures reveal the qualities of aesthetic masterminds whose art Holmes admires and seeks to decode with every mystery he untangles.

A Wilde Guess

Holmes himself is as queer in every sense of the word as his enemies and clients: his drug habits, sexuality, and supernatural powers of deduction translate into as acute an ability to perceive the true nature of people and things as Oscar Wilde. You may be aware that Holmes was inspired by Arthur Conan Doyle's mentor Joseph Bell, but it may come as a surprise to learn that Oscar Wilde was also Doyle's inspiration for the character. The two were colleagues and great admirers of each other's writing, and Doyle took Wilde as a muse. The 2010 documentary *Searching for Sherlock* visits the Langham Hotel where, in August 1889, Wilde and Doyle met. Doyle very much looked forward to Wilde's opinion of the first Holmes novel, *A Study in Scarlet*, and a year after their meeting, Doyle's second Holmes story was published in *Lippincott's Magazine*. According to scholars Graham Robb and Melissa Hope Ditmore, that meeting led to the publication of *The Picture of Dorian Gray* in *Lippincott's Magazine* as well.

Holmes's super powers of deduction are comparable to and perhaps not so different from Wilde's poetic sense. Wilde stuck up his nose at bourgeois English society the way Holmes belittles the same people for being philistines, and both made critics eat their words. Wilde followed the nineteenth-century Aesthetic Movement of fine artists and literary figures who endeavored to cultivate, define, and aspire to standards of taste.

Holmes might seem too morbid and sociopathic to be an aesthete, but as Wilde wrote in the preface to *Dorian Gray*, "No artist has ethical sympathies." He continues, "All art is at once surface and symbol. Those who go beneath the surface do so at their peril. Those who read the symbol do so at their peril. It is the spectator, and not life, that art really mirrors." If you look closely, Holmes has an affinity with artists that can't be explained by other theories of who it was that inspired Doyle's creation: Holmes's musical talent with the Stradivarius violin, for instance, and his admiration of androgyny—Irene Adler dons a male disguise to thwart the detective's plan to return a piece of evidence incriminating the King of Bohemia in "A Scandal in Bohemia."

Always at play in the stories and adaptations of Doyle's detective is the likelihood that Holmes may be, like Oscar Wilde, gay. The physical parallels are easy to miss but almost impossible not to see. Doyle's biographer Russell Miller compares Watson's description of Holmes in *A Study in Scarlet* to Doyle's revered teacher at the University of Edinburgh Medical School, but the physical description incidentally fits Wilde: "six feet," "so excessively lean that he seemed to be considerably taller," "sharp and piercing" eyes, "thin, hawk-like nose," prominent, square chin, and ink-blotted and chemical stained hands. Wilde's hair length is considerably longer and he appears younger than early Sidney Paget illustrations of Holmes in *Strand Magazine*, but in the story of the "The Adventure of the Blue Carbuncle," Holmes assumes a position Wilde was photographed in and later immortalized as a statue lying against a boulder in Merrion Square, Dublin: they are both lying across a day bed in their housecoat.

Watson mentions another intimate detail, which implicates his own queer sensibilities while insinuating that Holmes's delicate intellectual nature is commonly associated with such flamboyant men. Watson calls attention to the frequent occasions he saw Holmes "manipulating his fragile philosophical instruments." It sounds as if his hands were an extension of his aesthetic super-sight, instruments of a philosopher, more than just a detective's dirty fingers.

Sherlock Holmes is a fusion of the two influences in Doyle's life with a strong resemblance to both Bell and Wilde. Doyle's imbuing Holmes with keen aesthetic sense and artistic nature combined with a voracity for science and reason produced one of the most enduring and significant early private eyes.

Graham Robb suggests that the elevated awareness in Holmes is a trait similar to that identified by the first sexologists. These scientists took pleasure in studying "Homosexualität"— as least once the German word entered the wider vernacular. They behaved like detectives themselves, investigating into their clients' lives and fellow homosexuals. These sexologists, as Robb imagines, philosophized about the nature of homosexuals, "What was the secret sense that allowed these alien creatures to recognize one another at a glance and yet remain undetected? Was it innate or acquired? Could a normal person learn to identify them?" The questions are the same as to what gives Holmes his "secret sense" to identify those who demonstrate perverse nature. Edgar Allan Poe's earlier detective Dupin could see through "windows" into the hearts of men, a quality the narrator of "The Murder in the Rue Morgue," Dupin's dandy friend D., chalked up to a "diseased, intelligence" not unlike Professor Moriarty's diabolical hereditary tendencies.

The Aesthete and the Philistine

Watson's philistine nature makes him curious and practical but not especially clever or insightful. While Holmes tries to minimize his aesthetic sight as "elementary," Watson fails to see what, for Holmes, is self-evident. On a leisurely afternoon in *A Study in Scarlet*, a bored Watson leafs through a magazine article entitled "The Book of Life" by none other than Mr. Sherlock Holmes.

Watson recalls the gist of the passage:

> It attempted to show how much an observant man might learn by an accurate and systematic examination of all that came in his way. . . . The reasoning was close and intense, but the deductions appeared to me to be far-fetched and exaggerated.

The writer claimed by a momentary expression, a twitch of a muscle or a glance of an eye, to fathom a man's inmost thoughts.

When he comes to the infamous Holmes's remark "From a drop of water, a logician could infer the possibility of an Atlantic or a Niagara without having seen or heard of one or the other," Watson cries out "What ineffable twaddle!" Without the slightest grain of an aesthetic sense, Watson simply rejects Holmes's preposterous "rules of deduction" theories altogether. When Holmes reveals that he is the author, Watson is taken by surprise. He learns to trust Holmes's "intuition" as the detective calls it in later stories, but this first serious conversation between the new roommates that sets up the dynamic of their relationship for the entire saga.

As Wilde did during his famous libel trial against the Marquis of Queensberry, father of the author's lover, Lord Alfred Douglas, Holmes sticks up his nose at bourgeois English society and makes his skeptics eat his words. But unlike Wilde, Holmes was never imprisoned for "unnatural habits, tastes and practices" (otherwise known as sodomy). He rarely curtails his criticism of even the most prominent clients such as the King of Bohemia. Holmes throws around blatantly ugly remarks about his contemporaries, clients, and women, caring little if he offends anyone's philistine nature.

His relationship with Watson is peculiar not only because of the homosexual tensions but because Watson's philistine nature and Holmes's aesthetic sense are always at odds. The pair we know and love are polar opposites who debate like philosophers but deeply admire one another. Watson sees Holmes's cigar experiments as the work of a mysterious scientific genius, but, for Holmes, the cigar ash could be the clue to the character of the cigar smoker.

Finding the whereabouts of a criminal's identity is easily exposed by Holmes's aesthetic sight but it isn't enough to prove his conviction to the philistines who surround him. He must prove to the police, to the client, or to Watson, using hard evidence or eyewitnesses. Almost every story and adaptation leads us to the conclusion of a mystery, but Holmes always arrives there first in his mind, before Watson or we philistine readers figure it out for ourselves.

That Far-Away Look

In BBC's *The Case of the Silk Stocking*, openly gay Rupert Everett, as Holmes, shows up at the London morgue having heard through the grape vine of a recent murder possibly in connection with an aristocratic missing person, Lady Alice, daughter of the Duchess of Narborough. Holmes puts his aesthetic sense to work by noticing that the clothes the victim is dressed in were not her own, and, in fact, belong to a first undiscovered victim. He presses his fingers along the young girl's dead hands as an acupuncturist would check your vital organ functioning. His observations are mostly about Lady Alice's beauty and her well-groomed hands and feet, which later leads him to the conclusion that the killer seeks only flawless and untainted feet to fondle. Though Holmes doesn't blurt out this conclusion early on, the camera reveals the clues. The camera pans past worn dead women's feet before stopping at Lady Alice's body whose feet are well pedicured.

To gather more from the scene of Lady Alice's kidnapping, Holmes requests to see her bedroom. He enters with inspector Lestrade behind, and snaps into what Watson describes as that "vacant expression in his eyes" during his cocaine drug trips. A musical refrain starts playing that we only hear when Holmes is in this trance, hot on the trail of a criminal. We get a private showing of his aesthetic sight as the camera closes in on Holmes's face and our perspective switches to first person. He swiftly scans the room with his eyes and settles on the windowsill. Holmes mounts a bench and slides open the window. He climbs out and within seconds finds evidence that the young girl was seduced: a coat borrowed from the Dutchess, alcohol bottles, and smoked cigars. Holmes deduces that one cigar was put out by a lady's shoe and the other was left to burn out by a man.

Another victim is found shortly after Holmes finishes interrogating everyone in the Dutchess's mansion. Lady Georgina, daughter of Sir Massingham, is snatched from her bed in the middle of the night. In another showy demonstration of Holmes's aesthetic sight, he asks for a moment alone in the room. The return of the musical score from the first crime scene indicates Holmes's aesthetic sight is engaged. He hones in on the crumbs of clues left behind by the criminal: plaster from a ceiling tile, removed to enter Georgina's room unseen, the smell of chloroform sticks to the air, the same chemical used to sedate Lady Alice.

The climactic scene in which Holmes has tracked the serial killer to his lair is highly explicit and unsteadily straddles the line between suggesting that either Holmes's sexuality or his drug addiction help him identify with this criminal. Holmes tries luring the killer away from Roberta, the kidnapped fourth victim who is still alive. He admits his own cocaine addiction and relates it to the killer's fetish for feet and shoes. The atmosphere becomes very eerie when Holmes identifies himself with the criminal, yet this quality makes him a brilliant detective, like Dupin, who could see into the hearts of men.

The creators of *Sherlock*—starring Benedict Cumberbatch and Martin Freeman—imagine Holmes's aesthetic sight much like the Everett version. Upon Holmes's arrival at a crime scene, the point-of-view switches to first person. Our perspective joins with his, and we experience a taste of his heightened perception. His field of vision becomes narrower, more acute. We see some logic come into play visually in Sherlock, represented by numbers, algorithms, and words crisscrossing the screen, but Holmes's instinct to connect the dots to the killer make him invaluable to Scotland Yard.

After the fifth suspected suicide in "A Study in Pink," the first episode, Inspector Lestrade finally invites Holmes to lend his expertise. Holmes blusters through the police officers monitoring the perimeter of an abandon building with Watson hobbling in tow. Refusing to wear any protective gear except for a pair of latex gloves, he enters the top-floor bedroom of the skeletal house and gets to work. Lestrade and Watson stand aside silently while the camera closes in on Holmes's inquisitive face and the score signals he has entered the same trance-like state Everett displayed in *Silk Stocking*. Extreme close-ups force our perspective into Holmes's point of view as he deciphers a word the victim scratched on the floor, "Rache . . ." We close in on Holmes's hands feeling the wetness under her coat collar, examining her dry umbrella, polished earrings, necklace, and unpolished wedding ring. For each item, text descriptions and analyses blink onto the screen as if accessing a computer database in Holmes's mind.

When he comes out of the trance, Holmes concludes that the woman was unhappily married ten years, packed a small suitcase which is missing from the scene, and removed her wedding ring many times during affairs revealed by the polish on the inside but not the outside. All Watson can say is "Fantastic!" and "That's incredible!" We get the idea that Holmes is interested in keeping Watson, his new roommate, primarily as an admirer and not yet a protégé.

Watson does make some keen superficial observations of Holmes's investigative behavior in *A Study in Scarlet* that visually match with how

Holmes's methods are so faithfully portrayed in the two BBC adaptations mentioned here: "As he spoke, his nimble fingers were flying here, there, and everywhere, feeling, pressing, unbuttoning, examining, while his eyes wore the same far-away expression which I have already remarked upon. So swiftly was the examination made, that one would hardly have guessed the minuteness with which it was conducted."

Holmes makes another flashy demonstration of his aesthetic sight in the second *Sherlock* episode, "The Blind Banker." Watson tags along with Holmes to the Shad Sanderson investment bank where an anonymous, as of yet, indecipherable message was left in yellow spray paint across an antique framed portrait of the bank's former chairman. Holmes takes a few minutes to stand in every vantage point in the office, searching for the first person to have seen the painted message. He finally settles on the office of Edward Van Coon whom Holmes tracks down at his condo where the man is found shot. A young Detective Inspector Dimmock who now works with Lestrade shows up at the scene and immediately judges that it's a suicide. Holmes scoffs at his weak opinion and explains, "It's one possible explanation of some of the facts. You've got a solution that you like, but you're choosing to ignore anything you see that doesn't comply with it. The wound's on the right side of his [Coon's] skull. Van Coon was left handed." As usual, Holmes's observations are at first written off as insincere and absurd, but they inevitably lead to a Chinese murderess seeking a precious nine-million-pound hairpin Van Coon bought for his secretary.

While Holmes does offer an explanation linking facts, he fails to reveal how he concludes a case before gathering evidence. His penetrating aesthetic sight is enhanced by the details of a case, but the facts, testimonies, and clues do not produce answers on their own. Holmes applies his keen aesthetic sense to the case and draws out the true nature or motive behind a crime. He is both aware and clueless of his own ability.

He claims in "The Final Problem," "Of late I have been tempted to look into the problems furnished by nature rather than those more superficial ones for which our artificial state of society is responsible." This is all preposterous because Holmes is driven by the rare brilliance of his enemies and competitors, Dr. Moriarty, Inspector Lestrade, Mycroft, and the many criminals Holmes takes pleasure in analyzing.

The detective is not in the business of jailing or prosecuting criminals as in *The Hound of Baskervilles* or "The Speckled Band." Holmes's true payoff is a poetic one.

Chapter 19

A Touch of the Dramatic

Tamás Demeter

Is Sherlock Holmes a cold-blooded scientist, a human computer, a dessicated calculating machine? Or is he an artist, a visionary, a dreamer of strange romances?

Holmes keeps telling Watson, and telling us, that he's a scientist. And Holmes believes that being a scientist involves looking at the facts without prejudice, and then making deductions from those observed facts.

You would think from all this that if you accurately observe the facts, and are good at logical reasoning, you would be able to solve crimes like Holmes. But we know that there's more to it than that.

Holmes often insists that his own peculiar talents are cold, austere, logical, scientific, and unemotional. He prizes "that severe reasoning from cause to effect which is really the only notable feature" of any case. According to Holmes, "whatever is emotional is opposed to that true cold reason which I place above all things." He declares that "The emotional qualities are antagonistic to clear reasoning." Watson think s of him as "the most perfect reasoning and observing machine that the world has seen" Holmes often seems to imply that the solution of a case follows logically from the evidence. "I never guess. It is a shocking habit, destructive to the logical faculty." And yet, we know that Holmes often entertains one theory of a case, only to discard it later, in favor of a better theory.

Holmes's own description of what he does when solving cases is a somewhat misleading account of what he actually does. His description leaves out the crucial role of intuition, imagination, inspired guesswork, or artistic flair.

Between gathering the facts and solving the crime, Sherlock Holmes is a creator of stories: his stories are explanations of what might have happened, imaginative constructions of possible scenarios. Once the stories have been composed, they can then be compared with the observed facts of the case. These facts support or contradict the stories in different ways. It is here that Holmes uses his reasoning powers to pick the true story from among several alternative stories.

Creating Stories

However cold-blooded and methodical Holmes's technique of selecting a true explanation may seem, he first has to invent these stories—which we may also call scientific hypotheses. This crucial phase of inventing hypotheses is not a matter of observation and deduction. It requires something like artistic imagination.

Holmes's hypotheses are in fact different narratives each establishing possible connections among the various facts he has collected. These connections bestow significance upon the facts, and thereby they turn them into evidence: the way in which facts are interconnected within a particular narrative structure reveals their possible implications and relevance in various, and sometimes conflicting, ways.

Having arrived at possible hypotheses with different distribution of significance among various facts, selecting the true narrative can be deductive. Yet organizing facts into narrative patterns requires a set of values and sensitivities that go far beyond observation and deduction. In fact, Holmes's method requires an immense strength of *narrative imagination*, a quality he finds conspicuously missing in inspectors Lestrade and Gregory.

There are several passages in various stories in which Sherlock Holmes himself or other figures like Dr. Watson or Lestrade comment on the methods Holmes follows in his investigations. In these passages this method is described as purely deductive. However, as Peter Lipton has pointed out, it is not deductive in the strictly logical sense. According to logic, deduction means that the conclusion must be true if the premises are true. But typically in Holmes's 'deductions', Holmes's solution to the case is not logically guaranteed to be correct if the premises (the items are evidence) are correct.

Furthermore, collecting facts is at least as crucial a pillar of Holmes's method as drawing conclusions from them. Facts are collected by minute observations and an analysis of experience. Collecting peculiar and unusual facts is the key to solving the cases, because singular events can be explored through their singular features that distinguish them from more routine events.

As Holmes points out, "The most commonplace crime is often the most mysterious, because it presents no new or special features from which deductions may be drawn" (*A Study in Scarlet*).

Holmes emphasizes in "The Science of Deduction" (*The Sign of the Four*) that deduction and observation are two distinct phases of investigation. Working out the possible implications of facts collected leads to a pool of possible explanatory hypotheses.

The phase of creating hypotheses is not strictly deductive; given the total evidence Holmes collects in support of his hypotheses, the hypotheses may easily prove to be false—and sometimes indeed they do turn out to be false. But the process of selecting the true hypothesis from the pool of possible hypotheses can be made out to be deductive. As Holmes puts it: "when you have eliminated the impossible, whatever remains, *however improbable*, must be the truth" (*The Sign of the Four*; this statement appears again nearly verbatim in "The Blanched Soldier").

Holmes frequently applies this eliminative strategy not only in the final reconstruction of a case, but sometimes also while taking steps in the course of investigation, while deciding which hypothesis to accept for the moment as working hypothesis. If seen from this angle, Holmes is almost naturally represented as a "scientific detective"; even if his body of knowledge, consisting almost exclusively of information or collected evidence relevant for criminal investigation, is "without a scientific system" ("The Lion's Mane").

Closer to Art than Science?

This intermediate phase of Holmes's method, namely the one that lies in between collecting facts and selecting the true hypothesis, is the construction of the pool of hypotheses from which selection can proceed deductively. This consists in working out the implications and establishing connections among various pieces of possible evidence—the phase of finding out how things might have been.

You might think that this part of Holmes's method is closer to art than science: it requires more of an artistic imagination than the ability to make accurate deductions. It's a form of narrative explanation, and understanding this feature in Holmes's method allows the image of a "scientific detective" to be unmasked as the ideology of Holmesian inquiry which serves the purposes of advancing Holmes's profession.

In fact this creative use of the imagination is always vital to science. The description of science as purely logical is a huge blunder, a blunder that people were sometimes prone to make in the Victorian era. All the greatest scientific advances—those of Copernicus, Newton, Darwin, or Pasteur—involve vast leaps of the imagination. No logical method has ever been found for generating good hypotheses. This aspect of science was most famously captured by Albert Einstein, when he said: "I am enough of an artist to draw freely upon my imagination. Imagination is more important than knowledge."

Are Bizarre Explanations Better?

As Watson notes explicitly, Holmes had "a preference for a subtle and bizarre explanation when a plainer and more commonplace one lay ready to his hand." This is not always a virtue when searching for the truth, and thus it's hardly surprising that even Watson notes that some of Holmes's inferences are erroneous precisely because of this preference. Normally, simplicity is one of the main reasons for giving preference to one hypothesis over another, and if Holmes were in the business of inferring to the best explanation, this would be a value to keep an eye on. *Search for the most simple explanation!* should be one of his main heuristic rules. But in fact, for Holmes, it isn't.

Holmes has rules for discovering facts, and these rules help us to distinguish Holmes's method from that of professional detectives in Doyle's stories. An important methodological rule can be distilled from Holmes's warning that "There is nothing more deceptive than an obvious fact" ("The Boscombe Valley Mystery").

As we know from Watson's chronicles, Holmes's colleagues are inclined to rely on items of evidence according to their manifest weight, and therefore they are also inclined to ignore, or not even notice, facts which look insignificant. Holmes consciously avoids such prejudice concerning possible pieces of evidence. The unconscious preference for the obvious naturally leads Holmes's colleagues to overlook relevant or potentially relevant facts, and this inclination often leads to going astray in the course of investigation. Even Holmes sometimes makes this mistake, as early in "Silver Blaze" for example.

This rule can be generalized from the phase of fact-collecting to the entire process of investigation: "I make a point of never having any prejudices, and of following docilely wherever fact may lead me" ("The Reigate Puzzle"). While it seems that his professional colleagues are more inclined to cling to the first theory they have thought of, Holmes takes pain to collect facts as impartially and as completely as possible, and to speculate only after that. The inclination to build theories on conclusions hastily drawn diverts the proper course of investigation by making facts subservient to theories. As one of Holmes's central methodological rules has it: "It is a capital mistake to theorize before one has data. Insensibly one begins to twist facts to suit theories, instead of theories to suit facts" ("A Scandal in Bohemia").

Fact collecting may be distorted by trying to make the facts fit a prior theory, yet we can't avoid setting up hypotheses at some stage of the investigation. Our hypotheses may then lead us astray, as in "The Man with the Twisted Lip," but this danger is less threatening if hypotheses do not grow into prejudices and always remain liable to revision in the light of some new fact or by the recombination of already acquired ones.

Connecting the Dots

Holmes's egalitarian approach to facts, his reluctance to discriminate among them in the initial phase of fact collecting, poses the problem of weighing different items of evidence. Initially, all facts collected are equal with respect to their potential relevance to the case to be solved. But eventually some of them prove to be more significant than others: some prove to be highly relevant for the final explanation, and others are left out completely.

The weight of a piece of evidence may also change as the investigation goes ahead. So what is Holmes's method for apportioning weight to different pieces of evidence? Some obvious answers are ruled out. Preferring those pieces of evidence that lead to the simplest explanation is not an option for him, as we have seen. Relying on the most obvious facts is ruled out as well, as is organizing evidences so as to support the most plausible candidate among competing hypotheses—that would amount to twisting facts to fit theories.

Holmes's way of weighing evidences is that of finding *patterns* in the collection of facts. The core of Holmes's heuristics consists in establishing connections between various facts with an attention to their possible implications. Not every fact is turned into evidence in every pattern: different patterns may not agree on which facts count as evidences and which are mere disturbing noises. And so "when a fact appears to be opposed to a long train of deductions, it invariably proves to be capable of bearing some other interpretation" (*A Study in Scarlet*)—an interpretation which ascribes the fact some different significance or abolishes its status as evidence. And so, it is patterns that turn a fact into evidence by bestowing significance on them in a particular structure that establishes interconnections between facts and reveal their possible implications in various and sometimes conflicting ways.

Any particular pattern automatically distributes significance among facts: the weight of a piece of evidence is a consequence of its place within a pattern. This is why Holmes sometimes decides on "elucidating" hypotheses by further investigation even if there are "many grave objections" to them, as he does in "The Cardboard Box." Without doing so, it is much easier to overlook facts of potential significance, and to take obvious facts at face value. The process of elucidation results in a pool of possible hypotheses, possible patterns of facts, from among which the true one can be selected in the final phase of investigation by eliminating the impossible ones.

An Order of Significance

These patterns are organized by narrative principles. As Louis Mink has pointed out, a coherent narrative, whether historical or fictional, represents "actions and events . . . as it were in a single glance as bound together in an order of significance." The structure of events in a story enables us to understand it, by giving unity to a succession of events. The unity is not inherent in the facts, without the contribution of narrative imagination, and this unity cannot be inferred simply from a step-by-step analysis of effects and causes. Starting from an assortment of facts, unity can be created in many ways; the coherence of facts can be established in various patterns, and therefore several possible scenarios can be set up for further investigation.

The type of understanding given to us by Holmes's approach is, to use Mink's typology, *configurational* and differs from both *theoretical* and *categoreal* modes (as Mink calls them) that are characteristic to scientific and philosophical approaches respectively. In the theoretical mode, a number of instances are subsumed under, and understood as the consequences of, a generalization or law; in the categoreal mode, a number of instances are represented as belonging to the same category that gives form to experience itself. At this point it is easy to conclude that neither of these two is characteristic of Holmes's method; his preference for the bizarre and unusual excludes the possibility of theoretical comprehension, and his warnings against prejudices that distort observation excludes the categoreal approach.

It is the configurational mode of comprehension that informs Holmes's perspective; it holds together various pieces of information as elements in a single complex of concrete relationships. So understood, particular facts of a case are comprehended not under some abstract scheme of laws or categories, but they are smoothly woven together as evidences into a coherent narrative pattern.

Framing the Story

Various facts in these patterns acquire their weight as evidence due to the significance they posses in relation to the conclusion of the narrative. In this context facts can have "retrospective significance" which is accessible only if they are looked at from the teleological perspective of the narrative (Noël Carroll, *Beyond Aesthetics*, p. 127). This is the typical perspective Holmes adopts, and this explains why Holmes has a preference for seemingly irrelevant minutiae: facts that are not in themselves informative can be charged with significance by recognizing their possible implications in the light of the final outcome. They are thus "important . . . without being interesting" ("A Case of Identity"). This outlook also explains why Holmes needs an all-facts-are-equal approach in the initial stage of investigation: we can never know when a fact will turn out to be eventually relevant. This can be decided only in relation to the ending, which may be elusive in more mysterious cases.

Organizing facts into a narrative structure suits Holmes's preference for bizarre explanations. A plausible conclusion of a narrative, unlike that of an inductive inference from facts, does not need to follow with high probability; it does not need to be likely given the antecedents. And the same holds for the connection of facts within the narrative pattern.

Probability may be a good guide in some contexts, but it is also a kind of prejudice based on previous experiences. In a narrative framework, probability is not a good guide. Rather, antecedent events are expected to fill in some void, contribute some missing piece, however surprising or improbable. What matters is whether they enhance grasping the whole case together:

> "The more *outré* and grotesque an incident is the more carefully it deserves to be examined, and the very point which appears to complicate a case is, when duly considered and scientifically handled, the one which is most likely to elucidate it." (*The Hound of the Baskervilles*)

The fact that pieces of evidence are treated in a narrative framework sheds light on why Holmes is not concerned with simplicity and warns against any kind of prejudice (including some notion of probability prompted by previously observed regularities): they do not fit the logic of narrative explanation. But his preferences for subtle and bizarre constructions, as well as the search for unique features that do not fit with natural expectations, are consistent with looking at cases as if they had an inherent narrative structure.

Holmes's narratives are thus typically scenarios of how things might have been. They are constructed from facts collected in the initial stage of the investigation, and even if they are rarely put forward explicitly, they guide the second stage of fact collecting from the background.

Accepting a scenario, only if tentatively, guides the second phase of fact collecting, which may result in rejecting or strengthening the initial scenario depending on what further facts are collected and how they are related to other facts already at hand. We can see now why Watson's remarks are often helpful. His speculations, albeit typically mistaken, are useful in creating and eliminating possible, but untrue scenarios.

The Man with the Twisted Lip

The scenario before us, then, is that organizing facts into narrative patterns requires a set of values and sensitivities that are at odds with pure deduction. The resulting structure of facts and conclusions is a product of *narrative imagination*—a quality Holmes finds conspicuously missing in inspectors Lestrade and Gregory ("The Norwood Builder," "Silver Blaze")—and not of abductive reason. Abductive inference plays an important role in exploring the possible implications of facts, but not in creating scenarios of how those facts and implications may hang together. The most important work, we might say with Holmes, is done with "the scientific use of the imagination, but we have always some material basis on which to start our speculation" (*The Hound of the Baskervilles*).

Eventually, the outlines of Holmes's rules of discovery look like this: collect as many facts as you can, search for unique features, be attentive to seemingly unimportant minutiae, work out their possible implications and antecedents (this is the phase where abduction plays an important role), turn facts into evidences by organizing them into narrative scenarios whose conclusion is the mystery to be solved, collect further facts for finding and eliminating impossible scenarios and then you have the solution.

"The Man with the Twisted Lip" is an excellent illustration of this method. Neville St. Clair, a comfortably-off and respectable businessman, disappears in an opium den, and despite the fact that St. Clair's body is missing, a beggar, Hugh Boone is suspected of being his murderer. Holmes's first scenario, which he sets up after initial fact-collecting, is that Boone pushed St. Clair through an open window into the river underneath. Only St. Clair's coat, with its pockets filled with coins, remained in the room. Holmes sketches a scenario of how things might have happened:

> Suppose that this man Boone had thrust Neville St. Clair through the window, there is no human eye which could have seen the deed. What would he do then? It would of course instantly strike him that he must get rid of the tell-tale garments. He would seize the coat, then, and be in the act of throwing it out, when it would occur to him that it would swim and not sink. He has little time, for he has heard the scuffle downstairs when the wife tried to force her way up, and perhaps he has already heard from his Lascar confederate that the police are hurrying up the street. There is not an instant to be lost. He rushes to some secret hoard, where he has accumulated the fruits of his beggary, and he stuffs all the coins upon which he can lay his hands into the pockets to make sure of the coat's sinking. He throws it out, and would have done the same with the other garments had not he heard the rush of steps below, and only just had time to close the window when the police appeared.

This story is consistent with the facts, but some questions remain open, like: What was St. Clair doing in an opium den? And a question Holmes does not even bother to ask: Why did Boone kill him? Nevertheless, he sticks to this version even when he's presented with conflicting evidence: a letter most probably written by St. Clair to his wife after the time of his suspected murder. But eventually, the new fact leads Holmes to rethink the case, as "Sherlock Holmes was a man . . . who, when he had an unsolved problem upon his mind, would go for days, and even for a week, without rest, turning it over, rearranging his facts, looking at it from every point of view until he had either fathomed it or convinced himself that his data were insufficient."

As a result of rearranging the facts, Holmes realizes that St. Clair and Boone may be one and the same person. From this angle his earlier story or hypothesis is obviously misplaced. The facts are to be seen in an entirely different light, they count as different pieces of evidence supporting different conclusions. For example, the pockets filled with coins cannot count as evidence towards Boone's alleged intention of getting rid of St. Clair's coat.

So the very same fact is turned into different evidence in a different narrative. The elimination of the initial story is, in this case, due to some inconsistencies and a new scenario emerging from the imaginative recombination of available facts. The brute fact that St. Clair is missing is reinterpreted. Instead of being killed, he is in hiding. This brings along a different distribution of significance among the facts collected so that they contribute to the conclusion differently, and in this case even the conclusion is reinterpreted during the investigation.

After the initial phase of fact collecting, any further collecting and interpreting facts relies on the scenario Holmes accepts as his actual working hypothesis—until, of course, he decides such a working hypothesis needs to be reworked, and then he can look for a new item of evidence, demonstrating that that Boone and St. Clair are the same person.

An Inexact Science

Despite the key to Holmes's method being his narrative imagination—more art than science—he nevertheless takes pain to emphasize that his method is thoroughly scientific. This is his official ideology, which represents his actual practice in a distorted way.

Watson is inclined to paint Holmes's adventures in a way more colorful than Holmes would accept as appropriate. He comments on Watson's recounting of the events in *A Study in Scarlet* as follows:

> "Honestly, I cannot congratulate you upon it. Detection is, or ought to be, an exact science and should be treated in the same cold and unemotional manner. You have attempted to tinge it with romanticism, which produces

much the same effect as if you worked a love-story or an elopement into the fifth proposition of Euclid."

But while Holmes would prefer a reconstruction closer to scientific or even geometrical ideals, because that is how detection ought to be done, Watson insists that his presentation of the actual process of investigation was accurate: "But the romance was there . . . I could not tamper with the facts" (*The Sign of the Four*). Now the question is whether the public image Holmes would prefer for himself or Watson's perception is closer to truth. By now, you should not find it surprising that I side with Watson in this respect.

It seems that sometimes Holmes himself is inclined to admit that his capacities are in important respects imaginative and creative rather than deductive, and they cannot be acquired through systematic training. He even goes so far as to suggest that a hereditary gift is the basis for his unusual ability. When, in clear concert with what Holmes likes to think, Watson says: "it seems obvious that your faculty of observation and your peculiar facility for deduction are due to your own systematic training," Holmes very tellingly answers:

> "To some extent. . . . My ancestors were country squires, who appear to have led much the same life as is natural to their class. But, none the less, my turn that way is in my veins, and may have come with my grandmother, who was the sister of Vernet, the French artist. Art in the blood is liable to take the strangest forms."

And when Watson asks why he thinks his talent is hereditary, Holmes responds thus: "Because my brother Mycroft possesses it in a larger degree than I do" ("The Greek Interpreter"). This passage clearly suggests that Holmes's method is at most only partly founded in a strictly logical approach to mysterious cases.

In a similar vein, Holmes's well-known preference for taking drugs, mostly cocaine, fits fairly well with the central role of creative imagination in his approach to criminal cases. Were it only for rigorous deductions and logical connections, it would be far from obvious why he needs this stimulation: while it can enliven the imagination, it could hardly have a similarly positive effect on reliable logical capacities. Holmes is fairly clear that taking cocaine is relevant in the context of stimulating brainwork while arranging and rearranging facts, and as such, it has an effect similar to Watson's questions and objections to Holmes's scenarios.

But why is it then important for Holmes to maintain the "scientific" ideology of his practice?

On the one hand, appealing to the authority of modern science, as it was understood by Victorians, contributes to the legitimacy of his role as a consulting detective. His *persona* does not fit easily into the institutional framework of criminal investigation. Emphasizing the scientific character of his method lends him more credibility and makes his role more tolerable in a less than hospitable professional environment.

On the other hand, this ideology makes it possible for him to improve the skills and knowledge of fellow detectives. If Holmes were emphasizing his unique talents there would be no way for him to urge professional detectives, albeit in a sarcastic way, to be more careful in their investigations, more attentive to minutiae, and more systematic in reasoning. This educational aspect of Holmes's ideology has a potential for improving the existing practices of criminal investigation.

And criminal investigation is, after all, what he does.

A LITTLE
SCIENTIFIC FOR
MY TASTES

Chapter 20

Resisting the Siren Song of Rationalism
Jim John Marks

Sherlock Holmes was not the first fictional account of a modern detective. He was predated and influenced by Edgar Allan Poe's *C. Auguste Dupin* and Emile Gaboriau's *Monsieur Lecoq,* to name the best known. He was, however, the first to become a household name and to endure through several generations of fans. I believe that it is no accident that he was created, and experienced this singularly extraordinary publishing success, specifically in late nineteenth-century England.

Holmes, as detective *par excellence,* was by necessity the paragon Victorian. Holmes's complete faith in the power of the human mind, in the natural sciences, in technological progress, in hierarchical civilized society and in strict morality despite a nominal interest in matters of faith and the waning role of religion act as a nearly flawless mirror for the Victorian Era (subjects of the English Queen Victoria, who reigned from 1837 until 1901) in which he lived and worked. This is the Sherlock Holmes who, with outrageous style, taught me as a young man that critical thinking could benefit society, if properly applied.

We Meet a Man, the Epitome of His Era

Unexpectedly, for all his faith in deduction and absolute, objective facts, Holmes seems to have understood the limits of the human intellect. Let us not forget, Holmes rarely *prevented* crimes from being committed, he merely solved the mysteries of how they were accomplished and who was behind them, frequently preventing ultimate success by the criminal while many a dead body remained just as dead. On one such an occasion, at the conclusion of "The Adventure of the Cardboard Box" (published in 1892), he exclaimed, "What is the object of this circle of misery and violence and fear?" (He means life itself.) "It must have a purpose, or else our universe has no meaning and that is unthinkable. But what purpose? That is humanity's great problem to which Reason, so far, has no answer."

The very phrasing of the sentiment betrays Holmes's sharing of the fearful suspicion that had begun to creep into the collective conscience ever since Friedrich Nietzsche, the noted Modern (nineteenth-century) German philosopher, had spoken so unflinchingly about the impact that rapid secularization (removal of religion from civil society) would have on humanity's capacity to find meaning in the Cosmos. Victoria was not only the English queen, she was the head of the Church of England. In a society so explicitly intertwining Religion and Civics, how could one help but feel a certain fear when staring into the unknown of a society constructed on secular philosophies?

It is no coincidence that Nietzsche's notorious claim that "Gott ist tot" (God is dead) was published in its most complete form, in *The Gay Science*, in 1887—the same year that Holmes first made his appearance on the pages of *The Strand*. In fact, much of Modern philosophy was entirely focused on trying to reconstruct ethics, morality, justice and the social order once God, or rather Religion in general, for which God often stood in as a personification and scapegoat, was removed from the equation. Only a few decades before Nietzsche, Karl Marx had written "Religion is . . . the Opium of the People," and Charles Darwin had published *On the Origin of Species* (1859), which, through his theories about biological evolution, continued the trend of Natural Science displacing Religion as the final word of explanation.

European, and particularly Victorian English, society was fundamentally and inherently Christian in its foundations. It is easy to understand why so many of these Modern thinkers concluded that the social order would collapse entirely without the cohesive "glue" of Religion holding it together. Depending on how we choose to read the history of the first half of the twentieth century, we might conclude that it indeed *did* collapse. From Holmes's point of view in 1892, society might not be collapsing, but Reason (science, technology, reasonable discourse and information) was certainly failing to provide much comfort in the way of demonstrating either purpose or meaning to life. If one of the primary goals of philosophy is the pursuit of the knowledge necessary to construct a moral, ethical and just society, we might have to conclude that the secularization of society was not a very good idea, at least not from the philosophical point of view.

Fear at the Brink of Tomorrow, Even for a Genius

Holmes's reflection of Victorian society goes beyond the self-assured confidence we see on the surface to expose all the doubt, uncertainty and frustration which was lurking just below the surface. We can see that Holmes captures *both* the enthusiasm for progress *and* the paranoia of hurtling into the unknown which were the very fabric of late nineteenth-century Europe. Holmes's love of *avant-garde* composer-performers such as violinist Pablo Sarasate, and Watson's distaste for the same, help us see that when meaning and purpose come into question, aesthetic notions like beauty and taste begin to border on meaningless.

Holmes's use of cutting-edge pharmaceuticals such as cocaine, which he claimed cleared his mind and allowed him to think all the more clearly, contrasted with his abhorrence of the use of opium, which he always characterized as reducing people to useless dreamers—a completely individual morality, not rooted in any communally agreed upon norms, not even shared by his closest friend. His distaste for the traditional countryside which he frequently described as substantially more dangerous than London's darkest alleys, his accident-prone advances into the then dubious field of forensics, his fanatical devotion to the printed word, shows Holmes to be at the cutting edge of understanding that up-to-date, accurate, thorough information was essential for the kind of work that we are so often promised that science and technology can do.

Holmes made frequent use of the British railroad network, not only to reach the scenes of crimes, sometimes without a moment to spare, but also because their well structured time tables helped establish or refute alibis for witnesses and criminals. As the nation was tied together not only by railroad tracks but also telegraph wires, and as tariffs and taxes were reduced on the necessary supplies, the newspaper industry grew rapidly both in scale and in importance in British society. These baby steps towards what we would eventually call the Cloud Network had a seismic impact on the extent to which citizens were able to develop informed opinions about the world around them. Watson frequently complained about Holmes's refusal to ever dispose of anything printed and the controlling manner in which he insisted documents be filed and stored, and yet many a mystery was solved by the consultation of near-to-hand back editions and the ultimate success of a few crimes was prevented through details of information pulled from the evening edition, just off the presses. My own computer programming background sees this analog, proto-database as truly well ahead of its time, even simply as a conceptual technology.

These habits combine to give the stories their sense of fast-paced adventure which must have been truly breathtaking at the time they were first published. As the reality of such startlingly modern criminals as Jack the Ripper (London) and Herman Webster Mudgett (Chicago) exposed the fragility of civilized society, these fictional stories must have acted both as reflectors of reality and also as amplifiers of the sense of unease that permeated society. In 1883 (the earliest time setting for a Holmes tale, publication began in 1887), horse drawn carriages still dominated London streets and the smoke of wood, coal and tallow still dominated the skies overhead. While it's true that mechanized trains were commonplace both for mass transit and mass commercial transport, the Benz Patent Motorwagen (the first production internal combustion engine automobile) did not become available to the German public until 1888, and the Daimler Motor Company (England's first automobile production company) did not begin selling to the British until 1896.

Even the "safety" bicycle (the first style sold as usable by the mass public, including women) was a revolution in personal transportation so powerful that the consequences of the individual freedom it created, most notably for young, unmarried women, were at the very heart of one of the mysteries Holmes solved ("The Adventure of the Solitary Cyclist"). And yet, by the time *His Last Bow* is published in 1917, the First World War had ushered in not only motor vehicle travel, but motor vehicle warfare and tank warfare, not only powered air travel, but aviary warfare, not only petrochemical production, but chemical warfare. That collapse which the philosophers had predicted certainly seemed to have begun.

Humanity was literally thrilling itself to death with its capacity to harness the power of the mind to analyze data, innovate creative solutions to problems, and then to convert those solutions into mechanized slaughter. Surely this was all anathema to Holmes. Holmes loved the human capacity to deduce and reason precisely because it helped to retain law, order and civilized society. For all his Victorian bigotry (Englishmen of this era were notoriously racist, classist, and sexist by today's standards and neither Holmes nor Watson were an exception), Holmes is on the whole a humanitarian. He admired the French recognition of, and lenient sentencing for, "the crime of passion" and took as much pleasure in helping to free those wrongly accused as he did in bringing to justice the genuinely criminal. Is it any wonder that in the wake of such realizations about how distorted the pursuit of Science can become that Holmes enters quiet retirement to study something as banal and practical as bee husbandry? This is a Sherlock Holmes all too keenly aware that failing to understand the limits that The Cosmos imposes on us can have catastrophic consequences and wary of human arrogance.

And yet, roughly a hundred years after Holmes's career, long after sweeping projects in secularization such as Maoist China, Soviet Russia, and Nazi Germany bathed the first half of the twentieth century in oceans of blood, we still find ourselves in a society not yet entirely willing to admit that Reason (science, technology, reasonable discourse, and information) does not have all the answers. In fact, we see an ongoing, growing movement, which can be traced back all the way to the Age of Reason in the seventeenth century, spearheaded today by the likes of Richard Dawkins, Christopher Hitchens, and Bill Maher, advocating a Rationalist worldview. I use this term here to mean a blending of scientific Materialism (the view that only matter exists, and that all phenomena have a knowable explanation, as a boundary against the super natural or spiritual) with political positions regarding a secular society. Staunchly opposed to any even vaguely speculative approach to pursuing Truth, Rationalists are ever increasingly adamant that the longer we wait to cast aside superstitions (their assessment) like Religion in favor of Reason (science, technology, reasonable discourse and information), the longer we risk the obliteration of the human race. We have to wonder if these Rationalist thinkers have ever stopped to notice that humankind's best efforts at wiping itself off the face of the Earth, like Communism and National Socialism, have been direct products of radical secularization, not of misguided religious zeal. And so the question lingers, is Holmes the champion of Rationalism, or the harbinger of its inevitable doom?

A New Man Emerges for a New Era

In 1994, the late Jeremy Brett gave his final performance as the *definitively* Victorian Sherlock Holmes in the small screen adaptations which dominated the final decade of his life and career. In fact, the last sentences Brett ever spoke in the role are those which I quoted above from "The Adventure of the Cardboard Box."

Brett gave us a Holmes so obsessed with thinking, with reasoning, with deducing, and with The Chase that when the case was solved, his enthusiasm would get the better of him, often resulting in behavior which caused no end of embarrassment for his companion, Dr. Watson. But these eccentricities are mere symptoms of his great mind, not some kind of psychological profile.

We do not live in the Victorian Era, we live in the postmodern Era. The postmoderns were, and are, those post-World-War period philosophers who, often in direct reaction to the atrocities of those wars, voiced ideas starkly critical of the seventeenth-, eighteenth-, and nineteenth-century assertions that the human capacity for Reason could eventually drive social progress to an ideal end. They prefer to take a much more cautious view of humanity's ability to reason its way out of the mess it has made of the world.

No surprise then that in the recent Sherlock Holmes movies, Robert Downey Jr. gives us a postmodern Sherlock Holmes. A neurotic, tortured action hero who is solving crimes through adventure and violence, not deduction and Reason. He is calculating, but not deductive. He has amazingly precise timing, but not particularly precise thinking. He is emotional, often arguing and dismissive of his companion—showing far more strain on the friendship than is strictly speaking true to the original texts. Rather than Doyle's description of a physically fit, slim framed, well trained boxer, he is an anachronistic mixed martial artist and middle weight power house. Rather than being utterly disinterested in women and romance, he is a jilted and pining lover. Rather than a vocal champion of his innovations and methods, he is secretive about his work. Rather than a highly disciplined person for whom idleness bred a despair so complete that his discipline crumbled, he is a shambles of a man at all times who can barely pull himself together for long enough stretches of time to be presentable in public without causing a distasteful scene. To say that this film adaptation was a shock to the purist lovers of Holmes the Saint of Science would be an understatement in the extreme.

But, is this transformation of the Victorian Father of Forensics into a postmodern steam punk romper stomper a sign that contemporary culture is resisting the siren song of Rationalism? While it may make for arguably lower quality story telling, does it make for better philosophy? There are at least two reasonable interpretations of this film, and one of them allows us to see this film as a repudiation of the contemporary Rationalist position.

Who This New Man Is Not

Two conflicting interpretations of the film have occurred to me. The first interpretation appears to refute my claim that the film rejects Rationalism. In this interpretation of the movie, the villain, Lord Blackwood (played by Mark Strong), stands as the personification of Religion. Secretive, mystical, arcane, and ultimately evil, he uses elaborate ritual magic to spread fear as a tool to control government, and by extension the population at large, to gain power. Holmes stands as the personification of Reason; public, methodical, scientific, and ultimately good, he uses deduction and logic to prevent the success of Blackwood's schemes. The whole film becomes a neat and tidy morality tale about how Religion is patently false, irrational, a tool for duping the gullible and ultimately impotent when facing off against the power of the human mind, put to it's proper, that is to say scientific, use. However, there are serious problems with this interpretation of the film which ignores several key elements which render it an insufficient analysis.

Who This New Man Is

The second, I believe more accurate, interpretation of the movie takes these additional elements into account and reaches a very different conclusion. Lord Blackwood does not stand as the personification of Religion. He stands as the personification of Science in the hands of ambition—Technocracy. His rituals are a ruse. He does not rely on arcane magic, but chemistry, machinery, and psychology. Holmes does not stand as the personification of Reason. He stands as the personification of Science in the hands of the military—Dictatorship. The conflict between Blackwood and Holmes does not boil down to religious magic versus the logical mind, the conflict between Blackwood and Holmes boils down to who can dish out the most carefully aimed violence to eventually defeat the other through complete incapacitation—death, in fact. Holmes does not out-think Blackwood, he beats him to a pulp and then drops him off a bridge with a noose around his neck. And in the end, both Holmes and Blackwood lose to Professor Moriarty (who personifies Science in the hands of greed—Terrorism) who uses the distraction of their conflict to steal their most powerful tools. What could more perfectly encapsulate our post 9/11 cultural neuroses? But again, our question looms unanswered—Is Holmes the Victorian Scientist or the Postmodern Soldier? Can Reason save us, or will it destroy us in the end?

The New Man or the Old?

The twentieth century gave us a world in which almost all scientific and technological research is either conducted by the government (through the military or direct grant funding)—Dictatorship. What little technology is developed by the genuinely private sector remains in the hands of a select few very wealthy persons with personal ambitions—Technocracy. Sometimes these technologies, such as the nuclear material from the former USSR, get lost and ends up in the hands of criminals—Terrorism. The militarization of the Fruits of Reason have made those fruits decidedly unreasonable. It's all well and good to argue that the capacity of the human mind can ultimately save the world as a purely abstract, intellectual proposition, but the practical reality of the world around us is that the capacity of the human mind has been predominantly applied to ensuring that the poor stay poor, the powerful stay powerful, and that anyone who tries to change the rules gets reduced to a forgettable red smear—or less.

If we're honest about both the philosophy and history of the nineteenth and twentieth centuries, we must accept that while it *may be* that Religion is ultimately false, the role which Religion played within the fabric of society, shaping culture, politics and morality into some normative cohesion, may ultimately be not only crucial, but singular. The sweeping secularization experiments of the early twentieth century had a great hope that there existed some other normative, foundational principle upon which civil society could be based—Science, Social Progress, the Collective Good, Innate Superiority. A century into these experiments, our society is ever increasingly pluralistic, fragmented, contentious and violently uncivil. While we may have skirted the disasters of perpetual world war and deliberate nuclear holocaust, we remain on the brink of destruction because of climate change, terrorism, poverty and other consequences of nineteenth- and twentieth-century excesses. While it's true that we cannot produce an unassailable philosophical defense for faith or religion, ultimately those kinds of beliefs lie beyond the boundary of the reasonable mind, it's also true that Rationalism is a siren song. If we continue to insist that we can replace Religion with Science, we are eventually going to be dashed to pieces on the rocky shores from which that song is sung.

So where does this leave the boy who grew up enchanted by deductive reasoning applied with outrageous style? Can I love and enjoy Sherlock Holmes and reject the nineteenth-century philosophy and twentieth-century catastrophe with which it is inexorably intertwined? Which, then, is the "real" Sherlock Holmes: the devotee of science and technology, the last man of the Age of Reason, or the paranoid crank, begrudgingly among the first of the Postmoderns?

The answer, like the answer to so many big questions is not either/or, but is both/neither—Sherlock Holmes truly stands alone at the brink of a new age, with a foot on both sides of the divide. Perhaps this is why such a character can be as popular in the twenty-first century as he was in 1887.

Chapter 21

The Thing the Lion Left
Brian Domino

Nearly a decade after Mrs. Ronder's scheme for happiness went horribly wrong and left her disfigured, Holmes and Watson stand in her secluded apartment. After she has told them the truth of what happened that night, and that Leonardo, her one true love, recently died in a swimming accident, Watson and Holmes prepare to leave.

With his trademark perspicacity, Holmes detects that she's contemplating suicide. After a brief exchange, Holmes avers: "The example of patient suffering is in itself the most precious of all lessons to an impatient world." These words apparently stop Mrs. Ronder as two days later, a bottle of Prussic acid arrives by post for Holmes with the note, "I send you my temptation. I will follow your advice." Ostensibly, the hyper-rational Holmes (recall that in "The Adventure of the Mazarin Stone" Holmes tells his chronicler "I am a brain, Watson. The rest of me is a mere appendix.") convinces Mrs. Ronder of the truth of his quasi-Stoical life philosophy.

To interpret the story as the triumph of reason over the emotions misses what is most striking about the shortest story in the Canon. It is Mrs. Ronder but not Holmes who faces the challenge of constructing a rational basis for hope in the shadow of the death of God. She finds that solace in that most postmodern of constructs, the text—specifically in her case those of Dr. Watson. More pointedly, the crux of this story is hope, a word that occurs only once in it.

The Soul, Uneasy

Mention "hope" to an English speaker and he or she is likely to think of the cliché, "Hope springs eternal." This is a line from Alexander Pope's "An Essay on Man." The entire passage reads:

Hope springs eternal in the human breast:
Man never is, but always To be Blest.
The soul, uneasy and confin'd from home,
Rests and expatiates in a life to come.

Pope's poem is a rhymed version of Gottfried Wilhelm Leibniz's optimistic philosophy. Curiously, Holmes himself offers a version of it when he claims "The ways of fate are indeed hard to understand. If there is not some compensation hereafter, then the world is a cruel jest."

Leibniz hesitates less than Holmes, and wants to assert that the world is not a cruel jest. At the heart of his argument, Leibniz makes two claims about hope, both of which are encapsulated in Pope's poem. The first is a psychological claim that hope is necessary, if not for survival, then for human happiness. The second seems to also be a psychological one, but both Leibniz and Pope would understand it as a theological or metaphysical claim, namely, that hope requires the existence of a God who interacts in the world to bring about justice.

Leibniz charged his predecessor Descartes with failing to appreciate the first claim, due largely to his nearly wholesale adoption of Stoic and Epicurean ethics. The second claim is also lodged against Descartes, but Leibniz recognizes that since he subscribes to deism, Descartes is being consistent in rejecting hope as a rational possibility.

Possession of the Gods

When Holmes realizes that Mrs. Ronder intends to kill herself, he warns her: "Your life is not your own. Keep your hands off it." The claim that we are mistaken if we believe our lives are among our possessions to do with as we please, including terminating them, is at least as old as Plato. In his *Phaedo*, Plato has Socrates identify humans as possessions of the gods. He argues that just as we would be "angry if one of [our] possessions killed itself when [we] had not given any sign that [we] wished it to die," the gods will be angry with us for ending our lives when they did not want us to do so. Holmes is not the only fan of this dialogue, as Leibniz recommends it as holding views parallel to his own (pp. 241f, 283).

This can be a powerful argument when used on a believer who has failed to think of him- or herself as a divine possession. It is ineffective on Mrs. Ronder. In response to Holmes's claim about the rightful ownership of her life, Mrs. Ronder asks "What use is it to anyone?" The natural reading is that this is a rhetorical question since the life of a veiled hermit lacks value to others. In making this response, Mrs. Ronder ostensibly denies that a human life can have divine value. She does not retort "I don't see how God could find me useful" but keeps her answer on the human plane. Her earthly answer is consistent with both deism and atheism.

The Most Precious of All Lessons

Mrs. Ronder's implicit rejection of a god who remains active in the world after creating it means that Holmes cannot offer her hope; instead, he asserts that "The example of patient suffering is in itself the most precious of all lessons to an impatient world." Holmes's remarks and Mrs. Ronder's actions fit in nicely within a debate in ethics raised by Leibniz. In a letter to Molanus, Leibniz concludes that "Descartes has good reason to recommend, instead of felicity, patience without hope" (p. 242). By "patience" Leibniz means the intellectual fortitude to be unperturbed by the outcomes of fortune, over which we lack control. Stoic patience might be more accurately described as resignation, if that term is taken neutrally. Indeed, Leibniz himself uses this term elsewhere to describe the lives of many ancients who believed "there were neither providence nor an afterlife" (*New Essays*, IV.viii.9).

For Leibniz, the lack of hope stems from Descartes's conception of God. Hope requires the possibility of divine justice, or of God taking an interest in our well being. Leibniz's charge against Descartes in one sense turns on a psychological claim: "Patience without hope cannot last and scarcely consoles" (*G.W. Leibniz: Philosophical Essays*, p. 241).

Most of us believe that it is human nature to find something to hope for no matter how grim the situation. Most of us see this as among the most positive, laudable aspects of human nature. It will sound surprising, then, that the Stoics taught their followers to reject hope as ultimately harmful. For the Stoics, hope falls prey to the same problem as the other emotions, namely, that they are more indicative of an error on our part than any truth about the world. We hope for things that we believe are good, if only from our own often narrow perspectives. People who have recently ended a relationship frequently hope to be reunited with their former lovers even if, as it usually turns out, this would not be for the best.

If the world is mechanistic as Descartes thought it to be, hope amounts to saying "I would like it if it came to pass that . . . ." It is much like the situation of the gambler at the roulette wheel. She places a bet and hopes that her bet wins, but her bet is no more likely to occur than any other. Her bet is simply the outcome about which she has positive emotions. Hope can be seen as a particularly damaging emotion since it nurtures the expectation that one's hope will come to pass. It might be better to allow events to occur, and subsequently look for the good in them (Annette C. Baier, *Reflections on How We Live* p. 229).

In contrast to the Stoics and Cartesians, Leibniz connects hope with a morally perfect and omnipotent God. This gives a reasonable foundation to hope because no longer is the universe unfolding mechanistically but rather is controlled by a God who makes the morally right action occur. Of course I can be wrong about what the morally right action is. I may, for example, hope that my former lover wallows in anguish when she realizes she should not have left me, but that may not be the morally correct outcome. So to the extent that our hopes mesh with divine plan, in other words, to the extent that we are virtuous, we can rationally hope.

Alias Sherringford Hope?

Doyle originally christened Holmes as Sherringford Hope, a surname that for a variety of reasons would have been ironic.

In "The Adventure of the Second Stain" an important letter is entrusted to the Secretary for European Affairs, Trelawney Hope. Should this letter fall into the wrong hands, its contents could be used as an excuse to start a war. At night Hope puts the letter in his bedside box, surely a poor security practice. Indeed the letter is stolen from that very box. When Holmes later locates the letter and secretly returns it to the box, Hope is so happy that he unquestioningly accepts its magical reappearance. It turns out that Hope's wife, whom Watson describes as "the most lovely woman in London," had stolen the letter. She had taken the dispatch because she was being blackmailed. Holmes points out to her that had she confided to her husband about this matter, none of this needed to happen. She, however, views the situation emotionally and does not believe that a reasoned conversation would have solved the problem. In short, we have Hope described as irresponsible (who would bring such an important document home?), child-like in his acceptance of "magical" events, beautiful but irrational and entirely emotional (Mrs. Hope).

In *A Study in Scarlet* we meet another character named Hope, this time it's Jefferson Hope. In this story, Hope is a vengeful killer, who murders two men before himself dying. He suffers from an aortic aneurysm, but stays alive long enough to kill his two sworn enemies. To kill each man, he carries with him two sets of two pills, one poison and the other harmless. He offers each victim a chance to choose a pill, so that it is God who decides who shall die—thereby evincing Leibniz's claim that God and hope are connected. The first man follows Hope's demand, and chooses the poison. The other, however, refuses to play along, and Hope stabs him in the heart.

Here is what we learn about Hope in this story. Hope's true love, prevented from marrying him by these men, dies of a broken heart without Hope. God, at least a vengeful God reminiscent of the Old Testament God, sides with Hope. Hope can pierce your heart, and die happy. Nonetheless, it is important to remember that Holmes tracked down Hope and brought him to justice, thereby setting Holmes up contrary to Hope. In the end, Hope left four people dead (including himself), and did not leave an example of hope for others to follow.

Facing the Truth

"The Adventure of the Veiled Lodger" ends with Holmes believing himself to have prevented Mrs. Ronder's suicide. Holmes's explanation for her life's use should not have struck Mrs. Ronder as helpful. Until she unveils herself in front of Watson and Holmes, we're told of only two people who had seen her face, namely Mrs. Merrilow and a milkman, both of whom saw it accidentally. Unless Holmes is suggesting that Mrs. Ronder move to High Street and sit like a mannequin in a shop window, the only chance for her story to reach the world would be via Dr. Watson, a possibility to which we will return.

Whether Mrs. Ronder is an atheist or a deist is not a question about which we're likely to be able to make any progress. Whichever may be the case, Mrs. Ronder resembles a postmodern, someone living in an age characterized by Nietzsche's proclamation that "God is dead," by which he means minimally that God no longer plays a crucial role in our lives. It does not follow, however, that she accepts the theological claim, and thus must abandon all hope. Rather, hope is crucial to Mrs. Ronder.

The nagging question is, Why would Mrs. Ronder contemplate suicide now? It seems reasonable to think that her desire to commit suicide would have been most pressing shortly after the catastrophe. After all, that night began with the promise of ridding herself forever of her abusive husband and starting a new life, one rich in emotion, with her lover. The night ended with her being alone in the world and scarred in a way that ensured she would remain alone the rest of her days. She has been Mrs. Merrilow's lodger for seven years, so at least that much time has passed since the fateful night when her lover failed to protect her, and it became necessary to veil her once beautiful face. Presumably the desire to commit suicide would gradually wane, and so it is curious that she would consider killing herself now.

The most direct reasoning is as follows. The idea of confessing what happened that night appeals to Mrs. Ronder. She would like to do it before she dies, she tells Mrs. Merrilow. The reason she has not talked to anyone about the events so far is that her lover, who would've been implicated by her confession, remained alive. His recent death frees Mrs. Ronder to tell her life story. Having told Holmes and Watson what really happened, she was then free to kill herself, something that Holmes sensed.

This story line is complicated by Mrs. Ronder's selectivity in choosing her confessor. Mrs. Merrilow initially proposes that Mrs. Ronder talk either with a member of the clergy or with the police. Mrs. Ronder's objection to the police is interesting in that she does not object to them per se, nor does she mention that she would not want to be incarcerated. While she tells Holmes that she has not long to live, which presumably mitigates the threat of incarceration, the problem lies with the public. She does not want a scandal and publicity, as these would interfere with her wish to die peacefully. While ostensibly a good reason at the time—at this point in the story the reader assumes she has a terminal disease—we later learn that her death is imminent only because she plans to make it so.

While her dismissal of the suggestion to talk with the police is understandable, her reasoning about the clergy is not particularly cogent. She rejects Mrs. Merrilow's suggestion that she speak with a clergyman because "the clergy can't change what is past." While of course true, it isn't uniquely true of the clergy. No one can change the past, not even Sherlock Holmes. Her stated reason for selecting Holmes is that he is a "man of judgment," something that also seems true of the alternatives Mrs. Merrilow proposed, namely a clergyman or the police. While she might mean understanding, independent judgment, Holmes's response of "I do not promise you that when you have spoken I may not myself think it my duty to refer the case to the police" diminishes the difference between himself and the police.

Time Enough to Drink the Poison

Though we may not be able to say which with any certainty, Mrs. Ronder is an atheist or at least a deist. Not only is she far more concerned with earthly justice than divine justice but she also intends to kill herself, thereby violating a central precept of western religions. She has a strikingly postmodern conception of the clergy as impotent while the crowd wields the true power. So we're left facing the question, what reason would a suicidal atheist have to confess? Perhaps to assuage her conscience but then she might as well have told a clergyman since they traditionally keep confessions private. Or why not the more convenient answer of Mrs. Merrilow? Even if she were to report Mrs. Ronder to the police—something unlikely given her need for Mrs. Ronder's rent checks—there would be enough time to drink the poison first. Having no children or any family, it is difficult to think that any subsequent scandal would bother her.

Leonardo's death does not free her to do what she has wanted to do for nearly a decade. Rather, his death is precisely why she is now suicidal. What kept Mrs. Ronder going for the past seven or more years is the hope that perhaps she and Leonardo might be together again. In relating her story to Holmes, she confides that "at last our intimacy turned to love—deep, deep, passionate love, such love as I had dreamed of but never hoped to feel." This is the single use of "hope" in the entire story, which is fitting since its topic is suicide. Thinking about the chance of a post-mauling relationship, she contrasts Leonardo's love (as she imagines it) for her with hers for him: "He might as soon have loved one of the freaks whom we carried round the country as the thing which the lion had left. But a woman's love is not so easily set aside." She goes on to tell Holmes that Leonardo died the previous month. It is only a few quick comments after that that Holmes suspects that she is contemplating suicide.

Mrs. Ronder was kept alive by the hope that she might one day be with her lover Leonardo again. She had nothing else to hope for and so when he died, so did her reason to continue living. Her situation lends credence to both philosophical positions we have explored. The Stoics and the Cartesians would note that she had patience without hope she would not be devastated by Leonardo's death. And Leibniz would point out that without the proper conception of God her hope had no real foundation, it was as frail as human mortality.

It seems unlikely that she either relinquished hope or changed her mind about God. Rather, she found a new hope, one founded on Dr. Watson. Should he recount her case, she would indeed be able to set an example of patience in an impatient world. The clue to this is her desire for a confessor who can change the past.

While no clergyman or policeman or even Sherlock Holmes himself can change the past, a writer can. Indeed, Watson tells us at the very beginning of "The Adventure of the Veiled Lodger" that "I have made a slight change of name and place, but otherwise the facts are as stated," thus signaling the true nature of Mrs. Ronder's turnabout.

Chapter 22

Where the Most Logical Mind May Be at Fault

Miriam Franchella

"I should never marry myself, lest I bias my judgement." Strange statement, Mr. Holmes, strange statement. Is it a question of misogyny? Or a playboy's excuse for avoiding stable relationships? Evidently not, in Holmes's case.

But someone who talks like this is not isolated or outdated. The belief that emotion is at war with logic is still prevalent, and this raises a whole series of philosophical questions, beginning with: 'Do emotions interfere with the capacity for logical reasoning? And if so, how much?'

Dreaming of Difference

Andrea Nye has challenged the opposition of logic and emotion. Nye describes two approaches to the world, the "masculine" and the "feminine" approach. The masculine approach considers only the formal aspects and seeks to avoid emotions. The feminine approach considers the emotional aspects. According to Nye, logic has always been a property of men, and used by them to exert power. The masculine approach steers clear of emotions so as to avoid questioning the organization of society, while the feminine approach dreams of different social structures.

Holmes seems to be a genius because of his deductive capability, and he likes to give this impression, although he also often says that he has normal faculties, common to everyone. If we credit such capability only to a few men or women, we risk what Andrea Nye warns against: logic can be used as a super-power in order to oppress other people (for instance by opposing rational western-people to brutish savages). Holmes himself does not do that, but this can be the ultimate conclusion of a chain of reasoning beginning with labeling him a "genius," hence superior to other people.

Some shadows begin to appear when Doyle speaks of Tonga the cannibal in *The Sign of the Four*. Tonga is described as like an animal, governed by pure aggressive instincts:

> Holmes had already drawn his revolver, and I whipped out mine at the sight of this savage, distorted creature. . . . that face was enough to give a man a sleepless night. Never have I seen features so deeply marked with all bestiality and cruelty. His small eyes glowed and burned with a sombre light, and his thick lips were writhed back from his teeth, which grinned and chattered at us with half animal fury. . . .

> Tonga thought he had done something very clever in killing him, for when I came up by the rope I found him strutting about as proud as a peacock. Very much surprised was he when I made at him with the rope's end and cursed him for a little blood-thirsty imp. . .

This view of some humans as little more than animals was prevalent at the time, and linked with their lack of rationality or logic. At the time of the Holmes stories, exhibitions celebrating the triumph of science and rationality were popular, as were "human zoos" in which exotic peoples were depicted in their natural primitive living conditions. We have traces of this in Tonga's story. His master recalls: "We earned a living at this time by my exhibiting poor Tonga at fairs and other such places as the black cannibal."

If logic (in any of its forms) is not considered something common to all, something human (in the sense that is comprehensible by any human being in its basic forms), then this can be dangerous. But is logic really something universal?

A first hint for our reflections comes from Carlo Cellucci who maintains that our logic is the product of evolution—it's necessary for our survival—and that a kind of logic is present also in the most simple primitive unicellular beings.

> "All organisms" includes the most elementary ones, even unicellular organisms such as prokaryotes, the single cell organisms which were the first form of life on the earth in the Precambrian era. Such organisms perceive different states of the environment. The information about them is memorized in the genome and inherited, and is used by the organism to regulate its behaviour in accordance with the state of the environment. That the primary role of natural logic is to find hypotheses about the environment for the end of survival means that there is a strict connection between logic and the search of means for survival, and that, since generally all organisms seek survival, natural logic does not belong to humans only but to all organisms.

A further clue comes from Ignacio Matte Blanco, who explains that binary logic is a necessary part of life: it is necessary for distinguishing ourselves from the rest of the world, and the other beings one from another. There is a kind of "basic logic" that must operate in any human being, even if we may be unaware that it is going on. Starting from this basic logic, some types of logical argument automatically appear. Furthermore, they are useful in our social life (for choosing something or for detecting liars) wherever communication by means of words occurs.

There is a difference between being a logician as a profession and using logic in everyday reasoning. Still, it's necessary to use some logic in daily life. Aside from spirits and gods, every transaction by primitive humans satisfies the logical principles of bivalence and non-contradiction. Although logic is practiced by all people, consciousness of logical laws or rules develops culturally where some people are no longer preoccupied with finding food, where the language is very sophisticated, and where important decisions are stated after many discussions and arguments. So it is not helpful to expect a person from a "primitive" tribal background to think in terms of explicit logical rules.

Even when we reason on a problem expressed in our language, we have to comprehend it in depth first, by considering the conversational context. For instance, if Granny says to her grandson "If you practice your violin, then you can go and play with your sword," she says "If A then B," but she intends "B if and only if A." When logic is applied in everyday contexts, many of the logical steps are understood rather than explicitly announced. So we shouldn't evaluate the logic of primitive people by how well they understand formal statements. Such people are fully human and naturally employ logic, though usually without any awareness of the rules of logical argument.

The same holds for many first-world people—most of the readers of this book—who are sometimes not conscious of logic even when they use it. A conscious use of logical rules becomes more and more necessary as our society becomes more and more word-based and power is exercised through a mechanism of persuasion. So it was for "democratic" Athens, so it is for our democratic countries. A person who is not used to living in such a society may not feel the necessity of developing reflections about logical arguments, because in her society most communications are short and simple.

But this doesn't mean that we "civilized people" are superior to primitive people or that we're entitled to do what we want.

"Primitive" humans who actually exist and share the world with us cannot be put on a different stage of the evolutionary chain that the one on which we put ourselves, merely because we have more knowledge and a better capability of developing inferences. This would be an explanation like one based on the physical force: who is stronger is superior. An intellectual cudgel is in its essence not different from a material cudgel if it is used as a weapon of domination.

And we shouldn't forget that other cultures can offer something to us. The powder that is used in "The Adventure of the Devil's Foot" for letting relatives firstly enter into a state of lunacy and later die came from Africa, from primitive people. In this case, it was a poison, but it was however a new substance, that, in fact, Holmes—always interested in medicines that can let him have new mental experiences—tries and proposes Watson to try. "I told him how powerless European science would be to detect it" stated Dr. Sterndale: our interchanges with "primitives" are not one-way and cannot be confined to descriptions of our superiority.

Backwards Thinking

A further question concerns the kind of logic that Holmes uses. He himself describes it as "analysis," a procedure that starts from data—empirical data, left by victims and murders or found out by the detective—and goes on backwards: "People who, if you told them a result, would be able to evolve from their own inner consciousness what the steps were which led up to that result. This power is what I mean when I talk of reasoning backwards or analytically" (*A Study in Scarlet*). Its procedure is presented under the label "deduction" but some have remarked that it is in fact abduction. Carlo Cellucci can help us to tackle this question.

Cellucci offers a contraposition between the axiomatic (or "synthetic") method that starts from axioms and goes on by deduction and the analytic method. This is the method by which, to solve a problem, one starts from the problem, finds a hypothesis that is a sufficient condition for its solution by means of a non-deductive inference (inductive, analogical, metaphorical, metonymic, or diagrammatic), and finally checks whether the hypothesis is compatible with the existing knowledge.

If there is more than one hypothesis that can be a solution to the problem, we pick up the one which seems the "most solid." Cellucci stresses that it is a discovery method, bottom-up, where error is always possible: maybe not all possible hypotheses have been considered or the evaluation about the solidity of the hypotheses has been wrong.

In "The Adventure of the Yellow Face," Holmes believes that the anonymous person living in a cottage near his client is the first husband of his client's wife. But he later discovers that the mysterious person was instead the daughter of the client's wife and her first husband. Holmes had not even considered such a hypothesis.

Many criticisms have been raised against this method. According to philosopher and mathematician Gottfried Leibniz, this analytic method does not tell us how to come up with hypotheses, but only how to test hypotheses once we have thought of them. John Alan Robinson states that this analytic method is based on a procedure which is not rational, insofar as it requires intuition and divination.

Still, Cellucci observes, the situation is similar to that of the axiomatic method, as used in geometry. The latter defines a certain method of proof but it does not provide any indication as how to find a proof for a given proposition from given axioms. Similarly, the analytic method defines a certain notion of proof, but it does not provide any indication as how we could find hypotheses to solve a given problem.

This quest for the solution of a problem is an endless exercise and characterizes the method used by Plato. Many of his dialogues are not conclusive for this reason. In the *Republic* Plato states that the process of reasoning backwards arrives at what is no more than hypothetical. The *Republic* describes "the idea of a perfect Town, that—like every idea, according to Plato—can never be fully realized in this world. Only in the perfect City can the principle of everything be reached. Hence, in this imperfect world the search for hypotheses is a potentially infinite process" (Cellucci). And this long tradition of analysis is the method which Sherlock Holmes referred to.

We can observe that the difference between the analytic process executed inside an investigative context and within a theoretical context is that in the first case the quest has an end: when we caught the murderer (and know the reasons for the killing), we are satisfied. We do not need—for instance—to find the reasons why she had such and such feelings that led her to kill. When we establish that Mr. X had revenge reasons for a murder, it's enough. We don't ask why he could not forgive the victim's past actions. We can stop there.

According to what we have just specified, we should better express Holmes's being a genius in terms of capability of finding the right path upwards. We can agree with this opinion of Holmes's methods:

> Holmes's success at his brand of "deduction" is well described as a mastery of both a huge body of particular knowledge of things like footprints, cigar ashes, and poisons, which he uses to make relatively simple deductive inferences, and the fine art of ordering and weighing different competing explanations of a body of evidence. Holmes is also particularly good at gathering evidence by observation, as well locating and tracking the movements of criminals through the streets of London and environs (in order to produce more evidence)—skills that have little to do with deduction per se, but everything to do with providing the premises for particular Holmesian inferences. (www.wordiq.com/definition/Sherlock_Holmes)

Still, it should be stressed that mastering the paths upwards requires also mastering the paths downwards. In other words, the "right" hypothesis for a certain conclusion must be one that can be shown to lead to that conclusion. So, declaring that a hypothesis is right presupposes in any case the verification that that hypothesis leads to that conclusion, verification that consists of a deduction.

Emotional Rescue

At the same time that Andrea Nye was writing her book challenging our ways of considering logic, investigations of the psychology of reasoning looked at why we so often make errors. The role of emotions has been re-examined, and the results are that the role of emotions is at least ambivalent: sometimes emotions drive us away from the right path, but sometimes they help.

For instance, the Wason (Wason, not Watson!) test is one of the standard examples of how most people don't think logically. In the most talked-about version of this test, the experimenter places four cards on a table which have a letter or a number visible to the participant ("A", "D", "4", "7"). The participants are told that each card has a number on one side and a letter on the other side.

The problem for the subject is to choose which cards to turn over to determine whether the following rule is true or false about the four cards: "If a card has a vowel on one side, then it has an even number on the other side."

The correct answer would be "A" and "7" (and only "A" and "7"), because the only situations that do not obey the above rule

occur when a vowel on one side is accompanied by an odd number on the other side. So, the only relevant evidence is whether "A" has an even number on the other side and whether "7" has a consonant on the other side. Most people get this wrong.

However, that's not the end of the matter, because it was later found that the percentage of subjects getting this problem right goes up dramatically if it is cast in terms of a real problem from everyday life, especially one involving social obligations.

For instance the same logical principle can be presented as follows. There are four boys at summer camp, respectively aged 14 and 21, drinking beer and drinking water; the rule is "If a person is drinking beer then he must be over 18." In this case, if we put the question "Which of them should be checked out to establish if the rule is respected," then most people easily get the correct answer. It now seems obvious that the two examples to check up on are the boy aged fourteen and the boy drinking beer. Apparently the risk of being punished or deceived stimulates our capability for thinking logically. So it seems that some emotional involvement may sometimes help us to reason correctly.

BOY AGED 14	BOY AGED 21	BOY DRINKING BEER	BOY DRINKING WATER

Still, there are also reasons in favour of a strict symbolic-formal expression of reasoning. Gottlob Frege, who tried to design a new and purely logical language, understood that in everyday life, logic is all bound up with feelings and images, but that it can be helpful to identify the purely logical by stripping away these non-logical associations. According to Frege, "language does not simply express thoughts; it also imparts a certain tone or colouring to them. And this can be different even where the thought is the same." "In human beings it is natural for thinking to be intermingled with having images and feeling. Logic has the task of isolating what is logical . . . so that we should consciously distinguish the logical from what is attached to it in the way of ideas and feelings."

This Way Lies Madness

Logicomix by Apostolos Doxiadis and Christos Papandropoulos sheds some light on this desire of avoiding feelings inside logic. The authors consider the biographies of important logicians like Frege, Bertrand Russell, Ludwig Wittgenstein, and Kurt Gödel, claiming a link between logic and madness: some people devote their life to logic because they are incapable of managing their emotions. They're afraid of becoming mad, use logic as a way to live in a solid and sure world, but then their inability to manage their emotions results in the very thing they're afraid of: their madness—or that of their relatives. Russell's character says of Wittgenstein: "Like me, he constantly analyzed everything, a habit that annihilates emotions" and then the authors remark: "Russell's childhood had given him good reasons for annihilating emotions. Character, uncertainty, neurosis led him to logic" (p. 236). We're also informed that Russell's son suffered from schizophrenia, and that the same was true for Hilbert's son. The authors speculate that the fear of emotions which impels some people to study logic may make them bad parents.

Holmes has often been described as neurotic. Some diagnose Holmes as suffering from bipolar disorder. This can be inferred from the fact that he alternates between days or weeks of listless lassitude and periods of intense engagement with a challenging case or with his hobby, experimental chemistry. Some websites have instead diagnosed Holmes with Asperger syndrome, a light form of autism <http://kspot.org/holmes/autism.htm>.

Uta Frith, in her essay on "Autism: Explaining the Enigma," identifies the clues of Holmes's Asperger syndrome in Holmes's oddness, his socially detached mind, and his circumscribed but deep interests (as testified by his little monograph on the ashes of 140 different varieties of pipe, cigar and cigarette tobacco), that Frith describes as still vital ingredients "in all creations in art or science". Both the novel and film *The Seven-Percent Solution* give a psychoanalytic explanation for Holmes's behavior.

Logic can be a harbor for people escaping from emotions. In this case it represents a false harbor, since psychological problems should be faced and not simply put aside; otherwise they come back to bite us somewhere else. Strong emotions can also motivate us to concentrate better and become more logical.

Sherlock Holmes declares that he has to refrain from loving to keep his mind clear, but perhaps if he were open to love, he might even find his powers of analysis and deduction enhanced.

Chapter 23

What Mycroft Knows
that Sherlock Doesn't

Andrew Terjesen

Sherlock Holmes is the master of the science of deduction, a consulting detective with no equal. Everyone seems to think so. But is he really?

By Sherlock's own admission, his older brother is the true master at solving puzzles and problems. He tells Watson, "When I say, therefore, that Mycroft has better powers of observation than I, you may take it that I am speaking the exact and literal truth" ("The Adventure of the Greek Interpreter"). Sherlock makes it very clear that he considers Mycroft to be his superior in both observation and deduction.

We see this superiority of Mycroft on display in his first appearance. At the Diogenes Club, Mycroft and Sherlock engage in a series of deductions very reminiscent of Sherlock's skillful conclusion in *A Study in Scarlet* that Watson was recently discharged from Afghanistan. Sherlock and Mycroft engage in a series of deductions about someone who has recently served in India. In this instance, Mycroft picks up on a particular detail (that the man had more than one child) that Sherlock seems to have missed.

But what is it that makes Mycroft better than Sherlock?

Is it that Mycroft has a photographic memory that enables him to function as a living computer for the British government? Possibly. After all, Watson tells us the limits of Sherlock's knowledge, and there seems to be a lot he doesn't know about. If that were the issue though, it's unlikely that Sherlock would have called Mycroft better at observation and deduction.

Is it simply that Mycroft has had seven more years of practice than Sherlock? Again, that might be a viable explanation, but I imagine that Sherlock's pride and his dogged adherence to the facts would have caused him to mention that simple difference.

Instead, Mycroft's superior skills arise out of the one major difference between the brothers that Sherlock remarks on when he first mentions his brother to Watson: Mycroft has no interest in detective work.

Mycroft's Unique Insight

It's tempting to think that Mycroft's lack of interest is a result of laziness and not the product of some special insight into "the science of deduction." In both of the major appearances of Mycroft in the canon, Sherlock makes a point of telling Watson that his brother is lacking in ambition and energy.

Certainly the reason Mycroft gives for passing a case on to Holmes seems to back up this view. When he asks Sherlock to look into the case of stolen submarine plans, he is emphatic that he won't take care of it himself (even though it is a matter of national security). As he explains to Sherlock, "Give me your details, and from an armchair I will return you an excellent expert opinion. But to run here and run there, to cross-question railway guards, and lie on my face with a lens to my eye—it is not my métier" ("The Adventure of the Bruce-Partington Plans"). However, a lazy person would not bear the burden of running the British government (as Sherlock mentions that his brother is the government at times).

Of course, this could be a very specific form of laziness, like Sherlock's own aversion to spending time learning about philosophy or astronomy. As Sherlock points out, his brother

> will not even go out of his way to verify his own solutions, and would rather be considered wrong than take the trouble to prove himself right. Again and again I have taken a problem to him, and have received an explanation which has afterwards proved to be the correct one. ("The Greek Interpreter")

Mycroft is especially useless as a consulting detective because he will not take the time to work out the "practical points" that must be worked out before the case can be put before a jury. But it seems to me that it's quite likely that Mycroft sees no point in such endeavors because he appreciates the "Problem of Induction" in a way that his brother does not.

Lock and Key

"Induction" is the name logicians prefer to give to what Sherlock calls "The Science of Deduction." In everyday speech, we tend not to distinguish between induction and deduction and often use the terms interchangeably. Logicians think it is very important to differentiate between these two types of reasoning because each has its own problems that must be considered when evaluating an argument.

Deduction, as used by logicians, refers only to arguments that are constructed in such a way that their premises guarantee the truth of the conclusion. A classic example of a deductive argument is the process of elimination, in which one eliminates every other possibility and whatever remains (no matter how improbable) must be the truth. Holmes gives an example of this when investigating the theft of the Bruce-Partington plans as he reasons about how the suspect, Cadogan West, could have gotten the plans from the safe.

Holmes considers three possibilities: West used the clerk's keys, West used Sir James' keys or West had a copy made of one of those sets of keys. Holmes eliminates the clerk because he had only a key to the safe, he lacked the keys needed to open the building and the office. Sir James has all three keys, but they are always with Sir James who was in London at the time of the theft. The only possibility remaining is that West had a copy made and that must be what happened given the original premises of the argument. If there are only three possibilities and two are impossible then the one that is left must be what happened.

While most of Holmes' deductions end with a real bit of deductive reasoning, like this process of elimination, they almost always rely on quite a bit of inductive reasoning to establish the premises. Unlike the conclusions of a deductive argument, the conclusion of an inductive argument can only be known to be probably true. The conclusion of an inductive argument is never guaranteed to be true, even if all the premises supplied are true.

In the Bruce-Partington example, Holmes's process of elimination depends on there being only three possibilities. Holmes relies on inductive reasoning (in this case a bit of observation as to who had the keys and an inference from experience that keys can be copied) to establish these possibilities. When reasoning inductively there is always the possibility that we have missed some important bit of observation or that the experiences one is making inferences from are incomplete. In this case, Holmes had not considered the possibility that Sir James's brother Colonel Valentine had made copies of Sir James's keys so that he could steal the plans and sell them in order to pay off his debts.

This is the nature of induction, but it is not "The Problem of Induction" with a capital "P." Sherlock is very aware of the limits of reasoning from experience and observation. As he tells Watson at one point, "It is a capital mistake to theorize before one has data. Insensibly one begins to twist facts to suit theories, instead of theories to suit facts" ("A Scandal in Bohemia").

Holmes knows full well that insufficient data can lead to wrong-headed conclusions and so he usually plays things close to the chest until he has a critical mass of information. Scientists often rely on inductive reasoning in their experiments, so the scientific method strives to make sure that the sample size is sufficient and to test hypotheses. Holmes does the same thing before wrapping up a case. Although he suspected that West was not the culprit, he had to draw out the real thief and even he was surprised when it was Colonel Valentine. However, a simple awareness of the limits of probability and the possibility of missing an important clue are not the real problems of induction.

Billiard Balls that Don't Move

The philosopher David Hume is among the first to clearly identify what has become known as the Problem of Induction. In his *Enquiry Concerning Human Understanding*, Hume lays out the Problem as follows:

> When I see, for instance, a Billiard-ball moving in a straight line towards another; even suppose motion in the second ball should by accident be suggested to me, as the result of their contact or impulse; may I not conceive, that a hundred different events might as well follow from that cause? May not both these balls remain at absolute rest? May not the first ball return in a straight line, or leap off from the second in any line or direction? All these suppositions are consistent and conceivable. Why then should we give the preference to one, which is no more consistent or conceivable than the rest? All our reasonings a priori will never be able to show us any foundation for this preference. (Section IV, Part 1)

Hume's point is that when we see someone hitting one billiard ball so that it rolls straight towards another, we anticipate that the motion of the first billiard ball will be transferred to the second when they collide. After the collision, the first ball will stop and the second ball will move in the direction that the original ball was traveling. We would be astounded if the second billiard ball was not set into motion after the first had collided with it. If it did happen, we would begin to look for a logical explanation. For example, did the original billiard ball run out of momentum before getting to the second ball and only appeared to make contact? Or was it the case that the second billiard ball had been glued to the table or nailed down?

We look for intervening cause because we think that there is a fixed rule underlying our observations. The Problem of Induction is that we have no good reason for thinking that such a rule exists. If we were to ask someone watching a billiard game why they feel justified in thinking that the ball will go into a particular pocket, their answer would probably be: because that is where it has gone in the past. But we must then ask, what makes you so sure that the future will follow the same rules as the past? The answer cannot be that it will do so because it has done so in the past. That would be circular reasoning. We would be using our inductive reasoning to prove that our inductive reasoning always works. That would be like saying that someone is honest because they say they would never lie.

When Hume says that no "reasonings a priori" will show us that induction works, he is pointing out that deduction can't cut it. A priori reasoning is the reasoning we do without having to have any experience of the world. For example, I can understand 2 + 2 = 4 even if I have never seen 2 and 2 put together in the world. That is because I understand the rules of arithmetic. Those rules are such that if I am given a certain set of values then a certain result will necessarily follow. 2 and 2 do not equal 5. In order for the rules of arithmetic to be that certain, they cannot depend on any facts about the world that we need to observe before we add 2 and 2. There are no comparable rules that I am familiar with that govern billiard balls. We need to observe things like the slope of the table, the weight of the balls, and so on. Even with all that information, the geometry that many pool sharks rely upon will not predict with one hundred percent accuracy where the ball will go after it is hit.

A popular argument used in defense of induction is that we can observe regular patterns and therefore we have some sense of the underlying rules. In all my life, I have never seen a billiard ball go unmoved upon contact. The preponderance of evidence seems to go against a billiard ball remaining unmoved. The problem with that kind of argument is revealed by a variation on the thought experiment concocted by the philosopher Nelson Goodman in his book *Fact, Fiction, and Forecast*. Goodman asks us to imagine a property called "grue" which refers to an object that looks green if it is first observed before a certain date (let's say 2100) and it will look blue if it is first observed after that date. In 2012, you find an emerald that looks green. How do you know if it is green or grue? Green and grue have the same regular behavior up until a certain point. Grue may seem like an arbitrary property, but is it any different from a radioactive element turning into lead or a butterfly into a caterpillar? If you're dealing with a pattern that is so complex that we can't observe it in full, how can you differentiate between two possible explanations of that pattern? The Problem of Induction is that there is no definitive reason to prefer one explanation over the other as all the data you collect (until 2100) will support both explanations. After 2100, you'll know that when you find a green emerald it will really be green, but when you find a blue emerald you won't be able to tell if it is blue or grue.

Superficial Tricks

Conan Doyle seemed to be pretty well aware of the Problem of Induction. In a short parody he wrote entitled "How Watson Learned the Trick," Watson tried to turn the table on Holmes. Watson inducted that Holmes was preoccupied because he had not shaved that morning and that he had begun to engage in stock trading because he made a loud exclamation of interest when looking at the financial page.

It turns out that Watson is totally off the mark. Holmes hadn't shaved because he had sent his razor to be sharpened, and Holmes was showing interest in the cricket scores which are on the page beside the financial news. Holmes is bemused by Watson's failure to learn his "superficial trick," but when it comes down to it, there was nothing wrong with Watson's failed induction. His method was indistinguishable from Holmes's. The fact that his conclusion was wrong is not an indictment of his method. After all, scientists arrive at wrong conclusions all the time because induction is not guaranteed to lead you to the right conclusion. This doesn't mean scientists should abandon using induction.

One well-known attempt to defend the scientific method was proposed by the philosopher Karl Popper. Popper argued that scientists don't use induction to confirm things; instead they make hypotheses based on experience and test their predictions. If their prediction fails, then the hypothesis is thrown out. If the prediction is successful then that doesn't make the hypothesis true, it merely shows that it is still a viable option. Popper's theory is known as falsificationism because it holds that the main task for scientists is to try and falsify theories.

What Popper has done is respond to the Problem of Induction by claiming that science isn't based in induction. So, he hasn't dealt with the real Problem. In fact, the Problem of Induction haunts falsificationism because there is usually more than one way to understand a failed experiment. It could show that the hypothesis is false or it could show that our means for testing it was based on faulty assumptions. Once again, we can't easily decide between two explanations for the results we observed.

The best example of Conan Doyle's misgivings about taking the science of deduction too seriously can be found in his short story, "The Lost Special." It also illustrates the problems in deciding between explanations when the evidence is incomplete (as it must always be in a true mystery). The story is a report of a curious incident involving the disappearance of a chartered express train to London—the "special" that was "lost" between two stations and the appearance of the body of the special's driver. There was no sign of any wreckage and no point at which the train could have been diverted from the tracks, except for seven side lines leading to mines in the area. Four of those side lines had their tracks removed, which left only three possibilities, all of which were eliminated because someone would have noticed the train coming through.

The story excerpts a possible solution offered by an unnamed "amateur reasoned of some celebrity" who is thought by some to be Sherlock Holmes. At the very least, he begins his letter with his famous statement about eliminating the impossible. This amateur reasoner opines that one of the three available lines was manned by a crew that was paid by the culprits to assist in their endeavor. Nevertheless, the fate of the lost special remained unknown until the mastermind behind it confessed. One of the side lines where the tracks had been removed was prepared by laying down the missing rails so that railroad employees in the employ of the mastermind (which did not include the driver) sent the special along this abandoned side line and sent the train speeding into an abandoned mine pit. Once the rails were taken away again there was no evidence of the crime.

The case of the lost special is just another example of how far off one's inductive reasoning can be because the underlying principles are never known to us. If they were, we would simply use true deduction (like a process of elimination) to arrive at a conclusion that must be true. However, whenever we reason about events in the real world, there is always the possibility of another explanation no matter how outlandish it might seem. Had we never found out the truth, the amateur reasoner's conclusion would have been just as viable as someone who (unknowingly) gave an account of what actually happened.

The Kindly Whispered "Norbury"

In "The Adventure of the Yellow Face," Watson begins with a note that reminds us that our faith in Holmes's powers of reasoning might also be the result of a faulty induction. Watson did not usually write about Holmes's failures to solve a case, though he says there have been some. One notable exception was the case of Effie Munro, in which Watson reported Holmes's failure because he knew the actual facts. Effie was a widow from America who had remarried and had begun asking her husband for a sizeable sum of money. She had also begun to make surreptitious visits to a house down the road.

Holmes draws the tentative conclusion that Effie is not really a widow and that her first husband had come to visit her in England. The truth turns out to be far different. Effie had been married to an African-American man and had a child with him. Thinking that a biracial child would not be accepted by her new husband, she had brought the child in secret to live in the nearby cottage. The money she requested was for the child's upkeep. Holmes is chastened by the failure of his inductions and tells Watson, "If it should ever strike you that I am getting a little overconfident in my powers, or giving less pains to a case than it deserves, kindly whisper 'Norbury' in my ear and I shall be infinitely obliged to you" ("The Yellow Face").

Mycroft's deeper appreciation for the Problem of Induction keeps him from becoming as overconfident as Holmes. Knowing that there is no way to be certain our inductive inferences will be correct, he's always on the lookout for the facts that don't fit. Holmes appreciates the Problem enough to test his theories, but he dismisses the Problem after a certain point, which leads to his overconfidence. And because he becomes overconfident, he does not pay attention to the extra details that would lead him to a better solution.

Mycroft's appreciation for the Problem of Induction would also explain his disinterest in checking to see if his solutions are correct or in trying to prove his inferences to a jury. Since there is nothing that can guarantee an inductive inference, there is also no way to know when we have found proof that the inference is correct. All the evidence in the world might point to someone's guilt, but there is no way to be sure that we haven't missed something. "The Greek Interpreter" ends with just an ambiguity. The two villains flee England with the Greek Interpreter's sister. A newspaper later reports that they two men have been stabbed to death. The police conclude that they stabbed each other after an argument, but Holmes speculates that they were both killed by the sister as revenge for her brother's murder. He thinks, if he could just find the Greek girl, he could know for sure. (Of course in the Granada TV series with Jeremy Brett, the interpreter's sister is a willing accomplice, so she would not have sought revenge for her brother.)

Sherlock Holmes takes a Popperian approach to detective work as he seems to think that what he does is not really induction. Holmes develops a theory based upon the facts and then goes about testing it little by little. In "The Adventure of the Bruce-Partington Plans," he places an ad in the paper and then goes to see who shows up. Because he tests his theories before he exposes the culprit, it can make it seem as if he had the right answer all along. In some stories, he clearly changes his mind as he eliminates different suspects. Holmes's tests of his theories demonstrate impressive reasoning as he often recognizes implications and nuances that others have ignored.

But this reasoning almost always relies on knowledge of facts about human nature and the natural world to give it a starting point. At its heart, Sherlock's method is still about provisional observations. Even his ad relied on the assumption that no one else but the guilty party would show up. There would be no misunderstandings, curiosity seekers or anything else like that. Such a test would also not be very effective in ruling out someone who didn't show up. There could still be co-conspirators. Mycroft's superior intellect is not reflected in his ability to find the "right" explanation, it's in his ability to come up with other explanations that need to be considered and to see when the test of a theory might be compromised by its reliance upon induction. I'm not even sure that Mycroft has some extra special power of percipience that lets him see more alternatives. I think that truly understanding the Problem of Induction causes him to look longer and harder for other possible explanations.

Our Best Bet

Despite his appreciation for the Problem of Induction, Mycroft does not take it to extremes. It seems that Mycroft has embraced another possible response to the Problem of Induction originally proposed by the philosopher Hans Reichenbach. Reichenbach's defense of induction can be summed up as follows: as long as there is one method that enables us to predict the future, then induction will be at least as reliable as that method, if not more so. If the universe was completely chaotic, then induction would work just as well as any other method (which is not at all). If someone could predict the future through a crystal ball, then the rest of us would use induction to realize that we should start listening to the fortune teller's prediction.

Reichenbach's argument is known as a pragmatic justification because it simply argues that induction is our best bet, it doesn't try to prove that it is independently reliable. Mycroft seems to appreciate that the British government is best served when he uses induction to determine a solution to a problem. At the same time, he knows that he'll never be able to confirm that every bet was well-placed—so he doesn't bother.

Unlike Sherlock Holmes's Popperian attitude, Mycroft does not try and justify induction by pretending it is something other than what it really is: astute observation leading to an educated guess about the underlying pattern. Mycroft's wisdom is that he knows that the "Problem of Induction" is not simply about incomplete evidence. Sherlock appreciates the problem of false statements or misleading evidence and he knows that if new evidence were to come to light he would have to revise his thesis. What he fails to appreciate is that it's not clear how incomplete evidence can justify any conclusion.

Most of us are content to appeal to the most plausible explanation, but Sherlock is smart enough to avoid that pitfall. Following his famous dictum, he eliminates every other possible explanation until only one remains. But Mycroft knows that it's impossible to eliminate all but one explanation. Even if there aren't an infinite number of explanations for a particular set of clues, there seems to be an almost infinite number of ways in which once could be mistaken when concluding that a particular explanation has been "falsified." The only thing that really seems to motivate Mycroft to take a risk and act on conclusions arrived at by inductive reasoning is when the fate of England rests upon them.

If we were all more humble about our powers of "deduction," we could avoid a lot of embarrassing instances where we jumped to the wrong conclusions—especially since most of us lack the superior analytical skills of the Holmes brothers and are much more likely to run afoul of—and be frustrated by—the limits of inductive reasoning.

Music at Strange Hours

or

that Mixture of Imagination and Reality

Chapter 24

Why Sherlock Holmes Is My Favorite Drug User

Kevin Kilroy

Lazily he sits, in his wing back armchair, the heavy curtains pulled shut on Baker Street. A fire crackling in the deep chamber behind the hearth. He is in his robe and slippers, hair a mess, eyes bewildered—a far-away expression contemplating all he finds within.

On the mahogany table next to him, a vial of cocaine, precisely measured; morphine in another. With his long, white, nervous fingers he adjusts the delicate needle, rolls back his left shirtcuff.

Our existence contains more to be investigated than our senses will deliver, and Sherlock Holmes knows it. Intuition, imagination, daydreams, memories, esoteric knowledge gathered into books—he plunges the syringe into his scarred and pocked forearm. The scarlet thread absorbs the solution, rushing throughout his being.

His face and chest flush with the cocaine, he picks up his violin off the floor, neglecting the bow—to touch and pluck chaotically entices him more. Skillfully he navigates this time devoted to spontaneity and imagination.

Then to his reading. A tome of obscure criminal events which occurred in eighteenth-century Norway.

He lights a candle, skillfully administers another dose, and moves closer towards this communion of body and mind. Sherlock Holmes uses drugs with the intention to explore the intricacies of consciousness, to purposefully sculpt his collection of knowledge, and to grow more attune with the event of being.

And all this amounts to the source of his phenomenological powers. When at the scene of a crime observing intricate details and the hidden lives of objects, we trust he has access to an intelligence far more mysterious than most assume possible.

A Clue Isn't Helpful to the Case
until the Detective Notices Its Worth

Simply put, phenomenology is the study of essences. The essence of perception; the essence of consciousness. Phenomenology shares similar concerns with philosophy—reality, knowledge, being—yet it differs in that where philosophy has sought to analyze and explain these issues, phenomenology seeks to describe them.

Even before Plato, philosophers have been trying to articulate what constitutes reality. The pendulum of responses has been weighted heavily, causing swings from one side of the spectrum to the other: either the observer imposes order upon the outside world (subjectivity) or the world imposes order upon the observer (objectivity). Phenomenology, developed by Edmund Husserl in the early 1900s, was the first philosophical study to bridge the two—to say "Ah, one's experience of the murder weapon is the murder weapon itself compounded by the subject's understanding of murder weapons!" Both subjective mind and objective world work together to create a being's reality.

Add this all up and we can say that phenomenology is a branch of study which seeks to describe first-person experience through the understanding that reality is an intercourse between subject and object. Each of us experience the world in our own way, and the world imposes itself upon our experience. What this all means is that reality is an event. That subject and object are both criminal and scene of a crime. That all detectives are phenomenologists.

And there's no better demonstration of this than Sherlock Holmes in Sir Arthur Conan Doyle's novels, *A Study in Scarlet* and *The Sign of the Four.*

A detective's intentions are clear: to solve the case utilizing knowledge of crime and demonstrable logic; to make meaning out of the traces criminals leave behind. But not all detectives are created equal. A clue isn't helpful to the case until the detective experiences its intended worth. Clues can be misread and misinterpreted as much as they can be seen clearly. Phenomenological powers extend from a clear understanding of the interplay between the intentions of the detective (subject) and the intentions of the scene of a crime (object). We must transcend the assumed static quality of the objective world, and we must activate the exquisite tool of the mind. Sherlock Holmes, you fascinate me in this regard.

The Essence of Consciousness

The mystery and power of Sherlock Holmes lie in the expansiveness of his field of consciousness. No one doubts the extraordinary powers of detection and deduction Holmes commands, but there is more at work here than simply an excellent eye for detail. Sherlock Holmes represents a reality where knowledge lies in the field of consciousness—the event of an object's perception. What is there to be seen is not all that is there. We must not forget the workings of the detective's intelligence which beholds the room: an exalted sense of intuition fortified with countless hours of extensive research, experiments, and studying.

And inversely, there is more to be experienced than what is seen. Something is hiding, lurking in the object.

My intention is not to romanticize drug use, but to romanticize time spent in, what jazz musicians refer to as, the woodshed. Reading, listening, studying, practicing one's art, consistently and daily pursuing its exaltation—this is what matters when Holmes reaches the scene of a crime. The fact that Holmes uses drugs speaks more to his intense curiosity and his art of perception—he could not bear to interact with the unremarkable. He is addicted to the complex thrill of the mind intersecting with the outside world across his field of consciousness.

It is as if his study—Dr. Watson is such a sheepish roommate to let Holmes take over the apartment—is symbolic of his field of consciousness. Maps on the wall, small flames beneath beakers, pillows bundled up and loaded with bullets, candle wax deformities everywhere, books lined up neatly on the shelf and others as if tossed, yet open to excruciatingly specific passages, a home-made hand-collected skeleton, tobacco and pipe, fire roaring—add whatever else you like. Here we have the narrative manifestation of one half of our phenomenological equation—this is what Holmes brings to the table. Figuratively and literally.

In *The Sign of the Four*, Holmes lets Watson in on the three qualities of a great detective: Knowledge, Observation, and Deduction ("The Science of Deduction"). These are essential to transcendent detective work, and they mirror what phenomenology means when speaking about the intercourse—do forgive the philosopher Edmund Husserl's chancy word choice (or our translation of it)—of subject and object as it occurs across the field of consciousness. Knowledge is attributable to the subject—the intelligence which the detective has garnered and can apply to the crime. Observation is attributable to the object—the clues and evidence which the outside world contains, the way in which the scene of a crime is implicated in the crime. A superior detective is able to locate these clues even though they are hidden by the object which holds them—an inferior detective will misread or miss altogether that the beaker shows traces of an explosive substance. And Deduction—this is Holmes's particular recipe for arriving at truth; it is attributable to the intercourse between intelligence and evidence, subject and object. It is his description of the event which takes place across his field of consciousness.

Why Dr. Watson Has No Special Powers

Around this issue of drug use, not only do we gain a deeper experience of Holmes's intellect and being, but also we quickly see an underlying difference between Holmes and our stories' narrator, Dr. Watson. It is the differences between the two that amplifies the essence of Holmes's consciousness.

At the beginning of *The Sign of the Four*, Watson walks in on Sherlock Holmes shooting up.

> "Which is it today? Morphine or cocaine?"
>
> [Holmes] raised his eyes languidly from the old black-letter volume which he had opened. "It is cocaine, a seven per cent. solution."
>
> "Surely the game is hardly worth the candle. Why should you, for a mere passing pleasure, risk the loss of these great powers with which you have been endowed?"

Admonishing Holmes for his drug use, Watson's prudence and practicality are revealed. Qualities which never go hand-in-hand with special powers. He does not realize that it is Holmes's practices in his study that endow him with the acute insights into the observable world.

Watson at heart, I believe, is a romantic, but prior to having Holmes in his life, all the romance had been drained from his being by the Afghan war—suffering injuries, witnessing his infantry hacked to pieces, and the general malaise that extends from this. He is a doctor, a man of science and medicine—an empiricist to the core who relies on the order of the outside world to define his reality. He does not grow lost in the abstractions of his mind. He is a see-it-to-believe-it type of fellow. He continually challenges Holmes in this manner, though he is fascinated with the workings of the great detective's mind.

Holmes's answer to Watson does not disappoint:

> "My mind rebels at stagnation. Give me problems, give me work, give me the most abstruse cryptogram, or the most intricate analysis, and I am in my own proper atmosphere, I can dispense then with the stimulants. But I abhor the dull routine of existence. I crave for mental exaltation."

Watson knows neither transcendence nor exaltation—he offers nothing of his personal being to the objective world, as Holmes offers all.

But Watson is aware that he's missing something from his life, and he wishes to learn what this is. He is a character conflicted by the limitations of his empiricism, and driven towards the transcendence of phenomenology. In the first novel, *A Study in Scarlet*, Watson speaks of his life prior to meeting Sherlock Holmes. Back from the war and still healing, Watson sets up residence in London, but states that something is missing. "There I stayed for some time at a private hotel in the Strand, leading a comfortless, meaningless existence, and spending such money as I had considerably more freely than I ought." A meaningless existence, pursuing the luxuries of the outside world. He realizes he needed to cultivate an interior world similar to Holmes's study, and he states, "I must make a complete alteration in my style of living."

A friend introduces Holmes and Watson, seeing that they were both looking for a new apartment. This is where Watson's study begins. Having encountered such an unusual man who keeps odd hours, eccentric habits, and strange company, Watson's curiosity throws him into the middle of Sherlock Holmes's world. Accompanying Holmes on a case, Watson witnesses his extraordinary ability to thoroughly experience the scene of a crime—all of its details, all of its narratives, as if the room and its clues reverberate communicatively with Holmes's mind. Watson reflects on this, saying, "I had had such extraordinary evidence of the quickness of his perceptive facilities that I had no doubt that he could see a great deal which was hidden from me." And this is the mystery: how does one man see what is hidden from another when they are both staring at the same thing?

To answer this we must continue our examination of the observer and the object observed. Surely, Holmes's thorough homework allows him to understand what he sees at a deeper level than one such as Watson, who has never studied criminal history. And, according to phenomenology, the objects themselves—the scene of the crime, the murder weapons, footprints—have a life of their own. They appear differently according to the consciousness which beholds them. Holmes compares the mind to a room which we fill with furniture.

> "You see, I consider that a man's brain originally is like a little empty attic, and you have to stock it with furniture as you chose. . . . Now, the skillful workman is very careful indeed as to what he takes into his brain-attic. He will have nothing but the tools which may help him in doing his work, but of these he has a large assortment, and all in the most perfect order."

To describe this furniture, as phenomenologists, then this is what we must do.

Interior Design

There is a unity of Holmes's being. A balance which demonstrates his field of consciousness as the seat of his reality. As Dr. Watson points out, Holmes's body has been disfigured by the intentions of the objective world. He is deformed by his phenomenological powers, something few if any re-tellers of his tales have accounted for in the many visual depictions of Holmes. As Watson relates to us in *A Study in Scarlet,* his hands are mottled over with pieces of plaster and discolored with strong acids. His skin is invariably blotted with ink and stained with chemicals. His entire being is the meeting ground for the interplay of curiosity and the outside world.

When describing his courses of study, Watson notes the peculiarity of his specialties, and the gaping holes in his common knowledge. Holmes states that "he would acquire no knowledge which did not bear upon his object. Therefore all the knowledge he possessed was such as would be useful to him." Purposefully, Holmes has rid his intelligence of the superfluous—sure that no subjective nonsense would get in his way. He could do this only through understanding the nature of his objective: to make acute observations and accurate deductions. Only could he do this through a balance and unity between what one studies and the object of one's studies. On the other hand, Dr. Watson knows much about many things—sporadic knowledge; a liberal familiarity with many subjects.

Phenomenological powers begin with interior design of our knowledge. Whether or not we see our mind as an attic waiting to be filled with furniture, as Sherlock Holmes does, we must understand that there is a fluidity between what we study and what we observe. Knowledge in and of itself is not power. If intentional and unified with the objective situation, then power is there because consciousness is in immediate unity with the total situation determining it.

Reflecting on how he knew that the yet-to-be-captured criminal at the heart of *A Study in Scarlet* smoked Trichinopoly cigars, Sherlock Holmes tells Watson:

> "I have made a special study of cigar ashes—in fact, I have written a monograph upon the subject. I flatter myself that I can distinguish at a glance the ash of any known brand either of cigar or tobacco. It is just such details that the skilled detective differs from the Gregson and Lestrade type."

Sherlock Holmes Eats Roast Beef, Scotland Yard Has None

> "a motive so transparent that even a Scotland Yard official can see through it."
>
> —Sherlock Holmes, *A Study in Scarlet*

At the beginning of his career Sherlock Holmes did most of his work from his armchair. Citizens of London or Scotland Yard officers would themselves visit Holmes in his study and ask him to solve a crime through his intellectual powers. As Holmes describes it to Watson, "They lay all the evidence before me and I am generally able by the help of my knowledge of the history of crimes, to set them straight." Through his powers of intuition, imagination, and deduction, Holmes is able to conjure a facsimile of the case in his consciousness, and see it with a lucidity that those who have seen it first-hand cannot approximate. But what occurs in his consciousness when he gets up from his chair? It is as if every object in every room speaks to him, whispering its secrets.

To impose order upon the world and to believe that it revolves around your desires can be a frustrating experience in the detective business. And Scotland Yard detectives Gregson and Lestrade know this frustration very well. I compare it to square-peg round-hole—what you want it to be won't fit what the outside world says it is. Case after case they try so hard to solve, but never can they deal with what the evidence is, nor can they discover the clues necessary to get them on the right track. They do not see all that there is to be seen because they are biased by their theorizing and misconceptions. And because they have little to no knowledge of past cases or forensic particularities—meaning, they have intentions which are out of balance with their objective.

On the other hand, the scene of a crime is certainly activated through Sherlock Holmes's intelligence—he has studied enough of precise subjects and their interplay across his consciousness in order to differentiate and make sense of the sensory data he collects. And he's not afraid to boast about this, "No man lives or has ever lived who has brought the same amount of study and of natural talent to the detection of crime which I have done." Study, certainly, but what can be said of Sherlock Holmes's self-proclaimed "natural talent"?

Take *A Study in Scarlet*. Detectives Gregson and Lestrade quickly exhaust all the forensic and investigation techniques they know, and who do they call on?

> "Dear Sherlock Holmes, . . . There had been no robbery, nor is there any evidence as to how the man met his death. There are marks of blood in the room, but there is no wound upon his person. We are at a loss as to how he came into the empty house; indeed, the whole affair is a puzzler.
> "Yours faithfully, Tobias Gregson"

After a little nudging from Watson, Holmes decides to offer his assistance, and they hail a carriage. On their way, Watson is perplexed that Holmes is not anxious, concerned, or even speculating about the murder. Watson prods him about this, "You don't seem to give much thought to the matter in hand." And Holmes answers, "No data yet. It is a capital mistake to theorize before you have all the evidence. It biases the judgment." Here is the balance which a phenomenological view accounts for: all theory and no corresponding evidence would be a subjective blunder; all evidence and no corresponding theorizing about how it comes together would be an objective misreading—but Sherlock Holmes, seeks deftly for the phenomenal evidence of his case to trigger the theories and the intelligence to make sense of the evidence—*as he experiences it.* Not beforehand; not after the fact. While he is doing it. Let's see an example:

"His nimble fingers were flying here, there, and everywhere, feeling, pressing, unbuttoning, examining, while his eyes wore the same far-away expression which I have already spoke of." And I, as well, in the first section. Holmes's attention is cast in two directions simultaneously: the phenomenal world and the world of his being, his interior chambers. Attention to the objective world and his mind at the same time, producing the event of consciousness. He is absorbed by the moment before him as much as the moment is absorbed by him. After recounting for Watson how he was able to know so much about him in one quick glance, Holmes confesses that this is no trick, "From long habit the train of thought ran so swiftly through my mind that I arrived at the conclusion without being conscious of intermediate steps." These deductive conclusions are the interplay of knowledge and evidence occurring across his consciousness.

And reciprocally, Holmes understands how each of us play out across the physical world. We leave our mark. As Watson shows that he is learning the phenomenological foundations of Holmes craft in *The Sign of the Four,* "I have heard you say that it is difficult for a man to have any object in daily use without leaving the impress of his individuality upon it in such a way that a trained observer might read it." Gregson and Lestrade are not trained observers—they do not uncover the clues necessary to solve a case, and what they do see, they misinterpret.

Let's return to Gregson's letter requesting Holmes's assistance in order to reveal typical Scotland blunders.

> "There had been no robbery, nor is there any evidence as to how the man met his death. There are marks of blood in the room, but there is no wound upon his person. We are at a loss as to how he came into the empty house."

They have theorized prior to collecting data—surely, they believe, for a murder to occur, a robbery must be the motive. Because it is thieves who kill, right? Surely if there is blood at the scene of a murder, then it is the victim's? And when Lestrade uncovers the letters *R A C H E* scribbled upon the wall in blood, he and Gregson are of course correct to assume this to be the beginning of a woman's name—for a ring had been found on the floor near the body, and if not for money than a woman is motive enough for murder. Right?

Wrong on all accounts. All it takes for Sherlock Holmes to discover how this man met his death is a quick sniff of the lips— poison is foul and lingers upon the object. Ruling out all other possibilities, Holmes deduces that the blood must be from the murderer. Holmes assumes nothing. Through his compulsion to study the crimes of every country, Holmes knows that "Rache" is German. And it means revenge. As far as entry into the house goes, Holmes had that figured out before he entered the scene of the crime—observing the tracks outside instantly revealed all.

The phenomenal world of the scene of a crime holds all reverberations of the actions which took place; one must only trust the objective world and listen without bias to the intentions of the object, of the room, of the corpse—able to hold ambiguity in the mind without appealing to the false security of presumption. One must practice this talent—time spent in the woodshed, exploring one's consciousness.

The Essence of Perception:
Holmes's Intention and Objects Intended

So, we have seen the intentions and intuition cultivated by Holmes in his study. Now we must come to an understanding that the observable world is subject to our intentions, yet contains intentions of its own. And that objects possess various meanings.

In Edmund Husserl's book, *The Crisis of European Sciences*, he states "Things 'seen' are always more than what we 'really and actually' see of them" (p. 51). Take this chair for instance. There is nothing out-of-the-ordinary about it—a medical chair in a medical laboratory. For a detective searching for who stole the corpse, this chair offers little to no epistemological value. That is unless you've studied coasters made in the late 1800s—how they lock up once frozen. Yes, you say, the coasters are locked up, what of it? Well, what of it is that this chair just went from being nothing in relation to our investigation into being something. We observed this chair; we saw it—took note of it. Before we knew what to look for—that the coasters could tell the story of the chair's past—we didn't see all of it. There was more to the object than met the eye. We see this chair now as more than a place to sit—we see it as an object which has recently been in the deep-freeze; the same place the corpses are kept. According to our knowledge of coasters, that is; and according to the intentions of the chair. Edmund Husserl's famous slogan comes to mind: Knowledge is the grasp of an object that is simultaneously gripping us. Until the phenomenon of coasters is understood by the subject, the chair remains an object seamlessly stitched into the room.

A crime scene is a place where impact reverberates. A criminal's presence remains. Intention and execution are imprinted upon the physical world. But the detective must understand the properties of the physical world, how objects take in the presence of the criminal, how they shift in meaning according to what has occurred in the room. Cigar ashes, mud tracks, blood stains are no longer innocent bystanders.

Besides Edmund Husserl, Martin Heidegger is the other major philosopher to shape phenomenology. And it is helpful to turn to him to understand how an object has intentions of its own. Heidegger differentiates between the objects and meanings present at the scene of a crime, or anywhere, as being either "merely present" (*Vorhandenheit*) or "usefully present" (*Zuhandenheit*). In other words, a tablecloth across the dining table at the scene of a crime is something a detective would probably not spend too much time investigating—it is merely present; whereas, a wineglass stained with red lipstick would be taken into consideration—it is useful for solving the case.

The rooms Sherlock Holmes enters become abuzz with activity—the life of these objects in all their perceived, conceived, and actual manifestations is observable to him.[1]

Mysterious and powerful—a thick fog rolling across Baker Street slips into the room through the open window. Curtains billowing and stained with blood. An armchair and its view. A bureau drawer open, past crimes spilling out. Leaned against the closet door, a neck broken and limbs contorted. Hand-carved mannequins marked with entry and exit wounds. A trunk of curiosities from distant lands. A mirror's shattered pieces across the hardwoods. Glass tubes filled with a bubbling liquid above a burner. A revolver, six empty chambers, six bullets on deck. The feminine screech from the doorway. Across the floor, a Persian rug, ornate labyrinthine patterns stitched by hand. On the mantel, a candlestick heightened by all its cousins, its properties, its dense blow. One vial full, another rolling empty across the rug. On the desk, a letter to an heir interrupted mid-sentence. A wardrobe filled with books. A syringe stuck into an arm. This is neither study nor scene of the crime—this is Sherlock Holmes's Field of Consciousness.

---

[1] For more on this quandary, you may find "The Adventure of the Candle and the Dumbbell" (earlier in this book) worthy of examination. Clues abound everywhere, dear Reader, and circle back on themselves.

Chapter 25
Boredom on Baker Street
Daniel P. Malloy

Sherlock Holmes's greatest danger? His true nemesis?

It's not Professor Moriarty nor his associate Colonel Moran. It's not the interference of the company he keeps: the plodding Watson or the unimaginative Lestrade. It's not even Holmes himself—his tendency to self-destructive pursuits.

These are all perilous. But they pale in comparison to Holmes's only true nemesis: boredom.

Boredom plays a central role in making Holmes who he is. It's why he takes occasional refuge in cocaine and morphine when he has no interesting work to do. It's why he accepts certain cases and avoids others. His decision is not based on the urgency of the case or the potential monetary reward, but on the difficulty it presents. What attracts Holmes is the chance to fend off boredom for a little while.

At first glance it may not seem that boredom is an especially philosophical topic. Philosophical discussion of boredom is indeed quite limited—aside from an extended discussion by Martin Heidegger (1889–1976) and two books published in the last decade (Elizabeth Goodstein's *Experience without Qualities* and Lars Svensden's *The Philosophy of Boredom*), there are only a few short references in the works of Pascal, Kierkegaard, Schopenhauer, Nietzsche, and a few others. But boredom offers the philosopher an attraction not dissimilar from Holmes's attraction to his cases: it provides us the chance to exercise our faculties, and, perhaps, to stave it off for a bit.

When thinking about boredom, we're confronted with three related questions:

What is it?
Where does it come from?
And what do we do about it?

Unwelcome Social Summonses

It may seem odd to think of boredom as modern, but the evidence suggests that it is. None of Holmes's pre-modern predecessors struggled with boredom. It didn't motivate them. In fact, to all appearances, they never seem to have encountered it. Homer never mentions that Ulysses became bored. Likewise, it's hard to imagine Beowulf or King Arthur just passing the time. And yet that's often what we see Holmes doing. Boredom, in spite of its seeming universality, is a distinctly modern phenomenon. The word itself only appeared in the English language in the eighteenth century. It did, however, spread quickly. By the middle of the nineteenth century, it took on epidemic proportions. The turn of the century, where we find our hero, brought no abatement. Boredom continued to bore.

Boredom happens to us, we don't choose it. If Holmes had a choice, he would always have some new puzzle to work on, some case to solve or experiment to run. As he says, "My mind rebels at stagnation" (*The Sign of the Four*). This comment gives us some clue as to what boredom might be.

"What boredom might be? What are you talking about? We know what boredom is!" True. We've all experienced boredom at one time or another. But still, we may not have a good idea of what boredom is.

Suppose you met someone who had, somehow, never been bored. Could you explain it to them? We might say, with Holmes, that boredom means having nothing to do. But that isn't boredom; it's idleness. There may be a connection between the two, particularly for someone with an energetic disposition like Holmes. But it's possible to be idle and not be bored. Idleness can be quite pleasant, which boredom never is. And, it's possible to be bored and not idle. Many of us are both bored and busy. Someone doing chores around the house, for instance, is certainly busy, but could very easily be bored. For that matter, Holmes could, if he so chose, have more work than he could handle anytime he wished. Remember, he turns away cases that don't spark his interest.

Perhaps that's the key, then: interest. We get bored when nothing interests us. Thus we're bored when there's nothing to do, but also when there's plenty to do, but nothing that intrigues us. And herein lies boredom's connection to modern life. In pre-modern times, we considered ourselves as being here for the world—we were a part of it, and each of us had his or her own place in it. A serf working the land for his lord didn't have to wonder what was next. Either the next task presented itself naturally, or someone would tell him. In modern times, things are different. In part, perhaps, because of the degree of freedom we have achieved—from each other, from the state, from the church—we now have a different relation to the world around us. It's here for us. And we get bored when the things in it don't interest us. It's their responsibility to serve us, not the other way around.

Trifles, Our World, and Black Moods

So now we have a rough genealogy and definition of boredom; let's explore the phenomenon a bit more. At first glance, it seems that boredom is all the same, but on closer inspection (a MUST for Holmes) it appears that there are actually several distinct types of boredom, at least according to Heidegger. Each type is defined by the distinct way that it forces us to experience the world and the things in it.

The first type of boredom is the one we encounter most in the Holmes stories, and in our own lives. It's when we are bored *by* something. It may be a task or an object that bores us. But there's nothing inherently boring about the things that bore us, even though they cause our boredom. Being boring is not a property a thing might have, like being red or round. You can see this by thinking about the distinct reactions we often see coming from Holmes and Watson in relation to a single problem. For instance, when Holmes "reads" Watson's mind, demonstrating the ease with which one might ape the parlor trick of Poe's Dupin, the two characters plainly display how one and the same thing can be boring and not boring ("The Adventure of the Cardboard Box"). The demonstration, like many demonstrations, bores Holmes—it's a trifle, a gas, a thing hardly worth thinking about. But it astounds Watson (many things astound Watson).

Nevertheless, it won't do to say that it's entirely subjective whether one is bored by something. In this type of boredom, there is a very definite, though not easily definable, level of participation on the part of the object. The object is somehow attuning us to boredom. Some other object in its place would not be boring. Once again, think of Holmes. A case that initially bores him can have a peculiar twist in it that will suddenly change the face of matters in such a way that he is now quite interested. As in the case of the Red Circle, a single turn makes Holmes remark that "the case certainly grows in interest." Nothing about Holmes has changed—he remains as he ever was. But something in the nature of the case has gone from being the cause of boredom to the cause of excitement. Boredom, then, is neither subjective nor objective, but has to do with how those two spheres interact. When we're bored by something, there is a failure to engage the two spheres in an interesting way.

Sometimes, though, we are not bored by any particular thing—we are simply bored. Nothing engages us. This is what Heidegger calls *being bored with* . . .

Being bored with . . . is a strange mood, but a common enough one. Heidegger gives the example of being at a dinner party, engaging in usual small talk, having a nice meal, and only later realizing that we were bored out of our minds. Holmes, ever the astute observer, knows beforehand that he will experience this type of boredom. Upon receiving a note from his would-be client in "The Adventure of the Noble Bachelor," Holmes comments that it appears to be "one of those unwelcome social summonses which call upon a man either to be bored or to lie." There was nothing particularly boring about the party or the company. It is something about ourselves—we carry our boredom with us.

According to Heidegger, this second type of boredom is a deeper level of boredom, one that tells us more about our way of being-in-the-world. Because it's not simply about how we relate to individual objects, but about how we relate to our world as a whole (note: our world is not the same thing as the world). This deeper level of boredom tells us more about the kinds of beings we are, largely because of its connection to time. In truth, all forms of boredom have intimate connections to time. When we're bored by . . ., time moves slowly, sometimes incredibly so. We glance at our watches or clocks constantly, and despair of the end ever arriving. When we are bored with . . ., on the other hand, time does not seem to move at all. It is only in retrospect that we realize how fast time has gone by—not because we were enjoying ourselves, but because nothing really pinned us down. Time may fly when we're having fun, but we still have the sensation of time passing. When we are bored with . . . time simply does not pass. It has passed, and we wonder where it went.

To give a more modern example of this type of boredom, think about checking your e-mail. You sit down to accomplish a task that should take five minutes at the outside. And yet, often when we go to perform this simple task, entire hours pass while we complete it. One minute, I am just trying to send off a brief message or see if so-and-so has gotten back to me. The next minute, several hours have passed in which I've been watching Youtube videos of no real interest and getting angry at inaccurate articles on Wikipedia.

A further sort of boredom is well exemplified in the early Holmes stories. We can see it in Holmes's "black moods". This is the mood that Heidegger calls "profound boredom." Heidegger held that our moods reveal fundamental truths to us, truths about ourselves and our world. In this respect, profound boredom is second only to *Angst* (roughly, the fear of death)—some scholars, in fact, have argued that in Heidegger's writings after *Being and Time*, boredom overtakes *Angst* as the fundamental attunement of *Dasein* (or for Heidegger, *human entity*).

"Profound boredom," he says in his essay "What is Metaphysics?", "removes all things and human beings and oneself along with them into a remarkable indifference. This boredom reveals beings as a whole." In our normal lives, our predominant moods, everything is dictated by our temporal nature. We are creatures grounded in the past and rushing headlong into the future. This fact colors our experience of the world.

As I type this chapter, I experience the computer as a useful part of my world—I don't experience the computer itself. In a certain sense, I don't even notice it. I could notice it, if it suddenly froze. But then I experience it only as a hindrance—it would be getting in the way of my rush to the future. In profound boredom, however, that rush is suspended. I remain a temporal being but my connections to the past and the future are cut off. I am suspended in the present, forced to confront things as they are, as separated from my projects. Indeed, it is one of the few times when I am forced to confront myself and the world, with nothing in between. Given Holmes's energetic nature, and his laser-like focus on his projects, it's small wonder that he should find the mood of profound boredom intolerable.

Three Times the Solution, or . . .

We now have three problems, not one:

1. boredom by . . .

2. boredom with . . .

3. profound boredom

It's not simply a matter of overcoming or avoiding boredom—
we have to figure out how to deal with each type of boredom.
What works for one might not work for another. Our guide so
far is of no help. Heidegger's analysis of boredom includes no
clues as to how to avoid or escape it. Some have even gone so far
as to claim that boredom is inescapable. Arthur Schopenhauer
argued that life was a constant oscillation between pain and
boredom. Later, in "The Antichrist," Friedrich Nietzsche
said, "Against boredom even gods struggle in vain." In the
short philosophical tradition dealing with boredom, only three
solutions have been offered for this problem: amusement, work,
and religion.

When we're bored by something, the answer is relatively
simple: find something else. We can see this in the way Holmes
passes on cases. The ones that will bore him he passes by in
favor of the ones that interest him. In the same way we can cure
ourselves from being bored by things—it is a matter of diversion.
Immanuel Kant recommended work as the cure for boredom
(*Anthropology from a Pragmatic Point of View*, pp. 133–36). In this
case, he was talking about the boredom caused by amusements
of various sorts. One can see his point—a sustained burst of
focused effort is often a welcome antidote to the monotony of
repetitious amusements. But Kant never tells us how to overcome
the boredom of work. Still, either work or various forms of
amusement will be effective in helping us overcome being bored
by . . .

The second case is a bit more complex. First, it is difficult
to tell when we are being bored with . . . in the way Heidegger
describes. Once we realize that we have been bored in this way,
we are no longer bored. None of Holmes's typical escapes from
boredom seem to apply to this type. Escape requires an act of
will which itself requires some sort of desire. If you don't know
you're bored when you're bored then the unpleasantness of
boredom is not disturbing. At least, not until afterwards. That's
when you have that terrible revelation that you have just wasted
several hours of precious time.

Perhaps, on second thought, we can relate this type of boredom
to some of Holmes's activities—particularly to his non-work and
non-narcotic amusements. Holmes is a Victorian gentleman in
almost every way, including his status as an amateur scientist. He
has published a variety of monographs, including the fruition
of his retirement years, a manual on beekeeping. Some of these
are directly related to his work as a detective, but others, like
the "Practical Handbook of Bee Culture," reflect Holmes's

straightforward passion for learning. These monographs, along with the hobbies they often reflect, represent a way of warding off this second type of boredom. Unlike being bored by . . ., being bored with . . . cannot be fought against or escaped from; it must be evaded.

Profound boredom is the most difficult kind to shake. This may be why Heidegger recommends that we simply embrace it. It may also be why Holmes turns to narcotics to avoid it.

But why worry about it at all? Sure, boredom isn't pleasant, but there are worse things in the world, right? But boredom, while not especially distressing in itself, may be the source of many problems. At least two modern philosophers have argued that most of our self-inflicted problems are caused by boredom. Blaise Pascal says that "All human evil comes from a single cause, man's inability to sit still in a room" (*Pensées*, p. 47). More recently, Søren Kierkegaard goes even further and states on that "Boredom is the root of all evil" (*Either/Or*, Volume 1, p. 289).

Jeremy Paul's non-canonical play "The Secret of Sherlock Holmes" clearly displays the link between boredom and evil. In the course of the play Holmes hints that he may in fact have created his nemesis, the infamous Professor Moriarty. Why? Put yourself in Holmes's shoes. He's an unequaled intellect. On occasion he meets a puzzle that challenges him, but these occasions are infrequent and fleeting. How to relieve the boredom? What does he need? Drugs aren't helping anymore—Watson's a total square. Friends aren't working—their astonishment is briefly amusing, but not engaging. You need an opponent, an equal and opposite number. If one can't be found, make one.

Pascal and Kierkegaard have the same recommendation for avoiding this sort of profound boredom and its consequences, but I don't think it would really work for Holmes. Pascal and Kierkegaard argue that the way to escape from the sort of profound boredom is through a religious life. This touches on something we mentioned earlier: boredom's often caused by our lack of interest in the world, which can be traced to a lack of a sense of purpose. Religion, at least in theory, provides that purpose. Still, the purpose provided by religion depends on the ability to believe in religion. Holmes, being the modern character he is, has a murky relationship to religion at best. Aside from one rather uncharacteristic monologue about the beauty and uselessness of roses in "The Adventure of the Naval Treaty," he never seems to broach the subject, except when his quarry has some vague connection to a foreign and mysterious religion.

The Seven Percent Conclusion

There are several ways to combat the various types of boredom. Few of them are effective for very long. Much as I disagree with Pascal's and Kierkegaard's recommendation, it has the virtue of getting to the heart of the problem. The issue is that their solution depends on a complete change of worldview. It is not enough to simply "get" religion to combat boredom—one would have to shift one's entire way of living in the world to a medieval perspective. Modern religious people face boredom too, sometimes while engaged in the act of worship. Regardless of how appealing you may find the idea of combating boredom with religion—and some do—it's simply not possible. The modern world can be, among many other things, intrusive.

So how do we deal with boredom without the use of a time machine? Holmes offers a few possibilities: work, amusement, drugs, and evil. Clearly, we're going to want to avoid the latter two for a variety of reasons—the cure would be worse than the disease. As for work and amusement, they're quite effective when dealing with being bored by something, provided they are not the source of our boredom. They can help us avoid being bored with . . . as well. But they do nothing for profound boredom.

The problem with all of Holmes's solutions, indeed all of the common solutions to boredom, is that they confront a symptom rather than the disease. Boredom may be epidemic, but it is not the epidemic. There's something underlying it, something intrinsic in modern life that makes us bored. So, we have to learn to live with it, because modernity is not going anywhere.

Chapter 26

Willful Self-Destruction?
Greg Littmann

"But consider!" I said earnestly. "Count the cost! Your brain may, as you say, be roused and excited, but it is a pathological and morbid process which involves increased tissue-change and may at least leave a permanent weakness. You know, too, what a black reaction comes upon you. Surely the game is hardly worth the candle."

—Dr. Watson in *The Sign of the Four*

The greatest mystery in the Sherlock Holmes canon is this: How is it possible for a fellow as clever as Sherlock Holmes to be a habitual user of cocaine?

Holmes's cocaine use is more mysterious than the fate of Dr. Watson's bull-pup, the number of times Watson was married, or the issue of exactly which of the good doctor's limbs received a Jezail bullet at the battle of Maiwand.

Holmes is intelligent enough to know that he shouldn't inject cocaine and yet, for many years, he does so regularly when bored. Indeed, on at least one occasion he injects himself with a seven percent solution three times a day for several months, leaving his forearm "all dotted and scarred with innumerable puncture-marks" (*The Sign of the Four*). Had not Watson eventually "weaned him from that drug mania" ("The Adventure of the Missing Three-Quarter"), he may never have given it up, eventually retiring to the Sussex Downs to disastrously (if hilariously) combine heavy cocaine use and beekeeping.

It might be tempting to excuse Holmes's behavior on the grounds that the dangers of the drug were not well known at the time. After all, cocaine was legal in England until 1917 and many believed that it was harmless, or even medically beneficial. Some doctors prescribed cocaine for their patients, and cocaine-based medicines were openly and enthusiastically advertised—"A useful present for friends at the Front" promised one 1915 ad in *The Times*, unwittingly doing its bit to make World War I just a little more dangerous for the British soldier.

However, as Watson eloquently argues in *The Sign of the Four*, the drug may well be harmful for all that is known about it, and it makes no sense for Holmes for take any risks with the thing that matters most to him in life—his extraordinary brain. How could someone so intelligent do something so foolish? Baffling!

The Mysterious Nature of Weakness of Will

> I was horrified by my first glimpse of Holmes next morning, for he sat by the fire holding his tiny hypodermic syringe. I associated that instrument with the single weakness of his nature, and I feared the worst when I saw it glittering in his hand.
>
> —"The Adventure of the Missing Three-Quarter"

When people give in to the temptation to do something that they know isn't in their best interests, we say that their will fails them. What makes weakness of will of the sort Holmes displays so mysterious is that he is not choosing between two different goals, but between two different degrees of achieving the same goal—happiness. Yet with happiness as his goal, he chooses the path of less happiness over the path of more happiness.

Holmes shoots up because the cocaine is pleasurable—it helps to relieve his boredom when his mind is not absorbed by a case. However, his habit is liable to bring him less pleasure in the long run. If Holmes were ever to learn that he had damaged his faculties of reason, he would surely be plunged into despair for life. So Holmes takes cocaine for the sake of pleasure, but at the same time understands that he will likely receive less pleasure by doing so. How can it be?

To make the problem clearer, consider the absurdity of someone taking pleasure as their goal, and then choosing a course of action that brings them suffering instead. Imagine Watson returning to 221B Baker Street one evening to find Holmes sitting by the fire, repeatedly striking himself in the face with his violin. Shocked, Watson demands to know the meaning of this. Holmes explains, through swollen lips, that he had picked up the instrument because he thought it would be enjoyable to play it, but having reflected upon the fact that it would be most unpleasant to be repeatedly struck in the face with it, he had chosen that course of action instead. "Whatever is your object, Holmes?" cries Watson in amazement. "Pleasure Watson, though this activity gives me none and never shall," replies the great man and smashes his fifty-five shilling Stradivarius into his thin, hawk-like nose with a strength for which Watson should hardly have given him credit.

Such a scene would make no sense. If Holmes's object is pleasure, it is absurd for him to knowingly choose suffering instead. However, if it's absurd for one seeking pleasure to choose suffering instead, it is presumably no less absurd for one seeking pleasure to choose the lesser pleasure over the greater. It's akin to desiring money but, upon tunneling from your cellar into the bank vault next door, stealing only half of what is there. So how can it be that Holmes continues to take cocaine in the interests of his own happiness, knowing full well that his happiness would be better served by refraining?

A Mystery You Cannot Ignore

"Should you care to add the case to your annals, my dear Watson," said Holmes that evening, "it can only be as an example of that temporary eclipse to which even the best-balanced mind may be exposed. Such slips are common to all mortals, and the greatest is he who can recognize and repair them."
—"The Disappearance of Lady Francis Carfax"

There's nothing unusual about a human being giving in to pleasure by doing something that they know will not serve their happiness in the long run. You yourself do this. Perhaps you eat too much, or drive too fast, or smoke tobacco ("poison" as Watson reminds us). You might even gamble more than you can afford, like Sir George Burnwell ("The Adventure of the Beryl Coronet") or trifle with the affections of young ladies, like that king of bohemians, the king of Bohemia ("A Scandal in Bohemia").

Whatever exactly your vices may be, you know very well that you have them (shame on you!). However, as Holmes so often reminds us, the fact that an event is not exotic does not indicate that it lacks deep mystery. Indeed, it is the fact that such baffling behavior is so common that makes it so philosophically important. We'll be using Holmes as our touchstone because he provides such a clear example (perhaps literature's clearest example) of the problem at hand. However, this mystery directly concerns us all. How is it that, in the interests of happiness, we do things we know are likely to make us less happy? The answer to this question may provide us with clues about how to stop.

As Sherlock Holmes recognizes, a reliance on one's own

powers of observation and reasoning is most useful to one who considers the conclusions of other people. Holmes makes up his own mind, but this does not dissuade him from attending university, consulting the *Times*, or lounging for days in his armchair with his blackletter editions. Similarly, while you will have to make up your own mind about how human beings can knowingly act against their own interests, philosophers have been wrestling with this issue for about two and a half thousand years. The lines of battle were drawn early, in Ancient Greece.

Socrates Takes the Case

> "No crime, but a very great error has been committed," said Holmes.
> —"The Man with the Twisted Lip"

It was the philosopher Socrates (469–399 B.C.) who got the debate rolling by famously claiming that such weakness of will, *akrasia* in the Greek, is a myth. He thus took an approach to solving the problem of akrasia similar to that taken by Holmes to solving the problems of the Hound of the Baskervilles and the Sussex Vampire.

Denying the existence of akrasia does not resolve the mystery in itself, any more than Holmes had solved the Baskerville case when he first doubted that the supernatural hound persecuting the Baskerville line was real. For Holmes, it still remained to explain what was going on—who was really behind the strange events at Baskerville Hall, and who really killed Sir Charles. Similarly, it would not be enough for Socrates to simply deny that weakness of the will is real—he must provide an explanation of what is actually going on in cases of apparent akrasia. If Sherlock Holmes is not being "akratic" when sinking the needle into his vein, how the devil can he come to do such a thing?

Searching for clues to explain apparently akratic behavior, Socrates makes an interesting observation: whenever we choose a less pleasant course of action over a more pleasant course, the lesser pleasure is always nearer to us in time than the greater pleasure.

It makes sense to us that Sir George Burnwell might have ruined himself gambling by choosing the immediate thrill of the game over his long-term financial interests, but if he had ruined himself by exchanging a fortune now for some thrilling games many years in the future, his motivation would be a mystery. Similarly, it makes sense to us that Wilhelm Gottsreich Sigismond von Ormstein, King of Bohemia, might choose the immediate pleasure of Irene Addler's company even when he knows it is in his best interests in the long term to protect the house of Ormstein from scandal, whereas it would have made no sense if he had immediately thrown away his reputation in the interests of dallying with a woman he intended to abandon.

Again, we can understand that even someone as brilliant as Holmes might opt for the rush of cocaine right now rather than taking the best care of his brain, and thus, as Watson puts it, "for a mere passing pleasure, risk the loss of those great powers with which you have been endowed" (*The Sign of the Four*). On the other hand, it would be unimaginable for Holmes to subject himself to a chemical that he knew would destroy his great mental powers immediately, though it would give him a series of passing thrills at some time in the distant future. Similarly, in our modern world, smokers would not smoke if the onset of lung cancer was immediate, nor drunk drivers take to the road if they had to crash the car first.

Socrates likens this phenomena to the optical illusion by which an object appears to be larger when it is closer (and like the auditory illusion by which a sound seems louder when it is closer). Apparent cases of akrasia, then, are really cases of misjudgment in which we mistake the relative magnitude of pleasures due to their relative distances from us; nearer pleasures seem larger and more distant pleasures smaller. Thus, it simply isn't true that people knowingly choose the less pleasant alternative over the more pleasant alternative. Rather, beguiled by illusion, they choose the less pleasant alternative because they think it is the more pleasant alternative.

As Sir George Burnwell sat at cards, the pleasurable prospect of a big win on the next hand seemed more significant to him than the fact that he was slowly ruining himself; as the King of Bohemia gazed into the eyes of Irene Adler, the pleasure of her company seemed greater to him than the pleasure of his high position; and as for Holmes, the relief of his boredom loomed so large as he prepared his seven-percent cocaine solution, that it seemed more important to his happiness than any costs he might later incur. What they, and we, all need is not a strengthening of the will, but a greater mastery of the science of measuring the relative magnitudes of pleasures and pains. When we have mastered this ability, we will have the information needed to understand which pleasures are greater, and will no longer choose lesser pleasures over greater pleasures. What you and I must do, then, is develop this skill so that we can see things clearly. Exactly how we are to do this may remain to be determined, but at least we can know that what we are seeking is a refinement of our powers of reasoning.

Aristotle Examines the Evidence

> "There, that's enough," said Lestrade. "I am a practical man, Mr. Holmes, and when I have got my evidence I come to my conclusions. If you have anything to say, you will find me writing my report in the sitting-room."
> —"The Adventure of the Norwood Builder"

Mystery solved? Perhaps, but many philosophers think Socrates is accusing the wrong suspect. Playing Lestrade to Socrates's Gregson, Aristotle (384–322 B.C.) protested that the intellectualized Socratic account fails to match up with the way that akrasia manifestly appears to operate (*Nicomachean Ethics*). On Socrates's account, we never know that one course of action is best for us but take another course of action instead. Yet you and I and Aristotle are only too familiar with the feeling that we know what is best for us, yet choose to do something else instead. As you raise the lethal cigarette to your lips (or otherwise indulge your vices), it seems to you that you are perfectly aware of the consequences—consequences you would never choose directly.

Perhaps most powerfully, it seems absurd to suppose that Holmes is unaware of the danger he is placing himself in by indulging in heavy cocaine use. Holmes is a fellow who misses nothing, "the most perfect reasoning and observing machine that the world has seen" ("A Scandal in Bohemia"). Yet his cocaine use seems entirely plausible to us, a trait that is not incomprehensible, but compellingly human. We understand that the great Holmes could do something he knows he shouldn't because we do that too. Not only does akrasia seem horribly real, it feels not like an intellectual exercise, but a struggle of some sort, as if we wrestle with the Moriarty of our bad desires above the Reichenbach Falls of self-sabotage.

Aristotle, like Holmes, is aware that appearances need not reflect the way that things really are. What looks from the street like a chap in his dressing gown reading the *Times* might really be a wax dummy, while what clearly appears to be a case of murder may turn out to be misadventure by racehorse. However, like Holmes, Aristotle believed that our theories should not contradict what appear to be the facts without very good reason.

Aristotle held that akrasia is real, and results not from an error in measurement, but from a clash between reason and emotion.

When we fail to do what we know is in our best interests, we give in to our passions rather than following our reason. Sir George ruins himself at the card table because he follows his greed and excitement rather than calculating probabilities and cutting his losses, the king of Bohemia exposes himself to blackmail because he follows his attraction to Irene Adler rather than coolly considering his future and rejecting her, while Holmes injects cocaine simply because he's doing what feels good rather than heeding his extraordinary powers of reason.

Aristotle's disagreement with the Socratic account is not complete, though, for he thinks that while in one sense the akratic person knows what they're doing, in another sense they don't. He compares their condition to the state of one who is asleep, or mad, or drunk. There's a sense in which one is no less knowledgeable when half awake, or suffering from depression, or drunk. "Black Peter" Carey, the feared ship's captain who became "a perfect fiend" when drunk ("The Adventure of Black Peter") does not suddenly become ignorant of the fact that murderous violence is illegal when he's full of rum. Yet we may say that his reason is clouded in his drunken state. His case is not unusual. I can think of at least four cases that Holmes solved due to the foolish errors of drunken men who should have known better—"The Adventure of the Copper Beeches," "The Adventure of Abbey Grange," "The Adventure of the Illustrious Client," and "The Adventure of the Veiled Lodger"—while the number of villains who committed criminal acts when intoxicated, though they should have known better, is greater yet, including, at the least, "The Five Orange Pips," "The Gloria Scott," "The Adventure of the Solitary Cyclist," and *The Valley of Fear.*

Similarly, perhaps the rest of us become "drunk" with our very desire for drink, or cigarettes, or food, or whatever our vices may be. We would not expect even the great Holmes to be able to prevent his reason being clouded by enough alcohol, and so perhaps can understand through analogy how he, too, might become "drunk" with the desire for cocaine.

I shall leave aside the curious matter of Holmes's apparent resistance to opium smoke in "The Man with the Twisted Lip." Watson enters an underground opium den in the wharf district, a "low room, thick and heavy with the brown opium smoke" to the point that he can barely see through it. He soon learns that Holmes has been sitting in the thick of the cloud for many hours in disguise. Either Holmes has a unique immunity or he's high off his noggin and makes up the Isa Whitney case on the spot to avoid yet another lecture from Watson about drug abuse.

If Aristotle is right, then we will need more than an intellectual understanding of the relative magnitude of pleasures if we are to overcome our tendency to akratic behavior. We will have to master our emotions in order to resist temptation, a process that Aristotle thinks lies in consistent practice. Thus, it is through consistently practicing not giving in to his desire for cocaine, a desire that Watson assures us Holmes never loses, that Holmes manages to wean himself from the drug. Similarly, what you and I need to do is to practice resisting our own vices, until our new behavior becomes natural to us.

The Game's Afoot

"Here you are, doggy! Good old Toby! Smell it, Toby, smell it!" [Holmes] pushed the creasote handkerchief under the dog's nose, while the creature stood with its fluffy legs separated, and with a most comical cock to its head . . ."
—*The Sign of the Four*

Mystery solved now? Not yet, though the game's afoot and well worth the candle. At best, we have been given some telling clues. While Aristotle's theory accounts relatively well for our experiences of akrasia (and while he has far more to say on the subject than I've had space to convey), much remains to be explained. Most strikingly, it isn't clear that he ever resolves the problem that led Socrates to deny that akrasia is possible. If our goal is pleasure, and we are free to act, why would we choose to follow an emotion that we know will lead us to less pleasure? It seems to make as much sense of our hypothetical case above in which Holmes, having only music as his goal, chooses to strike himself in the face with his violin rather than play it.

How can someone as brilliant as Holmes use cocaine? Socrates and Aristotle would have been unable to agree, and philosophers still can't agree, two and a half thousand years later. Yet weakness of will is a mystery that we can't ignore, since we care about our own wellbeing and don't want to sabotage ourselves by opting for a lesser good over a greater one. The mystery of weakness of the will is the only case that Sherlock Holmes needed to solve for his own sake. It is also the only case that Sherlock Holmes failed to solve. Holmes could never break his cocaine habit on his own. It was good old Watson who "weaned him from that drug mania," not the power of his own reason and will. Let us hope that we do better on this case than Sherlock Holmes.

Chapter 27
Like Some Strange Buddha
Cari Callis

Do not dwell in the past, do not dream of the future, concentrate the mind on the present moment.
　　—The Buddha

My name is Sherlock Holmes. It is my business to know what other people don't know.
　　—"The Adventure of the Blue Carbuncle"

Sherlock Holmes has become my spiritual teacher, though it took me forty years to figure that out. Arthur—dare I be so familiar with Holmes's literary agent?—Arthur and I had something in common; we both loved Harry Houdini. And we both had a love-hate relationship with Sherlock Holmes.

For weeks, I carried around *The Original Illustrated Sherlock Holmes Complete Volume* from Wilson Junior High Library. The weight of it felt important. Back then I equated wisdom with the size and heft of the text. The Bible. *The Arms of Krupp*. The Tolkien Trilogy. Shakespeare. And this equation has for the most part remained true, at least until recently when nearly all of my books suddenly became digital and weightless, and yes, there might be a metaphor here.

You see, Houdini was a trained magician dedicated to conditioning his body to create illusions, and I wanted to be like him. His underwater feat of holding his breath for three minutes while extricating himself from handcuffs and various constrictions inspired me to practice everyday in the bathtub and the swimming pool.

It was his complex friendship with Arthur—I mean Doyle— that led me down the path of reading all of Sherlock Holmes's cases the summer I spent as a lifeguard. All that holding of my breath had paid off. If Houdini loved Sherlock Holmes then I would too.

What I discovered was that while Houdini used controlled breathing to free himself from handcuffs and locked chains, Holmes extricated the truth from criminal cases and unsolvable mysteries—both those that appeared to be foul play and those that appeared supernatural—through his awareness. His ability to find answers and solve mysteries depended upon what he saw that other people did not. In other words, Holmes was struggling to extract himself from illusion.

Watson and I were both amused by how simple his methods were once we knew them, and in "The Scandal in Bohemia," Holmes—sounding like a Buddhist teacher—instructs us, "You see, but you do not observe. The distinction is clear."

The Art of Masterful Control

Almost from the beginning of our introduction to Holmes, he's equated with Buddhism. In *The Sign of the Four*, he is described by Watson as speaking brilliantly "on miracle plays, on mediaeval pottery, on Stradivarius violins, on the Buddhism of Ceylon, and on the warships of the future." Watson adds that he spoke "as though he had made a special study of it."

Stephen Kendrick, a Parish Minister of the Universalist Church, draws on the teaching of Buddhists, Christians, and Judaism to explore the stories of Sherlock Holmes and compares the focus that Holmes uses to see things without theories or preconceived ideas to the Zen practice of Bare Attention. Kendrick notes in his essay, "Zen in the Art of Sherlock Holmes":

> That Holmes would study Hinayana Buddhism seems surprising, until one actually looks at the ancient sources of this rigorous minority branch of Buddhism. Then the attraction becomes quite clear. Hinayana Buddhism, which claims to be the oldest, most accurate account of Buddha's teachings, presents the Buddha as cool, rational, and emotionally distant, a strict and intellectually rigorous instructor.

Now that sounds like someone we know: cool, rational, and emotionally distant. In his first short story, "A Scandal in Bohemia," Watson describes Holmes by saying, "All emotions, and that one particularly, were abhorrent to his cold, precise but admirably balanced mind. He was, I take it, the most perfect reasoning and observing machine that the world has seen . . ."

We learn that Holmes has masterful control of his emotions. This is one of the fundamental techniques of Vipassana meditation in the Hinayana—or more commonly as it is called, the Theraveda—tradition. The main idea of Theraveda, which literally means "The Teaching of the Elders," is to promote the "Teaching of Analysis" which is not faith based, but originates with the idea that truth of any kind must be founded on critical analysis, personal experience, and reasoning as a means of coming to wisdom. To see things as they are is the ultimate aim of Vipassana or Insight Meditation.

In the Theraveda tradition there are many methods of meditation for developing mindfulness and concentration, and there are thousands of visualization techniques in the Tibetan tradition. The technique used is less important than the end result, which allows one to gain wisdom by eliminating the thoughts which obscure it. When we're prejudiced and subjective, it's impossible to be objective. The whole aim of Buddhism is to see *dukkha* (suffering) as *dukkha*, for what it is, not how we feel about it.

In Insight Meditation, when observing emotion, whether it is pain, pleasure, anger, or frustration, the practice is not to eliminate feeling, but to observe each emotion as it arises, recognize it's impermanence, and not react to it. If we're reacting and continuously justifying our reactions, those details that Holmes uses to solve his cases will elude us or worse, delude us.

> "It is of the first importance," he cried, "not to allow your judgment to be biased by personal qualities. A client is to me a mere unit, a factor in a problem. The emotional qualities are antagonistic to clear reasoning." (*The Sign of the Four*)

Throughout the stories Holmes is frequently instructing Watson on how to differentiate between that which is true and that which is not by demonstrating his use of his reason and observation. When we see something and make something out of it, we can't help but impose judgments upon it.

What "bare attention" in the Buddhist tradition means is a practice of Insight Meditation that uncovers or lays bare things as they really are. Holmes is telling Watson that he must practice not reacting to his expectations and that this will lead him to insight knowledge. He also reminds him, "It is a capital mistake to theorize before one has data. Insensibly one begins to twist facts to suit theories, instead of theories to suit facts." In this first short story, Doyle has already laid out for us the philosophy of Sherlock Holmes.

There is nothing more deceptive than an obvious fact.
—Sherlock Holmes in "The Boscombe Valley Mystery"

Consider Holmes as a roommate with his nocturnal violin playing, "self-poisoner" by morphine, cocaine and tobacco, "who keeps his cigars in the coalscuttle, his tobacco in the toe end of a Persian slipper, and his unanswered correspondence transfixed by a jack-knife into the very centre of his wooden mantelpiece." This doesn't conjure up the image of a Zen Buddhist. But perhaps there is more to the violin playing, which Watson admits he does well, but as eccentrically as all of his other accomplishments.

> That he could play pieces, and difficult pieces, I knew well, because at my request he has played me Lieder, and other favourites. When left to himself, however, he would seldom produce any music or attempt any recognized air. Leaning back in his armchair of an evening, he would close his eyes and scrape carelessly at the fiddle which was thrown across his knee. Sometimes the chords were sonorous and melancholy. Occasionally they were fantastic and cheerful. Clearly they reflected the thoughts which possessed him, but whether the music aided those thoughts, or whether was simply the result of a whim or fancy, was more than I could determine. (*A Study in Scarlet*)

Perhaps Holmes uses his focus on the violin as an Insight Meditation to uncover or reveal things as they really are. By keeping his body occupied with playing, he can observe his thoughts without classifying or clarifying, but by being a witness without commentary. This is much like what Buddhists do when they are performing Walking Meditation. As Thich Nhat Hanh, the Buddhist teacher and monk describes it,

> Walking meditation is not a means to an end; it is an end. Each step is life; each step is peace and joy. That is why we don't have to hurry. That is why we slow down. We seem to move forward, but we don't go anywhere; we are not drawn by a goal.

Holmes isn't focusing on what he is playing as Watson observes, he simply plays when he needs to passively register his ideas, thoughts, and concepts.

> The truth you believe and cling to makes you unavailable to hear anything new.
> —Pema Chodron, *The Places that Scare You*

After being "resurrected" by Doyle from his tumble over Reichenbach Falls with Moriarty in "The Adventure of the Empty House," Holmes appears to Watson in the street disguised as a bookseller carrying a strange book called, "The Origin of Tree Worship." Buddhists today still worship the Bodhi tree in Sri Lanka which protected Buddha while he was meditating to gain enlightenment. Early Buddhists struggled to figure out whether or not trees could be cut down lawfully, and though it was ultimately decided that they could be, it was documented that some trees contain sacred spirits, something people in India still believe today.

Holmes then follows Watson home only to expose himself as his long lost friend come back to life. Holmes is always disguising himself and allegedly fooling Watson, although whether or not Watson is really taken in is up for debate. But one thing is for certain; Sherlock Holmes loves to dress up, and does so ten times throughout his career. In addition to being a seaman, bum, an opium addict, and a woman, he's disguised himself as a clergyman in "The Scandal in Bohemia" and a priest in "The Adventure of the Final Problem." He's definitely fond of portraying himself as a spiritual seeker.

And where has he been while Watson has been mourning his demise? He confesses he's been traveling for two years in Tibet, where he "amused myself visiting llasa, and spending some days with the head lama." Some Sherlockians have speculated that Holmes may have used this time to become a Dharma Bum, a Buddhist initiate practicing the meditation of awareness and observation. It's a romantic idea, and certainly inspires all of the duality that Kerouac's life and ideals contained, in that Holmes like Kerouac was a truth seeker who was also a very flawed human being.

The Practice of Patient Attention

So how does he access his genius? Perhaps there are clues to his success in *The Yoga Sutras of Pantajali*. This is a Hindu text and the foundation of all yoga practice. It owes much of its origins to Buddhism, and the samadhi techniques are identical to the jhanas in the Pali canon (the scriptures of the Theraveda tradition).

The first step is Attention (dharana). Sir Isaac Newton once said, "If I have ever made any valuable discoveries, it has been due more to patient attention than to any other talent."

Most of us have driven somewhere and been thinking about something else and then suddenly realize we've arrived at our destination without any memory of how we got there. When we snap out of it and realize we've been functioning on "autopilot," we understand how Holmes must view his comrade Watson, who no matter how hard he tries can never quite achieve the level of attention that is indispensible to Holmes in solving his cases. Watson's whole life seems to function on autopilot. He is constantly amazed at the details that Holmes can discern from the smallest bit of evidence. But it's not enough for someone to be able to focus their attention on the details as Holmes does, for many times in the stories Watson tries to make assumptions based on what he observes when he focuses his attention. Inevitably, Holmes sets him straight and proves him wrong.

The prolonged holding of the perceiving consciousness in that area of the brain is meditation (dhyana). The second step that Holmes uses is to fix his attention on a visible object with a single penetrating gaze. By doing this he directs his attention on the smallest details until they reveal more of their characteristic nature to him than a single glance could take in. He focuses the laser-light intensity of his consciousness on the crime scene evidence and takes in all the details that are always overlooked by Scotland Yard. In *A Study in Scarlet*, he demonstrates how fiercely his attention can be focused:

> "The writing on the wall was done with a man's forefinger dipped in blood. My glass allowed me to observe that the plaster was slightly scratched in doing it, which would not have been the case if the man's nail had been trimmed. I gathered up some scattered ash from the floor. It was dark in colour and flaky—such an ash is only made by a Trichinopoly. I have made a special study of cigar ashes—in fact, I have written a monograph upon the subject. I flatter myself that I can distinguish at a glance the ash of any known brand either of cigar or of tobacco."

It is just in such details that the skilled detective differs from the Gregson and Lestrade type. No wonder Watson's head is in a whirl after witnessing the ability of his friend to discern such penetrating details. A couple of paragraphs later he tells Watson,

> "I'm not going to tell you much more of the case Doctor. You know a conjurer gets no credit when once he has explained his trick; and if I show you too much of my method of working, you will come to the conclusion that I am a very ordinary individual after all."

Was this a foreshadowing of Doyle's friendship—and the unraveling of that friendship over this very issue—with Houdini?

Holmes next task is to direct the perceiving consciousness to illuminating the essential meaning of the problem he's examining and to free himself from his personality and separateness. This is contemplation (samadhi). These are the moments we find Holmes sunk into his chair with a four-pipe problem or scratching on his violin struggling to comprehend the meaning of his evidence. He struggles to illuminate the truth. And none of this would be possible if he wasn't able to relinquish all personal bias, all desire to prove himself right (like Gregson and Lestrade), and all desire for personal recognition or profit.

Sherlock Holmes loves truth for its own sake. This is the essence of his spiritual core. He doesn't want publicity, wealth or accolades although it must be said that he's not above a bit of pride in his abilities. Watson tells us, "I had already observed that he was as sensitive to flattery on the score of his art as any girl could be of her beauty." But this is different than seeking truth or justice for recognition, and in fact Holmes seems to be quite the opposite in that regard. Watson says in "The Adventure of the Devil's Foot,"

> ". . . I have continually been faced by difficulties caused by his own aversion to publicity. To his somber and cynical spirit all popular applause was always abhorrent, and nothing amused him more at the end of a successful case than to hand over the actual exposure to some orthodox official, and to listen with a mocking smile to the general chorus of misplaced congratulation."

The Awakened One

Whether consciously or unconsciously Holmes appears to be following *The Yoga Sutras of Pantanjali* in his methods and techniques of deduction. When attention, meditation, and contemplation are exercised together, he achieves perfectly concentrated meditation. Holmes has the ability to set aside his personal limitations and judgment of his perceiving consciousness and can open himself to what can be called the All-consciousness to decipher his dilemmas. This is the place where his discoveries come from and where his spark of genius ignites.

We can't know if Holmes followed any particular spiritual path or whether he was a Buddhist or simply an agnostic as the lapsed Catholic Doyle defined himself. Later in his life Doyle became an avid Spiritualist believing in and promoting the supernatural, something Holmes disproves again and again. As did his friend Houdini, whom he took on in just such a public debate in the press. His desire to believe in charlatans and to even publish statements claiming Houdini was himself supernatural caused him to lose that friendship.

But what are we to make of the fact that Doyle was familiar with Buddhism and wrote a book called *The Mystery of Cloomber* the year after the first Sherlock Holmes novel was published, a mystery about a man who murders a Buddhist priest and is then avenged by his students (chelas)? It's a strange story about how the three chelas let the man live for forty years with an astral bell tolling over his head to keep him in misery. The priest's name is Ghoolab Shah, a Hindu-Muslim name, and the three students show up wearing red fezzes, so Doyle may not have had any direct experience with any actual Buddhists, but he did document in his autobiography that he'd read A.P. Sinnett's book, *Esoteric Buddhism*, which documents the life of the Buddha and his reincarnations and also introduces the laws of karma.

The word "Buddha" means the "awakened one" and this may have been what Doyle was thinking when he described Sherlock Holmes in "The Veiled Lodger" as sitting upon the floor "like some strange Buddha, with crossed legs, the huge books all around him, and one open on his knees." The yoga sutras suggest that the conscious cultivation of genius, whether the possessor recognizes it or not, is for certain the power and the vision of a spiritual seeker. Sherlock Holmes may not have consciously recognized that his spirit was full of reverence, of self-less devotion to truth, of humility—that his practice of constant awareness was mindfulness and rooted in the divine.

THE TRACING OF FOOTSTEPS

Chapter 28
Why *Sherlock* Is Like
a Good Hip-Hop Song
Rachel Michaels

"I'm Sherlock Holmes, the world's only consulting detective. I'm not going to go into detail about how I do what I do because chances are you wouldn't understand. If you've got a problem you want me to solve then contact me. Interesting cases only please.

This is what I do:

1.) I observe everything.

2.) From what I observe, I deduce everything.

3.) When I've eliminated the impossible, whatever remains, no matter how mad it might seem, must be the truth.

If you need assistance, contact me and we'll discuss its potential."

—the website of Sherlock Holmes (www.thescienceofdeduction. co.uk)

Mr. Sherlock Holmes and Dr. John H. Watson are often solely associated with the British Victorian era and its trappings—gas lights, horse carts, telegrams, petticoats, sexual prudery, the class system; sort of like Dickens's *A Christmas Carol* but with more sensational crimes.

But take them out of the 1890s and into the 21st Century, and we find Holmes and Watson still doing quite well. They have starred in scores of scholarly books (including this one), the popular Guy Ritchie steampunk-influenced Sherlock Holmes films, and the BBC television series entitled, simply, *Sherlock*. This series in particular explores the question many Holmes fans have asked themselves in the middle of the night: WWSHD? If Sherlock Holmes was here, now, what would he do?

Sherlock, which stars Benedict Cumberbatch as Sherlock and Martin Freeman as John, speculates that Holmes's methods and personality would be a great fit for the present day, with such newfangled contraptions as laptops, the Internet, and cellular phones. One hundred and twenty years after the first stories were published, we still need Holmes's unique abilities. Though the times have changed, the essential characters of Holmes and Watson have not. The way their stories are told, however, is quite different now from the 1890's. While Victorian readers enjoyed Sir Arthur Conan Doyle's stories in the monthly magazine *The Strand* (tagline: "A monthly magazine costing sixpence but worth a shilling"), modern readers have a multitude of media to get our Sherlock Holmes fix, including books, magazines, television, film, comics, websites, webseries, e-books, interactive tablets, and video games.

Not only are the ways we access the stories much more varied, we also have a century's worth of Sherlock Holmes stories and images to consciously or unconsciously reference. It's well documented that Sherlock Holmes stars in more movies that any other character in the world; the *Guinness Book of World Records* lists two hundred and eleven films with seventy-five actors playing Holmes. The world's only consulting detective has starred in eight television series, including his canine incarnation as *Sherlock Hound* (1984); *Sherlock Holmes in the 22nd Century* (1999), his animated venture into the future; as well as the great 1980s Granada series with Jeremy Brett. Both *Sherlock* and a comic series called *Victorian Undead* ("Sherlock Holmes vs. ZOMBIES!") appeared in 2010. Conan Doyle's stories have also had innumerable effects on subsequent incarnations of detective and thriller genres in fiction, films, and television.

Conan Doyle's original tales are straightforward, self-contained, and linear; they begin with a problem and end with its triumphant answer. The language is clear and sufficiently descriptive; the gentle hand of Dr. Watson guides us through all of the story's stages, from the client's first interactions with Holmes to the resolution of the case. Holmes applies his methods ("Eliminate all other factors, and the one which remains must be the truth") to the puzzle at hand, the mystery is subsequently resolved, and the reader finishes the story feeling that reason can, and in fact, does, rule the world.

For better or worse, the twenty-first century doesn't seem as simple. Our stories are told in ways that combine many different elements; we seem more mixed up. We blend various fragments—stories, visual techniques, genres, and media themselves—into innovative combinations, making new "originals" out of pieces that had not previously been linked. These stories are often told in a non-linear fashion, as well, making the viewer an active part of the process by having to piece together the narrative.

Think of films by Quentin Tarantino—they contain chunks of spaghetti westerns, kung fu, WWII espionage movies, stories of revenge, grindhouse, and American twentieth-century pop music. These movies blend these disparate sources into new, individual works. The material that comes out of this blending is called a pastiche, and once you start looking for them, you see that they are everywhere. Sherlock Holmes is involved in quite a few, including Sherlock (and the comics with the ZOMBIES!), and he would enjoy discovering his new adventures in the twenty-first century.

A Case of Pastiche

Postmodernism, like Victorianism and modernism before it, can be studied through its cultural output of stories, images, music, and media. Cultural theorist Fredric Jameson wrote in *The Cultural Turn* that one of postmodernism's significant features is "the erosion of the older distinction between high culture and so-called mass or popular culture." Postmodernists, Jameson continues, "no longer 'quote' such texts . . . they *incorporate* them, to the point where the line between high art and commercial forms seems increasingly difficult to draw" (emphasis mine). Our immense backlog of culture, from opera to comics, has become democratized and blended together. The modern world allows us to pick and choose strands of stories and images from across time; the playing field is now level.

Sherlock knowingly combines ingredients of prior works with new elements to create a unique work: a pastiche. This word is taken from the French language, and was based on the Italian word *pasticcio*, itself from the late Latin word for "paste," pasta. This multi-lingual word with multi-layered meanings is appropriate to describe the incorporation of different elements into a single whole. The creators of the pastiche are not only mixing together different pieces from their subconscious, they are consciously referencing and incorporating those elements into their own work.

We're surrounded by pastiches, from television shows (*The Simpsons, Family Guy, The Daily Show, Lost, Glee*) and movies (*Pulp Fiction, Moulin Rouge!, Marie Antoinette, Carlos, Repo! The Genetic Opera*) to genres of music—including hip hop, dub, dubstep, and other forms of electronic, rock, jazz, and pop.

An excellent example of pastiche is hip-hop music, a genre which can combine original beats and spoken or sung melodies with any combination of sounds sampled from other sources. Hip-hop songs are not "adaptations" of other works if they feature a Stevie Wonder horn sample, say, or a bit of a Hans Zimmer film score; they are something unique that has been constructed through the use of different parts. A pastiche is like Frankenstein's creature: sewn together to create a new being.

The most current—and trendy—term for this mixing of different pieces into new combinations is "mash-up." These days, anything that combines two different traditions is called a mash-up; a *New York Times* search of the hyphenated word in their pages includes over ten thousand uses of the term in the past thirty days as I write this, including as a description of the 2011 Oscars, various recipes, music videos, concerts, operas. A mash-up is a pulverized version of pastiche.

The Scientific Use of the Imagination

Sherlock frequently uses technology to illustrate this continuity throughout its first season. Watson's memoirs have become "The Personal Blog of Dr. John H. Watson." Sherlock uses texts and emails as the nineteenth century's Holmes uses telegrams— to communicate and receive information to solve a case. Both the Victorian and modern Sherlocks have a detailed map of London in their heads; now such systems are called GPS. Sherlock uses his PDA for information as Holmes scours the newspaper searching for information on weather conditions, possible cases, and clues.

As impressive as these toys can be, though, Sherlock is very explicit on one point: that modern technology aids Sherlock's deductions by providing data, but they alone do not solve the crimes. If the newer technology were solely responsible for the deductions, then even Lestrade could solve these cases. It is, of course, Holmes's singular ability to see a narrative chain from the data, and to draw connections between bits of information that seem otherwise unconnected.

Sherlock and John—we call them by their first names when we're talking about the new *Sherlock* series—still also investigate the old-fashioned way—by breaking into apartments, going to the library, visiting museums, and dodging bullets, with each mini-adventure developing their friendship. The Baker Street Irregulars, once a band of street urchins happy to get a shilling per day and a guinea (roughly one Pound Sterling) for an important clue, have evolved into the use of what Sherlock calls his "homeless network," whose investigative fee has become £50. Fees and technological tools may have changed, but Sherlock Holmes's ability to solve seemingly impossible cases has remained the same.

Eccentric or Sociopath: You Say Tomato, I Say Tomato?

How can we differentiate "postmodernism" from "modernism" or even "Victorianism?" Can society really have changed so drastically in only 150 years? Fredric Jameson answers this question by suggesting that different time periods do not involve total changes of content but rather a "restructuring of a certain number of elements already given: features that in an earlier period or system were subordinate now become dominant, and features that have been dominant again become secondary." Different values and interests become more prominent in one period, then become less culturally relevant in the next. Tendencies present in Conan Doyle's original stories (Holmes's misanthropy and superiority complex) are now played up and exaggerated to fit contemporary sensibilities. This is most evident in *Sherlock*'s portrayal of its main character as a self-proclaimed sociopath (a personality disorder featuring extremely antisocial attitudes and lack of conscience).

Sherlock stays true to Conan Doyle's portrayals of Holmes, with certain amplifications of his eccentricities that reflect a modern sensibility. Like Ritchie's films, the quirks and antisocial tendencies of Sherlock are the focus of his characterization. Sherlock describes himself as "a highly functioning sociopath," and he is indeed a difficult roommate and colleague. A recurring point of discussion between Sherlock and John is Sherlock's lack of empathy towards, well, anyone, as is his insistence that he solves crimes not to help others but to avoid being crushed by his own boredom. The Sherlock in this series is younger than has been presented before, and is accordingly both full of himself and highly concerned with others' respect for his abilities. John is able to guide Sherlock in how normal people think and how to speak to them—valuable skills when trying to gather the type of information that cannot be provided through an email.

While the oddities of Sherlock Holmes are certainly mentioned in the original stories—from the seven per cent solution to his lack of knowledge of the solar system to his mood swings—Conan Doyle presents them with more subtlety. The intervening century of psychology, modernism, and antiheroes (including fellow detective Sam Spade, *Taxi Driver*'s Travis Bickle, *Fight Club*'s Tyler Durden, and serial killer Dexter Morgan) have led to a greater level of acceptance (even expectation) of a flawed hero. Other parts of Conan Doyle's character can now be amplified in *Sherlock*, fitting with common heroes of the present day.

A Study in . . . Pink!

The first three episodes of *Sherlock*, "A Study in Pink," "The Blind Banker," and "The Great Game," are vivid examples of pastiche. "A Study in Pink" is particularly instructive in the differences between a straight-up adaptation and a postmodernist pastiche. The Jeremy Brett *Adventures of Sherlock Holmes* series is a straight-up adaptation—each episode's goal is to be a line-by-line duplication of Conan Doyle's stories, from dialogue to plot to costumes. "A Study in Pink," however, freely adapts from many different sources, as the title explains. "A Study in Pink" uses "A Study in Scarlet" as its basic text but tweaks it so much it becomes something different entirely.

The episode begins very much like *A Study in Scarlet*, with military doctor John Watson returning home from the war in Afghanistan with post-traumatic stress disorder. He runs into Stamford, a colleague from medical school, who introduces him to Sherlock Holmes after Watson mentions he is looking for lodging. Sherlock is then introduced to John (and the audience) in the laboratory at St. Bart's, where he is beating corpses with a stick to verify how bruises may be produced after death. He and John plan to meet the next day to visit the flat in Baker Street.

So far, so *not* a pastiche. This sequence of events in *Sherlock* is a direct adaptation of *A Study in Scarlet* and not a combination of different elements intermingling to create a new text. A "straight" updated adaptation of *A Study in Scarlet* would have continued in the previous vein. Sherlock would be called in to investigate a male murder victim covered in someone else's blood in Brixton. But the crime takes a different turn in "A Study in Pink;" the victim is female and is found in a shocking pink tailored suit. *Sherlock* is now *in pastiche territory*.

Cumberbatch's Sherlock uses a variety of tools to investigate the empty room where the body was found. He examines the body's fingers, jewelry, coat, and stockings with a magnifying glass and uses his PDA to obtain weather information. He systematically determines the five letters "Rache" scratched into the floor next to the body to be most of the word "Rachel." Viewers familiar with Conan Doyle's story will recognize the "Rache" element. In *A Study in Scarlet*, the police determine "Rache" to be the word "Rachel" but Holmes establishes it as "Rache," the German word for revenge. The situation is now reversed in "A Study in Pink": Sherlock recognizes the word as "Rachel" (later to be determined as the victim's email password) while the police come to the impractical solution of an angry note having been left in German.

Based on the state of her clothing and the day's UK weather forecast, Sherlock concludes that the victim is a media executive coming from the popular television center Cardiff, Wales. The pink-clad corpse is identified by Sherlock as the fourth victim in a string of serial suicides heavily covered by the British media. This creates a new storyline for the murders and eliminates Conan Doyle's plot about nefarious Mormons and an ocean-crossing act of revenge.

That original plot of *A Study in Scarlet* could have translated quite well into the year 2010, from smaller details to large. The letters found in the pocket of the dead man, Enoch Drebber, could have become printed emails, for example, and the motives of religious prejudice, greed, and revenge are still very much in style. The creators of *Sherlock* made a conscious decision, however, to use a multitude of elements to tell their story; they chose to employ the method of pastiche.

In this scene, Sherlock also refers to the "heavy rain" that the pink lady had to travel through. This is a direct reference to the video game *Heavy Rain* (Quantic Dream, 2010) that *Sherlock*'s visual style and theme strongly resemble. Both the game and the television series feature distinctive camera shots with a heavy blurriness around the focal point of the scene that directs the viewer's attention to particular details. *Sherlock* and *Heavy Rain* also share the same drab color palette as well as similar plotlines featuring an "Origami Killer" (a major plotline from *Sherlock*'s second episode, "The Blind Banker"). The strongest reference to *Heavy Rain*, however, is the use of on-screen text to illustrate Sherlock's deductive process. Even the font is the same—it's called Johnston and was been used for the London Underground since 1916 (coincidentally the year between the publication of Conan Doyle's *The Valley of Fear* and "His Last Bow"). All of these elements—from the font to filming techniques to plotlines to showing text on-screen in the first place—were conscious choices made by *Sherlock*'s creators.

So When Is the Lovely Couple Going to Get Killed?

Narrative content is not the only arena in which to find the pastiche, however. All of the choices made to convey the story to the audience—including camera angles, editing, color palettes, and acting styles—also create the experience of the episodes. Television programs have their own conventions, and, more specifically, so do genres of television programs like the detective thriller *Sherlock*.

We assume, for example, that contemporary detective thriller programs will consistently feature elements such as a murder-mystery, tense music, an investigation of the suspects, a red herring or false trail to ramp up the suspense, and the dramatic solving of the crime. Each of the *Sherlock* episodes features these elements, as do all of the *Law and Order* franchises, various real-crime documentary programs, and the *CSI* franchise. Florid acting styles, elaborate costumes, subplots other than how the detectives' dedication to their work makes their family life difficult, and romantic-sounding scores would all seem out of place in a detective thriller. They would, in fact turn the program into a drama, or perhaps a romance.

Therefore, when television programs (or films, or novels, or pieces of music, or nonfiction) share elements with other similar programs of the past and present, they are presenting codes to their audiences that reflect years of development. The programs mix different elements—some original, some not—to create a new individual work. They are pastiches.

The other two first-season episodes of *Sherlock*, "The Blind Banker" and "The Great Game," similarly combine a plot from a Conan Doyle story with new elements. "The Blind Banker" transforms the coded messages from "The Adventure of the Dancing Men" to street graffiti and mixes in a plot involving the continuing aftereffects of the 2008 financial crisis, an international smuggling ring, and a Chinese circus. Unlike the original stories, John is placed in mortal danger and must be saved by our brainy action hero Sherlock. This mixture of older and contemporary themes fits nicely with the postmodern blend of Victorian fiction, contemporary politics, and television thriller conventions in *Sherlock*'s "The Blind Banker."

"The Great Game" has Sherlock and John on the trail of no less than five mysteries, with their narrative strands interweaving to create a unique combination. In an adaptation of the Conan Doyle story, Mycroft Holmes asks Sherlock's help to find the missing flash drive holding the Bruce-Partington missile project.

The other mysteries feature the modern twist that each must be solved within a timeframe of a few hours or an innocent victim will die—placing Sherlock firmly within the realm of blockbuster action movies or TV's *24*. The whereabouts of a mad bomber, the death of a television "reality" star, the poisoning of a child, the disappearance of a businessman, and the possible forgery of an Old Master painting are crammed into its ninety minutes. The story climaxes in a standoff reminiscent of a cowboy movie and ends in a sensational cliffhanger. Echoing the purpose of Conan Doyle's original stories—that of thrilling entertainment—"The Great Game" is a vivid example of pastiche.

The Adventure of the Time-Traveling Detective

What could be in store for our heroes Mr. Sherlock Holmes and Dr. John H. Watson over the next 120 years? What kinds of crimes will we need them to solve, and with what tools? What parts of Sherlock will stand out to audiences in ten years, or twenty, or one hundred? Will they wonder what it was like to watch a program on a quaint old HD television and not on their head-screens, or how it would be possible to physically hold one of those massive-ancient-book-thingies without suction feelers? Will categories like "sociopath" and "banker" even exist?

One thing's for sure, though—no matter what the era, Sherlock Holmes can solve the most singular, improbable cases. His unerring powers of observation and deduction illustrate an apparently timeless faith in the applicability of empirical reason. And that, my dear, is elementary.

Chapter 29

Moriarty's Final Human Problem in *Star Trek: The Next Generation*

Zoran Samardzija

My fascination with Sherlock Holmes derives from the fact that I am huge *Star Trek* fan and nerd. I began to wonder why so many allusions to the fictional world created by Sir Arthur Conan Doyle appear throughout the numerous incarnations of *Star Trek*.

Upon reading the original Holmes stories, I began to understand that when they are referenced, quoted, or holographically recreated, the *Star Trek* writers do so in order to grapple with the philosophical, ethical, and geopolitical dilemmas for which the *Star Trek* franchise is best known.

In the timeframe occupied by the original *Star Trek* series, the first recognizable allusion to Sherlock Holmes occurs in the feature length film *Star Trek VI: The Undiscovered Country* (1991). After Captain Kirk and Bones are framed and imprisoned for assassinating the Klingon Chancellor Gorkon, Spock tells the *Enterprise* crew, before they begin searching for evidence to reveal the conspiracy, that "an ancestor of mine maintained, that if you eliminate the impossible, whatever remains, however improbable, must be the truth."

His appropriation of the famous quote about the power of logic functions as more than just an in-joke for Sherlock Holmes fans. For Trekkers like myself, it also slyly establishes thematic continuity between the original series and the first spin-off: *Star Trek: The Next Generation*, which is set several decades in the future. In particular, it associates Spock with Lt. Commander Data of the Starships *Enterprise D* and *Enterprise E*, a sentient android who wishes he were capable of human emotions. He, too, happens to be a fan of Sir Arthur Conan Doyle's Sherlock Holmes mysteries.

Upon hearing Spock's citation of Holmes in the movie, I was immediately reminded of two episodes of *The Next Generation* that aired prior to the sixth film: "Elementary, Dear Data" from 1988 and "Data's Day" from 1991. The former episode establishes Data's propensity to role play as Sherlock Holmes using the spaceship's holodeck. In the latter episode, Data is investigating an apparent transporter accident when he directly echoes Spock's dialogue as he, too, quotes the virtues of eliminating the impossible. In J.J. Abrams's recent "reboot" movie, *Star Trek* (2009), the "alternative universe" Spock utters the same famous Holmes quotation.

To use one of Spock's favorite words, I find it *fascinating* how *Star Trek* is able to dramatize competing definitions of human nature through its references to Sherlock Holmes. Since Spock is half-human and half-Vulcan (a race that privileges logic and reason at the expensive of emotion), in the *Star Trek* universe, it is an alien and a sentient android who identify with Sherlock Holmes and share his reasoning abilities. In other words, excessive rationality is characterized as a non-human trait, which means that *Star Trek* implicitly questions the core philosophical value of the Western Enlightenment that defines reason as the essential trait of humanity. This debate about human nature, however, is most compellingly dramatized in the Sherlock-Holmes-themed episodes of *Star Trek: The Next Generation* and the character of Data who engages in a battle of wits with Professor Moriarty who appears as a sentient holographic computer program.

Which Is More Human:
An Android Holmes or Holographic Moriarty?

The holographic Professor Moriarty in *Star Trek: The Next Generation* is introduced during Season Two in "Elementary, Dear Data." The episode begins with Captain Picard's usual captain's log, informing viewers that the *Enterprise* has arrived early for a rendezvous for their next mission and has nothing to do but wait. As is customary in the series, a pre-title credit sequence introduces the dramatic themes of each episode. In this particular case, Lt. Geordie La Forge, the ship's chief engineer, summons Data to engineering to show him his detailed model of a classic British battleship. After Data asks why he would be interested in a ship less technologically advanced than the *Enterprise*, La Forge responds, "That's exactly why this fascinated me, Data. See, it's human nature to love what we don't have."

His comment foretells how the episode frames its debate about human nature. In the broadest sense, the episodes explore whether logic and rationality or intuition and emotions are essential human traits. A careful consideration of its title, "Elementary, Dear Data," even hints at what answer the episode will provide. The first thing to note is that it's obviously a play on the famous phrase, "Elementary, my dear Watson," that Sherlock Holmes would utter in the early Basil Rathbone Sherlock Holmes movies whenever he wished to emphasize his reasoning to Watson. Here, however, the ironic interlocution of the episode's title positions Data against himself; while he role-plays as Sherlock Holmes, he is the one who needs to learn what is elementary about human nature. The line, in fact, is spoken to Data by the ship's doctor, Katherine Pulaski, who does not believe Data can ever become fully human. The context in which she says it is especially important.

For instance, after showing Data his model battleship, La Forge invites Data to participate in a holodeck simulation of a Holmes mystery. The holodeck, for those unfamiliar with the sprawling *Star Trek* universe, is a computer controlled virtual-reality simulator that crews use mostly for recreational purposes. While attempting the simulation, because of the brute strength of his computational skills and memory Data immediately solves the mystery, much to the annoyance La Forge. Upon leaving the holodeck, the two of them encounter Doctor Pulaski. Overhearing their conversation, she bets Data that he cannot solve a mystery that he was not previously familiar with, implying that he is only truly capable of computation and memorization. When the three of them enter the holodeck, Data once again immediately solves the mystery. This frustrates the doctor who then spins the "elementary" phrase against Data.

> **PULASKI:** (*to Geordi*) Now, now do you see my point? All he knows is what is stored in his memory banks. Inspiration, original thought, the true strength of Holmes is not possible for our friend. (*to Data*) I give you credit for your vast knowledge, but your circuits would just short out when confronted by a truly original mystery. It's elementary, dear Data.

In the guise of praising Sherlock Holmes's "true strength" and demeaning Data's computational skills, Doctor Pulaski offers a definition of human nature that privileges intuition. Interestingly enough she claims that it's not Holmes's exemplary reasoning that makes him so great. Rather, it is his eccentricities and originality, features which Data can never develop because he is incapable of overcoming his programming. In other words,

Data can only reason but Holmes can employ a wide-range of skills and behavior when solving mysteries. Doctor Pulaski's argument has a distinct Nietzschean flair to it. We can easily imagine that while in Starfleet Academy Doctor Pulaski must have read Nietzsche's *Human, All Too Human* where he writes in the aphorism "The illogical necessary" that:

> The illogical is a necessity for mankind, and that much good proceeds from the illogical. It is implanted so firmly in the passions, in language, in art, in religion, and in general in everything that lends value to life . . . Only very naïve people are capable of believing that the nature of man could be transformed into a purely logical one. (R.J. Hollingdale translation, p. 28)

The inability to be illogical and irrational, in other words, is what prevents Data from becoming fully human. Conversely, the fact that Moriarty in *Star Trek* has those traits makes him more recognizably human than Data. Consider, for example, how he comes into existence in the first place. After Doctor Pulaski's declaration of "fraud," La Forge yet again programs the computer, this time with the following directive, "in the Holmesian style create a mystery to confound Data with an opponent who has the ability to defeat him," in effect creating the sentient holographic simulation of Moriarty who is capable of "originality" and "inspiration," which are the very traits Data cannot develop.

This Moriarty that comes into existence, then, differs from the one Sir Arthur Conan Doyle describes in his original stories. Professor Moriarty plays a prominent role only in the notorious "The Final Problem" but his legacy as Sherlock Holmes's greatest arch-nemesis is unquestionable. In the story, Watson narrates how the Professor and Holmes fell to their deaths at Reichenbach Falls.

However, as devoted Sherlock Holmes readers are aware, a decade later Arthur Conan Doyle resurrected his most famous creation for a series of new stories after deciding against permanently killing him off. In "The Adventure of the Empty House" we learn that Holmes did in fact defeat Moriarty but faked his death in order to escape from Moriarty's criminal cohorts. Readers were thus deprived of subsequent battles between Holmes and his greatest antagonist. It also means that Doyle left unexplored several fascinating philosophical and ethical questions about the nature of Moriarty's criminal tendencies that are teasingly implied by the hyperbolic descriptions Holmes provides of him in "The Final Problem."

I often wonder about the intellectual legitimacy of Holmes's description of Moriarty. In the famous passage, Holmes tells Watson how Moriarty became a criminal:

> "He is a man of good birth and excellent education, endowed by nature with a phenomenal mathematical faculty . . . But the man had hereditary tendencies of the most diabolical kind. A criminal strain ran in his blood, which, instead of being modified, was increased and rendered infinitely more dangerous by his extraordinary mental powers."

After discussing how he became of aware of Moriarty's shadowy presence in London, Holmes tells Watson about Moriarty's criminal methodology. He adds:

> "He is the Napoleon of crime, Watson. He is the organizer of half that is evil and all that is undetected in this great city. He is a genius, a philosopher, an abstract thinker. He has a brain of the first order. He sits motionless, like a spider in the centre of his web, but that web has a thousand radiations, and he knows well every quiver of each of them. He does little himself. He only plans."

Given the hyperbolic intensity of Holmes's description of Moriarty—"a genius;" "extraordinary mental powers;" "The Napoleon of crime"—the question arises: What compelled Holmes, a master of logical abduction, to use his abilities to solve crimes while Moriarty uses his to become the definitive criminal genius of London? Especially from the perspective of a modern reader, Holmes's own answer to this intractable nature-versus-nurture dilemma relies on a regrettable idea that was no doubt commonplace during the Victorian and Edwardian Eras in which Doyle's stories were set. In other words, the recourse to biological determinism or "hereditary tendencies" to explain Moriarty's path to evil relies more on a hasty, inductive generalization rather than Holmes's usual impeccable abductive reasoning.

While the Moriarty in *Star Trek: The Next Generation* certainly appears to be a "philosopher" and "an abstract thinker," he in fact rebels against his "hereditary tendencies" and programming to be an evil mastermind. He exhibits an irrational and illogical commitment to securing his own right to exist. In essence, one can say that the Moriarty in "Elementary, Dear Data" has subconscious desires and intuitions, rather than deterministic "hereditary" traits, which he can use to gather knowledge about his "world." Consider what he says to Data and La Forge:

> **MORIARTY:** My mind is crowded with images. Thoughts I do not understand yet cannot purge. They plague me. You and your associate look and act so oddly, yet though I have never met nor seen the like of either of you I am familiar with you both. It's very confusing. I have felt new realities at the edge of my consciousness, readying to break through. Surely, Holmes, if that's who you truly are, you of all people can appreciate what I mean.

Moriarty, in other words, doesn't come to understand that he is a holographic simulation by using Holmesian reasoning. As his dialogue indicates, Moriarty is haunted by intuitions about which subsequently he must reason and make logical inferences. Reason, therefore, emerges as a secondary trait of the expression of human nature. Only later in the episode does Moriarty make philosophical and logical arguments about his sentience, such as in the following conservation he has with Captain Jean-Luc Picard and Data:

> **MORIARTY:** Is the definition of life "cogito ergo sum"? I think, therefore I am.
> **PICARD:** That's one possible definition.
> **MORIARTY:** It is the most important one for me, the only one that matters. You or someone asked your computer to program a nefarious fictional character from nineteenth-century London and that is how I arrived, but I am no longer that creation. I am no longer that evil character, I have changed. I am alive. I am aware of my own consciousness.

Moriarty refers to Descartes's famous *cogito ergo sum* proposition about existence, which is certainly one of the cornerstones of Western Philosophy. And the *Enterprise* crew are ultimately convinced, but there remains a pragmatic problem: As a holographic projection, Moriarty doesn't consist of matter. He's still only energy and light and, as such, he cannot ever leave the confines of the holodeck, which is a problem the sequel episode "Ship in a Bottle" revisits. He agrees, therefore, to be placed in protected computer memory until it can be determined what is to be done with him.

The Evil Genius that Turns Moriarty into a Brain in a Vat

Moriarty's story is resolved on *Star Trek: The Next Generation* in the episode "Ship in a Bottle." Instead of merely repeating the philosophical debates about human nature from "Elementary, Dear Data," the show cleverly presents a solution to Moriarty's inability to leave the holodeck. The solution offered represents a novel twist on the old philosophical dilemma of the "evil genius," which is updated as the problem of "a brain in a vat." In simple terms the idea is this: if some advanced species so desired, they could so completely deceive your senses that all your ideas about reality would be wrong. As you read this sentence, for example, you could be a brain in a vat receiving "false" stimuli, as some mad scientist forces you to read essays on Sherlock Holmes and philosophy. In the modern era, this radical skepticism about whether you can ever really know "external reality" was first articulated by René Descartes in *Meditations on First Philosophy* where he writes:

> I shall then suppose, not that God who is supremely good and the fountain of truth, but some evil genius not less powerful than deceitful, has employed his whole energies in deceiving me; I shall consider that the heavens, the earth, colours, figures, sound, and all other external things are nought but the illusions and dreams of which this genius has availed himself in order to lay traps for my credulity.

So how does the idea of existing only as a brain in a vat in some evil scientist's lab solve Moriarty's problem? "Ship in a Bottle" begins with Data and La Forge once again role-playing in a Sherlock Holmes mystery in the holodeck. However, they discover that it is malfunctioning because its "spatial orientation systems" project left-handed characters as right-handed and vice versa. That piece of techno-babble foreshadows what happens later in the episode. After encountering the system error, Data and La Forge summon Lt. Barclay to fix the holodeck, and he inadvertently releases Professor Moriarty from protected memory. Much to the concern of Captain Picard, the holographic Moriarty experienced the passage of time while stored in memory. As he states, he felt "brief, terrifying periods of consciousness . . . disembodied, without substance." Moreover, Moriarty no longer trusts the *Enterprise* to figure out how he can leave the holodeck, which is understandable after experiencing such terrible existential dread.

The subsequent plot of "Ship in a Bottle" resembles films about virtual reality such as *The Matrix* (1999) or David Cronenberg's *eXistenZ* (1999), though it aired several years before either (another example of how ideas in *Star Trek* are often ahead of our time). Moriarty takes control of the holodeck again, but this time he creates a simulation of the entire *Enterprise* within the Sherlock Holmes holodeck simulation he "exists" in. His aim in doing so is slightly convoluted. He wants to deceive Picard, Data, and Barclay into believing that through sheer will power alone, he is in fact capable of leaving the holodeck. Once he does that, he takes control of the ship and demands that the crew find a way to have the Countess Barthalomew, who is also a holographic simulation, leave the holodeck—knowledge he would use "in reality" to actually leave the holodeck himself.

In other words, Moriarty's plan recalls the idea of becoming trapped in dream within a dream, a concept popularized by Christopher Nolan's puzzle film *Inception* (2010). Unlike with *Inception*, however, audiences of "Ship in a Bottle" aren't meant to try and decode dream from reality by searching for textual clues. Whereas the former is constructed to allow for multiple interpretations and has an open-ended conclusion, the *Star Trek* episode advances the more radical proposition that, ultimately, humans can never have certainty about the nature of reality.

Only Data, who is not human, but an android, is able to deduce that he, Picard, and Barclay are still in a holodeck program because of its malfunctioning "spatial orientation systems." Because of his reasoning abilities, the three of them create a third holodeck simulation within Moriarty's simulation running within the initial Sherlock Holmes program—or think of it as a dream within dream within a dream. In their simulation, they convince Moriarty that he and the Countess have left the holodeck and the two of them take a shuttlecraft and leave the *Enterprise*.

Once that happens they exit all the simulations and keep Moriarty running in the program where he thinks he is freely roaming the universe. In his simulated reality, Moriarty apparently lives on thinking he has finally become human. Presumably he can never discern that he has been deceived. The final dialogue between Barclay, Picard, and the ship's counselor Troi nicely encapsulates the idea that complete certainty about the nature of reality is impossible. Picard asks hypothetically, "Who knows? Our reality might not be all that different from theirs. All this might be nothing more than an elaborate simulation being run inside a little device, sitting on someone else's table." In other words, humans can never deduce that we are "a brain in a vat," or part of an elaborate computer simulation. Like Moriarty in *Star Trek: The Next Generation* we choose to believe that we are not the subject of sensory experiments from some evil genius or deity. In the absence of evidence to the contrary, we believe in external reality and that we are human. Such a belief is not possible for Data. Unfortunately, his advanced reasoning allows him to know when he is being deceived by a computer simulation.

Since Data lacks the ability to have irrational beliefs, he can never become fully human. As Trekkers are aware, this dilemma is a reccurring storyline in the *Star Trek: The Next Generation* series and subsequent movies. For example, he experiments with an "emotion chip" and a program that allows him to dream, but these technologies meant to replicate the human experience of the irrational never succeed. Thus for Data a peculiar paradox emerges: only in death does he come close to achieving humanity. As the conclusion of the film *Star Trek X: Nemesis* (2002) reveals, he sacrifices himself to save the lives of others. In other words, believing he is still not human does not prevent him from acting humanely. In that regard, his fate is preferable to the holographic Moriarty trapped in a computer simulation, believing that he has become human.

I can imagine—in some distant future—the holographic Moriarty growing bored and restless from traveling throughout his virtual universe. Will he eventually long for death? Data at least found a way to terminate his programming, but Moriarty may never be able to escape the vast tomb of his computer simulation. Sometimes believing you are human has its limitations.

Chapter 30

The Curious Case of the Dog in Prime Time
Jonathan Clements

At 7:00 P.M. on 26th March 1984, the Japanese channel TV Asahi broadcast the first of twenty-six episodes of its new cartoon series *Meitantei Holmes* ("Famous Detective Holmes") directed by Hayao Miyazaki and Kyōsuke Mikuriya.

A children's show broadcast in primetime for all the family, it featured Holmes and Watson thwarting crimes by the evil Moriarty. Cases included someone tampering with the newly-established airmail service and the disappearance of the bell of Big Ben, alongside more canonical tales such as "The Speckled Band." The show's most obvious distinguishing feature is apparent in the title used for its English-language broadcast. It is known as *Sherlock Hound*, as all the parts are played by talking dogs.

The ancient Chinese philosopher Zhuangzi once asked if he was a man dreaming of a being butterfly, or a butterfly dreaming of being a man. In *Sherlock Hound*, we're not watching humans who behave like dogs (zoomorphism), we are watching dogs who behave like humans (anthropomorphism). Their reasons for doing so are buried in the long history of talking animals in Japan, in particular over the last century.

The process by which an Edwardian English detective can somehow find himself transformed into a Japanese cartoon canine is not as unlikely as it first seems. If we approach it through the context of detective fiction in Japan, the history of television in Japan, and the transnational aims of many animation studios, we can soon perceive the multiple influences that bring us to our mysterious case of the talking dog detective.

Sari Kawana's *Murder Most Modern: Detective Fiction and Japanese Culture* locates Holmesian sleuths as central icons in twentieth-century Japan's sense of modernity. Detectives became symbols of the onrush of change: its interpreters and guardians in an era when modern meant Western, even if the Western world did not live up to expectations.

The Japanese author Natsume Sōseki spent a miserable period as a student in Britain from 1900 to 1901, where he soon tired of boorish London locals. In his letters home, Sōseki even sourly observed "the Japanese, thanks to their diligent studies, now knew more about England than the average Englishman" (Donald Keene, *Dawn to the West*, p. 311). Sōseki's London sojourn coincided with the serialisation of *The Hound of the Baskervilles*, whose twelfth chapter mentions Holmes's "catlike love of personal cleanliness."

It was felines that would make Sōseki's name, on his return to Japan, when he published a satire on modern attitudes, as seen through the eyes of a disapproving pet in *I Am a Cat* (1905). He did so, however, at a time when many Japanese were ardent readers of detective fiction, both foreign and domestic.

The first Holmes story to be translated into Japanese was *A Study in Scarlet* in 1899, which was serialised in a radically altered form as "Chizo no Kabe" ("The Bloodstained Wall") in the newspaper *Mainichi Shinbun*. The translator remained anonymous, perhaps understandably, since Holmes and Watson were renamed as the Japanese investigators Homma and Wada, and the locale was shifted to contemporary Berlin. A legal translation of *The Adventures of Sherlock Holmes* commenced in the same year, serialised in the rival newspaper *Chūō Shinbun*.

Translations of Holmes continued throughout the early years of the twentieth century, with the character names changed variously to Holimi and Wada (1906) or Honda and Watanabe (1910), on the assumption that the protagonists needed to be "localized" into Japanese. However, there was an accurate, three-volume translation of Holmes stories available in Japan by 1916, maintaining the original illustrations from the *Strand* magazine along with the original nationalities and setting. Some, however, were still altered for Japanese readers, most notably "The Red-Headed League," refashioned as "The Bald-Headed League" for a country without redheads (Keith E. Webb, *Sherlock Holmes in Japan*, pp. 18–19).

Pastiches of Holmes were also common in the juvenile detective magazines of the period. Jūza Unno, the "father of Japanese science fiction" wrote a number of stories featuring the Japanese detective "Sōroku Homura" beginning in 1928 with "Denkifuro no Kaishi Jiken" ("The Case of the Mysterious Death in the Electric Bath"), serialised in the magazine *Shinseinen*. "A Soldier's Death" (1930), by Atsushi Watanabe in the same magazine, includes an unlicensed cameo by Sherlock Holmes as a baffled investigator, admitting that he has been defeated by the lack of evidence pertaining to the titular corpse. Holmes cannot work out how the lead character has died, allowing the readers, who have witnessed the whole death, a sense of smug satisfaction that they know something that he does not (Robert Matthew, *Japanese Science Fiction*, p. 21).

By 1933, the complete canon of Holmes stories was available in Japanese. A second "complete" translation was released in 1951–52, including in its first edition the apocryphal posthumous work "The Man Who Was Wanted," dropped from subsequent editions after it was discovered not to be the work of Conan Doyle. Some Holmes stories were also retold for younger audiences, leading to dilution of their content. Most infamously, a juvenile adaptation in 1958 replaced Holmes's addiction to cocaine with a penchant for coffee, and turned Watson into a small boy.

Cartoon Animals

There were other means of assigning more palatable, cuter aspects to foreign icons. Shaarokku Hōmuzu was named, of course, in the Japanese katakana syllabary, an alphabet used largely for foreign words and the noises made by beasts. Non-Japanese were not animals, but in a linguistic sense the use of katakana could imply that they were like animals, whatever that meant: unpredictable, perhaps? Potentially dangerous? Ultimately possible to master? Rendering foreign icons as animals could also render them subordinate, powerless, even cuter—an inadvertent by-product of the penchant for talking-animal cartoons, both already in existence in Japanese animation, and arriving from the West.

The use of anthropomorphism in cartoons masks more technical and cultural concerns than simply entertaining children. Animating realistic humans is expensive. Although Walt Disney experimented with complex fairy tales in the 1920s, he returned to simpler, animal-based narratives in the 1930s because too many fairytales required "plausible human characters at their core" (Barrier, *Hollywood Cartoons*, p. 90). The Disney studio eventually acquired realistic human motion by rotoscoping—in other words, filming human actors and using the material generated as a basis for tracing the movements of their animated counterparts. For a young animation industry, realistic human movement is a struggle, likely to lead storylines to skew towards something in which the capabilities of cartooning are a benefit rather than a hindrance. The Japanese animation business did not embrace rotoscoping, and was sure to use inanimate objects, fantasy creatures or animal figures as a means of reducing the number of naturalistic human figures required.

The burgeoning medium of cartoon animation established high levels of anthropomorphism in which animals did not merely interact with humans with a degree of intelligence, but actually spoke. On its release in Japanese cinemas in 1956, Disney's *Lady and the Tramp* was renamed *Wanwan Monogatari* ("Woof-Woof Story"). In an apparent attempt to cash in, *Deputy Dawg* was soon broadcast on Japanese television as *Wanwan Hoankan* (1959, "Woof-Woof Sheriff"). Japanese viewers were similarly assailed by a talking canine when *The Huckleberry Hound Show* was broadcast as *Chinken Huckle* (1959, "Curious Dog Huckle"). Japanese imitations were not far behind, including the cartoon feature *Wanwan Chūshingura* ("Woof-Woof Treasury of Loyal Retainers," 1963), a samurai epic in which all the main parts were played by dogs. The animators' decision was a cunning synergy of ideas, incorporating not only cartoon animals, but also a subtle historical reference. The original Treasury of Loyal Retainers kabuki play, perhaps better known as *The Story of the Forty-Seven Rōnin*, was set during the reign of the Shōgun Tsunayoshi (1649–1709). A real-life figure, born in the Year of the Dog, Tsunayoshi decreed that all canines were sacrosanct. As a result, the city now known as Tokyo was over-run with untouchable strays in an insane period now remembered as the "reign of the Dog Shōgun" (Clements, *A Brief History of the Samurai*, pp. 246–47).

Japanese cartoonists favored animal subjects themselves in children's works, at least in part because of the ease with which animals could be localized in other countries. The surreal or fantastic qualities of cartoons can often make them far easier to transfer between cultures than live-action footage. As long as the setting or plot is not incontrovertibly ethnocentric (and *Wanwan Chūshingura* certainly fails this test), a cartoon has the chance to make money for its maker in many foreign markets. Talking animal characters can even subtly sneak past certain viewers' prejudices, an idea certainly on the mind of Japanese animators in the selection of the Chinese story *Hakujaden* ("Legend of the White Snake") as the first feature-length animated film to be released by the Tōei studio in 1958, and intended to appeal across Asian markets.

"Famous" Animals

Meanwhile, in the world of live-action television, as TV ownership expanded beyond the Tokyo metropolitan area, viewers in outlying regions complained about the foreign dramas that were being fed to them. In particular, it was suggested that the humor of foreign comedies was unintelligible, the politics of cowboy shows incomprehensible, and Caucasian actors indistinguishable (Youichi Ito, "The Trade Winds Change"; Jonathan Clements and Tamamuro Motoko, *The Dorama Encyclopedia*, p. xvi). The nascent domestic television production industry began to generate its own materials, but the fact remains that Japanese TV in the 1950s, and Japanese color TV in the 1960s were each dominated in their early periods by a flood of mainly American programming—in 1957, ten percent of all broadcasting (Makiko Takahashi, *The Development of Japanese Television Broadcasting and Imported Television Programs*, p. 30).

Since foreign shows often began with an unintelligible logo in their native language which frequently failed to summarise the subject matter, the practice soon developed of adding a descriptive prefix or suffix in Japanese: a "foreground name and a background qualifier" (Clements and Tamamuro, p. xvi). This ensured, even in TV listings that only contained a programme's katakana title (denoted below by CAPITALS), that the title still provided an indicator of content. And so, in Japanese, familiar serials were rebranded as *Great Battle in Space STAR TREK*, or *Detective KOJAK*. Although less common, this tradition persists today, with examples as *Burn Notice* (broadcast in Japan as *Erased Spy BURN NOTICE*) and *The Shield* (*Futile Police Badge SHIELD*).

If one kind of show proved popular, Japanese programmers were not above retitling other serials to imply similarities that were not originally there, or even to accentuate a particular character. One of the first television import successes in Japan was *The Adventures of Rin Tin Tin* (1954) also a Western, but with a focus on a dog rather than any of the inscrutable cowboys. Broadcast as *Meiken RIN TIN TIN* ("Famous Dog Rin Tin Tin") on the commercial network NTV in November 1956, it achieved a peak 65.9-percent rating the following year, becoming the fourth most-watched programme on Japanese television in 1957.

Before long, *Sergeant Preston of the Yukon* was transformed into *Police Dog KING* in Japanese, and *The Pursuers* into *Police Dog IVAN*—it was, it seems, the dog that made the difference. The subtext was that the animals were the true stars and the humans merely an unwelcome supporting cast. Moreover, the assertion that Rin Tin Tin is already "famous" seems designed to suggest that Japanese viewers were missing out if they did not tune in. In order to imply a relationship, however tenuous, similar American shows were retitled: *Lassie*, as *Meiken LASSIE* ("Famous Dog Lassie," 1957), *Run, Joe, Run* as *Ganbare Meiken JOE* ("Keep It Up, Famous Dog Joe," 1977) and *The Littlest Hobo* as *Meiken ROCKY* ("Famous Dog Rocky," 1980).

The experience of emphasising animal images in selling to the Japanese did not escape the Japanese in considerations of selling animal images back to foreigners. If a locally made production was too ethnocentric, it was harder to sell in foreign markets. Ever since 1963, when Osamu Tezuka sold *Astro Boy* to the American network NBC, Japanese animators had actively searched for themes and characters that would be easier to sell to foreign markets because they were mukokuseiteki—"denationalized" (Chun, *A Nation of a Hundred Million Idiots?*, p. 279). An exotic setting was fine for local color, and a new audio track could remove the language barrier, but if characters were still demonstrably Asian or white, each was likely to cause dissonance in the other's market. Animal protagonists avoided this problem, as they were not racially distinctive. Tezuka, however, discovered a new problem: four-legged animals were more expensive to animate than humanoid figures. Anthropomorphic animals, on the other hand, were both transnationally appealing and technically simpler to animate.

Famous Animal Detectives

Perhaps we can already see the potential for a "Sherlock Hound" in such tensions—a foreign detective, "denationalized" through the use of talking-animal imagery, and de-fanged through adaptation for the children's market. It helps, too, if he is "famous", like Rin Tin Tin or Lassie. Best of all if he is a "famous detective".

Several foreign TV show titles gained the prefix Tantei ("Detective") or Shiritsu Tantei ("Private Eye") on Japanese broadcast, but a handful acquired the conjoined prefix Meitantei beginning with *Diamond / Call Mr D*, broadcast in Japan as *Meitantei DIAMOND* ("Famous Detective Diamond"). This practice persists, with retitlings such as *Barnaby Jones* as *Meitantei JONES* ("Famous Detective Jones"), and *Poirot* as *Meitantei POIROT* ("Famous Detective Poirot").

By 1978, the media strands of anthropomorphic animals and "famous" detectives had joined to create a genre of animal sleuths. A rising star of detective fiction, Jirō Akagawa, began the genre with his novel *Mikeneko HOLMES no Suiri* (1978, "The Case of Holmes the Tortoiseshell Cat"), in which a bereaved pet investigates the murder of his detective owner. The story has spawned thirty-two sequels to date, along with fourteen compilations of short stories, and several other spin-offs, including a cat-autobiography and a TV movie. Determined to cash in, the novelist and anime screenwriter Masaki Tsuji published a pastiche in a similar vein: *Meiken LUPIN no Meisuiri* (1983, "The Famous Case of Lupin the Famous Dog"). Albeit less successful than Akagawa's stories, the cases solved by Lupin the mongrel still ran to twelve volumes in the 1980s.

But Tsuji was not the only figure to attempt to capitalize on the bestselling *Mikeneko HOLMES* series. The beginning of the 1980s was a fertile environment for pitches that mixed family pets and famous detectives. The cartoon world, where animals would not need to be trained, would seem like a logical place to achieve the best synergy.

In November 1980, the animator Hayao Miyazaki attempted to gain the animation remake rights for the American anthropomorphic comic series *Rowlf* by Richard Corben, submitting a proposal for a feature-length cartoon in November 1980. Although nothing came of this, Miyazaki was instead soon working on a Japanese-Italian Sherlock Holmes coproduction that re-cast the characters as talking dogs.

Considering the timing of the production, it seems likely that both Japanese and Italian collaborators first assumed that the works of Arthur Conan Doyle would be out of copyright, as Doyle had died in 1930, and Japanese law allowed, and still allows, for works to come out of copyright fifty years after the death of their originator. This does not appear to have troubled the producers in the early stages, and they were perhaps given a false confidence by the previous transnational success of a science fiction remake of Homer's *Odyssey*.

Producer Keishi Yamazaki reported that *Ulysses 31*, a Franco-Japanese coproduction, had been well received in Europe, and that his only complaint was that Japanese crew names were left off the credits. He does not appear to have considered that the *Odyssey* was conveniently out of copyright and hence unlikely to invite lawsuits from its original creator's heirs. He may have also been spurred on by the recent success of the Spanish-Japanese coproduction *Dogtanian and the Three Muskethounds* (1981, *Wanwan*

Sanjūshi, literally "Woof-Woof Three Musketeers"), although this, too, faced no copyright issues, being based on a book long in the public domain.

Initial plans for a direct cartoon remake of *The Hound of the Baskervilles* were over-ruled, because the Italians feared it was too close to horror. Instead, writers were encouraged to keep to stories of simple larceny. Theft, however, was the issue at hand when the Conan Doyle estate protested at the use of material still in copyright. The estate appears to have first noticed Japanese infringements in 1981, with the broadcast of an unrelated cartoon, *Lupin vs Holmes*. It seems that the existence and potential illegality of *Sherlock Hound* only arose in the aftermath of the *Lupin vs Holmes* case, causing the production to be suspended when several episodes were already completed. A prolonged wrangle over ownership was patched up by the renaming of the characters in some territories, in particular in a feature edit of two early episodes, released in 1984. Miyazaki left the production during the hiatus, and instead directed his first feature anime, *Nausicaä of the Valley of Wind* (1984). *Sherlock Hound*'s later episodes were completed by a new director, Kyōsuke Mikuriya, and the series was subsequently broadcast around the world.

Although most scripts were written by anime regulars, one episode was written by Toshirō Ishidō, a crime author and prominent Japanese Holmes expert, who pitched an idea in which Moriarty would steal the Rosetta Stone from the British Museum, and the canine Holmes would seek the help of a famous Japanese author known to have been living in Edwardian London: Natsume Sōseki, famous in Japan as the author of *I Am a Cat*. It was a proposal that neatly brought the story of eminent, anthropomorphic Victorians full circle, although it faced opposition from participants who had never heard of Sōseki. The Italian producer Luciano Scafa resisted the idea until the Japanese producer Keishi Yamazaki suggested that he was only objecting because Holmes sought the help of an Asian. Scafa backed down, and the story went ahead as episode #19 (*Terebi Anime Damashi*, pp. 185-6).

In the episode as broadcast outside Japan, however, the plot element is garbled: Sōseki's name is mispronounced, and his knowledge of the Japanese parallels, to an infamous theft at Nagoya Castle by the samurai master-thief Ishikawa Goemon, is glossed over. European characters and themes can be sold to the Japanese if they are transformed into dogs, but there are still numerous linguistic and cultural difficulties in selling the Japanese to Europeans, whether as dogs or otherwise.

Dreams of Dogs and Butterflies

In a final coda, Jeremy Brett, who played the definitive Holmes for BBC television in 1984–94, was dubbed into Japanese on NHK by the actor Shigeru Tsuyuguchi. When Studio Ghibli required an actor to portray the tweedy, magisterial talking cat Baron in the anime *Whisper of the Heart* (1995), Tsuyuguchi was hired to provide the voice. Hence, in *Whisper of the Heart* in the original Japanese, the anthropomorphic cat Baron speaks with the voice of Sherlock Holmes. It is yet another strand in the odd alternate history of a foreign icon in Japan, in which a famous British detective has been slowly transformed, over decades of cross-media survival, from a magisterial, maverick London sleuth into a cartoon canine on primetime.

Zhuangzi's philosophical question on dreams and reality remains unanswerable, although his "butterfly" has undergone the oddest of transformations in Japan, emerging from its transnational chrysalis as an altogether different animal.

Chapter 31

A Study in Simulacra

Jef Burnham

A waste collector, retrieving a bin of discarded books from an alley one morning, tripped over the remains of a reality disfigured beyond recognition. It was the reality of a single fact rendered mercilessly untrue by some long-since fled assailant. Next to the remains, the word "simulacra" was scrawled on the pavement in the reality's blood as the desperate, final act of one whose authenticity is quickly fading.

The scene was cordoned off by the responding officers and a Detective Inspector from Scotland Yard (whose name has been omitted at the request of my editor) was brought in to investigate. No eyewitnesses were found and those living in the tenements overlooking the alley swore to having heard no screams as they had all been inside watching television. Unable to determine the reality's identity and with no clues to go on save for that curious word, simulacra, the DI turned to an expert on the term *simulacra*: the late French philosopher, Jean Baudrillard.

Baudrillard's postmodern philosophical text, *Simulacra and Simulation*, seemed the most logical starting point, but the DI reached an impasse in this line of inquiry when he found himself unable to apply Baudrillard's theories practically.

Thereafter, upon the urging of his wife, the DI attempted to enlist the services of legendary detective, Sherlock Holmes, in the solution of this beguiling case. Neither Holmes nor Watson were to be found in any directory of persons living or deceased and he concluded that their whereabouts must have been withheld by certain government entities to ensure the privacy of the detective and his biographer. Much to his embarrassment, the DI subsequently learned that Sherlock Holmes was in fact a fictional character created by Sir Arthur Conan Doyle.

Faced with a seemingly impossible case, the DI desperately turned to media representations of Sherlock Holmes for inspiration. He encountered Holmes outside of Doyle's writings in numerous works of film and television. However, many of the texts in which Doyle's characters were featured, especially those produced for television, did not focus exclusively on the great detective's exploits. For instance, he discovered Holmes, Watson, or Moriarty appearing in such television programs as *Saturday Night Live, Teenage Mutant Ninja Turtles, Star Trek: The Next Generation, Animaniacs, Batman: The Brave and the Bold, Muppets Tonight,* and *Remington Steele* to name a diverse few.

As a result, during the final stages of his investigation, the DI became fixated on a single episode of a 1980s children's cartoon series, *The Real Ghostbusters*: "Elementary My Dear Winston." With the aid of this unlikeliest of texts, he at last understood the practical applications of Baudrillard's theories and came face-to-face with the true destructive nature of the media and the images it perpetuates. Through his association with "Elementary My Dear Winston," the DI was finally able to solve the case, but not before being driven mad by what I can only describe as a paradox of perception. The murderer, he discovered, was none other than Sherlock Holmes himself, having transcended his fictional limitations through the process of hyperrealization. His ascendance would result in untold devastation.

I will attempt to reconstruct the case as presented by the DI in his final report to Scotland Yard. And as you will see, our intrepid DI discovered that the world's greatest detective has in fact perpetrated the world's greatest crime: the murder of the whole of reality!

I Ain't 'Fraid of No Holmes

"Elementary My Dear Winston" opens on the waters off the isle of Manhattan. An ominous, glowing orb rockets through the water at surface level toward two elderly fishermen who have cast their lines off the end of a dock. When the orb reaches them, the skeletal "remains" of Professor Moriarty burst from the water. Upon learning that he has arrived in New York City, Moriarty calls forth his flesh and clothing as the fishermen flee in terror. Moriarty then summons the Hound of the Baskervilles to inform the beast that his trip from England has left him hungry for evil—a hunger which sends him on a rampage through New York City. The scene cuts to Holmes and Watson traveling down the wrong side of a busy New York street in a turn-of-the-nineteenth-century automobile. Holmes enjoys a pipe in the passenger seat as Watson weaves the vehicle in and out of traffic precariously before passing ethereally through a large truck.

The viewer initially interprets this sequence to signify the arrival of Holmes, Watson, and Moriarty's ghosts in Manhattan. This interpretation is contradicted, however, when it's revealed that even in the world of *The Real Ghostbusters*, these characters originated as fictional creations of Arthur Conan Doyle. Therefore, it's impossible for them to have become traditional ghosts, having never been alive. But if they're not ghosts and they don't possess corporeal forms, what are they? A clue to the solution of this particular puzzle lies in the animators' depiction of Sherlock Holmes. Here, as in so many media texts, Holmes is characterized as tall and thin, with a deerstalker cap and an Inverness cape. While this is indeed the prevailing image of Holmes in the media, it is not in keeping with the character as originally depicted in the stories of Arthur Conan Doyle.

To understand the nature of this false image, we turn to Baudrillard's definitions of simulation and simulacra. In Baudrillard's writing, simulation is the selective imitation of a reality. Given that the perfect representation of one thing for another is a theoretical impossibility, simulations are at best partial representations, and are therefore separate from the realities they simulate. In this way, they are realities unto themselves yet falsehoods, in that they bear little or no resemblance to the realities they purportedly refer to. An excellent example of the non-referentiality of simulations is found in the close comparison of a painting to the prints of said painting found in a museum gift shop. Prints inevitably fail to represent every physical characteristic of the painting, including the artist's individual brushstrokes, the three-dimensionality of successive layers of paint, the texture and composition of the original canvas, the precise shades of colors, and so on. Since the print does not accurately embody all physical traits of the original painting, the print is therefore a reality unto itself—albeit a false reality in that it does not accurately capture the painting it is intended to represent.

When subsequent simulations reference previous simulations rather than the original reality, simulacra are created. Baudrillard described simulacra as orbitally recurring models. This would be like making prints of prints of a painting, or Xeroxes of Xeroxes. Each subsequent simulation is further from the truth and supports only the reality of the simulation. In this way, the Holmes depicted by the animators of *The Real Ghostbusters*—tall, thin, wearing a deerstalker cap and an Inverness cape, with a calabash pipe hanging from his mouth—is part of the Holmes simulacrum. After all, it is a reflection of the media's orbital simulation of Holmes, which is separate from the "real" Holmes of Doyle's texts.

Maybe Winston's onto Something

To begin with, the Holmes of Doyle's stories did not wear a deerstalker cap, nor did he routinely wear a cape. These were inventions of Sidney Paget, illustrator of the Holmes stories for *The Strand Magazine*. The calabash pipe was an invention of those earliest performers to portray Holmes on stage and screen, because it seems a calabash pipe is easier for actors to hold in their mouths than other pipes while performing stage business, due to its low center of gravity. In addition, most visual media texts featuring Holmes ignore the written character's drug addiction completely, while a widespread, false perception persists that Holmes's methods of sleuthing inspired the creation of forensic science, when precisely the opposite is true—a fact that Laura Snyder discusses at length in her essay, "Sherlock Holmes: Scientific Detective." Furthermore, Doyle's Holmes never uttered the phrase to which the title of the *Ghostbusters* episode alludes ("Elementary, my dear Watson"). Therefore, the media's depiction of Sherlock Holmes is a reality unto itself, separate from the works of Arthur Conan Doyle.

With this in mind, we return to the episode. Winston is the only member of the *Ghostbusters* to recognize the entities as Holmes and Watson upon their first encounter with the great detective and his biographer. Before divulging his conclusion to his more scientifically-minded colleagues, Winston consults an illustration of Holmes from his personal library for confirmation. Unsurprisingly, the illustration of Holmes, too, is in keeping with the Holmes simulacrum that saturates the media. So why is it that Winston makes this connection and not the others? Baudrillard asserts: "Everywhere socialization is measured by the exposure to media messages. Whoever is underexposed to the media is desocialized or virtually asocial" (p. 80).

Egon, Ray, and to a lesser extent, Peter, fall into the category of the desocialized, spending the bulk of their time in scientific research and experimentation rather than engaging with the media. Winston, on the other hand, is the everyman of the series—the only Ghostbuster who has not earned a doctorate and is not a scientist. (Although Winston does obtain a PhD at some point between the two films and the 2009 crossplatform video game from Atari, he is not a doctor at this point in the *Ghostbusters* timeline.)

Recall in the original film that it was not a passion for the paranormal that compelled Winston to respond to the Ghostbusters' help wanted ad. When asked during his interview if he believed in "UFOs, astral projections, mental telepathy, ESP, clairvoyance, spirit photography, telekinetic movement, full trance mediums, the Loch Ness monster, and the theory of Atlantis," Winston diplomatically responded, "If there's a steady paycheck in it, I'll believe anything you say." Winston is willing to work a job for which he has no passion simply for the monetary gain, and despite being a religious man, is reluctant to believe anything outside of his sensory experience or that which the media maintains to be truth. He's an average member of the modern social order and is therefore the most attuned to the media and the simulacra it perpetuates. Thus it is Winston who necessarily identifies the entities so in fitting with media-saturated simulacra.

Stepping outside of the text, we see that the Holmes simulacrum present in "Elementary My Dear Winston" is indeed the prevailing depiction of the character in the media at large. As a result, the masses have come to accept the simulacrum as the referent for the reality of Holmes. Thus, the simulacrum has taken precedence over the reality of Doyle's writings. When this occurs and simulacra become "more real than the real" in the public eye, reality is replaced by an order of the hyperreal.

I Have a Radical Idea

The theory of hyperreality is rooted in one of the fundamental concepts of postmodern philosophy, which asserts that universal truth is an impossibility. According to most postmodern thinkers, including Baudrillard, one of the key factors in this is the power of the media, which deals solely in simulations, to subjectively shape society's perceptions through indoctrination.

Consider once more the Holmes simulacrum: a distinguished gentleman and self-made sleuth, and again, tall, thin, with deerstalker cap, Inverness cape, and calabash pipe. Within media texts such as "Elementary My Dear Winston," these are but the signs of Holmes, perpetually referring back to previous mediated texts' simulations of Holmes rather than Doyle's writing. And it is this media saturation that allows the simulacrum to subsist.

Furthermore, consider how often Holmes and other canon characters appear on television alone, compared to how often the average person picks up a volume of Doyle's original works. *The Guinness Book of World Records* cites Holmes as the single most-portrayed character on screen. As such, modern society's increased reliance on visual media over print has allowed the simulacrum to become the prevailing representation of the character, creating a hyperreality.

Likewise, in "Elementary My Dear Winston," when the enigma of the simulacral entities' existence is posed to Egon, he proposes the theory that they are in fact "belief made manifest." Pursuing this theory further, Egon speculates that because so many millions of people believe in the simulacral forms of Holmes, Watson, Moriarty, and the Hound of the Baskervilles, they have achieved a "quasi-reality."

Replace Egon's chosen prefix of "quasi-" with "hyper-" and the concept is the same. These simulacra, empowered by the belief of the media-saturated masses, have murdered the reality that they were fiction and replaced that reality with their own existence. "Murder" is the term predominantly employed by Baudrillard when referring to the process of a simulacrum usurping a reality as referent. It personifies the simulacrum violently overthrowing the order of the real, emphasizing the way in which simulacra can quite literally take on lives of their own. However, the ramifications of this murder are far more devastating than the destruction of their fictional standing.

Here we must take a leap of faith with Egon's theory, for it is a stretch to believe that millions believe in Moriarty or the Hound, neither of which is defined by an identifiable simulacrum. The Watson in this episode does adhere to a Dr. Watson simulacrum, which depicts him as being shorter than Holmes, often round, and always with a mustache and a bowler hat—the perfect foil to the Holmes simulcarum. But there is no Professor Moriarty or Hound of the Baskervilles simulacrum as such.

Although the inspiration for the Hound came to Doyle from British folktales of black, phantom hounds, it has failed to evolve into a simulacrum. The Hound usually appears as a dog with a dark coat of fur, but it alternates between black and brown, with the breed of dog also fluctuating between the average hunting hound and something more akin to a wolf. However, in "Elementary My Dear Watson," the animators took major artistic liberties with this already extremely loose model, depicting the Hound as a bright yellow, lizard-like beast with an exposed rib cage; a spiked, red collar; and additional spikes protruding from its shoulders and forehead.

As for Holmes's arch-nemesis, Moriarty is very rarely depicted the same way twice. In fact, the lack of a Moriarty model is so prevalent that the writers of *Animaniacs* lampooned the villain for being model-less by depicting him as a kilted Scotsman in a sombrero piloting a flying machine. Moriarty is depicted in yet another unique form in "Elementary My Dear Winston," looking curiously like Batman's Solomon Grundy in a top hat. Later in the episode, a woman refers to this Moriarty as "Dr. Jekyll over there. Or was it Mr. Hyde?", indicating that even Robert Louis Stevenson's creations are more consistently simulated than Moriarty.

Murder with a Side of Hyperreal

Using "Elementary My Dear Winston" as a case study in the effects of hyperreality, let's assume that everything within the world of *The Real Ghostbusters* is real at the outset of the episode, save for the hyperrealizations of Holmes, Watson, Moriarty, and the Hound. Again, the reality murdered by these simulacra is the reality that they were fictional characters. As a result, they take on forms that are at once insubstantial yet "more real than real" as they can shift their molecular consistency from wholly insubstantial to completely solid at will, preventing the real from harming them. As such, the Ghostbusters' proton packs have no effect on the hyperreal specters, illustrating that once a hyperreality comes to be, the real is rendered powerless against it. After all, recall, hyperreality is the result of simulacra transcending reality—taking precedence over the real.

With but a single hyperreality identified, a flaw becomes apparent in our initial assumption about the Ghostbusters' universe. It's impossible, given the existence of the hyperrealities, to presuppose the presence of any definable realities within the world of *The Real Ghostbusters*. According to Baudrillard, when one simulacrum achieves hyperreal status, destroying the line between fact and fiction, the realistic standing of all other orders becomes indeterminable. True and false are rendered dubious distinctions; for once an order of the hyperreal is established, anything can become truth, no matter how unlikely or fantastic, so long as the masses believe in it. Thus, the classification of realities is contingent on the most fickle of authorities: human perception. The problem that faces those living in an order of the hyperreal is that anything they perceive to be a reality may in fact be a hyperreality. This creates a paradox wherein, although this person may be able to identify any number of hyperrealities, they can never be completely certain that the truths they invest in are not in fact hyperrealities facilitated by their own beliefs. As we'll see, this paradox of perception plagues our own society in no small part thanks to Sherlock Holmes.

From a distanced analytical vantage point, "Elementary My Dear Winston" appears to be a harmless exercise in realizing the catastrophic possibilities of simulation through Saturday morning cartoons. However, it would be more prudent to view the text as reflexive of the world at large, representing all of reality in today's media-driven society. Even in this "age of information," a quick Google search reveals that a constant debate persists surrounding Holmes's fictional standing. But this is no new trend, for further research reveals that Holmes achieved hyperreal status shortly after his creation. Accounts tell of numerous Britons in Doyle's time attempting to employ the services of Holmes and Watson (just as our ill-informed DI did in the opening of this text); and upon the publication of Holmes's death at the Reichenbach Falls in "The Adventure of the Final Problem," many Britons were seen wearing black mourning bands to work the next day in honor of the fallen detective (Sian Ellis, "On the Trail of Sherlock Holmes").

The prominence of the Holmes simulacrum in the media has continued to grow ever since. Shockingly, its hyperrealistic proportions have come to mirror those of the simulacral Holmes in "Elementary My Dear Winston." In 2008, a poll commissioned by UKTV Gold revealed that the speculative ascendancy of Sherlock Holmes detailed in "Elementary My Dear Winston" has indeed occurred in our own universe. The results of this poll, based on a series of questions posed to three thousand Britons regarding their perception of persons both real and fictional, showed that a staggering fifty-eight percent of the sample group believed Holmes to have been a real person. More people were found to believe in Holmes, in fact, than the real-life Twelfth Century figure, King Richard the Lionheart (forty-seven percent believed him to have been mythical), showing conversely how the reality of an actual person's existence may be murdered, rendering them fictional. Thus, the Holmes of our universe has become hyperreal as a result of media-saturated simulacra in an identical fashion to the Holmes of the Ghostbusters' universe.

Recall that, according to Baudrillard's theories, it takes but a single breach of reality for the whole of reality to be called into question. Such is the "murderous power of images" discussed by Baudrillard, which necessarily invalidates all of reality (p. 5). And certainly the ascendancy of the Holmes simulacrum in our universe represents a grievous breach of the order of the real. This is not to say that the Holmes simulacrum was the earliest simulacrum. Baudrillard cited capital as the earliest example. However, as Baudrillard asserted, since an order of the hyperreal is one without facts, it is also, by proxy, without causality. It then follows that within such an order, effects are not necessarily preceded by causes, making the historical precedence of capital irrelevant. Therefore, regardless of which simulacra achieved hyperreal status first, all simulacra are equally responsible for the murder of reality, including Sherlock Holmes.

Case Closed

This lack of a universal truth is a fundamental aspect of the postmodern condition. But how do we function in such a world? What we need, ironically, is a good detective. After all, the archetype of the detective is that of the analytic mind that discovers a reality hidden beneath a surface reality. In terms of this chapter, the detective is a philosopher—Detective Baudrillard, who solved the case of the hyperreal and discovered that at the heart of what we call reality is a series of potential simulacra undermining the very foundation of our reality. Whilst this appears vital to our comprehension of the world around us, it honestly doesn't do us a fat lot of good, for the question remains, how are we to operate in light of this information?

Certainly we cannot continue living as though everything we believe is empirical fact. However, we cannot simply adopt an attitude of universal skepticism either; nor can we live out our lives in despair. Surely there is a reasonable way to acclimate ourselves to this postmodern reality, and to this end we must enlist the services of a great detective, someone who can find a truth beneath our very lack of it. Until then, it's important to remain humble about that which we individually define as reality. Everything we think we know was potentially negated over a century ago by a make-believe drug addict in an ear-flapped traveling cap.

Thus our mystery is solved, and the truth of reality's demise is revealed. In a shocking twist that might have concluded a dimestore pulp novel, the murderer was in fact the very detective who may have otherwise been charged with solving the case.

Unfortunately, the Sherlock Holmes simulacrum, along with its accomplice, the Dr. Watson simulacrum, are still at large in the hyperreal, moving from one media text to another. They appear often with different visages, but their distinctive attire and builds render these disguises transparent.

Chapter 32

The Game Is Still Afoot!

Sean C. Duncan

> "But what's the game, Mr. Holmes—what's the game?"
> "Ay, what's the game?" my friend repeated thoughtfully.
> —*The Valley of Fear*, Chapter 5

Sir Arthur Conan Doyle's Sherlock Holmes Canon comprises fifty-six stories and four novels that have proven to be both durable and surprisingly malleable over the past century. Holmes and Dr. John H. Watson have thrived across a number of media, from faithful renditions by creators who have striven for verisimilitude with Doyle's works (say, the now-classic Granada series starring Jeremy Brett or the Soviet productions starring Vasily Livanov) to radical re-envisionings of the events and settings of Doyle's stories (Nicholas Meyer's *The Seven-Per-Cent Solution* or BBC's *Sherlock*, set in the modern day). Through these many versions and pastiches, there remains a recurring tension—that the Holmes Canon is at once both classic and modern, fixed and changing, created by Doyle and expanded by others through the playful exploration of the Canon that has come to be known as "The Game."

Living and Breathing

The Game is one of the defining activities of a century's worth of interest in Sherlock Holmes, and can be described as a communal and competitive intellectual exercise based on the conceit that Holmes and Watson were actual, real people, living, breathing, and solving mysteries in the London of the late Victorian and Edwardian era. Perhaps not such a strange idea today, in the era of *Twilight* fan fiction and enormous Wikis devoted to *Lost*, but in the early decades of the twentieth century, The Game was a unique way for fans of the Holmes stories to express their love for the material, flex their intellectual "muscles" on problems of interpretation, and to collaborate on making meaning of the worlds Doyle created in his fiction.

Fans and scholars of Holmes have played The Game for many reasons, including to reconcile the Canon's many inconsistencies—why, pray tell, does Watson's wife calls him "James" rather than John in "The Man with the Twisted Lip"? Or, who in the world might a real "King of Bohemia" have been, in "A Scandal in Bohemia"? Taking as an assumption that Holmes and Watson were real people, proponents of The Game have striven to flesh out answers to questions such as these, laboring long and hard to make sense of both the Canon's conflicting moments, as well as meaningfully tying the stories' narratives to actual events of the era (say, the Jack the Ripper murders, or early developments in forensic science). The Game, you might be able to tell, is as much about linking the Canon to what people do, know, and believe outside of Holmes fandom as it is an engagement with Doyle's stories and novels.

The Game has shaped the experiences of entire generations of readers of Holmes, with some of the most prominent Game-players identified within the notes in the best annotated editions (Baring-Gould's classic 1968 annotated editions, Leslie Klinger's recent *New Annotated Sherlock Holmes*, and Klinger's more exhaustive *Sherlock Holmes Reference Library* editions). And, though explicitly a "game" and an overt intellectual exercise regardless of how serious it may seem (or how dryly its players may describe it), The Game's influence has shaped the current resurgence of interest in Holmes. Modern Holmes variations illustrate the subtle ways Doyle's creation is still being amended, challenged, and expanded, even in recent Holmes adaptations, say, Guy Ritchie's Sherlock Holmes films (such as when Watson's disappearing "bull pup" mentioned in *A Study in Scarlet* is addressed), and *Sherlock*'s "A Study in Pink" (which gives us an explanation of what happened to poor James Phillimore, who disappeared after returning home to retrieve a forgotten umbrella, first mentioned but not explained in "The Problem of Thor Bridge").

That The Game has been influential and an important part of being a Holmes scholar, aficionado, and fan seems to be incontrovertible on one level—we're still talking about it a century after its inception, after all.

Yet, we're still left making sense of Game-players, why they do what they do, and what it all means. How can investigating

The Game illustrate the ways in which the active involvement of dedicated readers has fundamentally changed the ways that fans of many media make meaning of texts? Can The Game serve as a key example of changing epistemological stances toward media, and give us insight into theories of knowledge? And, what might The Game tell us about games and the role of identity play in everyday interaction with these stories?

The . . . Game . . . Is . . .

First, to unpack The Game, we need to address the notion of the term "game" itself, and think a bit about how an understanding of games might give us insight into its Sherlockian namesake. Most likely building off the famous "The game is afoot!" line from "The Abbey Grange," itself a reference to Shakespeare's *King Henry IV Part I*, Sherlockians quickly adopted the terminology of a "game" to describe their intellectual enterprise. As it was speculative, recreational, and, well, fun, why not? The playful exploration of the Holmes Canon was one for which the term "game" served to both clarify as well as deepen the meaning of interaction with Doyle's texts.

But, what is a game, exactly? Why this particular term to describe an activity that, on first blush, might appear like a form of playful scholarship? Are "games" and "work" necessarily that different from one another?

. . . Afoot!

Many of us have some implicit understanding of the term "game," one that often comes from our experiences in childhood, and the often conflicting relationships of "play" versus "work" that permeate our lives. Baseball, chess, *Team Fortress 2*, canasta, *The Settlers of Catan*, bingo, *Bejeweled*, lacrosse, *Super Smash Bros. Melee*, Texas Hold'em, xiangqi, *Halo: Reach*, soccer, Munchkin, cricket, go, and craps—all of these are commonly classified as games, all commonly considered fun, playful diversions. But, for some players, each of these has become a serious devotion, worthy of hundreds or even thousands of hours of play and study, much thought, and consideration. And, in some cases, developing expertise within them has become the project of a lifetime, worthy of devotion much like Holmes to his method. Historically, this has been more often seen with chess than with

Super Smash Bros., but times are changing. Like the world of Holmesian scholarship, games in general are simultaneously entertaining, diverting, and fun while also containing the potential for intense, driven study, and analysis. That games are entertaining by no means indicates that games are necessarily frivolous or without significance for those who play them.

The blurry boundaries of the term have long been a point of serious study by philosophers, game designers, and others who study knowledge and culture. In his classic *Philosophical Investigations*, Ludwig Wittgenstein famously illustrated the difficulty in defining the very notion of a "game." As a part of his larger project of language-games, formal definitions of concepts such as "games" were not insignificant. Rather, the notion of a "game" was extraordinarily important for illustrating his notion of family resemblances. For Wittgenstein, games presented an interesting case where no clear definition of the term was feasible, yet there were a number of overlapping similarities between many games that could be used to classify them as an intelligible, meaningful category. That is, rather than looking for a common feature present within all games that can describe them as a unified "thing," Wittgenstein argued that there was no such feature, only sets of similarities.

So, let's take Wittgenstein for granted for a moment and explore this notion's implications for our understanding of how the world of "games" might inform our thoughts on the Holmesian "Game"—if Wittgenstein is right, how do we understand the legitimacy of using the term "game" to describe an activity that many would find at least somewhat similar to the interpretive, argumentative "work" of academics?

Games are, for Wittgenstein, connected by their similarities to one another. What might work to link them are similarities in structure and intent of the players—an understanding of games as rules-based, as involving goals that can be achieved by players, and that serves to pull players out of their everyday concerns.

This leads to another interesting set of connections with the emerging field of "Game Studies." While used loosely and playfully by the Sherlockian scholars who play The Game, the term "game" itself has been the font of much thought and exploration over the last century, through a variety of fields of intellectual inquiry beyond philosophy. How do we conceive of a "game" separate from related concepts such as ritual, play, or even toys? Why might games and the use of games permeate human societies (as David Parlett so effectively cataloged in his classic *Oxford History of Board Games*)? Was Wittgenstein correct in describing the folly of attempting to discern the features that characterize a term that is used today so widely as to be applicable to fantasy football, *The Legend of Zelda*, and sharp-shooting?

. . . Play.

Wittgenstein's similarity argument notwithstanding, the field of "game studies" has emerged in recent decades to better understand these issues and try to refine our thought on what games are and games aren't. As the role of games has risen in Western popular culture—from the predominance of card games in the suburban America of the 1950s to the pervasiveness of Facebook games in the 2010s—scholars have sought to better understand what these are, how they work, and what meanings players draw from them. This is at once a pragmatic issue as much as a theoretical one.

Distinct from the mathematical endeavor of "game theory," this field has taken a largely socio-cultural bent, meaning many of the dominant theorists rose out of traditions in the mid-twentieth century that led them to considering games as cultural artifacts and social systems. In particular, one of the foundational texts for the new Game Studies came in the form of Johan Huizinga's *Homo Ludens* (or "Man, the Player"), originally published in 1938. Huizinga connected games to a much deeper cultural context than even Wittgenstein attempted—linking games to many other "high" and "low" culture activities. Huizinga stated:

> All play moves and has its being within a playground marked off beforehand materially or ideally, deliberately or as a matter of course... The arena, the card-table, the magic circle, the temple, the stage, the screen, the tennis court, the court of justice, etc., are all in form and function play-grounds, i.e., forbidden spots, isolated, hedged round, hallowed, within which special rules obtain.

Somewhat surprisingly, contemporary Game Studies scholars have taken Huizinga to task for one of those terms tucked away within the litany of forms or sites of play: The "magic circle." And it's this very notion that brings us back to the Sherlockian "Game"—what are the borders between the play activities within a game and the "real world"?

. . . Real?

In *Homo Ludens*, Huizinga described games as firmly circumscribed, with a clear line between the space of a game and the rest of human activity, which contemporary games scholars have now labeled "the magic circle" (though it is still unclear if this is exactly what Huizinga meant by the term; Katie Salen and Eric Zimmerman's 2003 book *Rules of Play* is often credited for reviving and perhaps misinterpreting Huizinga's use of the term). Regardless, the "magic circle" notion has taken hold to describe a theorized separation between games and "the real world." But has this ever really been true? Can we delineate what counts as a game from what counts as the social and cultural world outside the game? Can we see such a firm line between the Sherlockian Game and the rest of the world?

The barrier between everyday life and the world of the game has come under question, and in books like *World of Warcraft and Philosophy*, *The Legend of Zelda and Philosophy*, and *Halo and Philosophy*, that barrier has been more-or-less knocked down. Games demonstrably matter in everyday life, can be used to illustrate how humans make meaning, and provide an important lens by which we can understand not just the nature of media, but how we engage with them. Games, regardless of how we formally classify or define them, are complex, multifaceted engagements with the real world and with cultural systems.

In the case of the Sherlockian Game, it turns out, a blurring of lines between the "real world" and the "Game world" has been there since the very beginning. The study of games helps us to understand the ways that Holmes's admirers have been "playing" with the Holmes Canon, while at the same time, the example of "The Game" can help to better illuminate how and why hard declarations of a "magic circle" simply don't work. So maybe it's time to explore this idea a bit further, taking a look at the origins of The Game, as well as its role in defining a century's worth of Holmes fandom.

. . . Serious Business!

The better we understand the history of "The Game," the better we might be able to make sense of the ways that Holmes fans have long blurred the lines between "play" and "serious, intellectual activity." Unlike many other moments in fandom around other media texts, the historical genesis of The Game is clear. The publication of this very book in 2011 is fortuitous timing, in fact—this year, Holmesians and Sherlockians celebrate the centenary of The Game, as initiated by the classic essay "Studies in the Literature of Sherlock Holmes" written by Ronald Knox, delivered in 1911. Monsignor Knox, a British theologian, intended to parody the literacy analysis of the era by taking the much-loved "low" text of the Holmes Canon, and giving it a royal treatment typically only afforded "serious" works of literature.

Knox began the essay with this passage:

> If there is anything pleasant in life, it is doing what we aren't meant to do. If there is anything pleasant in criticism, it is finding out what we aren't meant to find out. It is the method by which we treat as significant what the author did not mean to be significant, by which we single out as essential what the author regarded as incidental. Thus, if one brings out a book on turnips, the modern scholar tries to discover from it whether the author was on good terms with his wife; if a poet writes on buttercups, every word he says may be used as evidence against him at an inquest of his views on a future existence. On this fascinating principle, we delight to extort economic evidence from Aristophanes, because Aristophanes knew nothing of economics: we try to extract cryptograms from Shakespeare, because we are inwardly certain that Shakespeare never put them there: we sift and winnow the Gospel of St. Luke, in order to produce a Synoptic problem, because St. Luke, poor man, never knew the Synoptic problem to exist.
>
> There is, however, a special fascination in applying this method to Sherlock Holmes, because it is, in a sense, Holmes's own method. 'It has long been an axiom of mine,' he says, 'that the little things are infinitely the most important.' It might be the motto of his life's work. And it is, is it not, as we clergymen say, by the little things, the apparently unimportant things, that we judge of a man's character.

Here, Knox explicitly makes a number of interesting connections—between "delight" and the pulling of unintended meaning out of Aristophanes's texts, the contradiction of knowing that Shakespeare never considered cryptograms but that we still "extract" meaning regardless, and, of course, that this "method" applies most clearly to Holmes, for it is a variant of the character's own. These are telling statements, and sets up Knox's essay on exactly the right notes. For Knox, playing with texts is something to delight in, something that involves our own creative capacities, and one that may connect us meaningfully with the themes of the original texts. Playing a game with literature may reflect the silly overextensions that some scholars engage with in their readings of other texts, but with Holmes, it actually seems oddly appropriate.

Given that the players of The Game have taken Knox's original, satirical essay as the starting point of their enterprise, we might then think of The Game and this form of gaming as an enterprise that's somehow hermeneutic in nature—the blurring of the "magic circle" in the Holmesian Game is reminiscent of the ways many fields have treated the interpretation of their core texts, be it religion, history, or comparative literature. The Game is treading that line between interpretation of a text and creation of new meaning from a text that may have not been originally intended by the author. The Game is a means to make sense of the source text, sure, but Knox's satire also points out that there's a creative act involved with the "gaming" of these texts— engaged scholars (and, nowadays, everyday fans) can insert their own meaning when diving into the interpretation of a text. For some, this perhaps makes problematic where the meaning actually resides in something like the text of the Sherlock Holmes Canon (or Aristophanes's plays or Shakespeare's sonnets), while for others it may only be problematic if we assume a singular conception of meaning within these kinds of texts.

. . . Not Just a Magic Circle.

For Knox, his satire of Holmes scholarship seems to indicate that he might assume Game-players are inserting too much of their own will into the Holmes texts, but for his followers (players of the Sherlockian Game), it certainly doesn't seem to be. Game-players in the twentieth and twenty-first centuries have gone to great lengths to both illuminate and expand upon Conan Doyle's original stories. The task of making meaning out of the Holmes texts is like the task of making meaning in any other textual interpretation. The "magic circle" between the game and the out-of-game activities is permeable, sharing common meaning-making practices with the rules of "The Game" being potentially shaped by out-of-game concerns.

As we consider the historical roots of The Game as well as challenges to Huizinga's (or, at least, Salen and Zimmerman's characterization of Huizinga's) conception of games, we're left considering how exactly the out-of-game desires, intents, and practices of Game-players impact the in-game activities, and vice versa. For some Game-players, playing The Game means adopting a role similar to Holmes himself, even going so far as to adopt a "Canonical name," as is done by the fan society Baker Street Irregulars and members of its scion organizations. In the spirit of full disclosure, my Canonical name is "Silver Blaze" as a member of the Madison, Wisconsin, scion society The Notorious Canary-Trainers—as Knox pointed out, one of the draws of such playful analysis of the Holmes texts was to put one's self in Holmes's shoes, and I can't deny that doing this myself has been a lot of fun.

So, is that what this comes down to? A sense of belonging to a social group, a sense of connecting one's self to the Canon, or developing an identity as one who can walk in the same footsteps as Holmes? Perhaps, but we should note that this also is not without epistemological consequence. As with many contemporary fan communities, players of The Game see texts as malleable, open to interpretation, and available for them to insert their own agency into. Knowledge and meaning do not reside purely within the "text" of the Holmes Canon for Game-players; far from it, perhaps Game-players see their task as playfully shaping knowledge at the same time as uncovering it. In the grand scheme of things, this is still playing games with stories; the knowledge created and uncovered in The Game is of a relatively inconsequential sort, but one that has, for over a century, driven fans and scholars to pick apart texts, connect their meanings to the real world, and then also augment or reshape Doyle's original stories.

. . . Blurring the Boundaries.

And yet, when stated like this, playing The Game again sounds quite a bit like some kind of academic exercise, or something that mirrors the kinds of work that academics (such as this author) often value. We're left thinking again about The Game and its relationship to "games" in which the "magic circle" seems to be inapplicable: Players of The Game blur the line between work and play, between informal and formal knowledge construction activities, and between analyzing Holmes and emulating him. To understand the epistemological implications of The Game, we necessarily need to undertake an analysis of the adventures of those Baker Street flatmates and how they were "picked up," retooled, and re-interpreted by others.

Since the beginning, partaking in The Game has meant "flexing" intellectual muscles and epistemological stances that hadn't seen much use in how everyday folks interacted with the popular literature of the era. But, beyond this, The Game shows us that the forms of knowledge, argumentation, and (most importantly) meaning made from popular texts helps us to understand that we can learn much from "gaming" the Holmes Canon. The Game is fun, it's diverting, and it's certainly a sign of devotion—but beyond that, it challenges us to rethink whether "magic circles" exist between authorship, texts, and knowledge. The "work" and "play" of Game-players' creative connection of the Holmes Canon to the real world means that as we attempt to understand the philosophical implications of media fandom, we need to wrestle with how meaning is made through playful communities such as these.

Chapter 33

The Final Final Problem

Magali Rennes

L'homme c'est rien. L'oeuvre c'est tout. ("The man is nothing; his work, everything.")

—Gustave Flaubert to George Sand, misquoted by Holmes in "The Red-Headed League"

A last unresolved mystery involving Sherlock Holmes? Ah, yes, dear Reader, despite our long and intimate acquaintance with this incomparable consulting detective, a single, all-important proposition lingers in the air like the smell of fetid ash from an Indian lunkah: Holmes is the greatest detective of all time. The question—and our final mystery—is *why*?

First responses praise him as the father of forensic science, the prince of personalized methods, the king of observation and deduction.

Indeed he is.

And yet many detectives who have followed in his wake have rivaled his abilities. Modern television and popular fiction have hijacked and proliferated the detective and crime drama genres—brandishing more precise forensics (*CSI*), more advanced reasoning (*Numb3rs*), and more stylized—and even more idiosyncratic—supersleuths (Poirot, Sam Spade, Columbo, Monk, Brenda Lee Johnson), all without producing anyone to rival our dear Holmes.

So why, more than a century later, does Sherlock still reign as king? Perhaps there's more to Sherlock's method than his hawk-like eyes and razor-sharp mind. Yes, dear Reader, perhaps Sherlock reigns not simply because of his abilities to observe and deduce, but (indulge here my methods and invoke your imagination) precisely because of another, overlooked, more important talent—his ability to *play*. If we examine Mr. Holmes through the eyes of theorist Mikhail Bakhtin, we see that

Sherlock transcends official convention by claiming the timeless, universal, unofficial spirit of the folk.

Sherlock crowns himself King of the *Carnivalesque*.

Two Bodies—or Two Corpses?

To be true to Holmes, let's start with the bodies. Sherlock appears on the scene in an England steeped in centuries of royal tradition. Queen Victoria continues the English political fiction—just as the reigning monarchs before her did—of having "two bodies." The monarch's "natural" (physical) body is single, mortal, material, and subject to infirmities, such as decay. It requires care, grooming, dress, modesty, and veneration—the royal treatment. The monarch's other body—the "body politic"—is collective, immaterial, consists of laws, policies, government, and includes the English people—subjects to the far ends of Empire. It also demands service, loyalty, patriotism, and the deepest veneration. When the Queen's natural body goes the way of all flesh, the *office* of Queen continues on in perpetuity through the body politic. The state and its institutions remain a fixed, protected collective—which explains the contradictory shout: "the Queen is dead. Long live the Queen" (Ernst Kantorowicz, *The King's Two Bodies*, p. 7).

Mikhail Bakhtin, a one-legged, Russian theorist writing under Stalinist rule, also talks about two bodies—not of the monarch, but of the folk. Inspired by the medieval traditions of popular feasts, pageants, fairs, and carnival, Bakhtin identifies what he calls "grotesque realism" in the two folk bodies (*Rabelais and His World*). A commoner has a "fleeting" mortal body as well as a "collective, ancestral body." Images of the folk mortal body include anything that degrades, that lowers the "high, spiritual, ideal, and abstract and transfers to the material level." In other words, the holes, the dips, the jiggling parts: "the open mouth, the genital organs, the breasts, the phallus, the potbelly, the nose." So celebrations (both live and literary) revolve around—what else?—the best things in life (or allusions to them): eating, speech acts, sweating, sneezing, blowing noses, lovemaking, urination, defecation, birth, and death. The line between man and earthly being blurs—orifices are the life of the party. In short, expect a complete liberation of the body.

Unlike the Queen's natural body and the body politic, the two folk bodies—mortal and collective—are "indivisible." The mortal body isn't a "private, egoistic form," but an integral part of the whole. Which means that any bodily function of the mortal body, including death, unites the individual to the "universal folk body, representing all the people." So the folk collective "has a cosmic and an all-people's character," and is "growing and renewed" until it becomes "immeasurable . . . in fertility, growth, and a brimming over abundance." The whole is more than the sum of its (ahem!) holes. This brimming folk collective body revels outside of the Queen's rule—it thrives in Nature, in the "biocosmic circle of cyclic changes, the phases of nature's and man's reproductive life." Its gods are the changing seasons: sowing, conception, growth, death. The essence of this kind of grotesque realism sports a "double-faced fullness of life"—negation (the death of something old) and affirmation (the birth of something new and better). So the collective romps as a "phenomenon in transformation, a yet unfinished metamorphosis of death and birth, growth and becoming." The lines between the "body and the world are overcome": the individual becomes the collective who communes with the cosmos. The folk's "growing and ever-victorious collective" is the cosmos's own "flesh and blood."

The folk are alive, then dead—but then undead, reborn, always living, always a collective. All for one, one for all. Long live the folk.

The Body Count Rises

So how does this apply to our dear Holmes?

Sherlock Holmes's London—and England, even to the ends of the Empire—groans in the struggle between the Queen's royal bodies and the folk's natural ones. On the one hand are the "serious, unconditional, and indisputable" institutions of the Queen that regulate the body politic. On the other hand are the real lives of the folk—the rising middle class corseted in bourgeois mores, the body's inborn connection to nature and seasons, the innate desire for liberation, humorous relief, and cosmic expansiveness. The Queen maintains order and decorum by cloaking her physical body in neck to toe modesty—and her body politic in progress, industrialization, and expansion, ensuring that the sun "never sets" on her Empire.

But Holmes shows us a different view.

Holmes parades us through tales of one-legged men, poisoned dart-spitting pygmies, ears sent in cardboard boxes, aging fathers who ingest ape serum, snakes that kill daughters, women chained in zoos, beggars with twisted lips, geese that lay blue carbuncles, men who keep court with corpses, pygmy-sniffing dogs, disfigured women, deranged opium addicts . . . crooked men in every sense of the term. "The more outré and grotesque an incident is," Sherlock says, "the more carefully it deserves to be examined" (*The Hound of the Baskervilles*). In an age when the Queen says "light or dark meat" so that no one will have to speak of a fowl's "breast" or "thigh" in polite company, Sherlock lifts the Victorian petticoat (oh!) and plunges us into the teeming underbelly of the Empire's grotesque.

So Who's the Victim?

The last time you staged a fake murder (April Fool's!), dressed up as Lady Irene Adler for Halloween, or crowned yourself King from a trinket found in a Mardi Gras cake, you probably didn't realize that you, dear Reader, were celebrating centuries-old relics of the carnivalesque—when folk escape from being subjects of authority into a time and space of sheer liberation. The carnivalesque "destroys seriousness, frees human consciousness, thought, and imagination for new potentialities" (*Rabelais*, p. 49). So this carnival spirit is deeply ambivalent—even subversive—towards official power structures. It defines itself, and invites individuals to define themselves, by unofficial means: laughter.

For Bakhtin, carnivalesque laughter is "an essential form of truth concerning the world," and the only power strong enough to oppose the "official tone" of institution. But folk laughter isn't a giggle, chortle, snort, or guffaw—although these are good starts, and Holmes has his fair share (poor Watson). Rather, it's a cosmic laughter rooted in a profound celebration of life. Consider it, dear Reader, a deep belly laugh *with* the cosmos about life itself. Not *laughing at* or *near*, but *laughing with* the order institutions try to put on a life cycle beyond their control.

The carnivalesque consecrates "inventive freedom"—it liberates from "conventions and established truths, clichés, and all that is humdrum and universally accepted." In the broadest sense, carnivalesque laughter includes:

- **communal gatherings in the marketplace—where life and art become one**

- **ritual spectacles—pageants, comic shows, parodies of sacred institutions**

- **comic verbal compositions—parodies of the extra-carnival life, oral and written**

- **verbal abuses—curses, oaths, derision, mocking**

- **hierarchies turned upside down—kings debased, clowns crowned**

- **a spirit of disguise—shifting identities, literal or figurative masks**

- **a sense of play—games, riddles, dice, cards, chess, prophecies, soothsaying**

- **timelessness—cosmic temporality, revolutions, seasons**

But it's difficult to pinpoint the carnivalesque—carnival spirit not only expands into the cosmos, but naturally transgresses boundaries. To define it smells suspiciously of official-ness. How can we contain the uncontainable?

To consider the carnivalesque, dear Reader, we must *be* of the carnivalesque spirit. Which means we may set aside reason momentarily (oh!) because we are offered the chance "to have a new outlook on the world, to realize the relative nature of all that exists, and to enter a completely new order of things." When we enter the carnivalesque, we embrace a never-ending process of "becoming and growth"—recognizing that the very nature of *being* is always and forever incomplete, unfinished, and in a state of change. We must be open to "uncrown" the "prevailing concepts of the world"—the ones the earth itself might shirk off, in a fit of cosmic, collective folk laughter, in another revolution or two.

Are you, dear Reader, prepared to topple (or is it tickle) a reigning Queen? Her body politic? Victorian mores? Industrialized time?

Is Holmes?

The Adventure of the New Marketplace

Where do the folk go to escape in Sherlock Holmes's London?

For Bakhtin, the center of the carnivalesque is the communal "marketplace"—the town fair, the festival center, the carnival square. Barkers, vendors, hawkers, actors, and clowns shout in cacophony. Speech that sells, speech that tells stories, speech that derides are indistinguishable in the din. All is performance, all a "show." The marketplace acts as the fulcrum of centripetal and centrifugal forces—it draws everyone in as a "world in itself, the center of everything unofficial," but also expands out into cosmic, cyclical time by corresponding to feast days, harvests, changes of season, revolutions of the earth. It combines the two folk bodies—mortal and collective, earthly and cosmic. And everyone participates: in the marketplace, actor and spectator are one and the same. It's not a spectacle *seen* by the people: the folk "*live* in it."

But Bakhtin's medieval marketplace is a far, hawking cry from London's. During Victoria's reign (1830–1901), London's population increases from two to six and a half million—the capital of the world's first industrialized nation and the British Empire. In 1811, the first high-speed press appears; by 1814, *The Times* is printed on it, inaugurating the age of mass media. Print material—countless newspapers and more than 170 new periodicals by 1860—proliferates through London and sails out through the globe. In it, hawkers, barkers, vendors—in the form of advertisements—sell their wares next to a cacophony of printed personal notices, news reports, society gossip, monographs, and literary and popular fiction. Absent a gathering place for six million people, a new festival is born. Where Victorian industrialization already competes with seasonal time—forcing a five- to six-day work week, with no medieval option of weeks off for seasonal festivals, white-collar Londoners now gather in space and time. They are drawn into a communal, "unofficial," abstract marketplace—the printed word.

Consider, dear Reader, how newspapers, journals, periodicals, and other print material litter the floor and the sideboard of 221B (Mrs. Hudson!). Holmes keeps an eye on London, often incognito, from within this print marketplace—watching for crimes (stolen blue carbuncles) and potential clues (monkey thefts). He stays in London even when he's abroad through print—warning Watson that Lady Frances Carfax is in danger, or knowing it's safe to return when Colonel Sebastian Moran finally fires his air gun ("The Empty House"). And Holmes decodes secret messages through print—he deciphers what Gennaro signals to Emilia ("The Red Circle") and outfoxes Valentine Walter's communications with his accomplice ("The Bruce-Partington Plans"). Sherlock's anonymous invitations invoke an endless parade through his drawing room, such as when adverts in the evening papers—"*Globe, Star, Pall Mall, St.*

James's, Evening News, Standard, Echo"—inspire Henry Baker to claim his goose. And, in one telling incident that shows how the new marketplace *is* life itself, Mr. Horace Harker of the Central Press Syndicate finds himself an almost-victim and reporter of the same crime ("The Six Napoleons"). Holmes himself complains when the newspapers are "sterile"—when his corner of London's marketplace isn't bustling ("Silver Blaze"). It's as if the sun rises and sets on Holmes's marketplace—so often a case begins with a printed notice of a large pearl or a Red-Headed League, and ends with—EXTRA!—Lestrade or Scotland Yard receiving the credit. And yet it is Holmes, all along, drawing us in and through the new vital media, connecting the unseen dots behind the pica.

And Watson actively beckons us in to this marketplace— as readers. Against Sherlock's wishes, Watson publishes the adventures, birthing them into print. Watson uses direct address, "laying facts" before us, the *reader*. He writes for *us*, in spite of Sherlock's perpetual grumblings. Where Holmes (at first) favors "scientific exercise," Watson gives us "point of view." Where Holmes prefers "classical demonstration," Watson shows us "sensational details" that "excite." Where Holmes would press Watson to "instruct," Watson clearly chooses to entertain, pitting Holmes as the star ("The Abbey Grange"). Watson draws us in with the intrigue, the excitement, the chase, the riddle, the fun. Perhaps because of Watson's clever enticements—and the inevitable readership the adventures create—even Holmes has a change of heart. He ends up encouraging Watson to write—and then also uses direct address to pen his own adventure, calling the reader "astute" ("The Blanched Soldier"). So we—along with the original Victorian audience—are not only invited guests to be told a story, but *detectives* who are challenged to solve the case. Elementary, dear Reader—we are fully-fledged actors in a participatory drama. In this marketplace, we, too, *live* what we read.

But Sherlock doesn't just star in this new marketplace, he revolutionizes it. In 1891, Conan Doyle publishes Sherlock's Adventures in *The Strand*—not as serial novels, but as single short stories to be read in "one sitting." Amidst proliferating periodicals with disconnected stories, for the first time in print history, Doyle focuses on one strong character—our dear Holmes—driving a new, self-contained story written for that particular issue. And *The Strand*'s circulation increases. This "one-sitting," cyclical romp at the end of the industrial work day or week quickly becomes festival-like—the new "season" of carnivalesque into which folk escape.

Because they can, just as easily, leave it to re-enter official, industrial time and space. Another adventure, another "one-sitting" escape, will soon return.

Extra! Extra!

Come, Watson! The Game Is Afoot!

When Holmes tugs at the sleeping Watson's shoulder—candle shining in his face—to wake the doctor up, to what *game* does he refer?

A spirit of play drives the carnivalesque. So, in Bakhtin's marketplace, games are a high priority—they pull players out of official, man-made time and space and into the timeless, cosmic world of play. Cards and sports, "forms of fortune-telling, wishes, and predictions," and metaphors of play abound. Games represent the life cycle—moving through "fortune, misfortune, gain and loss, crowning and uncrowning." Life itself becomes nothing more than a "miniature play," not to be taken (cosmic laugh) seriously! Games draw "players out of the bonds of everyday life, liberate them from usual laws and regulations, and replace established conventions by lighter conventionalities." So play "renews" time and player alike (*Rabelais*, pp. 230–39).

This spirit of play drives Holmes. He laments, on the fourth, crime-free day of fog in a row, how the "London criminal is certainly a dull fellow." Does Holmes want Londoners robbed, injured, or dead?

No.

And *yes*, if it means he can keep playing. What is a Chess Master without an opponent?

Holmes craves an equal, someone to rival his abilities so that he is not *bored*. Even if that nemesis is "pure evil." Sherlock sings Professor Moriarty's praises as his arch rival, the "Napoleon of crime": "he combines science with evil, organization with precision, vision with perception." Moriarty is his only criminal "intellectual equal" and Holmes, depressed, bemoans his loss. "Without him," laments Holmes, "I have to deal with distressed children, pygmies of triviality" (*The Eligible Bachelor*).[1] It is as if Holmes himself has died: "London has become a singularly uninteresting city. . . . The community is certainly the gainer, and no one the loser, save the poor out-of-work specialist, whose occupation has gone." Moriarty opens the field of play—"with

---

[1] Adventures given in italics are episodes of the Jeremy Brett TV series.

that man in the field," Holmes says, "one's morning paper presented infinite possibilities" ("The Norwood Builder"). Most lawmen would welcome the idea of justice being served. But not Holmes: his rival gone means *game over*.

Holmes's craft also suggests a field of play—and he makes the rules. As a self-titled "unofficial consulting detective," Holmes keeps himself at arm's length from royal authority and Scotland Yard (established just as Victoria assumes her reign). "I follow my own methods," he says, "and tell as much or as little as I choose. That is the advantage of being unofficial" ("Silver Blaze"). And Sherlock operates outside of the law, regularly picking locks, forcing safes, and burgling homes—even risking being a "felon" and time in a "cell" (*The Master Blackmailer*). And who can ignore Holmes's beloved "unofficial force"—the Baker Street Irregulars? They "go everywhere and see anything." Anyone who gets in Sherlock's way, if not met on his terms—including (pardon, your Majesty!) the Queen's authority—are as much of an opponent to Holmes as are the criminals on the other side of the chess board. What matters most is not the law but the game.

And Holmes openly jests—with the police, his clients, Watson. When Lestrade arrogantly taunts Holmes with fresh evidence about Jonas Oldacre's timber house fire, Holmes fires back. Literally. Holmes stages a fire of his own, smoking out the real culprit—the living Mr. Oldacre. "I owed you a little mystification," Holmes tells Lestrade, "for your chaff in the morning." And when Colonel Ross denigrates Holmes one too many times, Sherlock delights at having "a little amusement" at his expense. Holmes brings back a disguised Silver Blaze right before the bewildered Colonel's eyes, but only unveils the horse after tormenting its owner. Similarly, Sherlock plants the Mazarin stone in Lord Cantlemere's pocket, then calls outrageously for his arrest. And Sherlock prods Watson with a carnivalesque derision that can only show how warm-hearted he feels towards his friend—Holmes jabs at Watson both for writing adventures as well as for developing his own "powers of deduction." For all of his grand protestations of science, our dear Holmes surely enjoys having a bit o' fun at others' expense.

And, dear Reader, we rarely speak of (ahem, come closer as I whisper) how often, in defiance of his grand reputation, our dear Holmes *doesn't solve the case*. Holmes dissuades Violet de Merville from marrying Baron Gruner, yes—but there is no mystery per se. The scarred Mrs. Ronder reveals the murderous plot behind the "veiled lodger." But, again—no mystery to solve.

And Holmes himself confesses his many blunders to Watson—
"a more common occurrence than anyone would think"—such
as when he mistakenly assumes that Silver Blaze has returned or
when he diagnoses a case as "blackmail" only to find it a cover-
up of an innocent child. And, despite Holmes's best efforts,
(shhhhhhh!) *criminals elude him*—John Openshaw is murdered
and the masterminds of "The Five Orange Pips" escape by boat
(though they drown). Those who smash the engineer's thumb
also get away. Sherlock, in self-deprecation at one of his blunders,
tells Watson to remind him of his failures when he feels "overconfident" ("The Yellow Face").

So it's not the particulars of a case—the motive, the outcome,
or the moral issue at stake—that drives Holmes.

What matters most is that there's a game, that it's afoot, and
that he's afoot in it.

Come, Watson!

The Adventure of the King's Crown

Jeremy Brett—as Holmes—holds Henry Baker's large, beat-up
hat and challenges Watson to deduce why its owner has a large
"intellectual capacity." Watson can't. So Holmes playfully flips
the large hat onto his head. Its brim sinks low on Holmes's brow.

Why does Holmes do this?

The mask takes center stage in the carnivalesque.
Disguise encourages not only play, but the joy of "change and
reincarnation, relativity, and the merry negation of uniformity
and similarity" (*Rabelais*, p. 39). Masks fuel new identities—
folk can travel in and out of social spheres beyond their "real"
station—even to an outright "reversal of hierarchic levels." In
one classic carnival celebration called the "feast of fools," a fool
is elected king. The real king (old authority and truth) is brought
down—metaphorically killed—so that the king of fools (a new
authority, a new truth) can emerge. When the fool's reign is over
at carnival's end, his kingly disguise is removed and he retakes
his place as a clown. But the fool doesn't "die" in vain—he has
led the hierarchy and the folk through metamorphosis. Dying
brings change and rebirth.

Our dear Holmes is a master of masks. He travels, disguised,
up and down the social ladder to find the truth of his latest riddle.
We wonder which act he enjoys more—the rector, the bum, the
bookseller, the stable groom, the tramp, the plumber, the old
sailor, the opium addict. Maybe it's when he tricks poor Agatha

into becoming his fiancée (*The Master Blackmailer*). Perhaps it's the many times he fools poor Watson, even feigning sickness unto death (oh!). And Holmes sees *through* masks as if they aren't there—he identifies John Clay, recognizes Joe Barnes under the dress, discerns Flora Millar as playing a lunatic, catches the Resident Patient lying, and gets behind the deceptions of most other criminals. It takes a mask to know a mask: shape-shifting defines Holmes's methods (small wonder that the only one to fool him retains his highest affections—Irene Adler). Sherlock dons the hat—walks in the shoes—of others, *becoming* them. Watson explains: Sherlock "puts himself in the man's place, having first gauged his intelligence. Then he tries to imagine how he himself would have proceeded in similar circumstances" ("The Musgrave Ritual"). Our dear Holmes can become—literally or figuratively—anyone he chooses.

But Sherlock's greatest disguise is hiding in plain sight, when his chameleon-like abilities vaunt him upon a fool's throne. The body politic bows to Holmes when the monarch entrusts him with matters of state. Holmes acts as a royal agent when the monarch cannot (the "Illustrious Client" is none other than Edward VII). Holmes secretly resolves many cases that threaten Empire—he restores the lost Naval Treaty, recovers the Bruce-Partington plans, regains the Mazarin Stone, and retrieves the letter from the "ruffled foreign potentate" that would mean certain war ("The Second Stain"). So Holmes, in effect, becomes the surrogate embodiment of a royal authority. But Holmes also usurps royal authority without permission when he takes justice into his own hands. He pardons murderers: he burns John Turner's confession, letting him go free, and sends Dr. Leon Sterndale—"a law to himself"—back to Africa without reporting the doctor's devilish crime ("The Boscombe Valley Mystery," "The Devil's Foot"). And Holmes and Watson watch, from behind a curtain, the blackmailer Charles Milverton's murder—without stopping or reporting it. Here Holmes brandishes a kind of fool's justice beyond any royal decree. The fool as king independently creates and enforces a new law: his own.

But our dear Holmes shows his truest mettle when he defies all official protocol and crowns *himself*. Holmes unflinchingly dictates his terms to any client, to Prime Ministers, government Secretaries, nobility, and even kings. He levels patronizing nobility—Holmes tells Lord St. Simon he is "descending" by taking the Lord's case (his last client was a king). And Holmes refuses to bow to or shake hands with the King of Bohemia, exalting Lady Adler's character over his: "she seems indeed to be on a very different level to your Majesty." But Sherlock's most revealing and mystical self-crowning involves the divine right of kings, interrupted by Charles I's beheading in 1649. When Holmes helps school chum Reginald find the missing butler Brunton, he also recovers the sacred crown of Charles II. For more than two hundred years, none of the noble Musgraves has understood the family Ritual—and yet Holmes deciphers it in short order. Only Holmes recognizes the "battered and shapeless diadem" as fragments of the ancient crown. And only Holmes, of all the nobility in England, can metaphorically put the crown back together—as if, like Excalibur, it were rightfully his. As if Holmes, having recovered the divine right, is the *real king* of England.

And yet, game over, Holmes just as quickly steps off his throne. He faithfully returns Charles's diadem to the monarch. Holmes doesn't need a crown—sovereign authority seems to emanate from within him, from an independent source (dare we say a *cosmic* divine right?) that he can invoke at his choosing. His next adventure, perhaps.

So Holmes gives full credit to Scotland Yard and defers to royal authority, even when he's the mastermind. And outside of cases, Holmes upholds the Crown and lives as a respectful, law-abiding subject of the monarch. He keeps none of the vestiges of the throne for himself.

Only the thrill of the match—and the occasional satisfaction of checkmate.

Oh, and the spirit of rebirth after every new adventure.

All the Queen's Horses

So we return, dear Reader, to our final problem. Why is Sherlock the greatest detective of all time? Perhaps we might pose a different question.

Does Holmes serve the Queen or the folk?

Even amidst bodies piling up in Sherlock Holmes's *Adventures*, play for him means play for us. As readers, we don't feel the sting of death, the seriousness of crime, or rejoice in "official" justice in any meaningful, moral way. We know that the bodies (spoiler!) *aren't really injured or dead* anyway. What matters most is the puzzle, the chess match, the solution to the riddle. Will Holmes prevail? When it's all wrapped up, we don't remember victims or punishments, but *how* Holmes did it. It's all just a game. A game that continues to redefine modern entertainment.

Consider, dear Reader, how Holmes's "one character, one sitting" model still resonates in television media. Most sit-coms, dramas, detective shows, and crime dramas follow characters through half-hour or hour "sittings" of contained episodes. Who knew that the strength of Holmes's character would redefine carnivalesque time and space for the industrialized world? In effect, Holmes inaugurates "prime time."

And Sherlock Holmes will not *die*. When Holmes says "all the Queen's horses and all the Queen's men can't avail," he suggests he holds a power beyond the crown. The Queen's mortal body dies. But Holmes returns from Reichenbach Falls—inspired in part by Londoners wearing black arm bands in protest—and resurrects his adventures. With every daily revolution of the Earth, every yearly orbit around the sun, Holmes continues to appear across the hurtling globe—crowning and uncrowning himself as he puts Humpty Dumpty together again—in old and new media: comics, video games, novels, animation, television programs, and film. He's the man who protects the public, sports secret identities, wears a distinct costume, has a supporting cast, and cheats death because of special powers unique to him—powers not born just of reason, but of "imagination" and cosmic connection ("Silver Blaze"). It's no wonder that Superman appears in 1938—only a few short years after the last of Doyle's short stories is published. Holmes is his prototype: the first superhero.

So, does our dear Holmes "uncrown" the prevailing concepts of the world? Topple a monarch? Out with the old, in with the new? Perhaps, dear Reader, our mystery is best left for you to solve.

Your move.

In the meantime, in a cacophony of cosmic laughter, Holmes has left the building.

Holmes lives. Long live the King.

HE IS

A MAN OF

HABITS

AND I AM ONE OF THEM

The Very Smartest
of Our Detective Officers
For Whose Future Holmes Had High Hopes

ANATOLIA BESSEMER has been spotted in Chicago despite being equally at home in London. Knowing where she is at any given moment is difficult because Anatolia often travels under assumed names, disguises, and false passports, much like her hero Sherlock Holmes. Though for her, it's less about catching criminals and more about never quite being pinned down in terms of her analysis of religious, cognitive, Marxist or philosophical evidence. She likes to keep all options open.

JEF BURNHAM denies this reality. Only that which appears on television seems real to him. Indeed, he considers Egon Spengler, Crow T. Robot, and The Doctor among his closest friends and, to the horror of his wife and family, has gone through many a television set desperately trying to claw his way in. In spite of this debilitating perceptual handicap, Jef somehow managed to earn a degree in Film & Video from Columbia College Chicago and secure a position as Editor of FilmMonthly.com.

CARI CALLIS practices bare attention in her garden as she plucks drunken bees from grapevines, rescues the tomatoes from bindweed and investigates the death of eighty-six goldfish from an unexpected January thaw. She makes no claims that Holmes was a practicing Buddhist, but she's convinced that his creator intentionally cultivated that truth seeker with one foot poised upon the divine path. Houdini's pranayamic breathing lessons stayed with her and became a lifetime ritual on the yoga mat. But despite her invocations to the spirit of Holmes's genius, she still grapples with how to see things as they really are. In the classroom at Columbia College Chicago where she's an Associate Professor, she provokes her students to do the same. Oh, and if anyone has a copy of "The Origin of Tree Worship" she'd really like to borrow it.

JONATHAN CLEMENTS is the author of *Schoolgirl Milky Crisis: Adventures in the Anime and Manga Trade* and co-author of the *Dorama Encyclopedia: A Guide to Japanese TV Drama Since 1953*. As a contributing editor to the forthcoming new edition of the *Encyclopedia of Science Fiction*, he has been assembling details of Sherlock Holmes's many appearances in anime, manga and Japanese literature. He is a PhD candidate at the Faculty of Applied Design and

Engineering, Swansea Metropolitan University, writing his thesis on the industrial history of Japanese animation.

TAMÁS DEMETER has long been struggling with making people's behavior coherent. That's why he ended up with writing a thesis on the philosophy of psychology in Cambridge. There he argued that we are pretty much lore-abiding people who create reassuring narratives for making coherent otherwise unintelligible behavior. That's why he admires Holmes's immense capacity for creating coherence among divergent facts in various possible ways and deploying the resulting narratives while solving all those mysterious cases These days he is a Senior Fellow at the Institute for Philosophical Research, Hungarian Academy of Sciences, and he has been acting as guest editor for special issues on similar problems for *Monist* and *European Journal of Analytic Philosophy*.

Frequently accused of sharing Holmes's hyper-rationality, **BRIAN DOMINO** is an associate professor of philosophy at Miami University where, alas, he solves no crimes. He agrees with Holmes that "education never ends. It is a series of lessons with the greatest for the last." Unlike Mrs. Ronder, he is not contemplating finishing that lesson early, but is hoping for an extension of the due date. He would like the extra time to finish working on an essay on the meaning of life, and perhaps his monograph on Friedrich Nietzsche's *Ecce Homo*.

TOM DOWD spends way too much time as people other than himself. One of the co-creators of the table-top roleplaying game *Shadowrun* he has decades of credits in the role-playing and computer game industries, including the best-selling Xbox title *MechAssault*. Currently, he teaches game development and interactive and transmedia narrative at Columbia College Chicago where he oversees curriculum development as well as the large-team senior capstone class in game production. He also has a garage full of costumes and props from years of live-action role-playing and hard-disks full of computer adventure and narrative games that fill a similar purpose. Tom also currently oversees the text-based high-fantasy role-playing game *Castle Marrach* at www.skotos.net that blends mystery, intrigue, romance, and fantasy in an original narrative environment. With the exception of a few court orders, his fascination with costuming and personas—virtual or otherwise—hasn't gotten him into trouble... yet.

SEAN C. DUNCAN is Armstrong Professor of Interactive Media, an Assistant Professor within Miami University's School of Education, Health, and Society and Armstrong Institute for Interactive Media Studies. He studies games, learning, and participatory online cultures. In his free time, he enjoys vacationing in the island of Uffa (avoiding the Grice-Patersons, whenever possible).

DON FALLIS is Associate Professor of Information Resources and Adjunct Associate Professor of Philosophy at the University of Arizona. He has written several philosophy articles on lying and deception, including "What is Lying?" *Journal of Philosophy*, v. 106, n. 1, (2009) and "The Most Terrific Liar You Ever Saw in Your Life" in *The Catcher in the Rye and Philosophy* (Chicago: Open Court, forthcoming). He has also published on the philosophical implications of the work of Philip Marlowe and the work of Sam Spade. Finally, much like Professor Moriarty, he has done work in mathematics as well as philosophy (his Erdős number is 5), and he is responsible for "half that is evil" and "nearly all that is undetected" in southern Arizona.

MIRIAM FRANCHELLA is Associate Professor of Logic and Philosophy of Science at the State University of Milan. She feels that her washing machine has a deep empathy with her: they work in the same way. Miriam puts a set of different objects (a botanical t-shirt, some psychologised trousers, poetical gloves, logical socks) inside; then, they mix and renew everything. Looking at the clothes line, one can evaluate the result.

MIHAELA FRUNZA teaches Ethics at Babes-Bolyai University from Cluj, Romania. She holds a PhD in Philosophy and has recently published in applied ethics and bioethics. When not investigating Holmes's mysteries, she is involved in research in medical ethics and moral philosophy.

RONALD GREEN has endeavored to possess knowledge useful to his work. That relating to politics can be marked at zero, botany variable, geography profound only as regards the location of cults within fifty miles of town, sensational literature and self-mortification records unique. He teaches accordingly at Coastal Carolina University.

LAURI JÄRVILEHTO is a metaphysical explorer, an epistemic detective and a Sherlock Holmes fan. His master's thesis addressed Wittgenstein's ladder and his PhD focused on epistemology. His current research focus is on the workings of the human mind, and in particular intuitive thought. Lauri is passionate about trying to work out the mysteries of the mind and figuring out ways to share his findings with the world.

There are few places in the English speaking world further (both culturally and geographically) from 221b Baker Street than Montana. However, quite thankfully, when it comes to the science of deduction, wherever you go there is almost always room for at least one local dabbler. This is where you can generally find **JUSTUS SOLOMON JOHNSON**: poking his nose in other people's business and trying to convince local law enforcement that they need to hire a consulting detective. Justus can also be found running experiments at the University of Wyoming attempting to deduce precisely how moral appraisal and the distinction between doing and allowing interact.

As you emerge from the twilight quill, wondering whether it was the drug or the murder which knocked you down, **KEVIN KILROY** drifts and descends, drifts and descends—evaporating, cloudlike, across the city streets. Elsewhere, while you ponder the searchlights, he sits in his chair at The Office of Urban

Spiritual Research, the window open, a train rolling by, people, communion with the bruised weight—all of it criminal. He as well. And then there's his laughing, your drinking, his betting on horses. The newspaper, walking, ethically a detective as he ornaments these streets.

AMY KIND doesn't play the violin, doesn't smoke opium or tobacco, isn't a detective, and has never employed a band of irregulars to help her in her daily life. But other than that, she's exactly like Sherlock Holmes. (Then again, didn't Holmes say that women are never to be entirely trusted?) She's previously contributed to volumes on *Battlestar Galactica and Philosophy* and *Star Trek and Philosophy*, and she does her philosophical sleuthing at Claremont McKenna College.

RORY E. KRAFT, JR. first read a Holmes story when he was ten and there has been no going back since. Unlike Watson, he can tell you the number of steps up to his house and has never been fooled by a roommate in drag. In addition to wondering what Doyle had against dogs, he thinks a lot about questions about ethical theory and applied ethics. He is the editor of *Questions: Philosophy for Young People* and has been doing philosophy with children for a decade.

SAWYER J. LAHR prefers to see the world with pink glasses. The more normal things seem, the queerer they are. He seizes the opportunity to prove that "gay" doesn't begin to explain human behavior. Sawyer has grown the LGBT media coverage at FilmMonthly.com as Assistant Editor and Staff Writer while freelancing for Chicago's *Mindful Metropolis Magazine*. He's not shocked by much, but the audacity of Sacha Baron Cohen's gay social experiment, *Borat*, is still jaw-droppingly outrageous.

Sherlock Holmes approached the body, and, kneeling down, examined it intently. Standing, he announced "the dead man's driver's license reveals that his name was Dr. **GREG LITTMANN**. His low forehead and simian features indicate a professor of philosophy. The residue on his right heel attests that he received his doctorate from the University of North Carolina at Chapel Hill, but the residue upon the left demonstrates that he was employed at Southern Illinois University Edwardsville. His lips bear the distinctive odor of one who loved all philosophy, especially epistemology, metaphysics, and ethics. The ink stains on his fingers prove conclusively that he has published in metaphysics and the philosophy of logic, and has written chapters for popular culture and philosophy texts devoted to *Doctor Who, Dune, Final Fantasy, The Onion, The Terminator,* and *The Walking Dead.*"
"Good heavens!" I cried. "But what of the malignant and terrible contortion of his features as though in some grievous death struggle? And what of the mysterious letters scrawled in blood across the wall—TENUR."
Holmes shrugged. "I blame students," he sighed.

DANIEL P. MALLOY is a consulting philosopher and lecturer at Appalachian State University. The position of consulting philosopher is a unique one.

When other philosophers are stumped by a particularly complex problem, they seek out his aid and insights. Unlike a consulting detective, a consulting philosopher doesn't solve problems—he makes them more confusing.

JIM JOHN MARKS is not a philosopher, or a detective. At least not in any professional capacity. His formal education trained him to be a high school mathematics teacher, he eventually became a software engineer, and he now works in healthcare informatics. But there is something that mathematics, computer programming, informatics and philosophy all have in common: analytical, linear, rational thinking as the primary tool for problem solving. Knowing this, it should come as no shock to be told that a character such as Sherlock Holmes has been a hero of his since childhood. Sherlock Holmes illustrated with outrageous style that the critical thinking Jim learned in math and science classes could benefit society, if properly applied. He has, from a young age, always been dedicated to the idea that science, technology, reasonable discourse and information are our best hopes for achieving the humanitarian work that so much of our planet desperately needs. And yet, as he grew older and learned more about history, especially twentieth century history, the more it seemed as though the exact opposite were actually true. The more science, technology, reasonable discourse, and information humanity made available to itself, the worse things seemed to get! When Jim studied philosophy in college, he discovered that there are good reasons why the lesson Holmes taught about the seemingly limitless possibilities of what the human mind could achieve, might not be so black and white. After watching the recent film adaptation of his beloved role model, it has occurred to him that perhaps his young mind over-simplified what it was that his favorite detective wanted him to understand.

RAFE MCGREGOR tried to make a career writing pulp fiction, failed badly, and realised that he was better at *philosophy of horror* than *horror*. Some of his genre publications can still be found in print, but you have to look really hard. He has been a fan of *The Hound of the Baskervilles* for far too long, and although he has never been to Dartmoor, it is on his to-do list. He is in his second year of research at the University of York, where he is supervised by Professor Peter Lamarque. His thesis concerns the relationship between aesthetic and moral value in art, argues for some rather unpopular views, and is proving a major obstacle to the Dartmoor trip.

RACHEL MICHAELS's many disguises include those of a lecturer in English at Bronx Community College; a philosophy graduate student at The New School for Social Research; a common loafer; and a curly-haired spaniel.

One of our suspects is called **SAMI PAAVOLA** whose doings have some curious features. He seems to be a philosopher who believes that one can make some sense on processes and practices of discovery. He is searching clues on clues, and is a Sherlock Holmes enthusiast although acts more like Watson. He seems to be excited by weird terms and issues like 'abduction' (isn't it about UFOs or kidnapping?!), 'computer-supported collaborative learning', 'distributed cognition', or even 'trialogues' (come on ...). Besides, he suffers probably somewhat from triadomany (see the Commens Medical Handbook) diagnosed by his leaning on Charles S. Peirce, pragmatists, and others investigating mediated processes in various forms. So, what is he after?

One of the last surviving descendants of the original Red-Headed League, **MAGALI RENNES** only rarely copies the encyclopedia word for word in longhand. She spends most of her time in the cosmos writing, but returns to the hurtling earth to participate in festivals and the print marketplace. Like Sherlock, she takes on many disguises—writing across genres—and, teaching screenwriting, relishes the uncontainable, transgressive play of *story* in the same way the King of Detectives worships an elusive case. Her screenplays have won awards, but she sees her students (and our dear Readers!) as the real superheroes, folk kings and queens of cyclic renewal. She hopes, like our indefatigable Holmes, that there are always more games—and stories—afoot than feet to keep up with them.

Since they met in 1997, **MONA** and **JAMES ROCHA** have been solving murders and various other enigmatic cases for Scotland Yard, LAPD, NYPD, SFPD, Santa Barbara PD, and countless other investigative bodies across the planet. And they do this without ever leaving their couch—usually with the aid of books and their TV. To make it even more challenging, they must always solve these cases prior to their top rivals: Holmes, Poirot, Monk, Shawn Spencer, and Castle. To keep up appearances (and pay the bills) they also maintain day jobs: Mona studying for a PhD in women's history at LSU, and James teaching and researching applied ethics, feminism, and pop culture while an assistant professor, also at LSU.

When she's not fighting crime, **JULIA ROUND** teaches comics and literature at Bournemouth University (further details at www.juliaround.com). As a child she read Conan Doyle and Agatha Christie mysteries obsessively and watched extensive re-runs of *Blackadder*—laying the groundwork for the massive crush on Hugh Laurie that she would later develop. She has a penchant for many (but not all) of the vices shared by Holmes and House, such as playing the piano, guitar, and violin (badly), misanthropy and superiority, as well as an addiction to American TV shows (like *House*). Although well past the age of Scouts and Guides, she tries to practice 'Sherlock Holmesism' whenever possible: often setting herself cryptic puzzles that, when deduced in sobriety, invariably lead to little more than a brief shopping list—'Eggs (6)'—in her left pocket. She admits to being a fairly bad feminist, but seldom resorts to crying or *big eyes* to win a debate.

When not encouraging her unhealthy obsession with that delectable detective Sherlock Holmes, you'll find twenty-five-year-old, ace Investigator **KATE RUFA** rockin' a pixy hair style while teaching martial arts, trying not to kill people with her cooking, and desperately seeking a PhD program that will give her adequate funding to further advance her studies in philosophy and support her mystery mania. Recently graduated Summa Cum Laude from

Saint Xavier University in Chicago, Kate Rufa holds a BA in philosophy and has spent more time then she is currently willing to admit studying early modern philosophers with an emphasis on Spinozistic philosophy. This is, of course elementary, my dear reader.

ZORAN SAMARDZIJA is Assistant Professor of Film/Video at Columbia College Chicago. When he is not teaching, writing, and publishing on film, he's obsessively compulsively watching way too many films just for pleasure. Many are really bad like that one Western with a dinosaur that eats cattle. Occasionally this leaves time for a non-film related activity which is where interests in baseball, music, and *Star Trek* come into play. Sometimes he even bothers to read Sherlock Holmes, Enlightenment philosophy, and also compose a bio when asked.

Some say **FRANCINE J. SANDERS**'s first word, after "chocolate," was the question "Why?" There were other early warning signs of an investigator/ writer in the making, especially her obsession with hard-boiled detectives, trench coats, and frequent interrogations of the family parakeet. Later, she studied journalism (BS from the University of Illinois) and film studies (MA from Northwestern University). Her education on the human animal came from more than eight years working as a civilian investigator for the Chicago Police Department, and many more years riding CTA buses and trains (she doesn't own a car). Today, she teaches film and writing, and consults on police brutality issues. Her investigative team includes: Lili, a femme fatale posing as a white cockatiel, and Marlowe, a master sleuth in yellow cockatiel disguise. To no one's surprise, Francine's favorite film genre is noir.

TIMOTHY SEXTON is not retained by the readers of Associated Content from Yahoo! to supply their deficiencies, but he has filled the insufficiencies that exists in their singular acquaintance with the concept of popular culture as a plain Christmas goose by revealing that it is actually stuffed with rare and precious carbuncles. He achieved notoriety for his uncanny ability to deduce improbable truths from the connection of seemingly unrelated elements left behind after eliminating all impossible conclusions. The guiding premise behind his "The Poseur's Guide to…" is that what one man can invent another can discover. To him she will always be *the* woman: his wife, Skipper, who introduced him to Jeremy Brett and forever changed the course his life and philosophy would take.

JOSEF STEIFF always felt like he saw more than he was supposed to and longed for his own Watson to chide, "Did you just see that?" He initially tried to apply these observations to the mysteries of human behavior, working as a licensed social worker before becoming a filmmaker and writer. Now as a doddering professor, he walks into rooms and can't remember why, he tries to figure out where his reading glasses are, and he wonders what he had started to say as he loses his train of thought—that is the scale of the mysteries he tries to solve these days.

RUTH TALLMAN is an assistant professor of philosophy at Barry University, Miami Shores, Florida. She has written articles for several pop culture and philosophy books, including *Green Lantern and Philosophy*, *Rolling Stones and Philosophy*, and *Christmas and Philosophy*. Sherlock Holmes's extreme cool factor gave this nerd hope back before geek chic was a thing, and the friendship between him and Watson showed her what friendship should be.

ANDREW TERJESEN has a PhD in Philosophy from Duke University. He has been a visiting assistant professor at Austin College, Washington and Lee University and Rhodes College. Andrew's musings on the ethical questions related to fiction and "everyday" life can be found in a number of essays including contributions to *What Philosophy Can Tell You About Your Dog*, *The Onion and Philosophy*, *Supervillains and Philosophy*, and *Manga and Philosophy*. Thinking so much about the nature of intellectual property has inspired Andrew to attend law school in the Fall. His decision had nothing to do with the going rate for consulting *philosophical* detectives.

FIONA TOMKINSON teaches English Literature at Yeditepe University in Istanbul. She holds a BA in English from Oxford and an MA and PhD in Philosophy from Bosphorus University, Istanbul. She likes candles but has no use for dumbbells. She has always longed to be part of a real-life Sherlock Holmes adventure, but academic conferences are her substitute for scandals in Bohemia.

D.E. WITTKOWER, Assistant Professor of Philosophy at Old Dominion University, is a contemporary reboot of a genteel, old-fashioned profession. He is author of articles and book chapters on technology and digital culture, and editor of *Philip K. Dick and Philosophy*, *Facebook and Philosophy*, *Mr. Monk and Philosophy*, and *iPod and Philosophy*. He once shot a man in Thebes just to watch him die.

IVAN WOLFE splits his time between Arizona and Alaska, alternatively teaching English at Arizona State University and mowing lawns in the small town of Homer. He has a PhD in English from the University of Texas— Austin. The first time he read Sherlock Holmes (when he was eight years old), it was in an abridged edition that cut the Mormon sections out of *A Study in Scarlet*; he didn't find out about those chapters until his freshman year in college. He has many previous publications, all of which are part of his own personal canon. He also considers anyone else with the same name to be apocryphal.

THANKS TO Series Editor George Reisch, Editorial Director David Ramsay Steele, Shane Arbogast for the cover, Columbia College Chicago, Doreen Bartoni, Bruce Sheridan, Sara Livingston, Adam Barkman, Kristin Franseen, Bruce Krajewski, the 'Bou Crew (Laura, Joseph, Jori, Jen, Christin, Jayme, Allison, Dillon, Allie, Sarah H., Kelli, Kailey and Kari), and as always, thanks to Victor—yes, V., the book is done.

Abrams, Jerold J. 2009. The Logic of Guesswork in Sherlock Holmes and *House*. In Henry Jacoby, ed., *House and Philosophy: Everybody Lies* (Wiley-Blackwell).

Adler, Jonathan E. 1997. Lying, Deceiving, or Falsely Implicating. *Journal of Philosophy* 94.

Augustine. 1952. Lying (De Mendacio). In *Treatises on Various Subjects* (Catholic University of America Press).

Baden-Powell, Robert. 2005. *Scouting for Boys*. Oxford University Press.

Bakhtin, Mikhail. 1984. *Rabelais and His World*. Indiana University Press.

Baron, Marcia. 2003. Manipulativeness. In *Proceedings and Addresses of the American Philosophical Association* 77.

Barrier, J. Michael. 1999. *Hollywood Cartoons: American Animation in Its Golden Age*. Oxford University Press.

Baring-Gould, William.1967. *The Annotated Sherlock Holmes*. Volumes 1 and 2. Clarkson N. Potter.

Baudrillard, Jean. 1994. *Simulacra and Simulation*. University of Michigan Press.

Bell, J. Bowyer, and Barton Whaley. 1991. *Cheating and Deception*. Transaction.

Butler, Judith. 1990. *Gender Trouble*. Routledge.

Carnap, Rudolf. 1996. The Elimination of Metaphysics through Logical Analysis of Language. In Sahotra Sarkar, ed., *Logical Empiricism at Its Peak* (Routledge).

Carroll, Noël, 1990. *The Philosophy of Horror, or, Paradoxes of the Heart*. Routledge.

———. 2001. *Beyond Aesthetics: Philosophical Essays*. Cambridge University Press.

Carson, Thomas L. 2010. *Lying and Deception*. Oxford University Press.

Cawelti, John. G. 1976. *Adventure, Mystery, and Romance*. University of Chicago Press.

Cellucci Carlo. 1998. *Le Ragioni della Logica*. Laterza.

———. Forthcoming. Reason and Logic. In C. Amoretti and N. Vassallo, eds., *Reason and Rationality* (Ontos).

———. Forthcoming. *The Scope of Logic: Deduction, Abduction, Analysis*.

Chandler, Raymond. 1944. The Simple Art of Murder. *Atlantic Monthly*.

Cheng P. W., and K. J. Holyoak. 1989. On the Natural Selection of Reasoning. *Cognition* 33.

Chisholm, Roderick M., and Thomas D. Feehan. 1977. The Intent to Deceive. *Journal of Philosophy* 74.

Christ, Jay Finley. 1947. *An Irregular Chronology of Sherlock Holmes of Baker Street*. Fanlight.

Chun, Jayson Makoto. 2007. *'A Nation of a Hundred Million Idiots'? A Social History of Japanese Television 1953–1973*. Routledge.

Clements, Jonathan. 2010. *A Brief History of the Samurai*. Running Press.

Clements, Jonathan, and Tamamuro Motoko. 2003. *The Dorama Encyclopedia: A Guide to Japanese TV Drama Since 1953*. Stone Bridge.

Clements, Jonathan, and Helen McCarthy. 2006. *The Anime Encyclopedia: A Guide to Japanese Animation Since 1917*. Revised and Expanded Edition. Stone Bridge.

Cooper, J.M., ed. 1997. *Complete Works of Plato*. Hackett.

Cosmides Leda. 1989. The Logic of Social Exchange: Has Natural Selection Shaped How Humans Reason? Studies with the Wason Selection Task. *Cognition* 31.

Cross, Gary S. 2008. *Men to Boys: The Making of Modern Immaturity*. Columbia University Press.

Darwin, Charles. 2003 [1859]. On the Origin of Species. Facsimile of first edition. Wildside.

Delaney, Neil. 1963. Love and Loving Commitment: Articulating a Modern Ideal. *American Philosophical Quarterly* 33.

Derrida, Jacques. 1980. *Writing and Difference*. University of Chicago Press.

Deweese-Boyd, Ian. 2010. Self-Deception. *Stanford Encyclopedia of Philosophy*, <http://plato.stanford.edu/entries/self-deception>.

Didierjean, André, and Fernand Gobet. 2007. Sherlock Holmes—An Expert's View of Expertise. *British Journal of Psychology*.

Ditmore, Melissa Hope. 2006. *The Encyclopedia of Prostitution and Sex Work*. Greenwood.

Doxiadis, Apostolos, and Christos H. Papadimitriou. 2009. *Logicomix*. Bloomsbury.

Eco, Umberto, and Thomas A. Sebeok, eds. 1983. *The Sign of Three: Dupin, Holmes, Peirce*. Indiana University Press.

Edwards, Tim. 2006. *Cultures of Masculinity*. Routledge.

——. 1997. *Men in the Mirror: Men's Fashion, Masculinity, and Consumer Society*. Continuum.

Ekman, Paul. 2009. Lie Catching and Microexpressions. In *The Philosophy of Deception* (Oxford University Press).

Ellis, Sian. 2009. On the Trail of Sherlock Holmes. *British Heritage* 30:4.

Frege, Gottlob. 1972. *Conceptual Notation and Related Articles*. Clarendon.

——. 1979. *Posthumous Writings*. Blackwell.

Friedman, Marilyn. 2003. *Autonomy, Gender, Politics*. Oxford University Press.

Frith, Uta. 2003. *Autism: Explaining the Enigma*. Blackwell.

Gaylin, Willard. 1986. *Rediscovering Love*. New Viking.

Gettier, Edmund. 1963. Is Justified True Belief Knowledge? *Analysis* 23.

Goodman, Nelson. 1983. *Fact, Fiction, and Forecast*. Fourth edition. Harvard University Press.

Hamilton, Walter. 1882. *The Aesthetic Movement in England*. Reeves and Turner.

Harman, Gilbert. 1986. *Change in View*. MIT Press.

Heidegger, Martin. 1962. *Being and Time*. Blackwell.

Hiramatsu, K., ed. 2000. *Terebi 50-nen in TV Guide: The TV History of 50 Years*. Tokyo News Tsushinsha.

Hu, T. 2007. The Animated Resurrection of the Legend of the White Snake in Japan. *Animation* 2 (March).

Hume, David. 1999 [1748]. *An Enquiry concerning Human Understanding*. Oxford University Press.

Husserl, Edmund. 1989. *The Crisis of European Sciences and Transcendental Phenomenology*. Northwestern University Press.

Huizinga, Johan. 1971. *Homo Ludens*. Beacon Press.

Inui, N. 1988. *That's TV Graffiti: Gaikoku Terebi Eiga Sanjūnen no Subete [All About 35 Years of Foreign TV and Films]*. Film Art-sha.

Ito, Youichi. 1990. The Trade Winds Change: Japan's Shift from an Information Importer to an Information Exporter, 1965–1985. *Communication Yearbook* 14.

Iyoda, Y., et al., eds. 1998. *Terebi Shi Handbook [TV History Handbook]*. Jiyūkokuminsha.

Johnson-Laird, P.N., Legrenzi P., Sonino Legrenzi M. 1972. Reasoning and a Sense of Reality. *British Journal of Psychology* 63.

Johnston, Charles. 2010. *The Yoga Sutras of Patanjali: The Book of the Spiritual Man*. Project Gutenberg Literary Archive Foundation.

Kantorowicz, Ernst H. 1957. *The King's Two Bodies*. Princeton University Press.

Kawana, Sari. 2008. *Murder Most Modern: Detective Fiction and Japanese Culture*. University of Minnesota Press.

Keene, Donald. 1984. *Dawn to the West: Japanese Literature in the Modern Era*. Holt.

Kendrick, Stephen. 1999. *Holy Clues: The Gospel According to Sherlock Holmes*. Random House.

———. 2000. Zen in the Art of Sherlock Holmes. *Utne Reader* (January–February).

Kestner, Joseph A. 1997. *Sherlock's Men: Masculinity, Conan Doyle, and Cultural History*. Ashgate.

King, Laurie R. A Holmes Chronology, <www.laurierking.com/etcetera/lrk-on-holmes>.

Klinger, Leslie. Major Events, <http://webpages.charter.net/lklinger/Chrotabl.htm>.

Knox, Ronald. 1928. Studies in the Literature of Sherlock Holmes. In *Essays in Satire* (Sheed and Ward).

Leibniz, Gottfried W. 1991. *Discourse on Metaphysics and Other Essays*. Hackett.

Lellenberg, Jon L., ed. 1990. *Irregular Memories of the 'Thirties: An Archival History of the Baker Street Irregulars' First Decade, 1930–1940*. Fordham University Press.

Lipton, Peter. 2001. Is Explanation a Guide to Inference? A Reply to Wesley Salmon. In Giora Hon and Sam Rakover, eds., *Explanation: Theoretical Approaches and Applications* (Kluwer).

———. 2004. *Inference to the Best Explanation*. Routledge.

MacIntyre, Alasdair. 1985. *After Virtue: A Study in Moral Theory*. Duckworth.

———. 1988. *Whose Justice? Which Rationality?* University of Notre Dame Press.

Macintyre, B. 2010. *The Last Word: Tales from the Tip of the Mother Tongue*. Bloomsbury.

Magliola, Robert R. 1977. *Phenomenology and Literature: An Introduction*. Purdue University Press.

Mahon, James. 2008. The Definition of Lying and Deception. *Stanford Encyclopedia of Philosophy*, <http://plato.stanford.edu/entries/lying-definition>.

Mandel, Ernest. 1985. *Delightful Murder: A Social History of the Crime Story*. University of Minnesota Press.

Manning, Rita C. 1987. Why Sherlock Holmes Can't Be Replaced by an Expert System. *Philosophical Studies* 51.

Marx, Karl. 1977 [1843]. *Critique of Hegel's Philosophy of Right*. Cambridge University Press.

Matte Blanco, Ignacio. 1975 *The Unconscious as Infinite Sets*. Duckworth.

Matthew, R. 1989. *Japanese Science Fiction: A View of a Changing Society*. Routledge.

Merleau-Ponty, Maurice. 1973. What Is Phenomenology? In *European Literary Theory and Practice: From Existential Phenomenology to Structuralism* (Dell).

Metcalf, Andy, and Martin Humphries, eds. 1985. *The Sexuality of Men*. Pluto Press.

Mill, John Stuart. 1843. *A System of Logic*. John W. Parker.

Miller, Russell. 2008. *The Adventures of Arthur Conan Doyle: A Biography*. St. Martin's Press.

Mink, Louis. 1987. History and Fiction as Modes of Comprehension. In *Historical Understanding* (Cornell University Press).

——. 1987. Modes of Comprehension and the Unity of Knowledge. In *Historical Understanding* (Cornell University Press).

Miyazaki, Hayao. 2009. *Starting Point: 1979–1996*. Viz Media.

Moore, G.E. 1993. Moore's Paradox. In Thomas Baldwin, ed., *G.E. Moore: Selected Writings* (Routledge).

Moran, Richard. 2005. Getting Told and Being Believed. *Philosophers' Imprint* 5:5,<www.philosophersimprint.org/005005>.

Nietzsche, Friedrich. 1986. *Human, All Too Human*. Cambridge University Press.

——. 1988. The Greek State. In Giorgio Colli and Mazzino Montinari, eds., *Kritische Studienausgabe* (De Gruyter).

Nozick, Robert. 1989. Love's Bond. In *The Examined Life: Philosophical Meditations* (Simon and Schuster).

Nye, A. 1992 *Words of Power: A Feminist Reading of the History of Logic*. Routledge.

Painter, A. 1992. *The Creation of Japanese Television and Culture*. Ph.D. dissertation. University of Michigan, Department of Anthropology.

Parfit, Derek. 1984. *Reasons and Persons*. Oxford University Press.

Pascal, Blaise. 1995 [1670]. *Pensées*. Penguin.

Payne, David S. 1992. *Myth and Modern Man in Sherlock Holmes: Sir Arthur Conan Doyle and the Uses of Nostalgia*. Gaslight.

Peirce, Charles Sanders. 1995. *Collected Works of Charles Sanders Peirce. Volume 4: Science and Philosophy*. Harvard University Press.

——. 1998. *The Essential Peirce: Selected Philosophical Writings*. Two volumes. Peirce Edition Project. Indiana University Press.

Pierleoni, Allen O. 2006. Elementary, My Dear Kurland: A Petaluma Writer Takes on the Mysteries of Holmes and Moriarty. *Knight Ridder Tribune Business News* (21st August), <http://proquest.umi.com/pqdweb?did=11 01737551&sid=1&Fmt=3&clientId=3852&RQT=309&VName=PQD>.

Plato. 1973. *Theaetetus*. Oxford University Press.

——. 1997. *Apology*. In Cooper 1997.

——. 1997. *Gorgias*. In Cooper 1997.

——. 1997. *Phaedo*. In Cooper 1997.

——. 1997. *Phaedrus*. In Cooper 1997.

———. 1997. *The Seventh Letter*. In Cooper 1997.

Pollard P. 1981. The Effect of Thematic Content on the Wason Selection Task. *Current Psychological Research* 1.

Popper, Karl R. 1963. *Conjectures and Refutations: The Growth of Scientific Knowledge*. Routledge.

Pritchard, Duncan. 2005. *Epistemic Luck*. Oxford University Press.

Rehder, Wulf. 1979. Sherlock Holmes: Philosopher Detective. *Inquiry* 22.

Robb, Graham. 2003. *Strangers: Homosexual Love in the Nineteenth Century*. Norton.

Robinson, John Alan. 1965. Machine-oriented Logic Based on the Resolution Principle. *Communications of the ACM* 5.

Rosenberg, Samuel. 1988. *Naked Is the Best Disguise: The Death and Resurrection of Sherlock Holmes*. Ameron.

Russell, Bertrand. 2009. *Human Knowledge: Its Scope and Limits*. Routledge.

Rutherford, Donald. 2003. Patience Sans Espérance: Leibniz's Critique of Stoicism. In Jon Miller and Brad Inwood, eds., *Hellenistic and Early Modern Philosophy* (Cambridge University Press).

Salen, Katie, and Eric Zimmerman. 2003. *Rules of Play: Game Design Fundamentals*. MIT Press.

Saler, Michael. 2003. 'Clap if You Believe in Sherlock Holmes': Mass Culture and the Re-Enchantment of Modernity, c. 1890–1940. *The Historical Journal* 46.

Sata, M., and H. Hirahara, eds. 1991. *A History of Japanese Television Drama: Modern Japan and the Japanese*. Japan Association of Broadcasting Art.

Scruton, Roger. 1986. *Sexual Desire: A Philosophical Investigation*. Free Press.

Sedgwick, Eve Kosofsky. 1985. *Between Men: English Literature and Male Homosocial Desire*. Columbia University Press.

Shore, D. 2006. Developing the Concept. *Hulu.com*, <www.hulu.com/watch/21606/house-house---developing-the-concept#s-p2-st-i1>.

Shreffler, Philip A. 2006. Watson's Weird Tales: Horror in the Sherlockian Canon. *The Baker Street Journal* 56:2.

Smith, A. 2004. *Victorian Demons: Medicine, Masculinity, and the Gothic at the Fin-de-Siècle*. Manchester University Press.

Snyder, Laura J. 2004. Sherlock Holmes: Scientific Detective. *Endeavour* 28:3.

Solomon, Robert. 1991. The Virtue of (Erotic) Love. In Robert C. Solomon, Kathleen M. Higgins, and Arthur C. Danto, eds. *The Philosophy of (Erotic) Love*. University of Kansas Press.

Sorensen, Roy. 2007. Bald-faced Lies! Lying Without the Intent to Deceive. *Pacific Philosophical Quarterly* 88.

——. Forthcoming. What Lies Behind Misspeaking. *American Philosophical Quarterly*.

Spinoza, Baruch. 1992. *Ethics*. Hackett.

Stearns, Peter N. 1990. *Be a Man! Males in Modern Society*. Holmes and Meier.

Takahashi, M. 1992. *The Development of Japanese Television Broadcasting and Imported Television Programs*. M.A. dissertation. Michigan State University, Department of Telecommunications.

Thich Nhat Hahn. 1985. *A Guide to Walking Meditation*. Fellowship.

UKTV Gold. 2008. Is Robin Real? *UKTV* (February).

Waite, Geoff. 1996. *Nietzsche's Corps/e: Aesthetics, Politics, Prophecy, or, the Spectacular Technoculture of Everyday Life*. Duke University Press.

Walsh, Michael. 2009. Moriarty, Moran, and More: Anti-Hibernian sentiment in the Canon. In Martin H. Greenberg, Jon L. Lellenberg, and Daniel Stashower, eds., *Sherlock Holmes in America* (Skyhorse).

Wason, P.C., and D. Shapiro. 1971, Natural and Contrived Experience in a Reasoning Problem. *Quarterly Journal of Experimental Psychology* 23.

Webb, K. 1998. *Sherlock Holmes in Japan*. Next Church Resources.
Wittgenstein, Ludwig. 1981. *Tractatus Logico-Philosophicus*. Routledge.
———. 1953. *Philosophical Investigations*. Macmillan.
Wynne, Catherine. 2002. *The Colonial Conan Doyle: British Imperialism, Irish Nationalism, and the Gothic*. Greenwood Press.
Yamamoto, E. 1989. *Mushi Pro no Kōbōki: Ani Meita no Seishun [The Rise and Fall of Mushi Productions: The Youth of 'A. Nimator']*. Shinchōsha.
Yamazaki, K. 2005. *Terebi Anime Damashi [Spirit of TV Anime]*. Kōdansha Gendai Shinsha.
Zeisler, Ernest Bloomfield. 1953. *Baker Street Chronology: Commentaries on the Sacred Writings of Dr. John H. Watson*. Isaacs.

Hullo! Hullo! Good Old Index!